INDIGENOUS PEOPLES IN THE INTERNATIONAL ARENA

This book provides a definitive account of the creation and rise of the international Indigenous Peoples' movement.

In the late 1970s, motivated by their dire situation and local struggles, and inspired by worldwide movements for social justice and decolonization, including the American civil rights movement, Indigenous Peoples around the world got together and began to organize at the international level. Although each defined itself by its relation to a unique land, culture, and often language, Indigenous Peoples from around the world made an extraordinary leap, using a common conceptual vocabulary and addressing international bodies that until then had barely recognized their existence. At the intersection of politics, law, and culture, this book documents the visionary emergence of the international Indigenous movement, detailing its challenges and achievements, including the historic recognition of Indigenous rights through the adoption of the UN Declaration on the Rights of Indigenous Peoples in 2007. The winning by Indigenous Peoples of an unprecedented kind and degree of international participation – especially at the United Nations, an institution centered on states – meant overcoming enormous institutional and political resistance. The book shows how this participation became an increasingly assertive self-expression and even an exercise of self-determination by which Indigenous Peoples could both benefit from and contribute to the international community overall – now, crucially, by sharing their knowledge about climate change, their approaches to development and well-being, and their struggles against the impact of extractive industries on their lands and resources.

Written by the former Chief of the Secretariat of the United Nations Permanent Forum on Indigenous Issues, this book will be of interest to researchers, teachers, students, advocates, practitioners, and others with interests in Indigenous legal and political issues.

Elsa Stamatopoulou is Director of the Indigenous Peoples' Rights Program and Adjunct Professor in the Institute for the Study of Human Rights, the Department of Anthropology, and the Center for the Study of Ethnicity and Race at Columbia University, USA. Elsa is also Former (the first) Chief of the Secretariat of the UN Permanent Forum on Indigenous Issues (among other functions at the UN).

Part of the Indigenous Peoples and the Law series

series editors

Dr Mark A. Harris, *University of British Columbia, Canada*
Professor Denise Ferreira da Silva, *University of British Columbia, Canada*
Dr Claire Charters, *University of Auckland, New Zealand*
Dr Glen Coulthard, *University of British Columbia, Canada*

for information about the series and details of previous and forthcoming titles, see www.routledge.com/law/series/INDPPL

A GlassHouse Book

INDIGENOUS PEOPLES IN THE INTERNATIONAL ARENA

The Global Movement for Self-Determination

Elsa Stamatopoulou

Routledge
Taylor & Francis Group
a GlassHouse Book

Designed cover image: Claudio Ventrella / iStock/Getty Images Plus

First published 2025
by Routledge
4 Park Square, Milton Park, Abingdon, Oxon OX14 4RN

and by Routledge
605 Third Avenue, New York, NY 10158

Routledge is an imprint of the Taylor & Francis Group,
an informa business

a GlassHouse book

© 2025 Elsa Stamatopoulou

British Library Cataloguing-in-Publication Data
A catalogue record for this book is available from the British Library

Library of Congress Cataloging-in-Publication Data
Names: Stamatopoulou, Elsa, 1951- author.
Title: Indigenous peoples in the international arena :
    the global movement for self-determination / Elsa Stamatopoulou.
Description: Abingdon, Oxon [UK] ; New York, NY :
    Routledge, 2024. | Series: Indigenous peoples and the law | Includes
    bibliographical references and index.
Identifiers: LCCN 2024006785 (print) | LCCN 2024006786
    (ebook) | ISBN 9781032734170 (hardback) | ISBN 9781032734156
    (paperback) | ISBN 9781003464099 (ebook)
Subjects: LCSH: Indigenous peoples (International law) | Indigenous
    peoples—Civil rights. | Self-determination, National.
Classification: LCC KI280 .S73 2024 (print) | LCC KI280
    (ebook) | DDC 341.4/852—dc23/eng/20240214
LC record available at https://lccn.loc.gov/2024006785
LC ebook record available at https://lccn.loc.gov/2024006786

ISBN: 978-1-032-73417-0 (hbk)
ISBN: 978-1-032-73415-6 (pbk)
ISBN: 978-1-003-46409-9 (ebk)

DOI: 10.4324/9781003464099

Typeset in Sabon
by Apex CoVantage, LLC

*I dedicate this book to the Indigenous
Peoples' Movement*

CONTENTS

ACKNOWLEDGEMENTS

My deep appreciation goes to all those from around the world who encouraged the creation of this book with such care and expectation. There have been many over the years, as advocates, officials, colleagues, friends, or mentors, without whose multiple contributions to Indigenous Peoples' rights this book would not have been possible. I am grateful to all the participants at the numerous international, national, and local meetings, events, and projects, who, over the decades, gave their best to promote the rights of Indigenous Peoples: Indigenous representatives, UN system and other public service people, civil society advocates, academics, the Indigenous Elders, the women, the youth. They offered valuable insights from their rich experiences in public or private discussions, through their statements and writings, their art, or otherwise. These have been precious and have informed the outcomes of this book. I thank all those who inspired me to write the book to convey the stories and teachings of the Indigenous Peoples' movement, its visionary struggles, and inspiring achievements.

I am especially grateful to the people who spoke with me and were willing to give their time and share views and experiences about the broad questions that this book explores: Claire Charters, Antonella Cordone, Myrna Cunningham, Kenneth Deer, Binota Moy Dhamai, Lola Garcia-Alix, Moana Jackson, Mikaela Jade, Carson Kiburo, Wilton Littlechild, Oren Lyons, Les Malezer, Aehshatou Manu, Aroha Mead, Chhing Lamu Sherpa, Rodion Sulyandziga, Victoria (Vicky) Tauli-Corpuz, and Howard Thompson.

It would be impossible to list all the names of those I spoke to and learned from, over time, about Indigenous Peoples and their struggles and rights. Some have passed on, and I honor their memory. I honor the memory of my inspiring mentor at the UN, Augusto Willemsen Díaz, who introduced me to Indigenous Peoples' rights more than forty years ago.

Special thanks go to Mariam Wallet Mohamed Aboubakrine, Mattias Åhrén, Monica Aleman, James Anaya, Lars-Anders Baer, Albert Kwokwo Barume, Pierrette Birraux, Tone Bleie, Roberto Mukaro Borrero, Pamela Calla, Joan Carling, Andrea Carmen, Dimitris Christopoulos, Tim Coulter, Sandra Creamer, Roxanne Dunbar-Ortiz, Aviâja Egede Lynge, Karla General, Hurst Hannum, Edward John, Nina Kantcheva, Naomi Kipuri, Tom Kruse, Sheryl Lightfoot, Mariana Lopez, Victor Anthony Lopez-Carmen, Betty Lyons, Hui Lu, Otilia Lux de Cotí, Ole Henrik Magga, Mirian Masaquiza, Lucy Mulenkei, Binalakshmi Nepram, Ida Nicolaisen, Ishita Petkar, Carol Pollack, Cecilia Ramirez, Tarcila Rivera Zea, Mary Robinson, Devasish Roy, John Scott, Broddi Sigurdarson, Mililani Trask, Alexandra Xanthaki, Vassiliki Yiakoumaki, Teresa Zapeta, Amalia Zeppou, my dear daughter Sophia Stamatopoulou-Robbins, and many others. The International Indigenous Women's Forum (FIMI) and the Global Indigenous Youth Caucus have my appreciation, continuing friendship, and solidarity. The numerous Indigenous organizations I have worked with have accompanied and enriched my path, and I have been honored to accompany theirs.

I express my true appreciation to Colin Perrin, Commissioning Editor at Routledge, for his extraordinary care and collaboration, and my sincere thanks to Naomi Round Cahalin, his editorial assistant. Daniel Hanneman was my superb copyeditor for the book, committed as much to the substance as to the elegance of the texts.

For more than a decade now, I have greatly appreciated my enthusiastic and committed students at Columbia University for their sincere engagement and deep questions around Indigenous Peoples' rights. I have learned from them and tried to reflect some of these insights in this book. Columbia University, its Institute for the Study of Human Rights, the Center for the Study of Ethnicity and Race, and other departments provided an enriching research environment for which I am deeply grateful. I am also thankful to Columbia for sponsoring the creation by our Institute of the first massive open online course (MOOC) on Indigenous Peoples' rights.

Last but not least, I thank my family for their solidarity, care, and much more, for understanding and accepting the time I could not spend with them when I was giving endless hours to my work over the decades. I am deeply grateful to my life's companion, Bruce Robbins, for always supporting my work with Indigenous Peoples and for being an exacting but also encouraging, inspiring, and loving advocate of this book project, while keeping us fed at the same time.

The year 2027 will be the twentieth anniversary of the adoption of the United Nations Declaration on the Rights of Indigenous Peoples. This book is an homage to the continuing struggles and visions of the Indigenous Peoples' movement for a more just and sustainable world for all.

15 October 2023
Elsa Stamatopoulou

ABBREVIATIONS

CBD	Convention on Biological Diversity
CEDAW	Convention for the Elimination of All Forms of Discrimination against Women
CHT	Chittagong Hill Tracts
CSW	Commission on the Status of Women
DESA	UN Department of Economic and Social Affairs
DOCIP	Indigenous Peoples' Center for Documentation, Research and Information
EBRD	European Bank for Reconstruction and Development
ECOSOC	Economic and Social Council
EMRIP	Expert Mechanism on the Rights of Indigenous Peoples
FAO	Food and Agriculture Organization of the United Nations
FIMI	International Indigenous Women's Forum
FPIC	Free, prior, and informed consent
HRBA	Human rights-based approach to development
IASG	Inter-Agency Support Group on Indigenous Peoples' Issues
IFAD	International Fund for Agricultural Development
IFIs	International financial institutions
IGOs	Intergovernmental organizations
IITC	International Indian Treaty Council
ILO	International Labor Organization
IWGIA	International Work Group on Indigenous Affairs
MDGs	Millennium Development Goals
NGO	Nongovernmental organization
OD	Outcome Document
OHCHR	Office of the High Commissioner for Human Rights

PGA	President of the General Assembly
SDGs	Sustainable Development Goals
SPFII	Secretariat of the United Nations Permanent Forum on Indigenous Issues
UN	United Nations
UNCHR	United Nations Commission on Human Rights
UNCT	United Nations country team
UNDG	United Nations Development Group
UNDP	United Nations Development Program
UNDRIP	United Nations Declaration on the Rights of Indigenous Peoples
UNESCO	United Nations Educational, Scientific and Cultural Organization
UNFPA	United Nations Population Fund
UNGA	United Nations General Assembly
UNICEF	United Nations Children's Fund
UNOG	United Nations Office at Geneva
UNPFII	United Nations Permanent Forum on Indigenous Issues
WGIP	Working Group on Indigenous Populations
WCIP	World Conference on Indigenous Peoples
WHO	World Health Organization
WIPO	World Intellectual Property Organization
WTO	World Trade Organization

INTRODUCTION

Indigenous Peoples, in an organized manner, have pursued contact with the United Nations.[1] The fact that they have gone directly to interstate institutions and have been accepted there, and accepted with a unique status, deserves to be seen as a significant act of external self-determination and a significant moment in the history of the present.

In the 1970s, Indigenous Peoples from around the world began to approach the United Nations systematically as a site where they could pursue their quest for dignity, respect, and self-determination. On the face of it, this was an unlikely place for them to turn. The UN is after all a creation of states, many of which have been colonizers and oppressors of Indigenous Peoples. But what Indigenous Peoples accomplished by going to the international level is even more unlikely. That is the story I will be telling here.

In 1977, when I was in Geneva, Switzerland, as a graduate student, I saw various Indigenous persons walking around the city, including in the university areas where I was spending my days. By their clothing and hair styles, these visitors were quite distinct from those around them, and I was interested in them. For several days I wondered who they might be and why they were there. I was to learn years later that the historic International NGO Conference on Discrimination against Indigenous Populations in the Americas was being held those very days at the United Nations Office in Geneva, on 20–23 September 1977.[2]

---

1 There has been a trend to capitalize the terms "Indigenous" and "Indigenous Peoples." This book follows this approach. If a text is quoted that does not capitalize the initials, we follow the spelling of the original quote.
2 The conference is discussed in Chapter 1, section C, "Stepping Stones: Human Rights and Antiracism." Some information about the conference can also be found here: "Archives of

DOI: 10.4324/9781003464099-1

I hardly expected at that time that I would get to know several of those leaders later at the UN and that I would get deeply involved in Indigenous Peoples' rights. In 1981, when I was already employed at the then UN Center for Human Rights, the second such Indigenous conference took place at the UN Office, more global this time, and I witnessed it personally.[3]

One July afternoon in 1981, the office quiet was interrupted by the sound of drums coming from the yard surrounded by the building of the UN offices, Geneva's Palais des Nations. I leaned out the window and saw a procession of Indigenous people, in their traditional clothes, marching ceremonially through the yard. I noticed that in the front of the procession were old people leading the ceremony, walking slowly, some with difficulty, while being supported by younger people. The procession and the drumming lasted for some time. It was an extraordinary sight, and many UN staff members had come to their windows or down to the yard to watch. I was very impressed and intrigued myself and decided to find out who the people were, why they were at the UN, whom they were seeing – only to discover, to my delight, that they were in fact connecting with the human rights office, the UN Center for Human Rights, where I was working. In a few hours, I found the colleague who was the focal point for this event. It was the distinguished Augusto Willemsen Díaz, a Guatemalan political refugee, the first UN staff member who dealt with Indigenous Peoples' rights, and the man who would soon become my mentor.

I was initiated to the topic deeply by *Don* Augusto. His sincere devotion and insight, his courage to deal with huge obstacles and tell the truth were inspiring for a young UN worker like me. In addition, he had the generosity to open the possibility for me to enter the conference room in 1981, where consultations of Indigenous leaders were taking place, and to learn directly from these leaders. By 1982, Augusto had connected me with the UN Working Group on Indigenous Populations as well, and, in a sense, the rest is history, as the phrase goes. In this book, I try to tell some of this history that marked me profoundly as a person and a professional. In 2003, when I was brought on board at the Department of Economic and Social Affairs to establish the Secretariat of the new UN Permanent Forum on Indigenous Issues in New York, *Don* Augusto's was one of the first messages of support and encouragement that accompanied me in those challenging days.

Indigenous Peoples Day: A Documentary History of the Origin and Development of Indigenous Peoples Day," *Indigenous Peoples Day website*, ed. John Curl, accessed 2 November 2022, https://ipdpowwow.org/Archives_1.html.

3 See Elsa Stamatopoulou, "Walking the Talk? Including Indigenous Peoples' Issues in Intergovernmental Organizations," in *Indigenous Peoples' Rights in International Law*, ed. Roxanne Dunbar-Ortiz et al. (Kautokeino: Gáldu and Copenhagen: IWGIA, 2015).

Coming from Greece, a small European country, I have been aware of the suffering of peoples under occupation, marginalization, oppression, exploitation, and wars – and all this despite their glorious pasts. My interest in human rights was very much shaped by the repression I witnessed during the dictatorship in Greece and the struggles for democracy. I am proud to belong to the "*genia tou Polytechniou*" (the generation of the Polytechnical School), as it is called, the students and others who rose against the junta in our country.

Although I was born and raised in Athens, my parents came from villages of the Peloponnese, where I later spent school vacations throughout my childhood and youth. The hands of our village neighbors and family members were the hands of people who tend the land. I often saw those same hands when I was meeting many Indigenous Elders in the UN conference rooms. Their faces and eyes were marked by the sun and winds of the prairies, by the mountains and forests they took care of. Communicating through our eyes was eloquent, often better than through words, given the lack of common language between us. The life teachings I was receiving from Indigenous representatives were profound and marked me as a person and as a professional. In those early days Geneva was transformed into a space that was full of the steps of Indigenous Peoples, their voices, their drumming, their protests and aspirations. The place "spoke" many Indigenous languages.

I was lucky and humbled to be there from those formative times on and to be able to witness history in the making, the victories, one after the other, of the growing Indigenous Peoples' movement at an international level. It was one of the greatest privileges in my life to be part of the beginnings of the UN's relation with the Indigenous Peoples' movement, to walk together with the movement as best I could over the decades and see the results, including the adoption of the UN Declaration on the Rights of Indigenous Peoples (UNDRIP or the Declaration), the establishment of the Special Rapporteur on the rights of Indigenous Peoples, the UN Permanent Forum on Indigenous Issues (UNPFII), the Expert Mechanism on the Rights of Indigenous Peoples (EMRIP), an International Year of the World's Indigenous People, two International Decades of the World's Indigenous People, a World Conference on Indigenous Peoples, an International Year and then an International Decade of Indigenous Languages, and other policy breakthroughs.

These victories, which might have appeared impossible at the outset, given the power imbalances Indigenous Peoples were and are facing, are profoundly admirable and inspiring. Their roots can be seen to a large extent in the clear expression of Indigenous leaders as representing self-determined peoples, peoples who had experienced and are still experiencing injustice, and in the subsequent creation of distinct possibilities and tools for substantive Indigenous participation at the international level. I have felt for years that I needed to put on paper what I have learned, as best I could, to try and analyze why and how these achievements were possible. Obviously, the views expressed in this book are mine, informed by my experiences with the topic over the decades and by numerous discussions with many Indigenous representatives and other leaders. I take responsibility for those views. I place these writings in the hands of younger leaders, advocates, researchers, and other professionals as a humble contribution, also hoping to give back some of the Indigenous teachings I have received throughout my life.

A. Historical Context

Indigenous Peoples existed as sovereign entities long before the existence of states, let alone interstate organizations like the UN.[4] They did not need recognition by states or international organizations to bring them into existence. They knew themselves, and they know themselves. They have expressed their sovereignty and external self-determination over the centuries through decisions and actions to conduct commerce, wage war, pursue peace, conclude treaties, and develop various relations and arrangements with other Indigenous Peoples as well as states and nonstate entities. Still, what they achieved by making their issues matters of international concern is a major fact of world history.

This book shares stories and explanations of how Indigenous Peoples' issues became matters of international concern. They are the ones who decided to internationalize their issues. In following their actions, I also explore how the characteristics of this internationalization changed over the past sixty years and why. As a human rights advocate and expert, I also pay special attention to the important role of international human rights norms and processes as they relate to the Indigenous Peoples' movement.

After the First World War, there were mobilizations around various human rights causes, including minority rights, racial equality, and working conditions. Yet the League of Nations, the precursor of the United Nations, did not include the protection of human rights among its aims and did not even include issues of racial equality.

Negative experiences and friction with states prompted Indigenous Peoples' decisions to internationalize their issues, with different Indigenous Peoples doing so at a different pace, depending on their histories, circumstances, and knowledge of the opportunities available in the international systems as well as the availability of resources. For example, the Haudenosaunee and

---

4 In this book, especially given its topic and focus, the words "interstate organizations" are often used instead of "intergovernmental organizations," the common term. This is to signify that Indigenous Peoples have also had and have governments or governance systems and that having a government is not just a characteristic of states.

the Māori were already appealing to the League of Nations in the 1920s, as will be further discussed later and in Chapters 1, 3, and 4.[5]

In 1923 Cayuga Chief Deskaheh traveled to Geneva as the representative of the Six Nations of the Iroquois – also known as the Haudenosaunee – to the League of Nations to plead for the cause of his people. He waited one year, working behind the scenes for recognition by the League, but he was not received and finally returned to the United States. A few months before his death in 1925, Chief Deskaheh made a speech by radio in Rochester, New York, featuring some of the words he had prepared for the League of Nations. The following is an excerpt:

> *This is the story of the Mohawks, the story of the Oneidas, of the Cayugas – [I am a Cayuga –] of the Onondagas, the Senecas, and the Tuscaroras. They are the Iroquois. Tell it to those who have not been listening. Maybe I will be stopped from telling it. But if I am prevented from telling it over, as I hope I do, the story will not be lost. I have already told it to thousands of listeners in Europe. It has gone into the records where your children can find it when I may be dead or be in jail for daring to tell the truth. I have told this story in Switzerland. They have free speech in little Switzerland. One can tell the truth over there in public, even if it is uncomfortable for some great people.*
>
> *. . . I am the speaker of the Six Nations, the oldest League of Nations now existing. . . . It is a League which is still alive and intends, as best it can, to defend the rights of the Iroquois to live under their own laws in their own little countries now left to them, to worship their Great Spirit in their own way, and to enjoy the rights which are as surely theirs as the white man's rights are his own.[6]*

A similar journey was made by Māori religious leader W. T. Ratana. In protest against the breaking of the Treaty of Waitangi, concluded with the Māori in New Zealand in 1840, that gave Māori ownership of their lands, Ratana traveled to London with a large delegation to petition King George V, but he was denied access. He then sent part of his delegation to the League of Nations in Geneva and arrived there later himself, in 1925, but was also denied access.[7]

---

5 The Haudenosaunee were also known as the Iroquois Confederacy by the French during colonial times or as the League of Five Nations by the English; the Confederacy is now composed of the Six Nations, comprising the Mohawk, Oneida, Onondaga, Cayuga, Seneca, and Tuscarora peoples.

6 Deskaheh, "An Iroquois Patriot's Fight for International Recognition," in *Basic Call to Consciousness*, ed. Akwesasne Notes (Summertown, TN: Native Voices, 2005), 53.

7 Elvira Pulitano, "Conference Diplomacy at the United Nations and the Advancement of Indigenous Rights," *UN Chronicle* 51, no. 3 (December 2014), www.un.org/en/chronicle/article/conference-diplomacy-united-nations-and-advancement-indigenous-rights.

As these examples suggest, the history of Indigenous Peoples knocking at the doors of the institutions of the international community of "nations" is not new. Indigenous Peoples' understanding of themselves as sovereign nations, in parity with the other nations of the world, has always been strong. The fact that states, the colonizing powers, concluded treaties with many Indigenous Peoples is a testimony that Indigenous Peoples were viewed as sovereign, not only by themselves but also by states – those who actually developed international law in the modern era.

B. Issues and Challenges

Indigenous Peoples are estimated to number some 476.6 million in some ninety countries, representing 6.2 percent of the world's population.[8] It is also estimated that they represent as many as five thousand different Indigenous cultures, therefore accounting for most of the world's cultural diversity, even though they constitute a numerical minority. Indigenous lands make up around 20 percent of the earth's territory, containing 80 percent of the world's remaining biodiversity – a clear sign that Indigenous Peoples are the most effective stewards of the environment.[9]

The situation of Indigenous cultures in many parts of the world continues to be dire. Of the 7,000 languages currently spoken in the world, 6,700 are Indigenous, and it is precisely these that are most threatened.[10] Most of these languages are spoken by very few people, while most of the world's population speaks only a handful of languages. About 97 percent of the world's population speaks 4 percent of its languages, while only 3 percent speaks 96 percent of them. A great majority of these languages are spoken by Indigenous Peoples, and many of them are in danger of becoming extinct. Roughly 90 percent of all existing languages may become extinct within the next one hundred years. One can therefore imagine what the percentage of Indigenous languages this statistic represents.

But Indigenous Peoples also face systemic discrimination and exclusion from political and economic power; they continue to be overrepresented among the poorest, the illiterate, and the destitute. Although roughly 6.2 percent of the world's population, they constitute 15 percent of the world's

---

8 International Labor Organization, *Implementing the ILO Indigenous and Tribal Peoples Convention No. 169: Towards an Inclusive, Sustainable and Just Future* (Geneva: ILO, 2019), 13.

9 UN Permanent Forum on Indigenous Issues, *Indigenous Peoples Collective Rights to Lands, Territories and Resources*, Backgrounder (UNPFII, 2018), 1, www.un.org/development/desa/indigenouspeoples/wp-content/uploads/sites/19/2018/04/Indigenous-Peoples-Collective-Rights-to-Lands-Territories-Resources.pdf.

10 "A Decade to Prevent the Disappearance of 3,000 Languages," *UNESCO website*, 21 February 2022, www.iesalc.unesco.org/en/2022/02/21/a-decade-to-prevent-the-disappearance-of-3000-languages/.

poor.[11] Even in developed countries, Indigenous Peoples trail the non-Indigenous population in most well-being indicators: "They live shorter lives, have poorer health care and education, and endure higher unemployment rates. A native Aboriginal child born in Australia today can expect to die almost 20 years earlier than his non-native compatriot."[12] Indigenous women are more likely to be raped, with some estimates that over one-third are raped during their lifetimes.[13] Indigenous Peoples are more likely than others to be displaced by wars and environmental exploitation or so-called development projects. In Malaysia, for example, between five thousand and eight thousand Indigenous People were forcibly displaced by the large-scale clear-cutting of rainforest for the Bakun Dam project.[14] The weapon of rape and sexual humiliation is also turned against Indigenous women for the ethnic cleansing and demoralization of Indigenous communities.[15]

Indigenous Peoples are chased out of their ancestral lands and deprived of resources of survival – physical, cultural, and spiritual; and they are even robbed of their very right to life, simply killed when they are too much in the way of those who pursue other political and economic agendas. In more modern versions of market exploitation, Indigenous Peoples see their traditional knowledge marketed and patented without their consent and participation. One of the most serious shortcomings in human rights protection in recent years is the trend in states' action to penalize and criminalize social protest activities and legitimate demands made by Indigenous organizations and movements in defense of their rights. According to one study, about two thirds of human rights defenders killed annually are Indigenous and environmental advocates.[16] And last but not least, the endless hunger of the dominant development paradigm for natural resources leads to continuous land grabbing and exploitation of Indigenous lands by corporations, especially extractive industries, thus depriving Indigenous Peoples' communities of their basic livelihood and leading to further violence and marginalization.[17]

11 "State of the World's Indigenous Peoples," UN *Department of Public Information*, 14 January 2010, press release, 3, www.un.org/esa/socdev/unpfii/documents/SOWIP/press%20package/sowip-press-package-en.pdf.

12 "State of the World's Indigenous Peoples," 3.

13 "State of the World's Indigenous Peoples," 10.

14 UN Permanent Forum on Indigenous Issues, *Indigenous Peoples in the Asian Region*, Backgrounder (UNPFII, 2014), 2, www.un.org/esa/socdev/unpfii/documents/2014/press/asia.pdf.

15 "Fact Sheet: Violence against Indigenous Women and Girls in Bangladesh," *IWGIA website*, 30 November 2021, www.iwgia.org/en/news/4575-fact-sheet-violence-against-indigenous-women-and-girls-in-bangladesh.html.

16 Front Line Defenders, *Global Analysis 2022* (Dublin: FLD, 2023), www.frontlinedefenders.org/en/resource-publication/global-analysis-2022.

17 See, for example, Cathal M. Doyle and Andrew Whitmore, *Indigenous Peoples and the Extractive Sector: Towards a Rights-Respecting Engagement* (Baguio City: Tebtebba Foundation, 2014); Inter-American Commission on Human Rights, *Indigenous Peoples, Afro-Descendent Communities, and Natural Resources: Human Rights Protection in the Context of Extraction, Exploitation, and Development Activities*, OEA/Ser.L/V/II,

C. The Appeal to Human Rights

It was the unprecedented emergence of human rights norms and procedures after World War II and the openings thus created for the participation of civil society (that is, nonstate voices) that permitted the struggles of Indigenous Peoples to express themselves at the international level.

In 1945, the United Nations took a revolutionary step when it included human rights in Article 1 of the UN Charter as one of its three basic aims, along with peace and development. This meant that, for the first time, human rights were elevated to an issue of international global concern and action. The contribution of the United Nations to the codification of international law has actually been most pronounced in the field of human rights, with more than one hundred international human rights instruments – both declarations and treaties – adopted. One day before the adoption of the seminal Universal Declaration of Human Rights (UDHR) on 10 December 1948, the UN General Assembly adopted the Convention on the Prevention and Punishment of the Crime of Genocide. This *first* international human rights instrument marked the imperfect beginnings of a new era. In fact, the Convention and the UDHR were being negotiated simultaneously at the UN, in two different committees of the General Assembly. The discussion in this book will also bring us back to the connection between these two legal instruments.

Nothing shows more clearly how the concept of human rights is dynamic and developing than the gradual recognition of Indigenous Peoples' rights, epitomized by the 2007 UNDRIP.

In the earlier days of international law, Indigenous Peoples' rights were not recognized as separate issues. Apart from treaties to which Indigenous Peoples themselves were parties and the agreement that established the Inter-American Indian Institute in 1940,[18] no multilateral treaty or agreement addressed the issue of Indigenous rights per se prior to the adoption of International Labor Organization (ILO) Convention No. 107, the Indigenous and Tribal Populations Convention, in 1957.[19]

Bolivia was the first voice in the UN era to express the need for special attention to Indigenous Peoples. In 1949, Bolivia proposed the creation of a sub-commission of the UN Social Commission to study "the situation of the aboriginal populations . . . of the States of the American continent."[20]

Doc. 47/15 (IACHR, 2015), www.oas.org/en/iachr/reports/pdfs/extractiveindustries2016. pdf; Abigal Anongos, et al., *Pitfalls and Pipelines: Indigenous Peoples and Extractive Industries*, ed. Andy Whitmore (Baguio City: Tebtebba Foundation, 2012), 249–70.

18 "B-26: Convention Providing for the Creation of the Inter-American Indian Institute," *Organization of American States' Inter-American Treaties website*, www.oas.org/juridico/english/Sigs/b-26.html, accessed 26 October 2022.

19 Hurst Hannum, "New Developments in Indigenous Rights," *Virginia Journal of International Law* 28 (1988): 652.

20 UN Sub-Commission on Prevention of Discrimination and Protection of Minorities, Study of the Problem of Discrimination against Indigenous Populations: Final Report (First Part)

Given opposition to this initiative, the final resolution merely called upon the Economic and Social Council to undertake a study of "the situation of the aboriginal populations . . . of the States of the American continent requesting such help."[21] But even this proposal drew objections. Given objection to such study at that time, a study would not be undertaken until much later starting in 1972, under the UN Sub-Commission on Prevention of Discrimination and Protection of Minorities, as is explained in Chapter 1.

In the 1970s, there was a dramatic rise in the mobilization of Indigenous Peoples at the local, national, and regional levels. Little by little, these various struggles were coordinated, and an international Indigenous Peoples' movement came into being. Indigenous leaders realized that they could influence states by political and legal agitation and that international action would be an important strategy.[22] This is what it has become. Indigenous Peoples from different lands, languages, and cultures found themselves in the same rooms. While realizing the diversity among them, they also, perhaps especially, realized their common points, challenges, and aspirations. The nascent international Indigenous Peoples' movement realized it would need to gather around common narratives, principles, and strategies. Indigenous Peoples did just that.

The decision to try the international route manifested in two main ways. First, Indigenous Peoples organized nationally, regionally, and internationally among themselves. The various meetings from 1970 onward are a testimony to that.[23] The second route toward internationalization was to contact the UN to express their situation as well as their visions for a better and more just and sustainable future, a future where Indigenous Peoples would maintain and control their existence, their well-being, and their destinies.[24]

Submitted by the Special Rapporteur, Mr. José R. Martínez Cobo, Introduction, UN Doc. E/CN.4/Sub.2/476 (30 July 1981), para. 11–13, 84–85, https://social.desa.un.org/publications/martinez-cobo-study. See also Study of the Problem of Discrimination against Indigenous Populations: Final Report (Last Part) Submitted by the Special Rapporteur, Mr. José R. Martínez Cobo, Chapters XXI – XXII: Conclusions, Proposals and Recommendations, UN Doc. E/CN.4/Sub.2/1983/21/Add.8 (30 September 1983), para. 5–6.

21 UN General Assembly, Resolution 275 (III), Study of the Social Problems of the Aboriginal Populations and Other Under-Developed Social Groups of the American Continent, UN Doc. A/RES/275(III) (11 May 1949).

22 Douglas E. Sanders, *The Formation of the World Council of Indigenous Peoples* (Copenhagen: International Secretariat of IWGIA, 1977), 6, 8. Sanders lays out the history of the establishment of the World Council of Indigenous Peoples (WCIP) in 1975 and its connection to the UN, including through getting consultative NGO status with the UN Economic and Social Council. WCIP ended in 1996.

23 Secretariat of the Permanent Forum on Indigenous Issues (SPFII), *State of the World's Indigenous Peoples* (New York: UN Department of Economic and Social Affairs, 2009), 1–4, 10.

24 In the words of Native American leader Sam Deloria in the 1975 Indigenous conference in Copenhagen, "One limitation on the concept of national sovereignty is the existence of indigenous people . . . we have the right to maintain our political existence." Sanders, *Formation of the World Council*, 13.

Since the late 1970s Indigenous Peoples have been revealing to the UN and the world their plight due to colonization, settlement, and marginalization in general, as well as to specific atrocities. The UN, despite weaknesses that are to be expected from such an institution, and perhaps from any human construct, was and is viewed as an entity that is more than its component parts, an entity often perceived not just as representing its member states but as carrying the moral conscience of humanity. Indigenous Peoples have come to the UN to denounce states' behaviors within normative and political contexts that were framed by decolonization, human rights, and the fight against racial discrimination and for social justice. Indigenous Peoples have formulated their demands and visions about another future, one that would do away with these historic and current injustices and improve their well-being and the well-being of all humanity and nature. These demands and visions have been formulated by Indigenous Peoples in human rights terms, since, after all, this was the area where the first steps toward the internationalization of Indigenous issues were taken. At the beginning, it was not obvious that characteristic Indigenous issues – such as the theft of land and resources, the attack on Indigenous governance systems, rape of women, boarding schools – would be addressed in human rights terms. Human rights had been understood by many in a limited way, mostly as an instrument for redressing the wrongs of autocratic governments toward citizens. Indigenous Peoples reshaped the narrative and pursued the creation and interpretation of international human rights norms that would embrace and address their specific problems and concerns.

Early on in those steps of internationalization, Indigenous Peoples also realized that international processes were far from being just "technical." This was the case, for example, in complex UN procedures accrediting NGOs. It became clear to Indigenous leaders that their direct participation in these processes would be indispensable. For direct participation to be achieved, certain typical UN blockages had to be overcome. There had to be a decisive reshaping of rules. This was of course controversial.

In order to achieve such goals, Indigenous Peoples had to establish their legitimacy in the eyes of the non-Indigenous world, assert their distinctness, and show their numbers. That they managed to do so remains something of a miracle – all the more so because existing UN rules did not allow for the direct participation of Indigenous representatives. There had to be some creative revision of the rules – for example, the rule that consultative NGO status was a precondition of participation in certain UN meetings. As we will see, these difficulties have required exceptional strategies by Indigenous Peoples, including collaborations with supportive UN officials and states' diplomats within the UN. As a new UN official and, later, as a more experienced one, I had the chance to observe these strategies with respect and admiration for the creativity and strength of mind they required and the inspiring breakthroughs they made possible for direct Indigenous participation.

I discuss later the contribution of the UN Working Group on Indigenous Populations (1982–2005), the first UN body whose purpose was to deal with Indigenous Peoples' rights, as well as three Indigenous rights-related UN bodies that exist today: the EMRIP, the UNPFII, whose Secretariat I had the honor of heading, and the position of Special Rapporteur on the Rights of Indigenous Peoples.

In addition to the aforementioned actions, Indigenous Peoples took and continue to take initiatives to raise various cases with international human rights treaty bodies, including under the International Convention on the Elimination of All Forms of Racial Discrimination, the International Covenant on Civil and Political Rights, the Convention on the Elimination of All Forms of Discrimination against Women, and the Convention on the Rights of the Child, with other global human rights monitoring mechanisms and with regional human rights commissions and courts. They have achieved the creation of important legal precedents in their favor under international human rights law.[25]

As I have suggested, some demands that Indigenous Peoples made, especially those focusing on their direct international participation, were quite unprecedented in the UN system. But without these, they saw they could accomplish little. As a UN staff member and witness of the interactions between the Indigenous movement and the UN, I have been noting with admiration the special character of the demands and the acceptance of novel unprecedented approaches by states, an achievement of the Indigenous movement. In the environment of human rights norms in which these transformative processes were taking place, the demand of Indigenous Peoples for participation took various forms. One has been Indigenous Peoples' advocacy for them to co-chair UN meetings of relevance to them together with states.[26] Another form has been the increasing articulations of the right to self-determination and demands for this right to be implemented for

25 See, for example, Fergus McKay, *Indigenous Peoples and United Nations Human Rights Bodies. A Compilation of UN Treaty Body Jurisprudence, Special Procedures of the Human Rights Council, and the Advice of the Expert Mechanism on the Rights of Indigenous Peoples*, vol. 7, 2015–2016 (Forest Peoples Program, 2017), www.forestpeoples.org/en/law-policy-un-human-rights-system-guides-human-rights-mechanisms/report/2017/indigenous-peoples-and.

26 See, for example, the account of the July 2021 "Intersessional Roundtable of the UN Human Rights Council on Ways to Enhance the Participation of Indigenous Peoples' Representatives and Institutions in Meetings of the Human Rights Council on Issues Affecting Them," *UNHRC website*, www.ohchr.org/en/hr-bodies/hrc/intersessional-roundtable-indigenous-people, accessed 28 November 2022. It is indicated on the UNHRC website that the Roundtable would be co-chaired by "the President of the Human Rights Council and the Chair of the Indigenous Temporary Committee, Coordination Body."

Indigenous Peoples together with the principle of nondiscrimination.[27] The right to self-determination became the cornerstone of Indigenous Peoples' demands, together with land rights and cultural rights. States' reticence focused mostly on the first two.

Exercising their external right to self-determination as peoples, Indigenous Peoples got themselves first recognized *de facto* as Indigenous Peoples by the UN in order to participate at the UN. They then advocated to have themselves and their right to self-determination recognized *de jure*. This second step has been crucial and also an issue of nondiscrimination. They have stressed that they are *peoples*, and they should enjoy the rights recognized for *peoples*. Another fundamental aspect of the right to self-determination is that this right is seen as one crucial remedy for historical injustices to which Indigenous Peoples have been subjected. The recognition of the right to self-determination can also contribute to Indigenous Peoples more effectively negotiating power with and within the state, decolonizing the state, and reimagining and reestablishing the state. The rich international normative human rights framework has facilitated this process: already in 1966, the International Covenant on Economic and Social Rights and the International Covenant on Civil and Political Rights had recognized self-determination as a human right in their common Article 1.[28]

Taking stock of developments such as these, I would like to address three questions at this point: What has been the role of human rights discourses in the internationalization of Indigenous Peoples' issues? What has prompted the creation of an international Indigenous identity and the transformation of local movements into a global one? How did the dynamics between Indigenous Peoples and states change over time with the mediation of the UN?

It is important to underline that, by working through the human rights framework, Indigenous issues have succeeded in gaining international

27 Andrea Muehlebach refers to Indigenous politics at the UN as being infused with land and culture. Muehlebach, "'Making Place' at the United Nations: Indigenous Cultural Politics at the U.N. Working Group on Indigenous Populations," *Cultural Anthropology* 16, no. 3 (August 2001): 425.

28 Common Article 1 of the two International Covenants reads as follows: "1. All peoples have the right of self-determination. By virtue of that right they freely determine their political status and freely pursue their economic, social and cultural development. 2. All peoples may, for their own ends, freely dispose of their natural wealth and resources without prejudice to any obligations arising out of international economic co-operation, based upon the principle of mutual benefit, and international law. In no case may a people be deprived of its own means of subsistence. 3. The States Parties to the present Covenant, including those having responsibility for the administration of Non-Self-Governing and Trust Territories, shall promote the realization of the right of self-determination." See UN General Assembly, Resolution 2200A, International Covenant on Economic, Social and Cultural Rights, UN Doc. A/RES/2200A (16 December 1966), www.ohchr.org/en/instruments-mechanisms/instruments/international-covenant-economic-social-and-cultural-rights.

attention. Human rights bring out a political edge that not only makes states take notice but provokes states' annoyance or sensitivity because of the critique that is made of their practices. Other approaches do not necessarily have as much of an effect.[29]

Through their interventions, Indigenous Peoples have also brought culture into the human rights discourses. In fact, more than seventeen articles of the UNDRIP deal with cultural rights, including the right to education with a cultural perspective, language rights, traditional knowledge, and access to the means of dissemination of culture on the basis of nondiscrimination; the right of Indigenous Peoples to practice their religion; the freedom to maintain relations with their kin beyond national borders, and the right to participate in decisions affecting them through their own institutions; and the preservation of sacred sites, works of art, scientific knowledge (especially knowledge about nature), oral tradition, and human remains – that is, both the tangible and the intangible things that comprise Indigenous cultural heritage.

Special cultural rights also include the right to continue certain economic activities linked to the traditional use of land and natural resources. According to UNDRIP, Indigenous Peoples have the right to pursue their cultural development through their own institutions, and through those, they have the right to participate in the definition, preparation, and implementation of cultural policies that concern them. The education of the larger society about cultural diversity and Indigenous cultures must be pursued by the state. The media and other institutions should play a special role in promoting such knowledge.

The internationalization of the Indigenous movement did not just make new demands on states. It also saw the birth of a *new awareness* among Indigenous Peoples themselves, an awareness of their "*indigeneity*" as part of an identity and a category at the international level. In Latin America, for example, some social justice movements of peasants, *los campesinos*, originally included both Indigenous and non-Indigenous people. After the 1970s, however, more and more Indigenous Peoples established distinct political organizations, inspired by the international Indigenous movement and the empowerment that this brought. In the words of an Indigenous colleague of mine, who was analyzing the political movement in her country, "In the 1970s the social movement in our country became stronger through joint mobilization of *campesinos* and Indigenous communities, but we, at that time, didn't know we were Indigenous."

For Indigenous Peoples, the UN therefore became both a site for channeling their complaints of human rights violations and also for articulating

---

29 In fact, the women's movement realized this around the end of the 1980s and launched a campaign at the 1993 World Conference on Human Rights in Vienna under the slogan "Women's rights are human rights."

their aspirations for their future as Indigenous Peoples. The UN also became a public space through which a global Indigenous Peoples' identity was born, especially as Indigenous Peoples from all continents were joining this movement. Today, we see that Indigenous Peoples link up as a circle of old friends via email on an almost daily basis to comment on recent developments, to organize, and to strategize.[30]

We should add that academia always had a special interest in Indigenous Peoples, and academics have always attended the meetings of UN bodies that are dealing with Indigenous Peoples. Academics from two disciplines in particular have accompanied Indigenous Peoples at the UN from the early 1980s and, in the early days, supported them in articulating their identities and aspirations: anthropology and international law, especially international human rights law.

D.   Changes Over Time

While stories abound at the local and national level of political and cultural resistance of Indigenous Peoples to colonialism, domination, and exploitation, these did not always find resonance at the international level, in particular at the United Nations. In the post-World War II era, questions about ethnicity and minorities were viewed with suspicion by states. It is well-known, for example, that even the human rights body established in 1946 for this purpose, the UN Sub-Commission on Prevention of Discrimination and Protection of Minorities, was essentially politically prevented from doing its work on minority issues by its parent bodies, including the Commission on Human Rights, until after the end of the Cold War in the late 1980s/early 1990s.

However, there is something that clearly distinguished the minority agenda from the Indigenous Peoples' agenda internationally. And that important distinguishing factor has been the passing from local struggles to international ones, through the creation of a robust, committed, and sustainable international Indigenous Peoples' movement and its dynamic interface with the United Nations. No such movement was created by minorities.

What have been the main changes of position among states on Indigenous issues? At first, in the 1970s and early 1980s, some humanitarian feeling, perhaps a certain historical guilt, was expressed by some states. Later, states had to take account of a strong awareness of problems they had created and a political movement of Indigenous Peoples asking for the correction of these problems. We can note a differentiation of states' positions vis-à-vis

---

30 An increasing number of Indigenous Peoples' organizations join in attending the UNPFII annually; some two thousand persons preregister every year.

Indigenous Peoples over the years. For example, in the 1970s, when the issue of gross violations of human rights such as mass killings in Guatemala was brought up in the human rights bodies, states approached the issue mostly as a humanitarian one, one of "kindness" so to speak, to what they viewed as disappearing civilizations, in the process of what they viewed as inevitable assimilation. Overconfident, perhaps, that their antagonists would soon disappear, some states felt they could be permissive or generous with regard to exceptional, unprecedented, and extensive participatory procedures for Indigenous Peoples. But the result was increased numbers of Indigenous representatives at the UN, a strengthening of the global movement as well as its overall political impact.

By 1993, this relative permissiveness on the part of various states had itself disappeared. The balance of power and international solidarity had shifted. The Indigenous movement was stronger, and the Draft Declaration on the Rights of Indigenous Peoples included strong language on the right to Indigenous self-determination, on cultural rights, and on the right to lands, territories, and resources. In the Latin American region especially, the realities of exclusion of Indigenous Peoples, combined with their increased political awareness, were creating tense situations. Who does not remember the appearance of the Zapatistas in 1994 and of the mysterious Subcomandante Marcos, Rafael Sebastián Guillén Vicente, in Mexico, whose supreme commander was a council of Indigenous Elders? It was not uncommon in the 1990s to hear rumors in UN corridors that the next big issue to deal with internationally after apartheid would be the oppression of Indigenous Peoples. Indigenous issues had acquired a global profile.

What circumstances gave rise to the international Indigenous Peoples' movement after World War II? And what role was played in this process by the UN human rights system? How and why did Indigenous Peoples' issues become international after World War II? How did the characteristics of this internationalization change over time? These are questions that are discussed in this book.

Two main postwar periods can be identified. The first period, from 1945 to 1993, is characterized by the building of the first international normative and institutional foundations for Indigenous Peoples' rights. The second period, from 1993 to the present, is characterized by the establishment of human rights monitoring, policy, and programming institutions, aiming at the improvement of Indigenous Peoples' conditions on the ground.[31] Both these periods emerged alongside the growing international Indigenous movement and because of the systematic advocacy of Indigenous Peoples.

---

31 See also SPFII, *State of the World's Indigenous Peoples*, 1–4.

It should be pointed out that Indigenous Peoples have sought to be represented not only at the global level but also at the regional level. A good example is Indigenous representation at the Arctic Council.[32]

Regarding Indigenous active expressions of self-determination, we can distinguish three phases, which do not coincide with the two periods. Phase one started with the internationalization of Indigenous issues by Indigenous Peoples deciding themselves, in exercise of their external right to self-determination, to go to the central international playing field of states, the UN. As peoples, they decided (a) to organize among themselves and (b) to contact the UN, in particular through the area of human rights. While they were not states, Indigenous Peoples behaved like sovereign entities, or in a "state-like" manner. This has become more interesting given that their most dangerous antagonists have often come to be nonstate actors like corporations and extractive industries.

Phase two consisted of Indigenous Peoples defining the content of their right to self-determination vis-à-vis the state, through their active participation in the creation of international norms. This took place especially during the long years of drafting the UNDRIP, in which no fewer than fifteen articles deal with the right to self-determination in its various manifestations. Indeed, many Indigenous Peoples, as sovereign self-determined entities, have been able to define their parameters in practice, and often in law, to define their borders vis-à-vis states and beyond states through the human rights norms pertaining to self-determination, the right to lands, territories and resources, and their cultural rights.[33]

It is also significant that the word "partnership" appears in the mottos of both International Decades of the World's Indigenous People. While we note here that the "s" is missing from the word "People" in the title of the Decades, the first Decade, launched in 1995 and completed in 2004, adopted the motto "Partnership in Action." The second Decade that started in 2005 had the motto "Partnership for Action and Dignity." Among the five objectives for the second Decade, particularly relevant to this discussion is the one on participation and free, prior and informed consent:

> (ii) Promoting full and effective participation of Indigenous peoples in decisions which directly or indirectly affect their lifestyles, traditional lands and territories, their cultural integrity as indigenous

32 Dorothée Cambou, "Enhancing the Participation of Indigenous Peoples at the Intergovernmental Level to Strengthen Self-Determination: Lessons from the Arctic," *Nordic Journal of International Law* 87, no. 1 (March 2018), https://doi.org/10.1163/15718107-08701002.

33 Sheryl Lightfoot and Elsa Stamatopoulou, eds., *Indigenous Peoples and Borders* (Durham, NC: Duke University Press, 2024).

peoples with collective rights or any other aspect of their lives, considering the principle of free, prior and informed consent.[34]

Phase three of the process of defining the right of Indigenous Peoples to self-determination has been taking place after the adoption of UNDRIP in 2007, in the current times of rampant economic globalization. The Declaration confirmed Indigenous Peoples' right to self-determination as one of its three pillars, along with land rights and cultural rights. Phase three may come as a surprise as it is not necessarily or not only aimed at redefining the state. At this point Indigenous Peoples themselves and Indigenous-related UN mechanisms have been stressing other aspects of self-determination: self-determination as autonomous existence, as continuous existence, irrespective of the state or parallel to the state. Globalization and its weakening of the state have created a power vacuum, occupied largely by the private sector, especially in the form of corporate capital and extractive industries. Partly by necessity due to state neglect and attacks by extractives, partly because of the power vacuum, and partly because of the affirmation of UNDRIP, Indigenous Peoples express, with increasing strength, the value of and confidence in their self-determined existence, in their governance systems, in their traditional knowledge, and in the many ways in which they practice self-determination.

The time after the 2014 World Conference on Indigenous Peoples at the UN has seen efforts by Indigenous Peoples to highlight articulations of their own visions of well-being and sustainability. They do so, for example, through approaches to climate change, not only in relation to a specific state but by expressing their own philosophies and ways of existing in the global system and in relation to nature as distinct polities and by placing a sharpened focus on external self-determination. In other words, the intense and long involvement of Indigenous Peoples has expanded the concept of self-determination, allowing them to participate in the international community as polities having a distinct international status and stature. The hope is that these Indigenous expressions of self-determination at the international level will also have positive impacts at national and grassroots levels.[35]

---

34 See "Second International Decade of the World's Indigenous People," *UN Department of Economic and Social Affairs' Indigenous Peoples website*, www.un.org/development/desa/indigenouspeoples/second-international-decade-of-the-worlds-indigenous-people.html, accessed 28 November 2022.

35 IWGIA, the International Work Group on Indigenous Affairs, has been documenting rich practices of Indigenous Peoples in this field. See, for example, *Indigenous Peoples' Rights to Autonomy and Self-Government as a Manifestation of the Right to Self-Determination* (Copenhagen: IWGIA, 2019), www.iwgia.org/en/resources/publications/305-books/3316-indigenous-peoples-rights-to-autonomy-and-self-government.html. Other relevant IWGIA publications include Jens Dahl et al., *Building Autonomies* (Copenhagen: IWGIA, 2020),

E. Indigenous Participation in Indigenous Rights-Related UN Bodies

In 2001, the then UN Commission on Human Rights (UNCHR), later replaced by the UN Human Rights Council, decided to establish a Special Rapporteur on the human rights and fundamental freedoms of Indigenous people to examine the situation worldwide on the basis of communications received and of country-specific visits.[36] The high visibility of this mandate, for some time now held by Indigenous persons, has encouraged the protection of Indigenous Peoples' rights, but it has also created awareness among Indigenous Peoples' communities of the possibility of using the existing human rights instruments and procedures of the UN to seek redress.

The UNPFII was established as a high-level body creating policies for inclusion and changing paradigms, in response to strong advocacy of Indigenous Peoples. A ten-year process of international consultation led to its establishment by the Economic and Social Council (ECOSOC) in resolution 2000/22: its broad mandate (economic and social development, environment, health, human rights, culture, and education) and its unprecedented composition (eight state-nominated and eight Indigenous-nominated experts) make the UNPFII unique. UNPFII is mandated to advise the ECOSOC, coordinate and integrate Indigenous issues in the UN system, and raise awareness about Indigenous issues, producing material to inform about Indigenous issues. This high-level body in the UN's hierarchy, with an unprecedented composition,

---

www.iwgia.org/en/resources/publications/3815-building-autonomies.html; Romina Quezada Morales, *Dialogue and Self-Determination through the Indigenous Navigator* (Copenhagen: IWGIA, 2021), www.iwgia.org/en/resources/publications/3990-dialogues-in-iwgia. html; Alberto Chirif, ed., *Towards the Conquest of Self-Determination. 50 Years Since the Barbados Declaration* (Copenhagen: IWGIA, 2021), www.iwgia.org/en/resources/ publications/305-books/4524-barbados-50.html. See also the following studies of the UN Expert Mechanism on the Rights of Indigenous Peoples: Efforts to Implement the Rights of Indigenous Peoples: Indigenous Peoples and the Right to Self-Determination, UN Doc. A/ HRC/48/75 (4 August 2021); and Free, Prior and Informed Consent: A Human Rights-Based Approach, UN Doc. A/HRC/39/62 (10 August 2018). See also the report under the UNPFII, Study on Indigenous Peoples' Autonomies: Experiences and Perspectives: Note by the Secretariat (Jens Dahl), UN Doc. E/C.19/2020/5 (30 January 2020). Victoria Tauli-Corpuz, the Special Rapporteur on the Rights of Indigenous Peoples, issued two relevant reports in 2019: an introductory comment on the issue of Indigenous Peoples and self-governance (Rights of Indigenous Peoples: Note by the Secretary-General; Report of the Special Rapporteur of the Human Rights Council on the Rights of Indigenous Peoples, UN Doc. A/72/186 [21 July 2017]), and a report on the right of Indigenous Peoples to autonomy or self-government (Rights of Indigenous Peoples: Note by the Secretary-General; Report of the Special Rapporteur on the Rights of Indigenous Peoples, UN Doc. A/74/149 [17 July 2019]). The Inter-American Commission on Human Rights published a report on the *Right to Self-Determination of Indigenous and Tribal Peoples* in 2021; for an executive summary, see www.oas.org/en/iachr/reports/pdfs/self-determination-EN.pdf.

36 UN Commission on Human Rights (UNCHR), Resolution 2001/57, Human Rights and Indigenous Issues, UN Doc. E/CN.4/RES/2001/57 (24 April 2001).

demonstrates the increasing political will of states to engage in dialogue with Indigenous Peoples and to address Indigenous issues in some way.

The mandate of the Permanent Forum includes human rights, as previously mentioned. UNDRIP, in Article 42, explicitly mentions the Permanent Forum as a UN body that should promote the implementation of the Declaration. The Indigenous movement was born and bred in the human rights movement and reached such high international visibility because of the particular moral, legal, and political edge that human rights evoke in people, societies, and states. This point is not missed by the sophisticated Indigenous movement nor by states. About fifteen hundred Indigenous participants from all parts of the world attend the annual sessions of the UNPFII in New York, in addition to some seventy countries and about thirty-five interstate entities.

Following strong advocacy by Indigenous Peoples, the UN Human Rights Council also established the EMRIP in 2007 to advise the Council by conducting studies, and to provide advice to specific countries at their request. Indigenous participation in EMRIP is also extensive and direct, as in the UNPFII. The seven members of EMRIP have been almost all Indigenous persons in the past several years.[37]

F. Self-Determination, Corrective Exceptionalism, and Other Theoretical Underpinnings

Contradictions, paradoxes and surprises have never been uncommon as Indigenous Peoples continue to weave their existence as polities at national and international level.

While Indigenous Peoples have come into friction or collision with states through their lived experiences and struggles, historic and contemporary, they have at the same time contacted the UN, an organization of states, to seek a reversal of the injustices toward themselves. This contradiction that has generally borne certain positive results for Indigenous Peoples is compounded by another one that has also borne positive results: the fact that Indigenous Peoples entered the UN through the "door" of human rights, an area that makes states particularly alert or defensive and, as I have said, attracts their political attention. Such attention can lead to positive state actions in the field of human rights.

Although the Working Group on Indigenous Populations (WGIP), the first body to deal with Indigenous Peoples rights at the UN, discussed later, was under the radar for some time because of its *ad hoc* nature and low position in the hierarchy of UN bodies, it produced criticism against states through the human rights discourse, despite formidable resistance from states. Indigenous

---

37 UN Human Rights Council resolution 6/36 of 2007 established EMRIP, and resolution 33/25 of 2016 amended its mandate.

Peoples' participation in this process was massive – and it is still massive in the Indigenous-related UN bodies that succeeded the Working Group – thanks to the creation of positive deviations from regular UN rules, which might be described (though not everyone would agree) as benign and remedial. The concept of *corrective exceptionalism* that I put forward shortly, and the concept of *remedial* measures, used by various scholars, seem to coincide when we consider the broad spectrum of special results reached by Indigenous Peoples' advocacy, including the recognition of Indigenous Peoples' right to self-determination as well as land rights and cultural rights.[38]

The frame of Indigenous Peoples' participation at the UN as nonstate entities remains unique. There is nothing comparable in terms of the participation of other nonstate entities. Over time, it has become clear that Indigenous Peoples' participation was not only a means to achieve other important goals of the movement, especially the improvement of conditions of life in Indigenous communities. Such participation was also a goal in itself, an expression of Indigenous Peoples' external self-determination. Indigenous Peoples' participation in the international community as self-determined political entities has a value of its own, with Indigenous Peoples wishing to be international actors, putting forward their visions and approaches to global issues, including climate change, the environment, peace, human rights, gender, and development, among others.

Looking at the impressive results of Indigenous Peoples' advocacy at international level, one question that arises is why states, the ultimate decision-makers at the UN, have allowed for these exceptional practices. The phenomenon I call corrective exceptionalism helps explain the creation of space for such exceptional regimes due to an implicit, or occasionally explicit, understanding or admission of historical injustices imposed on Indigenous Peoples. The elements of corrective exceptionalism are the following: (a) that exceptions to existing rules or practices in the interstate system are applied that have positive effects for Indigenous Peoples, especially in terms of their participation; (b) such exceptions imply the intention or ethical desire to move toward correcting the injustices imposed on Indigenous Peoples by states. Chapter 3 places special focus on the concept of corrective exceptionalism.

At the same time, Indigenous Peoples have been reshaping the concept of self-determination itself. At the UN, after the so-called decolonization period, Indigenous Peoples have pointed out that, for them, this period has not ended. The understandable reluctance of states to reconsider the national borders that resulted from colonialism and its aftermath has meant that there was and is little appetite for anything but superficial discussions on

---

38 S. James Anaya sees the remedial nature and value of the recognition of Indigenous Peoples' rights. See Anaya, *Indigenous Peoples in International Law*, 2nd ed. (Oxford: Oxford University Press, 2004).

self-determination. States have avoided talking in-depth about the subject even if it was included in the annual agendas of the Human Rights Council and the General Assembly. They have also resisted timid efforts to "codify" self-determination and statehood. On the other hand, the creation of exceptions to established rules and practice, enabling Indigenous Peoples to participate, has kept self-determination in the spotlight.

In short, self-determination is a major part of this story, both in the strategies of Indigenous Peoples insisting on the subject and in the ways in which states may have changed their stand. This analysis reveals another kind of content that Indigenous Peoples are giving to the right to self-determination in its external aspects, beyond that given by states.

Some of the seminal, precedent-creating moments of Indigenous Peoples' international participation include (a) the process and methodology of the *Study of the Problem of Discrimination against Indigenous Populations* (1972–1984); (b) the creation of a procedure for Indigenous Peoples' participation at the WGIP (1982, and especially 1983 onward); (c) the establishment by the UN General Assembly of the Voluntary Fund for Indigenous Populations (now "Peoples") in 1985, and the replication of this for the Convention on Biological Diversity and the World Intellectual Property Organization; (d) the participation of Indigenous leaders at the opening of the International Year of the World's Indigenous People at the General Assembly (1992) and subsequent similar processes; (e) the procedure established for the participation of Indigenous Peoples in the Working Group of the Commission on Human Rights on the drafting of the UNDRIP (1995); (f) the composition of the UNPFII, the election/selection of Indigenous-nominated members based on the seven sociocultural regions decided by Indigenous Peoples (as compared to the five of states), and the continuing massive participation of Indigenous Peoples at the Permanent Forum; (g) the inclusion of Indigenous speakers from the seven Indigenous sociocultural regions *for the first time* at a *formal* plenary meeting of the General Assembly on 25 April 2017, at the commemoration of the tenth anniversary of UNDRIP;[39] and (h) the current process for Indigenous Peoples' enhanced participation *as Indigenous Peoples* at the General Assembly and other UN venues of their interest.

The idea of the remedial nature of Indigenous Peoples' right to self-determination is relevant to this research. James Anaya points out that remedies "do not necessarily entail a return to the status quo ante but, rather, are to be developed in accordance with the present-day aspirations of the aggrieved groups, whose character may be substantially altered with the passage of time."[40] Claire Charters puts forward the "legitimacy-positive

---

39 Agnes Leina, Maasai leader from Kenya, was the first Indigenous leader to speak on that occasion.
40 Anaya, *Indigenous Peoples in International Law*, 107.

impact of a 'contextual-participation approach' to Indigenous Peoples' participation in international law-making" and argues that Indigenous Peoples' participation is a matter of justice and "should be substantial where the issue being negotiated at the international level is of considerable interest" to Indigenous Peoples and Indigenous Peoples "have not consented to state representation."[41] According to Charters, the self-determination point is that Indigenous Peoples'

> *participation is legitimate for reasons above and beyond the justifications for civil-society participation in international law and policy making generally. It is premised on Indigenous Peoples' claims to historical sovereignty and the need to mitigate, as best as possible, the illegitimacy of [colonization].*[42]

What has also emerged is that seemingly small steps matter – steps on the part especially of Indigenous Peoples, but also of states, international bodies, or others. They are not lost. They become part of a trend or a wave of Indigenous Peoples' taking a distinct position in modern international law and international politics; creating, reinterpreting, or bending rules; transgressing the status quo; and shaping new theoretical breakthroughs, international customs, norms, and institutions. Indigenous Peoples, through their actions at national and international levels, aim at resetting their relations to the state and their position in interstate organizations. Sheryl Lightfoot points out that the way the Indigenous Peoples' movement engages in global politics serves as a "transformational norm vector, pointing the way toward some alternative ways of doing global politics and new imaginings of political order."[43]

The concept of constructivism in international law and international relations also offers a tool to help understand the achievements of Indigenous Peoples' participation at the international level. The idea is that "law is most persuasive when it is created through processes of mutual construction by a wide range of participants," focusing "upon a particular understanding of legal legitimacy, rooted in adherence to internal morality and the specificity of legal rationality."[44]

---

41 Claire Charters, "A Self-Determination Approach to Justifying Indigenous Peoples' Participation in International Law and Policy Making," *International Journal on Minority and Group Rights* 17, no. 2 (2010): 215, https://doi.org/10.1163/157181110X495872.

42 Charters, "Self-Determination Approach," 216.

43 Sheryl Lightfoot, *Global Indigenous Politics: A Subtle Revolution* (London: Routledge, 2016), 4.

44 Jutta Brunnée and Stephen J. Toope, "International Law and Constructivism: Elements of an Interactional Theory of International Law," *Columbia Journal of Transnational Law* 39, no. 1 (2000): 19.

Borrowing liberally from the concept of relative autonomy in political theory,[45] we note that the various institutions within the UN system have "relative autonomy" that can open them up to the issues raised by Indigenous representatives. For example, the UN Secretariat, as one of the organs of the UN under the UN Charter, not only carries out the requests of the political bodies of the UN, such as the Human Rights Council or the General Assembly, but also has the possibility to act in ways that are relatively independent. Thus Article 100 of the UN Charter, for example, proclaims the independence of the international civil service.[46] This means that the UN Secretariat and UN agency officials have the capacity, within certain parameters, to act with autonomy and to facilitate Indigenous Peoples' participation in interstate processes.

G. The Purpose of This Book

What is the main purpose of this book? By examining significant periods or moments in the international Indigenous Peoples' movement since the late 1970s, it tries to shed light on why and how Indigenous Peoples have made such important achievements at the international level. Why and how has substantive participation been a characteristic aspiration and pursuit of Indigenous Peoples at all levels? What have been the philosophies, strategies, and approaches that Indigenous Peoples have selected to put their issues forward as self-determined peoples? How do they express external aspects of self-determination at international fora? How have they created a positive international environment that was and is receptive to their visions and aspirations? How were and are their initiatives received by states and by the interstate system and with what impact? How has Indigenous Peoples' international self-presentation and representation changed over time? What are the theoretical foundations and creations of the Indigenous Peoples' movement? What has been the role of human rights discourses in the internationalization of Indigenous Peoples' issues? What are the lessons – political,

---

45 According to the *Oxford Dictionary of Politics*, relative autonomy is "the theory that any social totality has four separate and distinct sets of practices – economic, political, ideological, and theoretical – which act in combination, but each of which has its own relative autonomy according to the limits set by its place in the totality." *A Concise Oxford Dictionary of Politics and International Relations*, 4th ed. (2018), s.v. "relative autonomy."

46 "1. In the performance of their duties the Secretary-General and the staff shall not seek or receive instructions from any government or from any other authority external to the Organization. They shall refrain from any action which might reflect on their position as international officials responsible only to the Organization. 2. Each Member of the United Nations undertakes to respect the exclusively international character of the responsibilities of the Secretary-General and the staff and not to seek to influence them in the discharge of their responsibilities." Article 100, Chapter 15: The Secretariat, United Nations Charter, 26 June 1945, www.un.org/en/about-us/un-charter/chapter-15.

cultural, legal, and other – that can be learned from the Indigenous Peoples' movement for younger generations of leaders and for other social justice and anticolonial movements? How can national power structures veer toward a hybrid balance once issues are internationalized? I hope to answer these questions.

I also hope this book will serve as a reference tool of the history of the international Indigenous Peoples' movement, as well as a tool for the intergenerational transmission of knowledge regarding the movement. The many years of the Indigenous Peoples' movement and its broad geographical presence across continents lead to the realization that there are many histories – local, national, regional, and global – that have been lived and sometimes captured in writings of various forms over time. So much information and knowledge, one could say, cannot be contained in just one research project, since it is held by many. In this sense, this book sees itself as one modest contribution among others.

The book's main novelty lies in the approach to a specific aspect of Indigenous Peoples' right to self-determination – namely, the aspect expressed through Indigenous participation in international fora, especially at UN fora. The research brings out, among other things, my notion of corrective exceptionalism as one theory that underlies the expansion of Indigenous Peoples' participation in international processes. There are of course other aspects of external self-determination exercised by Indigenous Peoples, including treaties among Indigenous Peoples and between Indigenous Peoples and states,[47] as well as other relations developed by Indigenous Peoples across state borders. The research is future-oriented and reveals the dynamic and evolving nature of Indigenous participation. It also takes into account a gender and an intergenerational perspective and weaves both a historical perspective and recent developments, including the 2014 World Conference on Indigenous Peoples and its Outcome Document on the topic of enhanced Indigenous participation in the UN system. It is important to mention here the visionary Alta Outcome Document from the 2013 Global Indigenous Preparatory Conference (also known as the Alta Conference) for the World Conference on Indigenous Peoples. The Alta Outcome Document has several references to the right to self-determination in its various forms, and the Outcome Document of the 2014 World Conference reflected some of those.[48] The negotiations on enhanced participation, under the aegis of the President of

---

47 See the discussion of this topic in Dalee Sambo Dorough, "The Significance of the Declaration on the Rights of Indigenous Peoples and Its Future Implementation," in *Making the Declaration Work: The United Nations Declaration on the Rights of Indigenous Peoples,* ed. Claire Charters and Rodolfo Stavenhagen (Copenhagen: IWGIA, 2009), 272–274, www.iwgia.org/iwgia_files_publications_files/making_the_declaration_work.pdf.
48 The Alta Conference took place 10–12 June 2013, in Alta, Norway, to prepare for the World Conference on Indigenous Peoples, held 22–23 September 2014 in New York.

the General Assembly, are discussed further in Chapter 4, Section L ("The Vision of Enhanced Participation"). Consultations were still underway as of the time of this writing, and no solution had yet been found. However, various ideas have surfaced that demonstrate a direction toward enhanced Indigenous participation at the interstate level.

H. Methodologies

This book is interdisciplinary. It is primarily located within the disciplines of international law, international relations, political science, and, more broadly, Indigenous studies. Qualitative and primary sources include my own professional and research experiences on Indigenous Peoples' rights since 1981; numerous related UN reports that I either authored or studied; numerous international meetings I organized or participated in, including those on the drafting of the UNDRIP; country-specific missions I was part of over the years; numerous consultations; relations with Indigenous and other organizations; research for various books, articles, or book chapters I published; as well as research for my academic teachings and presentations at various fora over the years. Documents published by the UN, other interstate organizations, Indigenous Peoples and their organizations, and individual states are used as primary sources. Academic literature and testimonies of Indigenous persons that appear in published literature are also cited as primary sources.

Numerous discussions with Indigenous representatives over the decades of my involvement are precious sources contributing to understandings of complex issues reflected in this book. Discussions with state representatives, staff of interstate organizations, and academics have added to the explanation of questions and have informed my knowledge and views on various issues.

I also conducted specific interviews with Indigenous leaders and other engaged stakeholders who experienced the processes of Indigenous Peoples' participation and expressions of self-determination or have otherwise been actively involved. Eighteen persons were interviewed between 2016 and 2022 specifically for this research project; these were mostly Indigenous leaders, in addition to one official of a UN agency and one official of an NGO working on Indigenous Peoples' rights. I knew the interviewed personalities within the context of my work over the years. The following people were interviewed, and their titles and dates of interviews appear in Annex 1: Claire Charters, Antonella Cordone, Myrna Cunningham, Kenneth Deer, Binota Moy Dhamai, Lola Garcia-Alix, Moana Jackson, Mikaela Jade, Carson Kiburo, Wilton Littlechild, Oren Lyons, Les Malezer, Aehshatou Manu, Aroha Mead, Chhing Lamu Sherpa, Rodion Sulyandziga, Victoria (Vicky) Tauli-Corpuz,

---

See the Alta Outcome Document, 2013, www.un.org/esa/socdev/unpfii/documents/wc/AdoptedAlta_outcomedoc_EN.pdf.

and Howard Thompson. I am deeply grateful for the generosity, time, and insights that these extraordinary leaders offered. I am obviously the only person responsible for opinions I express in this book.

The questions that animated these interviews were broad enough to give the opportunity for interviewees to express their thoughts as extensively as they chose on the fundamental question of Indigenous Peoples' participation and expression of self-determination at the international level. The purpose of this research project was explained to each interviewee, and all were asked for permission to quote them by name in the book; they all agreed. I also asked whether they would first like to see the quotations I would use from their interviews; a few interviewees asked to see them, and I sent those quotations to those who requested them.

The following questions were discussed with each person interviewed:

1. Why did/do Indigenous Peoples come to the UN and its organizations?
2. How did Indigenous Peoples pursue participation during the decades of their interface with the UN? What were some special moments of opportunity during those decades?
3. Regarding UN General Assembly processes, what is Indigenous Peoples' vision for participation after the World Conference on Indigenous Peoples Outcome Document asked for consideration of enhanced participation of Indigenous Peoples?
4. How do you see Indigenous Peoples' participation at the UN as compared to that of states?
5. What expectations do Indigenous Peoples have from or within their own communities regarding participation?
6. What have been/are major difficulties in Indigenous Peoples' participation?
7. Why do you think states have allowed Indigenous Peoples' participation at the UN through exceptional procedures?
8. What changes do you see in Indigenous Peoples' participation over time in terms of quality and results?
9. How does participation of Indigenous Peoples at the UN (and other interstate organizations) impact relations between Indigenous Peoples and states at the national level? How does it change relations within the state (if it does)?

The book places significant focus on human rights, the first area of international law and relations where Indigenous Peoples presented their concerns and aspirations. As is well-known, Indigenous Peoples' international advocacy has expanded to other areas – including environment, development, health, education, climate change, peace, culture, traditional knowledge, and other areas – always providing a focus on human rights and stressing the need to implement the UNDRIP. In addition to the human rights field and the Indigenous-related UN fora, the book examines at some length the field of "development" at the interstate level, where significant international attention and resources are concentrated and in which Indigenous Peoples have devoted substantive participation and advocacy. In an effort to keep this book to a manageable length, the research does not expand equally on every field of international Indigenous participation. My hope is that, within the parameters of this research, the book brings out a worthwhile analysis of Indigenous Peoples' external self-determination at the international level.

I. The Chapters

The book combines the history and analysis of Indigenous Peoples' expressions of self-determination at the international level, weaving the various aspects into five chapters.

Chapter 1, "The Formative Years," discusses the first organized efforts of the Indigenous Peoples movement in the post-WWII era to contact the UN, seeking recognition of their situation and proclamation of their rights. What were the results of these efforts? The chapter analyzes the strategies, methods, and narratives of Indigenous Peoples, starting with the launch of the UN Study of the Problem of Discrimination against Indigenous Populations in 1972, the interventions of Indigenous Peoples at the 1977 International NGO Conference on Discrimination against Indigenous Populations in the Americas, and ending, at this first phase, in 1983, with the unprecedented acceptance of direct Indigenous participation in the WGIP. These efforts, immersed in concepts of human rights, decolonization, and social justice, achieved the internationalization of Indigenous Peoples' issues, the creation of a global Indigenous Peoples' movement and a global Indigenous identity, and the establishment of a new "Indigenous" space in the interstate system, a space that was to expand considerably in years to come. The chapter includes an account of how issues of minorities, "inherited" by the First and Second World Wars, compounded fears of states and contributed a certain resistance to Indigenous issues.

Chapter 2, "The Victory of Nondefinition," discusses the linkages between the understanding of the term "Indigenous Peoples" and decolonization and self-determination. By stressing this link as well as their right to self-determination and self-identification, Indigenous Peoples insisted on and achieved not being defined formally by the UN, while also claiming their rights. By critiquing the "doctrine of discovery" and other concepts of colonization, Indigenous Peoples created an understanding of indigeneity that goes beyond the "blue water principle" and establishes a global political, human rights, and legal category of Indigenous Peoples valid for all continents. A discussion of Palestinian participation in the UN's Indigenous-related bodies shows, among other things, what can be at stake in a definition.

Chapter 3, "The Rise of Corrective Exceptionalism," lays out what the "normal" UN procedures were for accepting nonstate actors as part of the interstate processes and what the battlefield looked like when Indigenous Peoples attempted to open these processes for themselves. This chapter also discusses the moral and political leadership that bent UN procedures and gradually transformed the UN from a space just for states into a space in favor of Indigenous Peoples' direct participation, where Indigenous Peoples could and can own at least part of the narrative. The drama of the confrontation between Indigenous Peoples and states has played out visibly at the UN, and it has often been virulent, including state resistance to documenting their abuses against Indigenous Peoples. Yet the paradox is that states either acquiesced or proactively cultivated direct Indigenous participation at the UN. This phenomenon of corrective exceptionalism has had an ever-increasing impact on the political visibility and normative and institutional achievements of the Indigenous Peoples' movement.

Chapter 4, "Self-Representations and Demands of Indigenous Peoples," has a central position in the book. It is an especially long chapter, as it combines a broad analysis of the issues with accounts of concrete examples from practice that bring key points to the surface. The chapter explores the question of how Indigenous Peoples represent themselves at the international level on their own terms, while laying out their often politically controversial demands on states; and it examines how and why these self-presentations create a cultural, legal, and political space that impacts positively on political outcomes. The long negotiation process of the UNDRIP provides the ground for the analysis of these questions, including new concepts engrained in the Declaration and Indigenous protocols that represent Indigenous philosophies. What has been the form and impact of Indigenous women's participation? What role is played by Indigenous youth? How have Indigenous protocols been expressed and interwoven in Indigenous participation? The early internationalization of the case of the Yanomami gives further insights of novel approaches promoted by Indigenous Peoples. The chapter finally asks what the limits are of Indigenous Peoples' participation within the international interstate system, including an analysis of efforts to enhance Indigenous participation at the UN General Assembly and elsewhere.

Chapter 5, "The Right to Self-Determined Development," deals with another central topic and the position and advocacy of Indigenous Peoples within it: how Indigenous Peoples have been questioning the dominant development paradigm – in fact the very concept of "development" – through their participation, especially at the international level, since the beginning of the WGIP and, later, at the UNPFII, as well as in major international debates on the Millennium Development Goals (MDGs) and the Sustainable Development Goals (SDGs). The latter two have been major battlegrounds on such issues, where Indigenous Peoples have articulated what could constitute a just development and well-being for all people and the planet. A section at the end of the chapter is devoted to the SDGs and Indigenous Peoples' participation, and another section focuses on the concept of "good examples" of Indigenous Peoples' participation in development processes. Given the emphasis on development in the international system, and the active involvement of Indigenous Peoples in such policy efforts, this chapter unveils additional opportunities and challenges for Indigenous participation. The issues woven under the concept of development, including environment, climate change, and traditional knowledge, also help us understand what self-determined development would mean for Indigenous Peoples.

It is my sincere hope that this book will spark further dialogues, research, and actions that are substantively informed by Indigenous Peoples' rights and their continuing struggles and advocacy.

Bibliography

Alta Outcome Document. "Global Indigenous Preparatory Conference for the United Nations High Level Plenary Meeting of the General Assembly to Be Known as the World Conference on Indigenous Peoples." Alta, 10–12 June 2013. www.un.org/esa/socdev/unpfii/documents/wc/AdoptedAlta_outcomedoc_EN.pdf.

Anaya, S. James. *Indigenous Peoples in International Law*. 2nd ed. Oxford: Oxford University Press, 2004.

Anongos, Abigal, Dmitry Berezhkov, Sarimin J. Boengkih, Julie Cavanaugh-Bill, Asier Martínez de Bringas, Robert Goodland, Stuart Kirsch, Roger Moody, Geoff Nettleton, Legborsi Saro Pyagbara, and Brian Wyatt. *Pitfalls & Pipelines: Indigenous Peoples and Extractive Industries*. Edited by Andy Whitmore. Baguio City: Tebtebba Foundation; Copenhagen: IWGIA; London: PIPLinks, 2012.

Brunnée, Jutta, and Stephen J. Toope. "International Law and Constructivism: Elements of an Interactional Theory of International Law." *Columbia Journal of Transnational Law* 39, no. 1 (2000): 19–74.

Cambou, Dorothée. "Enhancing the Participation of Indigenous Peoples at the Intergovernmental Level to Strengthen Self-Determination: Lessons from the Arctic." *Nordic Journal of International Law* 87, no. 1 (March 2018): 26–55. https://doi.org/10.1163/15718107-08701002.

Charters, Claire. "A Self-Determination Approach to Justifying Indigenous Peoples' Participation in International Law and Policy Making." *International Journal on Minority and Group Rights* 17, no. 2 (2010): 215–240. https://doi.org/10.1163/157181110X495872.

Chirif, Alberto, ed. *Towards the Conquest of Self-Determination. 50 Years Since the Barbados Declaration*. Copenhagen: IWGIA, 2021. www.iwgia.org/en/resources/publications/305-books/4524-barbados-50.html.

Dahl, Jens, Victoria Tauli-Corpuz, Shapion Noningo Sesen, Shankar Limbu, and Sara Olsvig. *Building Autonomies*. Copenhagen: IWGIA, 2020. www.iwgia.org/en/resources/publications/3815-building-autonomies.html.

Deskaheh. "An Iroquois Patriot's Fight for International Recognition: The Last Speech of Deskaheh." In *Basic Call to Consciousness*, edited by Akwesasne Notes, 41–54. Summertown, TN: Native Voices, 2005.

Dorough, Dalee Sambo. "The Significance of the Declaration on the Rights of Indigenous Peoples and Its Future Implementation." In *Making the Declaration Work: The United Nations Declaration on the Rights of Indigenous Peoples*, edited by Claire Charters and Rodolfo Stavenhagen, 264–78. Copenhagen: IWGIA, 2009. www.iwgia.org/iwgia_files_publications_files/making_the_declaration_work.pdf.

Doyle, Cathal M., and Andrew Whitmore. *Indigenous Peoples and the Extractive Sector: Towards a Rights-Respecting Engagement*. Baguio City: Tebtebba Foundation; London: PIPLinks and Middlesex University, 2014.

Front Line Defenders. *Global Analysis 2022*. Dublin: FLD, 2023. www.frontlinedefenders.org/en/resource-publication/global-analysis-2022.

Hannum, Hurst. "New Developments in Indigenous Rights." *Virginia Journal of International Law* 28 (1988): 649–678.

Inter-American Commission on Human Rights. "Executive Summary to *Right to Self-Determination of Indigenous and Tribal Peoples*." 2021. www.oas.org/en/iachr/reports/pdfs/self-determination-EN.pdf.

Inter-American Commission on Human Rights. Indigenous Peoples, Afro-Descendent Communities, and Natural Resources: Human Rights Protection in the Context of Extraction, Exploitation, and Development Activities. OEA/Ser.L/V/II, Doc. 47/15. IACHR, 2015. www.oas.org/en/iachr/reports/pdfs/extractiveindustries2016.pdf.

International Labor Organization. *Implementing the ILO Indigenous and Tribal Peoples Convention No. 169: Towards an Inclusive, Sustainable and Just Future*. Geneva: ILO, 2019.

International Work Group for Indigenous Affairs (IWGIA). *Indigenous Peoples' Rights to Autonomy and Self-Government as a Manifestation of the Right to Self-Determination*. Copenhagen: IWGIA, 2019. www.iwgia.org/en/resources/publications/305-books/3316-indigenous-peoples-rights-to-autonomy-and-self-government.html.

Lightfoot, Sheryl. *Global Indigenous Politics: A Subtle Revolution*. London: Routledge, 2016.

Lightfoot, Sheryl, and Elsa Stamatopoulou, eds. *Indigenous Peoples and Borders*. Durham, NC: Duke University Press, 2024.

McKay, Fergus, ed. *Indigenous Peoples and United Nations Human Rights Bodies. A Compilation of UN Treaty Body Jurisprudence, Special Procedures of the Human Rights Council, and the Advice of the Expert Mechanism on the Rights of Indigenous Peoples*. Vol. 7, 2015–2016. Forest Peoples Program, 2017. www.forestpeoples.org/en/law-policy-un-human-rights-system-guides-human-rights-mechanisms/report/2017/indigenous-peoples-and.

Morales, Romina Quezada. *Dialogue and Self-Determination Through the Indigenous Navigator*. Copenhagen: IWGIA, 2021. www.iwgia.org/en/resources/publications/3990-dialogues-in-iwgia.html.

Muehlebach, Andrea. "'Making Place' at the United Nations: Indigenous Cultural Politics at the U.N. Working Group on Indigenous Populations." *Cultural Anthropology* 16, no. 3 (August 2001): 415–448. https://doi.org/10.1525/can.2001.16.3.415.

Pulitano, Elvira. "Conference Diplomacy at the United Nations and the Advancement of Indigenous Rights." *UN Chronicle* 51, no. 3 (December 2014). www.un.org/en/chronicle/article/conference-diplomacy-united-nations-and-advancement-indigenous-rights.

Sanders, Douglas E. *The Formation of the World Council of Indigenous Peoples.* IWGIA Document 29. Copenhagen: International Secretariat of IWGIA, 1977.

Secretariat of the Permanent Forum on Indigenous Issues (SPFII). *State of the World's Indigenous Peoples.* UN Doc. ST/ESA/328. New York: UN Department of Economic and Social Affairs, 2009. www.un.org/esa/socdev/unpfii/documents/SOWIP/en/SOWIP_web.pdf.

Stamatopoulou, Elsa. "Walking the Talk? Including Indigenous Peoples' Issues in Intergovernmental Organizations." In *Indigenous Peoples' Rights in International Law: Emergence and Application,* edited by Roxanne Dunbar-Ortiz, Dalee Sambo Dorough, Gudmundur Alfredsson, Lee Swepston, and Petter Wille, 172–199. Kautokeino: Gáldu; Copenhagen: IWGIA, 2015.

Tauli-Corpuz, Victoria. Rights of Indigenous Peoples: Note by the Secretary-General; Report of the Special Rapporteur of the Human Rights Council on the Rights of Indigenous Peoples. UN Doc. A/72/186, 21 July 2017.

Tauli-Corpuz, Victoria. Rights of Indigenous Peoples: Note by the Secretary-General; Report of the Special Rapporteur on the Rights of Indigenous Peoples. UN Doc. A/74/149, 17 July 2019.

UN Charter, 26 June 1945. www.un.org/en/about-us/un-charter/.

UN Commission on Human Rights (UNCHR). Resolution 2001/57, Human Rights and Indigenous Issues. UN Doc. E/CN.4/RES/2001/57, 24 April 2001.

UN Department of Economic and Social Affairs (DESA). "Second International Decade of the World's Indigenous People." UN DESA's "Indigenous Peoples." Accessed 28 November 2022. www.un.org/development/desa/indigenouspeoples/second-international-decade-of-the-worlds-indigenous-people.html.

UN Expert Mechanism on the Rights of Indigenous Peoples. Efforts to Implement the Rights of Indigenous Peoples: Indigenous Peoples and the Right to Self-Determination. UN Doc. A/HRC/48/75, 4 August 2021.

UN Expert Mechanism on the Rights of Indigenous Peoples. Free, Prior and Informed Consent: A Human Rights-Based Approach, UN Doc. A/HRC/39/62, 10 August 2018.

UN General Assembly. Resolution 2200A, International Covenant on Economic, Social and Cultural Rights. UN Doc. A/RES/2200A, 16 December 1966. www.ohchr.org/en/instruments-mechanisms/instruments/international-covenant-economic-social-and-cultural-rights.

UN General Assembly. Resolution 275 (III), Study of the Social Problems of the Aboriginal Populations and Other Under-Developed Social Groups of the American Continent. UN Doc. A/RES/275(III), 11 May 1949.

UN General Assembly. Resolution 61/295, United Nations Declaration on the Rights of Indigenous Peoples. UN Doc. A/RES/61/295, 13 September 2007. www.un.org/development/desa/indigenouspeoples/wp-content/uploads/sites/19/2018/11/UNDRIP_E_web.pdf.

UN Permanent Forum on Indigenous Issues. Indigenous Peoples Collective Rights to Lands, Territories and Resources. Backgrounder. UNPFII, 2018. www.un.org/development/desa/indigenouspeoples/wp-content/uploads/sites/19/2018/04/Indigenous-Peoples-Collective-Rights-to-Lands-Territories-Resources.pdf.

UN Permanent Forum on Indigenous Issues. Indigenous Peoples in the Asian Region. Backgrounder. UNPFII, 2014. www.un.org/esa/socdev/unpfii/documents/2014/press/asia.pdf.

UN Permanent Forum on Indigenous Issues. Study on Indigenous Peoples' Autonomies: Experiences and Perspectives: Note by the Secretariat (Jens Dahl). UN Doc. E/C.19/2020/5, 30 January 2020.

UN Sub-Commission on Prevention of Discrimination and Protection of Minorities. Study of the Problem of Discrimination against Indigenous Populations: Final Report (First Part) Submitted by the Special Rapporteur, Mr. José Martínez Cobo. Introduction. UN Doc. E/CN.4/Sub.2/476, 30 July 1981. https://social.desa.un.org/publications/martinez-cobo-study.

UN Sub-Commission on Prevention of Discrimination and Protection of Minorities. Study of the Problem of Discrimination against Indigenous Populations: Final Report (Last Part) Submitted by the Special Rapporteur, Mr. José R. Martínez Cobo. Chapters XXI – XXII: Conclusions, Proposals and Recommendations. UN Doc. E/CN.4/Sub.2/1983/21/Add.8, 30 September 1983. https://social.desa.un.org/publications/martinez-cobo-study.

1

THE FORMATIVE YEARS

A. Indigenous Voices

Indigenous Peoples have come to the United Nations for diverse reasons. They have in common, however, a sense of history that reflects the systemic discrimination they have suffered, their struggles to overcome it, and their aspiration for more just futures. Despite some skepticism about the UN, based on its own history – and Indigenous Peoples could enumerate their reasons – they managed to arrive at a view of the UN as a positive space where it made sense for them to seek recognition of their cause, where they could get a hearing for their opinions and visions of justice, where it was not implausible for them to expect solidarity, where Indigenous Peoples could also share with the rest of humanity the hard-earned knowledge from their own experiences. While exclusion and lack of positive action are realities for Indigenous Peoples in the countries where they live, they have won acceptance for themselves as international actors and subjects of international law at the UN, thereby participating in the creation of norms and policies that impact their lives and also the broader well-being of humanity and nature.

I interviewed several historic and younger Indigenous leaders from various regions of the world and their reflections are eloquent.[1] We explored the questions of why Indigenous Peoples went and continue to go to the UN, what the impact of such international mobilization is, and what some threshold moments in the Indigenous Peoples' movement have been. I start this

---

1 The list of persons with whom discussions were held appears in Annex 1. The questions discussed with interviewees are listed in the introduction.

DOI: 10.4324/9781003464099-2

first chapter with extensive excerpts from these discussions.[2] Other excerpts are included in other chapters. I am deeply grateful and feel honored as an author and as a reader that people gave their time with commitment and sincerity for these interviews, sharing wisdom from their lifelong experiences.

Why did Indigenous Peoples come to the UN, and why do they continue to come? Oren Lyons, the Elder and Faithkeeper of the Onondaga Nation, a leader who was there from the beginning of international mobilizations with other Haudenosaunee, recalled that Mohawk and Onondaga Chiefs visited England and Queen Anne in 1701.[3] He also recalled that the Six Nations, the Haudenosaunee, had one of their Chiefs, Deskaheh, go to the League of Nations in 1923, but he was not accepted.

> *International participation is part of a broad spectrum of levels of battle that we are engulfed in. We have to be at every level. We have to fight at the international level, the national level, the local level. And that's a continuous process. Decisions are made on our behalf in these international levels, and if you're not there, as I've said before, if you're not at the table, you're on the menu. . . . So it's important, it's fundamentally important to be there as a presence and as a statement, a general statement to the public at large: yes, here you are. Regardless of what anybody else says. Being there and being seen, and understood, and speaking, is fundamentally important to identity, and the continuation of ourselves.*

Chief Lyons linked the global mobilization of Indigenous Peoples with the history of colonialism and the pivotal 1977 International NGO Conference on Discrimination against Indigenous Populations in the Americas, discussed further in this chapter.

> *The watershed moment of course was when we went to Geneva, when we decided that that was where we had to go. That was in 1977, but a lot of discussion [took place] prior to that, preparation. In 1972 they assigned Chief Powers and myself to be the guard, the advance guard, to move that. . . . When we went to Geneva, in '77, it was a delegation of leaders that were fighting for their recognition as nations because they couldn't find any justice in the lands that we were on. . . . We never left that position, and we always gathered every year, and it gave us time at least once a year to sit and talk amongst ourselves about what was going on around the world. I would say that that was a premier watershed moment, and it was a revelation*

---

2 In presenting excerpts of interviews, I tried to preserve their spontaneity, depth, and frankness, for which I am eternally grateful to the interviewees, without including in the text some words that are sometimes used to link parts of thoughts and sentences in oral communication.

3 Lyons interviewed by the author, 20 September 2016.

to many people around the world that Indigenous People were still here. Because the policies of the colonial governments, of both the United States and [others], whether it was England, or the UK (it has to bear the responsibility) of advocating the extinction of the reality of the political body called Indigenous nations. And they [those states] were determined. [They]were based on Christian policies, and the Christian doctrine, which later became better known as the doctrine of discovery, and illustrated how long ago those roots were set. The doctrine of discovery, it wasn't the first time it was used – it was used in Africa, it was used in India, it was used in Asia. . . . It's a Christian doctrine. Further, [this doctrine posited that] if there are people there, and they are not Christian, they do not have a right to title of land. They have only the right of occupancy. Which was the same right applied to the deer, and the bears, and the rabbits, and the raccoons. And to the Native people. And that was not only offhand, but it was a standard remark.

Kenneth Deer of the Mohawk Nation of the Kahnawake territory is an award-winning journalist, educator, and internationally known Indigenous rights activist. He was also an active participant in the development of the UN Declaration of the Rights of Indigenous Peoples (UNDRIP). He addressed the question of why Indigenous Peoples went and continue to go to the UN:[4]

The Haudenosaunee in North America, particularly in Canada, felt that the government of Canada was not living up to its obligations. And we felt as a sovereign people, we had a right to take our complaints to the League of Nations. So the Haudenosaunee sent a Cayuga Chief to the League of Nations, here in Geneva, in 1923. His title was Deskaheh. His English name was "Levi General." He came to the League of Nations to complain that Canada was not living up to its obligations or its treaties. He tried hard to get into the League of Nations. But when Canada found out he was here, Canada, with the help of Great Britain, prevented him from speaking.
. . . If you go forward to Wounded Knee in 1973, in the aftermath, in 1974, there was a gathering of leaders in the United States. And they concluded that they couldn't get justice in America. So they had to have a campaign to take our issues internationally. We started a process to assign people to open the doors of the UN. And that led to the 1977 meeting of the NGO Conference on Racial Discrimination against the Indigenous Peoples of the Western Hemisphere. That's a seminal meeting in '77. . . . About 200, 250 Indigenous people came to Geneva. And the Haudenosaunee sent a delegation.

4 Deer interviewed by the author, 6 April 2016.

> *. . . When our people decided to come, they said, "Well, we're not going to come as Canadians or Americans. We're going to come as Haudenosaunee. When Deskaheh came, he made his own passport to come to Geneva. So when our delegation came in, in '77, they made their own passports too, on a piece of leather and paper. . . . So when they arrived here in Geneva, the Swiss didn't know what to do with them. Who are these people with this strange passport? So they held them at the airport. They wouldn't let them enter Switzerland. That's where the issue started, [how] to get them in. And when the Mayor of Geneva heard about it, he said to let them in on his authority. So they let them in. And then the Mayor invited them to dinner at City Hall. When they went to City Hall, they met the Mayor, and lo and behold, that little boy that was tugging on Deskaheh's shirt in the 1920s was now the Mayor of Geneva.*

Victoria Tauli-Corpuz, the famous Igorot leader from the Philippines and former UN Special Rapporteur on the Rights of Indigenous Peoples as well as former Chairperson of the UNPFII, when interviewed, also addressed the question of why Indigenous Peoples came and continue to come to the UN.[5]

> *Indigenous Peoples can hardly find any remedy to social problems that they face in their own countries. So, they are seeking ways to bring the issues to a body which can address them, or at least where they can raise the issues in a more direct way and get some suggestions or reactions in terms of how they can deal with the problems. But I think the other [reason they are coming to the UN] is also a realization that international standards can also help influence the domestic laws or domestic policies which might be helpful for Indigenous Peoples in terms of their issues being addressed. I think that is really why they persist in coming to the UN.*

On the question of what the threshold moments of the international Indigenous movement were, Tauli-Corpuz identified a number of events and circumstances:

> *I think the coming together of Indigenous Peoples supported by NGOs, and institutions like the World Council of Churches was a catalytic moment, because that really brought together Indigenous Peoples from different parts of the world to talk about their situations and identify what are the common problems or elements that they face as Indigenous Peoples. . . .*

---

5 Tauli-Corpuz interviewed by the author, 18 October 2016.

But the other part was the 1977 Conference in Geneva. I think that was also [a special moment]. Generally at that time, there were really strong Indigenous Peoples coming into the picture because of the issues that they faced. And there was this consciousness that they would like to develop a movement where they can influence some processes. And the UN of course provided that kind of a setting.

I think the other moment is the establishment [realization] of the study, this Martínez Cobo Study [of the Problem of Discrimination against Indigenous Populations]. This was really important in terms of raising awareness within the UN itself, which led to the creation of the Working Group on Indigenous Populations and the objective of having to draft a Declaration [on the rights of Indigenous Peoples]. So, the establishment of the Working Group and the decision to start drafting the Declaration in '85 was another moment, it was a seminal moment. . . .

Those were the moments where those sorts of ideas gelled and were put before the UN. . . . Even in '92 [there was] another way that Indigenous Peoples participated – and I say this because I did . . . [They participated] in the World Conference on Environment and Development. Because we really thought that you cannot have such a theme [and not participate], and it does capture much of the thinking of Indigenous Peoples in terms of being holistic and all that. So we did participate, I myself participated in Rio. Before that I took part in the preparatory meetings in New York, because I was invited to make a paper on Asian Indigenous Peoples' perspectives on environment and development. On that basis, I came into . . . two preparatory meetings, and then the Rio Conference. That was also a [pivotal] moment because Indigenous Peoples were there. I remember Ole Henrik Magga was there too, and there was a big group of Indigenous Peoples. Even during the preparatory meetings, we were already proposing that Indigenous Peoples be considered part of the major groups which would enter into the Agenda '21 agreement, and its plan of action. . . . That was a very good moment as well. Then, after that, every year we come to the UN to take part in the CSD, the Commission on Sustainable Development, sessions and that's where we pursue a lot of the [Indigenous] agendas as well.

Then of course the Permanent Forum on Indigenous Issues was established. Even when it was being shaped, one of the [crucial] moments was [the discussion about] its composition, the geographical regions [on the basis of which the membership of the Permanent Forum would be determined]. The states were just pushing that there be five regions.[6] But Indigenous

---

6 States divide themselves into five regions for various purposes at the UN, one of them being elections to UN bodies. The regions are African States, Asian States, Eastern European States, Latin American and Caribbean States, and Western European and Other States.

Peoples asserted that [the composition of the Permanent Forum] has to also reflect the [seven] regions where Indigenous Peoples come from.[7] That was another change [that Indigenous Peoples achieved]. [Indigenous Peoples] change the way the UN conceived those regions, and this is good, even now with the new EMRIP [Expert Mechanism on the Rights of Indigenous Peoples] resolution; states finally agreed [for EMRIP]to have seven representatives [members]. Those are the moments when [Indigenous Peoples] sort of changed the rules.

And then the participation of Indigenous Peoples in the Permanent Forum was of course established. The same method of participation was also agreed upon where [as an Indigenous organization or institution] you don't have to have . . . ECOSOC [consultative] status, to be able to take part in the Permanent Forum. Those are the kinds of ways that participation has been shaped and Indigenous Peoples[have] managed to change the rules of procedures of the UN and get themselves to be actively engaged with many of these different processes. We [Indigenous Peoples] also decided to be active in the Convention on Biodiversity, as well as Climate Change Conventions. We are covering a lot of ground because we don't think that Indigenous Peoples should only be limited to human rights. If we are talking about the UN Declaration on the Rights of Indigenous Peoples, it has to have or own [to cover] the different arenas as well.

Wilton Littlechild, Grand Chief for Treaty #6 in Western Canada and world-renowned Cree Indigenous leader, when interviewed, expressed his respect for the strategies and achievements of the women's movement in their struggles and how much he has learnt from it.[8] He also spoke about the 1977 antiracism conference in Geneva and other significant moments in the history of Indigenous Peoples participation at the UN:

You remember in '77, we really couldn't get in to the meeting, to the UN itself. We held a march – Elders, spiritual leaders leading the way with our sacred pipes. That entry into the building itself was a significant entrance into the discussions being held within the walls of the United Nations, which eventually allowed us in.

Thanks to Madame Daes,[9] who said, "Well this is about Indigenous Peoples. Wouldn't it be important to hear from them?" And that really

---

7 Indigenous Peoples see themselves as belonging to seven sociocultural regions: Africa; Arctic; Asia; Central and South America and the Caribbean; North America; Pacific; and Central Europe, Russian Federation, Central Asia, and Transcaucasia.
8 Littlechild interviewed by the author, 28 January 2017.
9 The late Erica-Irene Daes was the Chairperson of the UN Working Group on Indigenous Populations from 1984 to 2001, and her important contributions are covered in this book.

opened the meetings for us to come in and present our views on each of the articles [of the then draft declaration on the rights of Indigenous Peoples] as the discussions were happening. That was a significant moment.

The other highlight for me was when the UN Permanent Forum on Indigenous Issues was established, and the Secretary General said, "Welcome to the UN family". I thought that was a very, very important signal to me that, yes, we've struggled to get our voice heard. From 1923 to 1977 we were silent, and all of a sudden now we have the opportunity through a working group to express our views. Of course, we didn't get the full participation [recognized], because we still couldn't make resolutions or motions or vote on issues, but the important thing was we were able to present our views on important items that were being discussed. To be welcomed into the UN family was a very, very significant step forward in terms of participation of Indigenous Peoples in the international arena.

Wilton Littlechild explained the reasons he and his people came and continue to come to the UN:

For us [participation] is very unique in a way, because it was very specifically focused on treaty. Our Elders and our spiritual leaders at home had been very, very concerned about violations of Treaty #6 – our treaty – by our treaty partners. After ceremony, and after a lot of prayer and deliberation, they came together. I was just a very young lawyer at the time in terms of having graduated from law school. They called me in, after ceremony, to talk with me along with another lawyer. This was in the '70s. And they said to me, well, to us, that we have to go back to the international arena because our treaty was with Great Britain and Northern Ireland. They felt very strongly that it was an international treaty, and we needed to go to the international arena to try and get our treaty honored and respected, as they said. When I asked them, years later, "What is it that we really want?" they said to me, "Just 3 things: We want recognition of who we are. We are Cree nation. We want respect because we have a sacred agreement with the British crown. And we just want justice." That's what they said. So those were guiding principles for me going forward in terms of the treaty advocacy.

Before we left on our very first journey to the international arena, they gave us four instructions in our language. One of the words that they used is "kikbactingosomin," which means in our language that we have inherent rights. You're born with these rights, you don't ask a government, or you don't ask another person to give you those rights because you already have them. So, remember these are "kikbactingosiyak" – they are inherent rights. Secondly, that our treaties are sacred agreements, "kitch-ieoyecweganak," they said. That means that our treaty is a sacred agreement. And because of that, it needs to be understood as we understand it, in our language. It was important, they said, that we tell the world, this is how we understand treaty from our perspective, that [our rights are] inherent, that it's a sacred agreement, that it's about self-determination.

And then they [our Elders and spiritual leaders] gave us the instruction: "Don't ever stand back from these instructions when you're out there, arguing for us." And the other one was that it [this process, the treaty, and our participation] was about peace. It was about peaceful coexistence. Those were the four instructions they gave me, in the ceremony and after. Those have been my guiding principles.

In frustration of resistance that we were facing over the years, I asked them, "What is it that you really want?" That was the other [response] that they gave me. It was about treaty; it was about violations of treaty. Really all they wanted, they said, was to have our treaties honored and respected. But we need to go back to the international arena, because this is an international agreement. So that was the main purpose for my community in sending me to the international arena.

The late Moana Jackson was a New Zealand lawyer of Ngāti Kahungunu and Ngāti Porou descent, specializing in constitutional law, the Treaty of Waitangi, and international Indigenous issues. He was a famous advocate for Māori rights, leading work on constitutional reforms, and supporting the rights of Indigenous Peoples internationally. When he spoke with the author, he reflected on the Māori's path, including his personal path, to the international field:[10]

I think it was inevitable that our people would make the decision to go to Geneva, and I was asked – told – by our people that I should go as part of Māori delegation, because Great Grandmother had been to the League of Nations in 1923 – we were then denied admission. But the process is really difficult. The way I have described it to a lot of our young people at home is that at home we deal with government, and at the UN we're dealing with nearly two hundred, many of whom were colonizing states and still are colonizing states. And after a number of years of frustration during the drafting [of the UNDRIP], we were asked by our people to withdraw from the process. And so we did. It was never meant to be a permanent withdrawal but an indication to the New Zealand state that we were not prepared to be involved in a process where the New Zealand state in particular was being obstructive, dishonest.

. . . We started going again [to the United Nations] in the later stages of the drafting [of the Declaration]. And our involvement in the later

10 Jackson interviewed by the author, 16 May 2017.

stages was mainly to protect what we could, to protect Article 3, self-determination.[11] And also because it was fairly clear at home that the New Zealand government was going to fight against the Declaration, and we wanted them to know that we were there. Eventually we got [the Declaration] to the General Assembly of course [in 2007, where New Zealand] along with Canada, Australia, and the USA voted against it. . . .

In the '70s and '80s, our people were beginning to establish links and relationships with other Indigenous Peoples, in the Pacific of course, but also in the Americas. When we first went, it was very much because of the situation at home, because of the need, in our view, to stand in solidarity with other Indigenous Peoples. That remained an important reason for us being there. We like to feel that we contributed something to help other Indigenous Peoples, and we certainly received support and assistance from them. Since the Declaration was adopted, most of our focus has been at home to keep pressure on the government. . . .

I think the Declaration and the Permanent Forum on Indigenous Issues were worthwhile achievements for Indigenous Peoples, and different Indigenous Nations will use them in the future in different ways. But I think our sense at home is that we will focus on the Declaration at home. We won't isolate ourselves from international places. The bigger issue now is that we have much, much stronger links among Indigenous Peoples.

Myrna Cunningham is a Miskita senior Indigenous rights advocate from Nicaragua, former President of Fondo Indígena, Executive Director of CADPI (Centro para la Autonomía y Desarrollo de los Pueblos Indígenas), President of Pawanka Fund, Chair of Land Tenure Facility, former Chairperson of UNPFII, and a medical surgeon. Dr. Cunningham shared reflections about the reasons Indigenous Peoples have been going to international fora:[12]

Indigenous Peoples came to the UN because we were not able to solve our problems in our countries. When the countries became countries, they left out Indigenous Peoples, so historically all of the policies and legislation and everything is defined without Indigenous Peoples' participation. . . , without Indigenous Peoples' rights included. It has become very difficult for a lot of Indigenous Peoples in different parts of the world to really find solutions to their problems in their countries.

The second reason is because we understand that at the international level the governments are setting standards, and we need our voice to be

---

11 Article 3 of UNDRIP reads: "Indigenous peoples have the right to self-determination. By virtue of that right they freely determine their political status and freely pursue their economic, social and cultural development."

12 Cunningham interviewed by the author, 17 May 2016.

heard at those levels. We need that those standards that are being defined include Indigenous Peoples' rights and Indigenous Peoples' perspectives.

The third goal maybe we have [in participating at international level] . . . is because we believe that we have something to give to the rest of the world. . . . Maybe the resilience capacity, maybe our knowledges. There's something that we need to share with the rest of the world.

Les Malezer is an Aboriginal leader, Chairperson of the Foundation for Aboriginal and Islander Research Action (FAIRA) in Australia, and a person that held various international Indigenous-related mandates, including as member of the UNPFII. Malezer commented on the various impacts of the international mobilization of Indigenous Peoples:[13]

It was the language of the UN that we were speaking at home. We have a right to this. We have a right to that. . . . It was also the perception that we were providing that it's not the governments that call the shots. They don't tell us what to do, what not to do. We have rights as peoples. . . . So, if you recall those times back in the '80s in particular, we were actually taking our home messages to the UN. It wasn't the UN sending messages to home, it was Aboriginal peoples, North Americans, the Sámi, the Māori. And for Aboriginal people, everything we talked about was land rights, that was our word, land rights. We were going to the UN saying we want land rights. And that's exactly what we were also saying to the governments back home. . . . What was really going on was, in the '70s, during the civil rights movement, [was that] Indigenous delegations were talking to each other. People were communicating, from the Sámi, from North America, from New Zealand, from Australia, particularly those countries. We were also having bilateral delegations to other countries. Like China invited Aboriginal people to come to China in the mid '70s, about '74, '75. There was a lot of interest in what was going on in Australia from places like Africa, from Europe.

Aehshatou Manu of the Mbororo People in Cameroon, a lawyer and the National Women Coordinator of the Mbororo Social and Cultural Development Association, also analyzed the reasons why Indigenous Peoples came and continue to come to the UN:[14]

They have faced a lot of human rights violations since years and centuries, and they decided to come to the UN because they felt that the UN is the biggest body where everything can be heard and solved. So, they came in to tell the UN that, we have human rights violations [against us], and

13 Malezer interviewed by the author, 8 April 2016.
14 Manu interviewed by the author, 29 November 2016.

they are not considered. Try to give us the space so that we can express this, and try to see how we can solve those violations. There are many violations. Though we are all citizens, we have our own particularities. As Indigenous Peoples, we have our identity and we want to maintain our lifestyle. It's not like we want to create another state, but we want our things to be respected, our way of seeing things, our own way of governing, our own way of preserving our culture and languages. So that is why we came. That is why Indigenous Peoples came to the UN. . . .

In terms of the strategy: Indigenous Peoples saw it like a dream come true, most of them, because, they saw it like, "Wow, the UN has allowed us to come and express what we feel." And now at the UN we have the Permanent Forum, and the Secretariat in the UN at the Headquarters. Already this is something, it's already a big success for the movement itself and for the Indigenous Peoples at large. Our Elders have fought for us, and now us too, we are coming to join them, and others also joined them. This will continue growing. It's a very big step, a very important success for the [Indigenous] movement and for the communities.

Māori leader Aroha Mead, Māori Elder and an active representative at international fora for decades, also commented on the question of why Indigenous Peoples have been coming to the UN and discussed her own path to the international level:[15]

Indigenous Peoples participate in UN meetings for diverse reasons. In some cases, it's because they have been sent by their communities to relay quite specific concerns about their situation in their home countries. They hope that by elevating news of their situation to a higher level it might have greater influence than they are able to achieve at home. In other cases, Indigenous representatives participate for information gathering or because word has circulated through networks that issues of significance to Indigenous Peoples are being discussed and we are needed to influence decisions so they benefit Indigenous Peoples and at the very least do not cause harm. Much of our effort is spent ensuring we are present and have our own voice. "Nothing about us, without us."

In my case, I was sent by my community to table a formal complaint that our tribe (Ngati Awa) had made against the New Zealand government. The claim involved confiscation of lands and, amongst other things, the repatriation of an ancestral house called Mataatua. The Mataatua meeting house was dismantled and taken from us in 1879 and for over one hundred years was moved from museum to museum in Australia,

---

15 Mead interviewed by the author, 5 April 2016.

England, and back to NZ, ignoring requests from our chiefs to return it to our home community.

I never understood why my community chose me, because I was a painfully shy person, and suddenly I was told, you must go to the United Nations in Geneva, to table this complaint and let the world know what has happened and what we are trying to achieve. And so I traveled to the UN Working Group [on Indigenous Populations, WGIP] in 1985 as part of the first Māori delegation to participate in WGIP sessions. By then there was already an Indigenous modus operandi. The ones who were more experienced with the WGIP and the drafting of the UN Declaration on the Rights of Indigenous Peoples would mentor the new ones coming in. I remember people such as Tim Coulter, Dalee Sambo, Sharon Venne, Lars Anders Baer, and others, who would approach the "newcomers" and ask, "What are the pressing concerns of your people?" and suggest how they could frame their intervention to feed directly into the text negotiations on the draft declaration on the rights of Indigenous Peoples.

I will never forget when I gave that intervention. My first time of speaking publicly was in that room, and the strength to overcome shyness to do it came from my sense of responsibility to my own. When I pressed the button on the microphone, aware that my statement was being translated across the UN's official languages, well, it was life changing in many different ways. The pressing of that button is for me a symbol of the beginning of a new chapter in my life. As well as completing the instruction given to me by my tribe, at a personal level it brought a new level of confidence. At the global level the issues we brought of misappropriation of Indigenous cultural sacred items and repatriation were included in the Declaration [on the Rights of Indigenous Peoples] and subsequently went on to inform a series of studies by the UN Special Rapporteur on cultural and intellectual property rights of Indigenous Peoples, which in turn influenced the World Intellectual Property Organization (WIPO) to include Indigenous intellectual property rights concerns in its work.

When I returned home and reported the experience and the reaction of others to the call to repatriate our Mataatua meeting house, I recommended that we organize an international meeting as not many people had examined in any detail how the intellectual property rights system could impact Indigenous heritage, tangible and intangible. Few had ever really heard of "intellectual property" in the 1980s. We spent a year researching intellectual property rights, and in 1993 we convened in my birthplace, Whakatane, the meeting that produced the Mataatua Declaration on the Cultural and Intellectual Property Rights of Indigenous Peoples. And the rest, as they say, is history.

So, the journey to come to the UN Working Group [on Indigenous Populations] had multiple impacts for me personally, for my tribe Ngati Awa, for the Declaration text, and for what would become a full-time career in advocating for the rights of Indigenous Peoples, particularly in relation to cultural and intellectual property rights.

UN meetings can be amazing laboratories, for ideas, networking, learning, advocating, and advancing understanding about your peoples, their hopes, aspirations, and also their truths in how they were, and still are, impacted by colonization. It's important to look beyond the negotiations of the day at any specific UN meeting, as there are so many competing interests at play outside our influence. Rather, the benefit of participation comes from knowing that advocacy for your own people supports and assists the global Indigenous community as well.

Binota Moy Dhamai, leader and Indigenous rights activist from Bangladesh, and member of the UN Expert Mechanism on the Rights of Indigenous Peoples (EMRIP) for several years, summarized why Indigenous Peoples have been coming to the UN:[16]

They do so because they do not have other places to share their grievances, the impact of colonization, discrimination, injustices. At the domestic level, Indigenous Peoples often face not only discrimination but also a systematic process of assimilation. Drivers are land grabbing dispossessions, territorial demarcation or eradication; militarization; human rights violations; no grievance mechanism at the national level; losing of their own political, social, and economic institutions that force them into a vulnerable situation. The decolonization process let growing nation-state building, where Indigenous Peoples were excluded. There were also suppressive policies towards those who raised voices for maintaining self-governance, autonomy, and self-determination. Most importantly, Indigenous Peoples wanted to maintain their own ways of life through the participation in the nation-state building process; they expected to maintain their political, economic, cultural, and social institutions, which are embedded in their own identity and existence. Due to exclusion and suppression [that people suffer], the UN is the most important platform that has been realized; the Charter of the UN itself stresses equality, nondiscrimination, and peoples' right to self-determination.

Dhamai also refers to the distrust and betrayal of Indigenous Peoples by states not implementing the treaties, agreements, and other constructive arrangements. He points out that

Indigenous Peoples started a journey to reach out to the international community, to the United Nations, and the Indigenous Peoples' movement and

---

16 Dhamai interviewed by the author, March 2016.

representative organizations led this journey. Now Indigenous Peoples have a place at the United Nations to address their grievances, injustice, discrimination, genocide, massacre, assimilationist policy implementation at the national level.

It has also been important for small Indigenous Nations to be represented at the UN. As Mikaela Jade – an Indigenous rights advocate from Australia, and founder and CEO of Indigital, a business that aims to help embed Indigenous stories and history into the mainstream – points out,

> *I came to the UN because I live in a community of three hundred people in a very remote area of Australia where I run a technology company, and I came here because the struggles I was facing in my own community suddenly became global when I realized how data is used for and against Indigenous Peoples, and I recognized that there was a gap in strategy, a gap in policy, a gap in people's knowledge about how data flows impact them. So I wanted to raise awareness about that. . . .*
>
> *My people expect me to report back to my community about what's happened here [at the UN]. There's a lot of people in the digital space in Australia that have requested interviews with me when I return home.*[17]

Is there an impact at home from Indigenous leaders' UN participation? Jade says,

> *I think there is, I think being able to say you come to the UN as a delegate to the Permanent Forum on Indigenous Issues does something in opening doors. I met with our Prime Minister February this year [2016], so I think that really helped, when you make contact with those state officials, to show you know the system and how everything works. I think it's a little bit harder to be ignored when you know how things work. . . . [Also] I think people [who participate at the Permanent Forum on Indigenous Issues] are much more willing to commit to side events [during the sessions of the UNPFII]. I've been to lots of side events over the last week, and they are overflowing with people. Our peoples understand that we need to know more. So I think there's a concerted effort to come here, not just to intervene at the UN, but also to network with everyone else and find out how other people are dealing with issues.*

Chhing Lamu Sherpa is a respected Indigenous leader in Nepal and Founder and member of Mountain Spirit. She said that the reasons for Indigenous

17 Jade interviewed by the author, 16 May 2016.

Peoples coming to the UN are so their voice can be heard and so they can express and receive solidarity.[18] She pointed out that

Indigenous Peoples have different issues in our countries, and we don't have the space to express the reality, there is no environment for that. So the UN offers this space. Indigenous Peoples' speaking power has increased, and so has empowerment and confidence. They can talk actually a lot to the community, to the people. . . . With the Indigenous and non-Indigenous, we need to also create harmony and an inclusive society; that has to be realized by our non-Indigenous people. We are in the process of convincing them.

B. Participation as Methodology: The Pivotal UN Study

The concept of human rights has progressed over the decades following the struggles of people, the constant movement of international relations and multilateralism, and the dynamism of history that is the result of numerous actors and actions. The process for strengthening human rights mechanisms in the United Nations emerged together with a new anticolonial and antiracist consciousness and discourse. The recognition of self-determination as a human right in common Article 1 of the International Covenant on Economic, Social and Cultural Rights and the International Covenant on Civil and Political Rights in 1966 also shed new light on the rights of Indigenous Peoples, paving the road, not only toward the acceptance of their identities by states, but also toward the strengthening of those identities.[19]

As more voices were raised against the plight of Indigenous Peoples, a major international breakthrough occurred in 1971. The Economic and Social Council (ECOSOC) unanimously requested the Sub-Commission on Prevention of Discrimination and Protection of Minorities, an organ of the then UN Commission on Human Rights, to prepare a Study on the Problem of Discrimination against Indigenous Populations (the Study). Authored under the name of Sub-Commission member José R. Martínez Cobo of Ecuador, as Special Rapporteur, this monumental historic study took thirteen years to complete and became the most voluminous UN human rights study, composed of many documents.[20]

---

18 Sherpa interviewed by the author, 21 November 2016.
19 Elsa Stamatopoulou, "Indigenous Peoples and the United Nations: Human Rights as a Developing Dynamic," *Human Rights Quarterly* 16, no. 1 (February 1994): 60.
20 A collected edition of the final version of the Martínez Cobo Study was reissued in UN Doc. E/CN.4/Sub.2/1986/7 and Addenda 1–4. The conclusions and recommendations of the Study are in Addendum 4. José R. Martínez Cobo, *Study of the Problem of Discrimination against Indigenous Populations*, UN Doc. E/CN.4/Sub.2/1986/7 (vol. 1) and UN Docs. E/CN.4/Sub.2/1986/7/Add.1–E/CN.4/Sub.2/1986/7/Add.4 (vols. 2–5) (New York: UN, 1986–1987).

The drafting process of the Study was key to the development of relations between the UN and the international Indigenous Peoples' movement that was being built at that time. A major consideration among Indigenous Peoples and some people in various positions at the UN or in state institutions and civil society was that the Study had to reflect the views and aspirations of Indigenous Peoples about their own future. The legitimacy of the Study depended on that.

The dynamism of the rising Indigenous movement and anticolonial and antiracist ethics resulted in a radical shift in the Study's methodology. Rather than the usual interstate or mainstream comparative law approach, the Study included a diverse range of Indigenous Peoples' inputs. This methodology was adopted by the UN Secretariat and expressed the vision of Augusto Willemsen Díaz, the person in charge of the study in the UN Secretariat and the first one to work on Indigenous rights at the UN. Despite the political challenges and resistance that he faced within the UN bureaucracy and certainly on the part of certain states, Willemsen Díaz fought for and facilitated Indigenous Peoples' input in the Study. Credit also goes to José Martínez Cobo, who took the political risk and responsibility within the Sub-Commission to support the initiatives of this new methodology. (The Study is also referred to as "the Martínez Cobo Study.") Augusto Willemsen Díaz has written that he was free to determine the content of the study, presumably speaking of his relation to Martínez Cobo. The exception was the area of Indigenous Peoples' own legal systems and the exercise of jurisdictional powers by their communities and community authorities, which Willemsen Díaz was asked not to include or rather include in minimal terms.[21]

The drafter of the Study had to overcome not only the political and bureaucratic obstacles that were to be expected but also the relative difficulty for inputs by the Indigenous movements in different countries that were in various stages of organizing themselves. Normally, a UN study would take at most four or five years to complete in those times, and the outcome would have a comparative international law angle, such as a comparison among various state systems regarding their handling of specific issues in law and practice. Had the Study followed the usual methodology of most UN studies, the force of its conclusions – no matter how progressive – would have stumbled upon a historic vacuum. By this, we mean two things. First, there would not have been adequate time for the Study to have the input of the

---

The original editions of the individual reports in the Study are available on the UN DESA's "Indigenous Peoples" website: https://social.desa.un.org/publications/martinez-cobo-study.

21 Augusto Willemsen Díaz, "How Indigenous Peoples' Rights Reached the UN," in *Making the Declaration Work: The United Nations Declaration on the Rights of Indigenous Peoples*, ed. Claire Charters and Rodolfo Stavenhagen (Copenhagen: IWGIA, 2010), www.iwgia.org/iwgia_files_publications_files/making_the_declaration_work.pdf.

Indigenous Peoples themselves, therefore it could not have responded to their realities as they saw them themselves; it would not have the moral credibility required nor, actually, the practical effect required, since the views of the peoples concerned would not have been brought in. Secondly, if the Study had come out too soon, by the mid-1970s, the then emerging international Indigenous Peoples' movement would probably not have been able to sustain the international political momentum the Study would have produced. It would have been challenging for the movement to press for and achieve a concrete significant follow-up to the Study, as happened later.

Therefore, the Study had to change methodology from the usual ways. First of all, it had to slow down so as to allow Indigenous Peoples and their communities to contribute; and then, the actual inputs of Indigenous Peoples had to be collected. The thirty-seven monographs that went into the Study did just that. Moreover, eleven country missions were undertaken to collect information. In addition, the process of preparing the Study created new bonds and alliances among Indigenous Peoples, who, despite their immense diversity, realized that they shared problems from similar historic injustices and that they had to act together at the international level. This realization was only enhanced after the establishment of the UN Working Group on Indigenous Populations (WGIP) in 1982 and continues to be strengthened through the participation of more Indigenous delegates every year at sessions of the UN Permanent Forum on Indigenous Issues (UNPFII) and the EMRIP. The strength of an international Indigenous identity became well-established through these repeated annual gatherings that fomented solidarity, visions, and strategies.

It is through such slow international processes of participation over many years, starting with the preparation of the Study, that the Indigenous articulations of values, norms, rights, and demands evolved and have been marking international institutions. These slow processes, or, more precisely, sloweddown processes, have been significant in broadening democracy in international institutions. This approach was also followed in the drafting of the UNDRIP, gathering the substantive input of numerous Indigenous delegates in a span of twenty-five years.

One year before his passing in 2014, a group of Mayas of Guatemala paid homage to Augusto Willemsen Díaz for a life dedicated to seeking justice for the Indigenous Peoples of the world.[22]

---

22 I was asked to send a message to that event, which took place in the home of Rigoberta Menchú. The message I sent on 3 June 2013 read as follows:

"I have learned that your Indigenous brothers and sisters in Guatemala are honoring you today (June 7) at a gathering in Rigoberta's house. I would like to be there to express my respect and gratitude and the deep bonds of friendship that we have tied us over so many years.

The extraordinary Study on the Problem of Discrimination against Indigenous Populations became a catalyst for the Indigenous Peoples movement to strengthen itself, to articulate its critiques and aspirations, to make its voice heard, and to establish itself as a strong international actor for years to come.

C. Stepping Stones: Human Rights and Antiracism (1977 and 1981)

One hot July afternoon in 1981, a year after I had joined the Division of Human Rights of the UN in Geneva, as the human rights program was called at the time, the office quiet was interrupted by the sound of drums coming from the yard surrounded by the buildings of the Palais des Nations. I leaned out the window and saw a procession of Indigenous people, dressed in traditional clothes, marching ceremonially through the yard. I noticed that at the very front of the procession were old people leading what looked like a ceremony, walking slowly and with some difficulty due to their age. They were supported by younger Indigenous people. The procession and the drumming lasted for some time. It was an extraordinary sight, and many UN employees had come to their office windows or walked down to the yard to watch. It was the first time in my still brief UN life that I saw a large group of organized people personally coming to the UN to claim justice – and doing so by using strong cultural manifestations of their own. I could see from the expressions of UN staffers watching that they were as impacted by the procession as I was.

"You have been in my mind very often. Dear Augusto, you are my much-respected mentor, and I continue to be inspired by your example and all that you have taught me. During the long years that I worked in the United Nations and especially the eight years I spent heading the Secretariat of the UN Permanent Forum on Indigenous Issues until 2010, I always had in mind your example and your strategic teachings.

"Since January 2011, I am at Columbia University, teaching Indigenous Peoples' rights! I am also Director of the Indigenous Peoples' Rights Program at the Institute for the Study of Human Rights at Columbia and, through various activities, I am trying to give visibility to our issues.

"Your strategic steering of the historic Study on the Problem of Discrimination against Indigenous Peoples in the 1970s and 1980s, and your synergies with the Indigenous Peoples' Movement, gave birth to the UN institutions devoted to Indigenous Peoples' rights. I would like you to know that I never stop recognizing you, dear Augusto, in the various teachings and speeches I give, including at my farewell speech at the UN that the Indigenous women organized for me through FIMI (Foro Internacional de Mujeres Indigenas). And of course, I speak a lot about you to the students at my course and we also read your writings about the Declaration.

"You are always an inspiration for me, for us, with your commitment, your energy and your deep sense of justice.

"Thank you for all you have given to the Indigenous Peoples of the world and to each one of us."

Augusto responded with an email to me a month later; this was our last contact.

The images I have in my memory from the 1981 entrance procession of the Indigenous leaders are similar to the historic pictures taken by Jean-François Graugnard of the 1977 International NGO Conference on Discrimination against Indigenous Populations in the Americas.[23] I saw the 1977 pictures many years later, in 2013, when the Documentation Center of Indigenous Peoples (DOCIP, now the Indigenous Peoples' Center for Documentation, Research and Information) distributed them at an anniversary celebration of the 1977 historic meeting. The anniversary meeting took place in the same room at the Palais des Nations in Geneva, with the surviving Indigenous leaders who had been there in 1977. Indigenous youth also participated in the 2013 anniversary meeting that was intended to transmit knowledge and experience across generations.[24]

Impressed and intrigued by what I saw that July afternoon in 1981, I sought to find out who the people were, why they were at the UN, and whom they would meet. I soon discovered, to my delight, that they were in fact visiting the Division of Human Rights, the office where I worked. In a few hours, I found the colleague who was the focal point for this visit: it was Augusto Willemsen Díaz, a Guatemalan jurist and political refugee, as I learned – the first UN staff member who was dealing with Indigenous Peoples' rights and who would soon become my mentor. I realized only later the tremendous significance of his teachings that had nothing to do with UN hierarchies and formalities but were cutting through them and dealing with the substance of what justice should be for the marginalized, in human rights terms.

Augusto Willemsen Díaz was extremely busy. He had one assistant, Luz Cuellar, from Colombia, a great team worker and a person who cared about Indigenous rights. She called him "Don Augusto" or "Professor Augusto," with respect and affection. The gathering in 1981 was the second international meeting of Indigenous leaders, beyond the Americas. The 1981 meeting was called the International NGO Conference on Indigenous Peoples and Land. Indigenous Peoples from Russia and Africa were not yet present in such international fora. They would come onto the international scene by the early 1990s.

To my delight, *Don* Augusto said yes to my shy request whether I could attend the July 1981 meeting. I started attending on the second day of the meeting. *Don* Augusto explained things quickly, in a voice hardly concealing excitement, as we walked through the *Salle des pas perdues* to the conference

---

23 Jean-François Graugnard, Photographic report of the "International Conference against Discrimination against Indigenous Populations of the Americas," United Nations, Geneva, 1977.

24 The 2013 Symposium was entitled Indigenous Peoples at the United Nations: From the Experience of the First Delegates to the Empowerment of the Younger Generation, Geneva, 10–13 September 2013, www.docip.org/en/oral-history-and-memory/symposium/.

room. The room was full to capacity, the atmosphere was charged. People speaking were addressing injustices of centuries, the impacts of colonization, land grabbing and displacement, genocides, ethnocides, suppression of Indigenous governments, forced assimilation, systemic discrimination, and more.

The year 1981 was a pivotal one. It was also the year that the ECOSOC approved the establishment of the WGIP, the first UN mechanism to address Indigenous Peoples' rights. In retrospect, I understood that the July 1981 meeting functioned as a strategic space for Indigenous leaders on how they would pursue their visions of survival and well-being through the UN. It was an organizing space, a space where representatives from many local Indigenous Peoples' struggles around the world, while aware of their rich diversity, were learning from each other, strengthening ties among themselves, and becoming a global movement that would grow year after year. In fact, strategy meetings and trainings on international law and human rights were taking place before every session of the WGIP, either at the Palais des Nations or at the offices of the World Council of Churches in Geneva, where Indigenous Peoples shared experiences and knowledge and planned for next steps. Every year, new leaders arrived from different Indigenous Peoples and their communities, making the circle bigger. This trend continues to this day.

Another important and helpful UN insider at that pivotal time, in addition to the lead of Augusto Willemsen Díaz, was Theo van Boven. The visibility that the UN Study on the Problem of Discrimination against Indigenous Populations (the Study) gave to Indigenous Peoples resulted in increasing political reverberations. Theo van Boven, the Dutch Director of the UN Division of Human Rights since 1977, was taking major and politically courageous steps those very years. Already in February 1981 he had made an important statement at the UN Commission on Human Rights (UNCHR) on the need for the human rights system to take measures for "the protection of vulnerable populations, people in slavery-like conditions, children and indigenous populations."[25] The term "Indigenous Peoples" was not yet used at that time, and it was to take decades of advocacy by Indigenous leaders and the adoption of the UNDRIP in 2007 for the term to become the accepted and established legal and technical term in international affairs. A few Indigenous leaders were able to speak at the UNCHR those days, as representatives of nongovernmental organizations (NGOs) in consultative status with the UN ECOSOC. Russell Means, the famous leader of the International Indian Treaty Council (IITC), used to come to the Commission and make statements about the inequitable conditions of Indigenous Peoples in the United States. One of the goals of IITC was and is to seek to promote and build

---

25 Bertrand Ramcharan, *The Advent of Universal Protection of Human Rights: Theo van Boven and the Transformation of the UN Role* (New York: Springer, 2018), 31–32.

participation of Indigenous Peoples in the UN and its specialized agencies, as well as other international fora.[26]

Leif Dunfjeld, a Sámi leader from Norway, was posted to Geneva by the World Council of Indigenous Peoples and by the Nordic Sámi Council and had started engaging with the UNCHR, informing states about the dire situation of Indigenous Peoples. Roxanne Dunbar-Ortiz, the acclaimed Native American academic and human rights advocate, was also very active in placing political visibility on Indigenous rights from the earliest days.[27]

The Indigenous Peoples' movement continued to engage with the international human rights agenda, including the struggle against racial discrimination, in the formative year of 1981. In his speech at the Commission on Human Rights on 2 February 1981, van Boven addressed the topic of "world order and vulnerable groups" and referred to "children, women, migrants, victims of ethnic or racial oppression or indigenous populations."[28] Among other things, he said:

> If a human rights programme has any relevance to people, it should first and foremost be concerned with the vulnerable, the weak, the oppressed, the exploited. . . . The plight of indigenous peoples is often a very acute one. Frequently they are the most under-represented parts of the population, they often have no voice in policies and decisions which directly affect their basic existence or even their survival.[29]

Theo van Boven continued to push for Indigenous rights. In his opening speech at the Sub-Commission on Prevention of Discrimination and Protection of Minorities on 17 August 1981, he addressed the topic "Survival of the Fittest" and stated:

> Questions of survival affect the vulnerable, the disadvantaged, the dispossessed, the deprived and many weak groups of society. Today's world is one which often demonstrates a lack of solidarity. Ideologies and practices proliferate which are based on, and propagate, unbounded freedom for the powerful and the strong. The free play of the activities of the powerful and the strong as well as of naked market forces may, and often

---

26 See the International Indian Treaty Council website, www.iitc.org.
27 Roxanne Dunbar-Ortiz, "The First Ten Years, from Study to Working Group: 1972–1982," in *Indigenous Peoples' Rights in International Law*, ed. Roxanne Dunbar-Ortiz et al. (Kautokeino: Gáldu and Copenhagen: IWGIA, 2015). See also Roxanne Dunbar-Ortiz, "How Indigenous Peoples Wound Up at the United Nations," in *The Hidden 1970s: Histories of Radicalism*, ed. Dan Berger (New Brunswick, NJ: Rutgers University Press, 2010), https://doi.org/10.36019/9780813550336.
28 Ramcharan, *Advent of Universal Protection*, 31–32.
29 Ramcharan, *Advent of Universal Protection*, 32.

do, . . . threaten their very survival. "Survival of the fittest" is an anti-human rights notion. Freedom is not only for the strong, but for the weak also, and any society which is incapable of demonstrating the will and the solidarity that is necessary to provide and guarantee human rights for the weak is a society which is far removed from the realization of human rights.[30]

Later in the Sub-Commission's session, van Boven again spoke on the issue:

Is there not a special responsibility upon the international community and upon the United Nations to take measures to protect the human rights of these people and to save them from the dangers of extinction? Should not the international community assume a responsibility for their preservation, the enjoyment of their economic, social and cultural rights as well as civil and political rights, the preservation of their culture and the protection of their lands?[31]

Referring to the Study on the Problem of Discrimination against Indigenous Populations that was at its final stage, van Boven noted,

It has become clear, first of all, that there is need for further standard-setting regarding the human rights of indigenous peoples. It has also become clear that indigenous peoples need an appropriate forum within the United Nations to which they can address themselves on a regular basis and which may give regular consideration to their problems. Thirdly it has also become clear that there is need within the United Nations for an ongoing system of fact-finding into problems affecting the enjoyment of human rights by indigenous peoples. It may be asked whether the time is not ripe for the Sub-Commission to request permission, as it has done for the problem of slavery, for a regular working group on the human rights of indigenous peoples.[32]

In the same year, 1981, a draft resolution at the Sub-Commission for the establishment of the Working Group was actively steered through by the Norwegian member Asbjørn Eide, a respected human rights scholar and later first Chairperson-Rapporteur of the WGIP.[33] Various Western states, specifi-

---

30 Ramcharan, *Advent of Universal Protection*, 32.
31 Ramcharan, *Advent of Universal Protection*, 38.
32 Ramcharan, *Advent of Universal Protection*, 38.
33 Asbjørn Eide, "From Prevention of Discrimination to Autonomy and Self-Determination: The Start of the WGIP, Achievements Gained and Future Challenges," in *Indigenous Peoples' Rights in International Law*, ed. Roxanne Dunbar-Ortiz et al. (Kautokeino: Gáldu and Copenhagen: IWGIA, 2015).

cally Australia but also others, were resisting this initiative. Roxanne Dunbar-Ortiz's advocacy and consultations with the prominent Egyptian member of the Sub-Commission, Ahmed Khalifa, ensured the broader support of Third World members of the Sub-Commission.[34]

At the end of the 1981 session of the Sub-Commission on Prevention of Discrimination and Protection of Minorities, the Sub-Commission finally proposed the establishment of a Working Group on Indigenous Populations. The establishment of WGIP was subsequently approved by the UNCHR and its parent body, the ECOSOC, in ECOSOC resolution 1982/34. The Working Group became the first UN mechanism specifically devoted to Indigenous Peoples' rights.

D.   The First Indigenous-Related Body at the UN (1982)

It was August 1982. After the meeting of Indigenous Peoples from around the globe in 1981 at the UN in Geneva, the first meeting of the first session of the WGIP was about to happen. It was to take place in a UN conference room, on the third floor of the Palais des Nations. Augusto Willemsen Díaz, senior official in the Section on Prevention of Discrimination and Protection of Minorities, was in charge of the Working Group in the Division of Human Rights, as the human rights office was called at the time. The division was under the Department of Political Affairs that was headquartered in New York. Some states had pushed to move the human rights program to the UN Office in Geneva in 1973, as a way to reduce the political visibility of the topic away from UN Headquarters, a visibility that bothered some states by the rising sharpness of international human rights work.

Willemsen Díaz had allowed me, a junior staff member, to enter the 1981 meeting of Indigenous Peoples at the Palais des Nations. I did not belong to his section, but he needed staff and, even more, needed people within the Secretariat to share his struggle within the bureaucracy; and, particularly relevant in my case, he needed young people to be educated about the issues. He was allowing me to learn by absorbing what was happening in the room. Everything seemed historic in my eyes, and it was. As a young person, I felt it was as if a big and prestigious history book was being written live by the Indigenous leaders speaking at that meeting.

Willemsen Díaz was special, different from various other UN officials around me, and, as a novice at the UN, I was appreciating that. I felt impatient and underused with the scarcity of assignments I was given at the other section where I was assigned at the time. In contrast, *Don* Augusto was always very busy, even out of breath in a way that somebody making history, taking risks, and creating revolutionary steps would be. He spoke in a low

34 Ramcharan, *Advent of Universal Protection*, 40.

voice when talking to me, as if confiding something special. I realized later that, indeed, all this was special and unprecedented. *Don* Augusto's eyes were shining and sincere when he spoke, his demeanor revealing passion for the work he was doing. He was eager to explain what he was doing and to share his difficulties within the Division of Human Rights.

I would walk up from the second floor, where my office was, to the fourth floor of our building, where *Don* Augusto's office was at the Palais. His office had high ceilings and dark furniture, as did all others in that building. The first time I knocked at Augusto's door and slowly opened it was in 1981. It was a revelation. That office did not look like a "regular" office. There were piles and piles of documents stacked from the floor up to the last point where the pile would not tilt and fall. In order to reach *Don* Augusto's desk, you had to walk through a winding path, through the forest of documents, careful not to stumble or hit a pile by accident. *Don* Augusto explained that these documents had been collected during the preparation for the Study on the Problem of Discrimination against Indigenous Populations, the Martínez Cobo Study. He was really concerned that UN archives could no longer host the material – they had told him it was too voluminous. The first volumes of the study started being issued in 1982 and the full study was out by 1984.

Taking positions of principle as a UN official, especially taking such positions with visibility, is laudable and necessary, but it can be risky. Theodoor Cornelis van Boven, the Dutch jurist and later professor emeritus in international law, became the head of the UN Division of Human Rights in 1977 but was to abruptly resign from his post in March 1982, at a time that was critical for Indigenous issues in the UN. He was a sincere human rights advocate, a person of principle, respected and beloved by the world of human rights NGOs and other advocates. He was supporting the efforts for Indigenous Peoples' rights and the nascent WGIP, as mentioned earlier. His opening speech at the Commission on Human Rights in February 1982 was an act of courage, where he decided to critique the violations of human rights in the Soviet Union, in the United States, and in Latin American dictatorships that were ravaging those societies. His speech defending the right to life was never cleared by his superiors at the UN Department of Political Affairs in New York, the Secretary-General's entourage; he was told that if he gave such a speech, he would do so at his own risk. Van Boven did deliver that speech at the opening of the UNCHR. At the end of it, he announced his resignation, drawing the awe of those attending the Commission. The human rights world expressed its deepest respect for Theo van Boven. Forty NGOs sent a letter of protest to UN Secretary-General Perez de Cuellar.[35] In a monumental

---

35 *The Subversives: Theo van Boven at the UN*, directed by Miles Roston (Naarden, Netherlands: Ethan Films, 2017; distributed 2019), 81 min, www.ethanfilms.com/work/subversives-2019. Van Boven also testified at the trial of the Argentinian junta in 1985.

event in the biggest auditorium of the University of Geneva, at the end of March 1982, van Boven was celebrated. Soon after, Hans Thoolen edited a book collecting van Boven's views on a number of human rights topics.[36]

Theo van Boven and devoted staff around him were crucial in creating the space for protection of human rights and a precedent through the establishment of the Working Group on Disappearances in 1980, the first international thematic monitoring human rights mechanism.[37] Van Boven has been a courageous, principled human rights advocate who occupied an important and visible public position in the UN at a crucial moment in international politics. I was on maternity leave when he gave that speech at the UNCHR and, along with so many others, I heard with shock that he had to resign. It was inspiring, especially for younger staff, to see that such integrity is possible even in the midst of the UN's heavy politics and also to appreciate the painstaking steps it took to create independent UN human rights procedures. Of course van Boven was not lost to the human rights world after he left this UN position. Apart from his teaching, he continued his deep engagement, including as Special Rapporteur at the Commission on Human Rights.[38]

Theo van Boven was succeeded by somebody quite different, Kurt Herndl, an Austrian jurist and diplomat, who led the UN human rights program, renamed to the Center for Human Rights, from 1982 to 1987. Herndl became the first Assistant Secretary-General on Human Rights. He was viewed as conservative and willing to keep human rights advocacy under control, following states' strict guidelines. It did not take too long for Augusto Willemsen Díaz to feel the pressure of the new situation. He was telling me that he felt obliged to explain the approach to the Study to the new leadership repeatedly – one of his memoranda was no fewer than seventeen pages.

Within the context of this rich and complex background, there came the first day of the first session of the WGIP, 9 August 1982. This day became so significant in retrospect that August 9 was proclaimed in 1994, and still is, International Indigenous Peoples' Day, in order to recall that significant moment in the history of the global Indigenous Peoples' movement.[39]

---

36 Theo van Boven, *People Matter: Views on International Human Rights Policy*, ed. Hans Thoolen (Amsterdam: Muellenhoff, 1982).
37 For a description of the mandate and work of this Working Group, see UN Office of the High Commissioner for Human Rights, *Enforced or Involuntary Disappearances*, Fact Sheet no. 6, rev. 3 (OHCHR, 2009), www.ohchr.org/Documents/Publications/FactSheet6Rev3.pdf.
38 He was the UN's Special Rapporteur on the Right to Reparation to Victims of Gross Violations of Human Rights from 1986 to 1991 and Special Rapporteur on Torture from 2001 to 2004. He is also a member of the International Commission of Jurists. From February to December 1994, van Boven was the first registrar of the International Criminal Tribunal for the former Yugoslavia.
39 The International Day was established by the United Nations General Assembly in its resolution 49/214, in December 1994, and was first marked in 1995. See UN General Assembly,

The atmosphere outside and inside the conference room assigned to WGIP in the Palais des Nations was electrified. Inside were the members of the Working Group, nervous diplomats, and several human rights NGOs, including three Indigenous ones – the IITC, the Indian Law Resource Center, and the World Council of Indigenous Peoples – and eleven others – namely, Anti-Slavery Society for the Protection of Human Rights, Afro-Asian Peoples Solidarity Organization, International Commission of Jurists, International Federation for Human Rights, International Movement for Fraternal Union among Races and Peoples, Women's International League for Peace and Freedom, Survival International, Procedural Aspects of International Law Institute, Bahá'í International Community, Commission of the Churches on International Affairs, and Friends World Committee for Consultation.[40]

Nine Indigenous organizations and institutions are recorded in WGIP's first report as having "furnished information to the Working Group with its consent"; namely, the Haudenosaunee-Six Nations Iroquois Confederacy, Oglala Lakota Legal Rights Fund, Lakota Treaty Council, Nishaniwbe-Aski Nation (Grand Council Treaty No. 9), Native Council of Canada, Standing Rock Sioux Tribal Council, Santeioi Maoaiomi Mikmaoei (Grand Council Mikmaq Nation), Indian Council of South America (CISA), and the National Federation of Land Councils (Australia).[41]

Outside the room where the WGIP was meeting, in the corridor, were many Indigenous people, representatives of their peoples, communities, institutions, and organizations. They were visibly there, many in traditional attire, but they were not yet recognized to formally attend the meeting, as they had no formal standing. Minutes before 10 a.m., the official starting time for the meeting, our secretariat team was on the podium arranging our papers. Augusto Willemsen Díaz was speaking with several people. There was nervousness in the air, a sense of something important about to happen. I was in the back of the podium when the Director of the Center for Human Rights approached the podium and, without much looking at us, tilted his head slightly toward us and walked past, giving his instructions in a tone that could only be heard by us: "Low profile, low profile." It was as if we were about to do something a little illegal and had to keep it under wraps. We learned later that ambassadors from Latin America had been in his office that morning calling for vigilance over this new body.

Resolution 49/214, International Decade of the World's Indigenous People, A/RES/49/214 (17 February 1995).

40 Participants in the 1982 session of WGIP are recorded in its report. UN Sub-Commission on Prevention of Discrimination and Protection of Minorities, Report of the Working Group on Indigenous Populations on Its First Session, UN Doc. E/CN.4/Sub.2/1982/33 (25 August 1982), para. 3–9.

41 UN Doc. E/CN.4/Sub.2/1982/33, para. 8.

The Working Group elected Asbjørn Eide, the Norwegian scholar and jurist, member of the Sub-Commission on Prevention of Discrimination and Protection of Minorities, as its Chairman-Rapporteur. At the end of the morning meeting at 1 p.m., participants opened the doors to a corridor full of Indigenous representatives who had not been able to get in. The discomfort among the members of the Working Group and some state delegates was clear, and whispers were loud about how unacceptable it was that the Indigenous representatives could not get in to attend a working group established to deal with their issues. I do not know exactly how the Indigenous representatives even got onto UN grounds that day. In retrospect, I understand that *Don* Augusto must have facilitated that together with UN colleagues in charge of NGO matters at the UN Office in Geneva, including the committed and feisty Raymonde Martineau, from Quebec, Canada, who played a significant role on this in later years as well.[42]

Kenneth Deer[43] recalls the challenges of those first years.

One of the things that was interesting about having the Working Group on Indigenous Populations was that to have a traditional opening was a battle. We had a big fight with them, we tried to – I mean, we had to – the five experts [the members of the Working Group] . . . no matter who they were, they had to be educated about Indigenous. They knew nothing about us. So I have to give credit to Madame Daes, who was the Chair [of the WGIP] since 1984. She went out of her way to learn about us. She travelled, and she met. . . . And from knowing almost nothing about us she become our biggest champion in the UN system. So I give her credit, but even still, in those days, in the '80s and early '90s, it was a battle to get them to [agree] – for us to have a traditional opening. And it [the traditional opening] was in [the form of] a prayer. It was a Thanksgiving, an invocation. They [would] say, "Well we don't know what you'll really say, but, you know, people don't pray at the UN." And so, we had to convince them that it's not a prayer. So, that was a big battle. And now it's common [to have an Indigenous traditional opening], it's so common today.

In the corridor outside the WGIP's conference room at its first session in 1982, *Don* Augusto introduced me to Rodolfo Stavenhagen and Rigoberta

---

42 Raymonde Martineau represented the International Movement for Fraternal Union among Races and Peoples (UFER) at the UN from 1973 to 1975. Once recruited at the UN, she became the Liaison Officer in charge of relations with NGOs and other civil society at the United Nations Office in Geneva in 1975 and later participated in United Nations missions in Namibia from 1989 to 1990 and in South Africa from 1992 to 1994. Raymonde Martineau, interview by James S. Sutterlin, 7 July 1998, Geneva, transcript in UN Dag Hammarskjöld Library, https://digitallibrary.un.org/record/503509?ln=en.
43 Deer interviewed by the author, 6 April 2016.

Menchú Tum for the first time. Professor Stavenhagen, an anthropologist from Mexico, was to become the first UN Special Rapporteur on the rights of Indigenous Peoples from 2001 to 2008. He had a close friendship with *Don Augusto*, and they both shared the passion for the Indigenous Peoples' cause. Rigoberta Menchú was twenty-three in 1982. She became a major symbol of Indigenous Peoples' struggles in Guatemala[44] and was later honored as a Nobel Peace Prize laureate in 1992 and as the UN's Goodwill Ambassador for the International Year of the World's Indigenous People in 1993.

What was the mission of the WGIP? The mandate of the Working Group, according to resolution 1982/34 of the UN ECOSOC was "to review developments pertaining to the promotion and protection of human rights and fundamental freedoms of indigenous populations" while also giving "special attention to the evolution of international standards concerning the rights of indigenous populations."[45]

Indigenous Peoples' direct participation was the core issue at the 1982 first session of WGIP. About twenty-five people were in the room attending that session. Willemsen Díaz recalled his concern about the restrictive effect of the simplistic, across-the-board application of the requirement for consultative status with the ECOSOC, which had been strictly demanded for participation on NGOs in the sessions of UN organs and bodies for more or less thirty years.[46] Under this system, non-ECOSOC-accredited Indigenous Peoples' representatives could not be accredited. He felt it absurd, and contradictory in the extreme, for the UN to create a working group to listen to Indigenous organizations' representatives and then to demand that they have consultative status before they could participate in its sessions, which was the same as destroying with one hand what you had just finished building with the other.

At the end of the first session of WGIP, it was clear to its members that the work would hardly have legitimacy if the WGIP could not hear from Indigenous representatives themselves. The Working Group decided that, starting in 1983, it would open its meetings to Indigenous Peoples' representatives who could make oral presentations under the various agenda items, especially the one on "recent developments regarding the situation of indigenous populations." This moment sowed the seed for the most inclusive UN procedure ever, a procedure that has led to the exceptional participation of Indigenous Peoples in several UN processes, starting with the field of human rights.

---

44 See her book *I, Rigoberta Menchú*, where she tells the tragic story of her family's killing by the Guatemalan military and the trajectory of her struggles. Rigoberta Menchú, *I, Rigoberta Menchú: An Indian Woman in Guatemala*, ed. Elisabeth Burgos-Debray, trans. Ann Wright (London: Verso, 1984).

45 UN Economic and Social Council, Resolution 1982/34, Study of the Problem of Discrimination against Indigenous Populations (7 May 1982), para. 1–2.

46 Willemsen Díaz, "How Indigenous Peoples' Rights Reached the UN," 26.

That year, 1982, I was informally helping *Don* Augusto out, without formal permission from my regular supervisor. I would in principle not be allowed to offer work time in another unit, as this might signify that the unit I was formally positioned in did not have enough work to occupy its staff. *Don* Augusto was preparing the oral presentation for the Study on the Problem of Discrimination against Indigenous Populations that José Martínez Cobo, the Special Rapporteur, would need to read out at the meeting of the Sub-Commission plenary. It was August 1982. I was accompanying Willemsen Díaz and Martínez Cobo as they walked to the Sub-Commission's conference room. There was tension in the air as both men knew that the topic was politically sensitive, the Study had taken long to complete by comparison to all other Sub-Commission studies, and its methodology, led by *Don* Augusto, had allowed for the direct inputs of Indigenous Peoples, in addition to those of states.

This approach to the methodology of the Study was unprecedented and, as was proven with time, created the first exceptional procedures that paved the way for other exceptional procedures that are discussed in this book. Those exceptional procedures, compounded together, paved the way for a new underlying doctrine when it comes to Indigenous Peoples at the UN, the doctrine that I call "corrective exceptionalism." It is the phenomenon of states, the formal decision-makers at the UN, accepting or acquiescing to exceptions to rules or practices that are positive for Indigenous Peoples. The second element tries to address the question, why states have allowed such exceptions, while they have the power to oppose them. The concept of "corrective" in "corrective exceptionalism" refers to the idea that states are aware of the deep, historic, and also contemporary injustices of colonialism, racism, and overall discrimination against Indigenous Peoples. They are pushed, to a large extent by the need to have a certain positive public image, to adopt policies that will somehow correct these evils. Even if many or most states do not hold positions of principle that come out of deep moral commitment to anticolonial and human rights principles, it is clear that they will prefer to show a moral face when they come to the international arena, and even, for various reasons, at the national level. These first steps of corrective exceptionalism previously described during the formative years facilitated an ever broader and more significant Indigenous Peoples' participation at the UN in subsequent years and decades.

The day came, in August 1982, that the Study, or some finalized parts of it, would be presented to the Sub-Commission on Prevention of Discrimination and Protection of Minorities. Willemsen Díaz and Martínez Cobo felt they had to be ready for a pushback from Sub-Commission members. *Don* Augusto sat next to Martínez Cobo, whose hands were trembling while he was reading his introductory remarks. It was a big moment. Martínez Cobo, the Sub-Commission expert from Ecuador, had taken the risk and political responsibility for the Study, and its special characteristics, under his name. The Study was the substantive work of *Don* Augusto – or Professor Augusto, as we called him with respect. We all felt nervous in the Secretariat. We did not know what to expect. But the Sub-Commission members were diplomatic, cooperative, and, overall, accepting. It was a threshold moment when this monumental Study could be considered politically endorsed by the Sub-Commission, its parent body. The various final parts of the Study were published between 1982 and 1984. It was this UN study that received a substantive input through participation of the stakeholders themselves, the Indigenous Peoples, in addition to that of states. It was the most voluminous UN human rights study and the one that took the longest to complete.

Lola Garcia-Alix, a long-time executive of the International Work Group on Indigenous Affairs (IWGIA), former Executive Director and now Senior Advisor on Global Governance, and a well-known advocate for Indigenous Peoples' rights, underlined the significant collaboration that was achieved between the UN and Indigenous Peoples for their direct participation in international processes.[47]

> *Participation has always become a key issue, because the basis for Indigenous Peoples is their participation in international processes, but of course also at the national level. In international processes, it has been the right approach to participate in discussions of all the issues that affect them. I think that has been the line from the very beginning. And I think they [Indigenous Peoples] have been very, very consistent in this demand, if you can call it that. And they have had great achievements. A lot of challenges, but there are a lot of achievements. . . . One of the things is how the UN somehow always tries to find a way to ensure this participation in some way. And the legitimacy that Indigenous Peoples have achieved in regard to that demand for the right to participate, I think is a great achievement of Indigenous Peoples. . . . The processes at the UN have given them the possibility to make visible, and to legitimize also, their struggle. Another important component is also the possibility to meet with other Indigenous Peoples, to network, to [self-]identify, to learn also about the strengthening of their rights.*

At the end of its 1982 session, the Sub-Commission recommended to the UNCHR that it renew the mandate of the WGIP for the subsequent year. The Commission agreed and passed on the request to its own parent body, the ECOSOC, which took the decision that the WGIP would again be held in 1983. The WGIP was not a permanent body of the UN. So fragile was its

47 Garcia-Alix interviewed by the author, 29 April 2016.

existence that every year the same procedure of the renewal of its mandate had to be followed. It was barely one month before each annual session of the Working Group that the holding of its session could be formally confirmed by the ECOSOC. Years later, this fragility and low position of the WGIP in the hierarchy of UN bodies would prompt the Indigenous Peoples' movement to ask for a *permanent* body on Indigenous issues at the UN – an effort that culminated in the establishment of the UN Permanent Forum on Indigenous Issues (UNPFII) as a subsidiary body of the ECOSOC in 2000. The word "permanent" in the title of the UNPFII reflects the fact that the WGIP was not a permanent UN body.

In the fall of 1982, I spoke directly to my supervisor, asking that he allow me to formally work for the Secretariat of the WGIP, at least during its one-week annual session in the summer. The answer was negative. I was disappointed and decided to send a memorandum to my supervisor with a copy to the Deputy Director of the UN Center for Human Rights, asking for the same. I also explained that I did not have enough work to occupy me fully in the Treaty Section. Rereading that memo after my many years of experience in diplomacy at the UN, I had to marvel at the youthful courage bordering audacity of the entry-level professional woman from a small country that I was, in a UN environment. I was elated when my request was granted by the higher echelons. After more than two years as a UN staffer, I was finally getting really excited to be there. Something meaningful and historic was happening in front of my very eyes. I had much to learn. Augusto Willemsen Díaz became my mentor, explaining things again and again, in his generous and inspiring way, not sparing time and effort. His words conveyed commitment and optimism, that many good things were possible, despite obstacles in the UN and in states, and that there was significance in pushing to open these human rights spaces together with Indigenous Peoples. History proved him right.

Kenneth Deer of the Haudenosaunee shared reflections about the significance of building the global Indigenous caucus since the early days.

> I started going to the UN in '87, '88, '89. Academics and others were saying, "You're not peoples. . . . You don't have a right to self-determination. This declaration will never see the light of day." And so there is tremendous resistance to Indigenous Peoples. So when we finally got the Declaration [on the Rights of Indigenous Peoples adopted] in 2007, which people said would never happen, people analyzed, what was our success. And they credit the success to the caucus. The Indigenous caucus, we started it right from the beginning where we had Indigenous Peoples from all around the world, and speaking different languages, and with different experiences, sort of, but they all had [also common experiences] – and we were able to gel, to come to work by consensus and together, to move

together, and all because we were all dispossessed. We are all colonized, we were all disempowered. So we had all that common experience, and that's what held us together. That's what was common. And we were able to channel that in one direction. Now, mind you, we had our differences, but that caucus operated differently from other movements. Other movements were fractionalized – all had the same goal, but they had their own groups going.

. . . And then personally, my role was to coordinate the caucus. I had coordinated every Indigenous caucus from 1994 to the present in Geneva.

E. Consolidating Direct Participation (1983)

The second session of the WGIP in 1983 was a watershed moment in Indigenous Peoples' direct participation at the UN. People were glad that Asbjørn Eide was the Chairman-Rapporteur of WGIP, as we felt he was a friend of the cause. We also knew it was the last time he could hold this position, since 1983 was his last year as member of the Sub-Commission on Prevention of Discrimination and Protection of Minorities. We were concerned about that. I use "we" to convey a feeling of togetherness and solidarity around an uphill battle, a feeling that prevailed among Indigenous representatives, pro-Indigenous Working Group members, UN Secretariat staff, and NGO and academic friends of the issue.

At the first meeting of the second session of the WGIP, on 8 August 1983, Eide announced that the Working Group had agreed to allow representatives of Indigenous Peoples' communities to attend the meetings and make statements, especially under the item "review of developments pertaining to the promotion and protection of human rights and fundamental freedoms of indigenous populations." That meant that Indigenous representatives could take the floor and speak in this public UN forum to describe their situation.

Eide had to explain this approach to an audience now strong with a visible Indigenous presence as well as the presence of representatives of states witnessing what some felt was a controversial decision. The small conference room was packed and could no longer fit the swell of people attending, soon to grow to over eight hundred or one thousand annually in subsequent years.

In order to appreciate the diversion of this decision of the WGIP from established UN practice, we have to remember that there were and are specific and strict rules about how NGOs can participate at the UN. In order to participate at UN meetings formally – that is, to be accredited, receive passes, and make oral or written statements – NGOs must have consultative status with the ECOSOC of the UN. I discuss this in more detail in Chapter 3.

The decision of the WGIP to allow direct Indigenous participation was outside the UN's written rules regarding NGO participation: with a few exceptions, such as the IITC, which was the first Indigenous organization to receive ECOSOC NGO status in 1977, Indigenous representatives did not belong to NGOs. *The peoples and communities they represented were not NGOs.* It would actually sound quite strange to even think such a thing those days, when the concept of "NGOs" would hardly be familiar to many Indigenous leaders attending the Working Group and new to this international system of rules. They represented their nations, their communities, their peoples, their own governing institutions. Being fully cognizant of the courageous step the WGIP was taking and of states' possible reactions, Asbjørn Eide explained that the Indigenous representatives could "only" make oral statements; in other words, they would not provide written statements. Eide was implicitly trying to tell states, in an effort to appease them, that the Indigenous representatives would not have the full range of privileges of NGOs "in consultative status with the Economic and Social Council."

One after the other, Indigenous representatives were given the floor, laying out the grave situations they were facing, including killings, torture, rape, displacement, land grabbing, continuing settlement of their territories, systemic discrimination, forced assimilation, and illiteracy. Rigoberta Menchú also spoke. The words "genocide" and "ethnocide" were resonating throughout the room. Aboriginal representatives from Australia spoke about how their children were being stolen and placed in institutions away from their families. Speaking with indignation, they placed their Aboriginal flag on the table, for the Working Group to see. Mario Ibarra, a political refugee and Mapuche from Chile, was there too. Mario had for years been the only Indigenous person present at the UNCHR, having made Geneva his temporary home and representing the IITC since 1977, when IITC became the first Indigenous organization to receive consultative status with the ECOSOC.

Many Indigenous nations from North America were denouncing the breaking of treaties their ancestors had concluded with states. The Haudenosaunee unfurled and explained the Two Row Wampum, which

> codified an alliance between the Haudenosaunee and the Dutch in the early 1600s: the white shells symbolize the purity of the agreement and represent a river. Three beads of white wampum separate the purple rows, and those three beads represent peace, friendship and respect; the two rows of purple, which "have the spirit of your ancestors and mine," symbolize two vessels traveling the river together, one for the Indian people and one for the non-native people. "We shall each travel the river together, side by side, but in our own boat. Neither of us will try to steer the other's vessel."[48]

---

48 Wampum: Memorializing the Spoken Word, Oneida Indian Nation website, www. oneidaindiannation.com/wampum-memorializing-the-spoken-word/, accessed 2 July 2022.

The reaction of states was tense, and the display of frustration by some was hard to conceal under the diplomatic protocol. Brazil and Peru in particular took the floor several times and said that this procedure of allowing people to speak without having UN NGO status was against the UN rules and that it was therefore illegal. They threatened that the Working Group could be closed down for allowing this. They repeated this position in the informal discussions with Working Group members and Augusto Willemsen Díaz, not just in 1983 but also in 1984. We were aware of the political danger and therefore of the fragility of the Working Group. The countries that were threatening to close down the WGIP, overtly or covertly, we knew, had a lot to hide in terms of their actions against Indigenous Peoples. But the threat was there, nevertheless.

The 1983 report of the Working Group recorded a new category of observers – in addition to states, UN agencies, and NGOs in consultative status. We called this category "indigenous nations and organizations." We felt this was an important step, to write "indigenous nations" in a UN document.[49] The following were recorded under this category in the 1983 report: Haudenosaunee, Mikmaq Nation, Lakota Sioux, INNU National Council, Ad Mapu, Indigenous Delegation of Nicaragua, Metti National Council, Committee for Rural Unity (International Indian Treaty Council), Nordic Sámi Council, National Indian Brotherhood-Assembly of First Nations, National Aboriginal Conference, Federation of Aboriginal Land Councils, National Aboriginal and Islander Legal Service Secretariat, Movimiento Indio "Pedro Vilca Apaza," Interethnic Association for the Development of the Peruvian Jungle, Alianza National de Profesionales Indigenas Bilingues A.C., and Indigenous World-Mundo Indígena. In addition to the aforementioned category, there was one of "Indigenous peoples' NGOs in consultative status with the Economic and Social Council." Present in 1983 were the IITC, the World Council of Indigenous Peoples, the Indian Council of South America (CISA), the Indian Law Resource Center, and the Circle of the Four Directions.

Chief Wilton Littlechild's profound engagement for decades gives precious insights with a time perspective. During our interview,[50] he reflected on why states allowed Indigenous Peoples to participate directly.

I think it was for internal advocacy because we had experts in the Working Groups that were willing to actually allow that discussion to happen within the four walls of a room where both state delegations were and Indigenous Peoples' delegations were. . . . The frequency of the Working

49 UN Sub-Commission on Prevention of Discrimination and Protection of Minorities, Report of the Working Group on Indigenous Populations on its Second Session, UN Doc. E/CN.4/Sub.2/1983/22 (23 August 1983), para. 7–8.
50 Littlechild interviewed by the author, 28 January 2017.

*Group meetings, the intersessional Working Group meetings, the fre-
quency of opportunity to meet global perspectives galvanized our efforts,
and we were able to go forward in places, and we learned from each other
as we went along. So, yeah, I think that's still [like that], it kind of mirrors
that. Like I said earlier, we mirrored the women's advocacy process. Now
we have our process. . . .*

*I remember the day, it was August 27, 1977, at the World Conference
on Indigenous Issues, and I proposed that we should have World Indigenous Games.*

It is also interesting to hear the thinking of a younger Indigenous leader
and appreciate the intergenerational aspect of engagement with the UN. Discussing with various leaders on the question of why Indigenous Peoples did
and do come to the United Nations and other international fora, we can get
various perspectives.

Claire Charters is a professor at Te Wāhanga Ture, Faculty of Law, Waipapa Taumata Rau, University of Auckland, Aotearoa, New Zealand, and
a well-known Indigenous rights advocate. Charters was also an adviser
appointed by the President of the General Assembly for consultations on
enhanced participation following the 2014 World Conference on Indigenous
Peoples, discussed in Chapter 4. According to Charters,[51]

*The international system offers some recognition of self-determination or
some recognition of an external sovereignty or something along those lines
for Indigenous Peoples, something that domestic states can't recognize or
don't recognize, something that seems to be beyond the domestic legal
system. Obviously the international legal system can and does recognize
some determination of peoples and of states, and for Indigenous Peoples
who have lost out on recognition of sovereignty or self-determination historically, wrongly. It's incredibly enticing to have an institution such as
the UN or an international legal order that can recognize sovereignty, or
something akin to what we feel that we wrongly lost out on. . . .*

*I also think that the human rights movement of the '60s – these things
happen in particular eras and times, '60s and '70s, the Indigenous Peoples'
movement – Indigenous Peoples recognized that there are other Indigenous Peoples around the world that are in similar situations, that the cohe-
sion and warmth of coming together, the power of working together and
at an international sphere, I think that's incredibly enticing and powerful
as a political movement, so I think that's another reason why Indigenous
Peoples come to the UN.*

51 Charters interviewed by the author, 2 November 2018.

In terms of special moments in the Indigenous movement, they included of course, in the early '80s, a sort of opening the doors of the UN, and this is what I'm teaching now. I have pictures and it looks like they're literally opening the doors and going through the doors, and that was the early '80s. . . .

Another special moment that I have in mind was when the Declaration [on the Rights of Indigenous Peoples] went through the Sub-Commission and up to the Commission on Human Rights Working Group. And then there was the question on whether Indigenous Peoples and states would have equal voice. And so a big thing for me was the push, of which Moana Jackson was in a leadership role, to ensure Indigenous Peoples had an equal voice in the Working Group of the Commission on the Draft Declaration negotiations, which led to him walking out, among other things.

In the early days of transition toward establishing and normalizing a process of direct Indigenous participation in UN processes, it was the field of human rights that opened the space. Several actors and circumstances contributed to that. The fact that the human rights field had already started opening up to the participation of nonstate actors was a facilitating factor for the participation of Indigenous Peoples. Indigenous Peoples themselves clearly and strongly advocated for their participation. As more Indigenous leaders were joining in from around the world, their voices asking for participation were more effective, and the moral high ground they represented had an impact. Various individuals, whether UN employees, state diplomats, Sub-Commission members, independent experts, or academics, also played a role in helping navigate the complex UN procedures and culture, formal and informal, in order to achieve the acceptance of Indigenous Peoples' direct participation. Subsequent chapters will analyze these efforts further, explaining how the phenomenon of corrective exceptionalism was created at the UN regarding Indigenous Peoples.

F. Indigenous Peoples Are Not Minorities

At the second session of the WGIP in 1983, the Secretariat consulted with the members of the Working Group informally about how to arrange the agenda of each annual session. We proposed that the Working Group should have two main agenda items as per its official mandate: (a) review of developments pertaining to the promotion and protection of human rights and fundamental freedoms of Indigenous populations; and (b) development of international standards concerning the rights of Indigenous populations. "Indigenous populations" was the term used in the UN resolutions at that time, and this lasted long, until it was replaced by "Indigenous Peoples," especially after the adoption of the UNDRIP in 2007. Item (b) in the proposed agenda was a way to paraphrase what had been articulated in the mandating resolution of the ECOSOC that established the WGIP. The phrase in that resolution was "special attention to the evolution of international standards concerning the rights of indigenous populations." This phrase in ECOSOC resolution 1982/34 was admittedly weak and was quite an indirect way of saying that the WGIP should develop new international human rights standards regarding Indigenous Peoples. This vague language showed the disagreement of some states that did not wish to see the development of such standards. This part of the Working Group's mandate, as with so many other things in UN mandates, was a matter of interpretation. Ivan Tosevski, the member of the Working Group from the then Yugoslavia, objected vehemently during those consultations, saying that it was not at all clear in the mandate, according to him, that the Working Group should be developing new international standards. In order to understand this position, we have to give the context of other, parallel international discussions, human rights standard-setting processes, and politics that were taking place those very years regarding minorities.

Tosevski, a seasoned Yugoslav diplomat, had been, since 1981, the Chairperson of an Informal Working Group of the UN Commission on Human Rights to consider drafting a declaration on the rights of persons belonging to national or ethnic, religious, or linguistic minorities. This declaration was, formally speaking, an initiative of Yugoslavia after the completion, in 1979, of the influential study of Special Rapporteur Francesco Capotorti on persons belonging to national, ethnic, or linguistic minorities. The study had been prepared under a mandate of the Sub-Commission on Prevention of Discrimination and Protection of Minorities.[52] I was assigned to provide secretariat support to the Informal Working Group of the Commission on Human Rights from 1981 to 1984, which meant, among other things, that I was to attend the meetings and prepare brief reports. The informal working group would meet only three times during each session of the UNCHR, for three hours each time, or less, if the working group completed its discussions earlier. Two things surprised me during those years that I supported this informal working group. There was not one NGO present in the room during the meetings of the working group, attendance being limited only to members of the group – namely, states representatives that had an interest in the matter. The second thing that struck me, and that was perhaps enough to deeply disappoint a young person working in human rights at the UN, was

---

52 Although completed in 1979, the study was so politically sensitive for states that it remained only as a UN document for years; it came out as a UN publication only in 1991. See UN Sub-Commission on Prevention of Discrimination and Protection of Minorities, Special Rapporteur Francesco Capotorti, *Study on the Rights of Persons Belonging to Ethnic, Religious and Linguistic Minorities*, ST/HR(05)/H852/no. 5 (New York, 1991).

that no state, from the East, West, North, or South, appeared to have any interest in engaging and making progress on the draft declaration. Not one article of a draft declaration was adopted from 1981 to 1984. It would be accurate to say, from the positions expressed in the informal working group, that all those states attending were actually there to prevent any international declaration on the rights of minorities from being adopted. It took the avalanche of the dissolution of the Soviet Union and of Yugoslavia by 1991 for states to rush into a recognition of minority rights, by adopting, in 1992, the UN Declaration on the Rights of Persons Belonging to National or Ethnic, Religious or Linguistic Minorities.

It was against this background of tremendous skepticism of states toward minority rights, a well-known political sensitivity since the establishment of the UN,[53] that Ivan Tosevski and other state representatives were watching, with trepidation, the unique dynamism enveloping the WGIP. Tosevski repeated his position, in informal discussions, that issues of minorities and Indigenous Peoples were similar and international human rights standards in one area would be relevant to the other; so the work had to be very cautious, and the UN could not rush to adopt standards on Indigenous Peoples that may be considered as applicable to minorities. Tosevski's positions in the WGIP and in the informal working group on a declaration on the rights of persons belonging to national or ethnic, religious or linguistic minorities were compatible. The international political stature of Yugoslavia at the time as leader of the Non-Aligned was strong, and its views carried weight in the human rights field as well. Yugoslavia was walking a fine line between supporting decolonization in its various aspects, including for Indigenous Peoples, and also defending positions of states, including Yugoslavia's, that feared ethnicities and minorities.

Finally, Tosevski's position did not prevail in the WGIP, and, as a result, the item "evolution of standards concerning the rights of indigenous populations" was included in the WGIP's annual agenda. In fact, some time was spent by advocates of the cause in the first four years of the Working Group to defend the idea that a human rights instrument, a human rights declaration,

---

53 Asbjørn Eide has often discussed the issue, detailing the many ways in which states had prevented the work of the UN body that included the word "minorities" in its very title, the UN Sub-Commission on Prevention of Discrimination and Protection of Minorities, from doing its work. See his 2012 "Statement at the Fifth Session of the Forum on Minority Issues at the UN" (Geneva, 27–28 November 2012), www.ohchr.org/Documents/HRBodies/HRCouncil/MinorityIssues/Session5/Statements/ItemII/2.%20MinorityforumGenevepresentationAsbjornEide.pdf. See also Asbjørn Eide, "Working Paper on the Relationship and Distinction between the Rights of Persons Belonging to Minorities and Those of Indigenous Peoples," in *Indigenous Peoples' Rights in International Law*, ed. Roxanne Dunbar-Ortiz et al. (Kautokeino: Gáldu and Copenhagen: IWGIA, 2015); and Dunbar-Ortiz, "How Indigenous Peoples Wound Up at the United Nations."

specific to Indigenous Peoples was necessary. The main arguments were that Indigenous Peoples were suffering gross and systematic violations of human rights and that they had various areas of concern that were not explicitly covered under existing human rights instruments, especially the right to land, territories, and resources, collective rights, governance rights, and especially the right to self-determination and the preservation of their own cultures and ways of life. The idea was that the international human rights standards already proclaimed in existing human rights instruments needed to be detailed and explained as to how they were applicable to Indigenous Peoples in a declaration devoted to their rights. This would promote the implementation of those rights.

The notional proximity of Indigenous issues and minority issues was in the minds of states, at least in those earlier days. The political reverberation from that proximity, as explained earlier, is just one example of the political fluidity of issues that is sometimes observed, at both national and international levels. This can lead to the promotion or obstruction of some actions that are not necessarily linked to the substance of the issues at hand. In this way, we can explain, for example, why there was a certain delay of Indigenous-related actions at the UN because some states wanted to prevent similar actions on minority issues. When such fluidity is detected, the various actors need to engage in dialogue to explain in more depth the distinction among issues. In the case of Indigenous issues, from the very beginning, Indigenous representatives and rights advocates did exactly that. One of the topics that appeared relevant was the understanding of the term "indigenous" and its distinction from the term "minority," as discussed in Chapter 2. While an extended analysis of the historical, political, and international law differences between the two categories is beyond the purview of this book, academic writings have been devoted to these questions and will probably continue to be written as well.[54] We should note here, however, that these two categories mostly evolved separately, both historically and politically, and have ended up in separate international law categories and regimes, with separate normative instruments and international mechanisms and processes. There is more emphasis on group rights for Indigenous Peoples, especially regarding the right to land, territories, and resources, and the right to self-determination.

54 Agar-Erdene Gankhuyag, "Has the Minority Rights Framework Suffered Because of the Advancement of Indigenous Peoples' Rights within the United Nations System?," working paper, 2019, www.academia.edu/41719967/Has_the_minority_rights_framework_suffered_because_of_the_advancement_of_Indigenous_peoples_rights_within_the_United_Nations_system; the author answers the question in the title of his essay in the negative. See also Anna Meijknecht, *Towards International Personality: The Position of Minorities and Indigenous Peoples in International Law* (Antwerp: Intersentia, 2001); and Daes, "Working Paper on the Relationship and Distinction between the Rights of Persons Belonging to Minorities and Those of Indigenous Peoples."

Importantly, there has not been a global movement of minorities or for minority rights, while there has been an impressive and strong global Indigenous Peoples' movement, which, through its intense and sustained participation over decades, has played a pivotal role in international achievements in this field.

In this chapter, we have followed the first organized, strategic, and decisive efforts of the Indigenous Peoples movement in the post-WWII era to contact the UN and seek justice for their cause. Impressive results came out of these efforts early on. Significantly, strategies, methods, and narratives of Indigenous Peoples, accompanied by their supporters, led to exceptional and impressive Indigenous participation: in the UN Study on the Problem of Discrimination against Indigenous Populations launched in 1972, at the 1977 International NGO Conference on Discrimination against Indigenous Populations in the Americas, and ending, at this first phase, in 1983, with the unprecedented acceptance of direct Indigenous participation in the UN Working Group on Indigenous Populations.

These efforts, immersed in concepts of human rights, decolonization, and social justice, achieved the internationalization of Indigenous Peoples' issues, the creation of a global Indigenous Peoples' movement, and a global Indigenous identity, as well as the establishment of a new "Indigenous" space in the interstate system, a space that was to expand considerably in subsequent years. The chapter has shown how issues of minorities compounded fears of states and contributed a certain resistance to Indigenous issues. Despite this and other challenges, the organized entry of the Indigenous Peoples movement to the international arena in the 1970s and early 1980s responded and strengthened the anticolonial and human rights ethic of that period. The international dynamic initiatives of Indigenous Peoples have become an important expression of their self-determination in its external aspects.

Bibliography

Daes, Erica-Irene. "Working Paper on the Relationship and Distinction between the Rights of Persons Belonging to Minorities and Those of Indigenous Peoples." In *Indigenous Peoples' Rights in International Law: Emergence and Application*, edited by Roxanne Dunbar-Ortiz, Dalee Sambo Dorough, Gudmundur Alfredsson, Lee Swepston, and Petter Wille, 130–135. Kautokeino: Gáldu; Copenhagen: IWGIA, 2015.

Dunbar-Ortiz, Roxanne. "How Indigenous Peoples Wound Up at the United Nations." In *The Hidden 1970s: Histories of Radicalism*, edited by Dan Berger, 115–134. New Brunswick, NJ: Rutgers University Press, 2010. https://doi.org/10.36019/9780813550336.

Dunbar-Ortiz, Roxanne. "The First Ten Years, from Study to Working Group: 1972–1982." In *Indigenous Peoples' Rights in International Law: Emergence and Application*, edited by Roxanne Dunbar-Ortiz, Dalee Sambo Dorough, Gudmundur

Alfredsson, Lee Swepston, and Petter Wille, 42–87. Kautokeino: Gáldu; Copenhagen: IWGIA, 2015.

Eide, Asbjørn. "Statement at the Fifth Session of the Forum on Minority Issues at the UN." Geneva, 27–28 November 2012. www.ohchr.org/Documents/HRBodies/HRCouncil/MinorityIssues/Session5/Statements/ItemII/2.%20Minorityforum-GenevepresentationAsbjornEide.pdf.

Eide, Asbjørn. "From Prevention of Discrimination to Autonomy and Self-Determination: The Start of the WGIP, Achievements Gained and Future Challenges." In *Indigenous Peoples' Rights in International Law: Emergence and Application*, edited by Roxanne Dunbar-Ortiz, Dalee Sambo Dorough, Gudmundur Alfredsson, Lee Swepston, and Petter Wille, 98–121. Kautokeino: Gáldu; Copenhagen: IWGIA, 2015a.

Eide, Asbjørn. "Working Paper on the Relationship and Distinction between the Rights of Persons Belonging to Minorities and Those of Indigenous Peoples." In *Indigenous Peoples' Rights in International Law: Emergence and Application*, edited by Roxanne Dunbar-Ortiz, Dalee Sambo Dorough, Gudmundur Alfredsson, Lee Swepston, and Petter Wille, 122–129. Kautokeino: Gáldu; Copenhagen: IWGIA, 2015b.

Gankhuyag, Agar-Erdene. "Has the Minority Rights Framework Suffered Because of the Advancement of Indigenous Peoples' Rights within the United Nations System?" Working Paper, 2019. www.academia.edu/41719967/Has_the_minority_rights_framework_suffered_because_of_the_advancement_of_Indigenous_peoples_rights_within_the_United_Nations_system.

Graugnard, Jean-François. *Photographic Report of the "International Conference Against Discrimination Against Indigenous Populations of the Americas."* Geneva: United Nations, 1977.

Martineau, Raymonde. Interview by James S. Sutterlin, 7 July 1998. Geneva. Transcript in UN Dag Hammarskjöld Library. https://digitallibrary.un.org/record/503509?ln=en.

Martínez Cobo, José R. *Study of the Problem of Discrimination against Indigenous Populations*. Collected Edition. UN Doc. E/CN.4/Sub.2/1986/7 (vol. 1) and UN Doc. E/CN.4/Sub.2/1986/7/Add.1–UN Doc. E/CN.4/Sub.2/1986/7/Add.4 (vols. 2–5). New York: UN, 1986–1987.

Meijknecht, Anna. *Towards International Personality: The Position of Minorities and Indigenous Peoples in International Law*. Antwerp: Intersentia, 2001.

Menchú, Rigoberta. *I, Rigoberta Menchú: An Indian Woman in Guatemala*. Edited by Elisabeth Burgos-Debray. Translated by Ann Wright. London: Verso, 1984.

Ramcharan, Bertrand. *The Advent of Universal Protection of Human Rights: Theo van Boven and the Transformation of the UN Role*. New York: Springer, 2018.

Roston, Miles, dir. *The Subversives: Theo van Boven at the UN*. Naarden: Ethan Films, 2017; distributed 2019. 81 min. www.ethanfilms.com/work/subversives-2019.

Stamatopoulou, Elsa. "Indigenous Peoples and the United Nations: Human Rights as a Developing Dynamic." *Human Rights Quarterly* 16, no. 1 (February 1994): 58–81. https://doi.org/10.2307/762411.

UN Economic and Social Council. Resolution 1982/34, Study of the Problem of Discrimination against Indigenous Populations, 7 May 1982.

UN General Assembly. Resolution 49/214, International Decade of the World's Indigenous People. A/RES/49/214, 17 February 1995.

UN General Assembly. Resolution 61/295, United Nations Declaration on the Rights of Indigenous Peoples. UN Doc. A/RES/61/295, 13 September 2007. www.un.org/development/desa/indigenouspeoples/wp-content/uploads/sites/19/2018/11/UNDRIP_E_web.pdf.

UN Office of the High Commissioner for Human Rights (OHCHR). Enforced or Involuntary Disappearances. Fact Sheet no. 6, rev. 3. OHCHR, 2009.

UN Sub-Commission on Prevention of Discrimination and Protection of Minorities. Report of the Working Group on Indigenous Populations on Its 1st Session. UN Doc. E/CN.4/Sub.2/1982/33, 25 August 1982.

UN Sub-Commission on Prevention of Discrimination and Protection of Minorities. Report of the Working Group on Indigenous Populations on Its Second Session. UN Doc. E/CN.4/Sub.2/1983/22, 23 August 1983.

UN Sub-Commission on Prevention of Discrimination and Protection of Minorities, Special Rapporteur Francesco Capotorti. Study on the Rights of Persons Belonging to Ethnic, Religious and Linguistic Minorities. ST/HR(05)/H852/no.5. New York, 1991.

van Boven, Theo. *People Matter: Views on International Human Rights Policy.* Edited by Hans Thoolen. Amsterdam: Muellenhoff, 1982.

Willemsen Díaz, Augusto. "How Indigenous Peoples' Rights Reached the UN." In *Making the Declaration Work: The United Nations Declaration on the Rights of Indigenous Peoples*, edited by Claire Charters and Rodolfo Stavenhagen, 16–31. Copenhagen: International Work Group on Indigenous Affairs, 2009.

2

THE VICTORY OF NONDEFINITION

A. Why There Is No Definition of "Indigenous Peoples"

The use of the term "indigenous," "native," or "aborigine" in international documents before World War II referred to colonized populations under foreign domination, to non-Westerners, regardless of whether or not they had been born there or were newcomers.[1] The meaning of the term after World War II changed to what its new understanding is today, especially through the work of the International Labor Organization (ILO) and the United Nations.

The working definition or understanding of the term, and the most quoted one, was originally offered in the UN Study of the Problem of Discrimination against Indigenous Populations (the Study). It was linked more to the concept of Indigenous populations in classical colonialism. As we will see, this understanding was reinterpreted and complemented by Indigenous delegates that participated in the Working Group on Indigenous Populations (WGIP) as well as by others outside the UN. The working understanding in the Study read as follows:

> Indigenous communities, peoples and nations are those which, having a historical continuity with pre-invasion and pre-colonial societies that

---

1 Albert Kwokwo Barume, *Land Rights of Indigenous Peoples in Africa: With Special Focus on Central, Eastern and Southern Africa*, 2nd ed., IWGIA Document 128 (Copenhagen: IWGIA, 2014), www.iwgia.org/images/documents/popular-publications/land-rights-of-indigenous-peoples-in-africa.pdf. Barume provides an excellent account of the work of the International Labor Organization – the first such organization to use the term "indigenous" – since 1936, and how, through the decades, the use of the term in ILO treaties changed to what today's understanding is.

DOI: 10.4324/9781003464099-3

developed on their territories, consider themselves distinct from other sectors of the societies now prevailing on those territories, or parts of them. They form at present non-dominant sectors of society and are determined to preserve, develop and transmit to future generations their ancestral territories, and their ethnic identity, as the basis of their continued existence as peoples, in accordance with their own cultural patterns, social institutions and legal system.

This historical continuity may consist of the continuation, for an extended period reaching into the present of one or more of the following factors:

(a) Occupation of ancestral lands, or at least of part of them;

(b) Common ancestry with the original occupants of these lands;

(c) Culture in general, or in specific manifestations (such as religion, living under a tribal system, membership of an indigenous community, dress, means of livelihood, lifestyle, etc.);

(d) Language (whether used as the only language, as mother-tongue, as the habitual means of communication at home or in the family, or as the main, preferred, habitual, general or normal language);

(e) Residence in certain parts of the country, or in certain regions of the world;

(f) Other relevant factors.

On an individual basis, an indigenous person is one who belongs to these indigenous populations through self-identification as indigenous (group consciousness) and is recognized and accepted by these populations as one of its members (acceptance by the group).

This preserves for these communities the sovereign right and power to decide who belongs to them, without external interference.[2]

In other words, one fundamental element is that the Indigenous People's group exercises agency, *considers itself* distinct, and considers that *the group itself* is determined to preserve, develop, and transmit to future generations

2 José R. Martínez Cobo, *Study of the Problem of Discrimination against Indigenous Populations*, Volume V: Conclusions, Proposals and Recommendations, UN Doc. E/CN.4/ Sub.2/1986/7/Add.4 (New York: UN, 1987), para. 379–382. Volume 5 of the Study is the most quoted one. The Study was launched in 1972 and was completed in 1984, thus making it the most voluminous study of its kind, with thirty-seven monographs. A reprint edition of the Study, collecting all thirty-seven of the original individual reports in five volumes, was published in 1986–1987. The original reports in the Study are available at https://social.desa. un.org/publications/martinez-cobo-study.

their territory and culture. Another fundamental element is that the group forms at present a *nondominant* sector of society.[3]

Similar elements of understanding the term "indigenous" also appear in ILO Convention No. 169, the Indigenous and Tribal Peoples Convention, 1989.[4]

Article 1 of ILO Convention No. 169 contains a statement of coverage rather than a definition, indicating that the Convention applies to

    (a) tribal peoples in independent countries whose social, cultural and economic conditions distinguish them from other sections of the national community, and whose status is regulated wholly or partially by their own customs or traditions or by special laws or regulations;

    (b) peoples in independent countries who are regarded as indigenous on account of their descent from the populations which inhabited the country, or a geographical region to which the country belongs, at the time of conquest or colonization or the establishment of present state boundaries and who irrespective of their legal status, retain some or all of their own social, economic, cultural and political institutions.

Self-identification of a group as Indigenous or tribal is considered a fundamental criterion. At the level of the individual, self-identification and acceptance by the group as such are the decisive criteria. The aforementioned conceptual elements found their way in various forms in the UN Declaration on the Rights of Indigenous Peoples (UNDRIP), advocated by Indigenous Peoples, as is discussed later.

Self-identification, closely linked to the right of Indigenous Peoples to self-determination, is the practice followed in the United Nations system and other intergovernmental organizations as well. This practice is especially important when it comes to accrediting Indigenous representatives in Indigenous-related meetings, such as the UN Permanent Forum on Indigenous Issues (UNPFII) and the Expert Mechanism on the Rights of Indigenous Peoples (EMRIP) or other relevant international meetings and projects as, for example, those around the Convention on Biological Diversity (CBD) and the World Intellectual Property Organization (WIPO).[5] The exceptional

---

3 This chapter has some elements from the author's contribution on this topic in the introduction to Sheryl Lightfoot and Elsa Stamatopoulou (Eds.), *Indigenous Peoples and Borders* (Durham NC: Duke University Press, 2024).

4 International Labor Organization, C169: Indigenous and Tribal Peoples Convention, 1989.

5 For example, at the CBD Working Group on Article 8(j), and at WIPO's Intergovernmental Committee on Intellectual Property and Genetic Resources, Traditional Knowledge and Folklore (IGC).

procedure of the WGIP to accept the participation of persons representing Indigenous Peoples and their communities, institutions, and organizations since the early 1980s later became the regular procedure in the UNPFII and other UN bodies.

The discussions at the UN around issues of definition of Indigenous Peoples lasted a few years. At the second and subsequent sessions of the WGIP, experts of the Sub-Commission on Prevention of Discrimination and Protection of Minorities, Indigenous Peoples' representatives, states' diplomats, and independent international law experts launched efforts to identify differences between Indigenous Peoples and minorities and, also, to address the term "Indigenous Peoples." From the beginning, the WGIP adopted a flexible, progressive approach to the issue of definition because the information brought before the group included situations that could not be included in the "classical" context of colonialism, such as situations of tribal peoples in India and Bangladesh. The same was true when African Indigenous representatives started coming to the WGIP, such as the Korongoro Integrated Peoples Oriented to Conservation (KIPOC) from Tanzania.[6]

Based on the UNDRIP, ILO's work, and the conceptual work on Indigenous Peoples carried out by the African Commission on Human and Peoples' Rights, Albert Barume points to the human rights-based understanding of the term "Indigenous" in current times – namely, the need for protection of people who suffered discrimination, injustice, and dispossession.[7] Focusing more on the African context, Barume underlines that the concept of Indigenous Peoples is indeed a human rights construct aimed at redressing specific violations of rights linked to cultural identities, livelihoods, and cultural existence as community.[8] Robert Nichols sees indigeneity as a political identity based on historic and current experiences and institutionalized systems of dispossession.[9] Indigeneity may also be seen as a contemporary political construct, in that it is used by certain communities as a way to claim specific rights denied to them, rights proclaimed internationally in recent times thanks to the mobilization of Indigenous Peoples from around the world.

6 UN Sub-Commission on Prevention of Discrimination and Protection of Minorities, Report of the Working Group on Indigenous Populations on Its Ninth Session, UN Doc. E/CN.4/Sub.2/1991/40/Rev. 1 (3 October 1991), 3.

7 African Commission on Human and Peoples' Rights, *Report of the African Commission's Working Group of Experts on Indigenous Populations/Communities: Submitted in Accordance with the "Resolution on the Rights of Indigenous Populations/Communities in Africa"* (Banjul: ACHPR and Copenhagen: IWGIA, 2005), www.iwgia.org/images/publications/African_Commission_book.pdf; Barume, *Land Rights of Indigenous Peoples*, 30–34.

8 Barume, *Land Rights of Indigenous Peoples*, 34.

9 Robert Nichols, *Theft Is Property! Dispossession and Critical Theory* (Durham, NC: Duke University Press, 2020).

During UN discussions on the concept of "Indigenous Peoples," a number of countries were particularly resistant on the issue of definition. China, India, and Bangladesh, also joined by the former the Soviet Union, fiercely resisted the Working Group's flexible approach, stating also that they had no Indigenous Peoples on their territory.[10]

For example, India, whose Indigenous population – or "tribal" population, the term used in the country's constitution – is estimated at 104 million.[11] India, however, does not recognize that it has Indigenous Peoples and has opposed the term "Indigenous," stating that all inhabitants of India are indigenous to India – a position it has held since the beginning of the WGIP in the early 1980s. In those times, India also insisted, along with Bangladesh and the Soviet Union, that a definition of "Indigenous Peoples" was necessary before the UN could draft a declaration on the rights of Indigenous Peoples. This position was not accepted by the Working Group, which, following a broader consensus, decided that a formal definition of the term "Indigenous Peoples" was not necessary. Moreover, with time, India stopped even attending the meetings of Indigenous-related bodies, including the UNPFII in New York, even though India was brought up at the Permanent Forum by Indigenous speakers. On the positive side, India voted in favor of the UNDRIP at the UN General Assembly in 2007. While not participating at formal meetings of the Permanent Forum, India has in recent times tried to avert the practice of open Indigenous participation at the UN, using as an argument the fact that there is no UN definition of Indigenous Peoples. This was also India's position, following the 2014 World Conference on Indigenous Peoples, during the discussions on enhanced Indigenous Peoples' participation at the UN. On another occasion, in 2010, during consultations on the status and participation of NGOs at the UN, India attempted to question open Indigenous participation at the Permanent Forum, but there was no follow-up to that; the delegation of India did not press the point further.

India's positions matter internationally, given the country's strong geopolitical presence. Its positions have repercussions on the Indigenous Peoples in India as well. While other countries in the area, such as the Philippines and Indonesia, have accepted, in different degrees, that they have Indigenous Peoples in the international sense of the term, it is disconcerting that India has not done the same. After decades of UN work in this field, the reason India gives – that is, that "all Indians are indigenous to India" – is inadequate at international level, especially coming from a big country like this. India,

10 The author witnessed their representatives taking these positions at many relevant UN meetings.
11 Dwayne Mamo, ed., *Indigenous World 2022* (Copenhagen: IWGIA, 2022), 201, www. iwgia.org/en/resources/indigenous-world.

together with Indonesia, has the largest Indigenous population of Asia, making Asia the continent with the highest number of Indigenous Peoples.

Indigenous politics are taking place within the context of national, regional, and global politics of their time. The broader antiracism, decolonization, and social justice frameworks that Indigenous Peoples were creating for their struggles since the 1970s found resonance, among others, with Cuba in the polarized politics of the Cold War. Cuba also aspired to play an important role among newly independent countries that had emerged through decolonization. Moreover, at least at the beginning of the internationalization of Indigenous affairs, the general idea was that these were matters of major concern for countries of the West, including obviously the United States, and also other countries with conservative, often military-backed regimes in Latin America. There was little broad awareness early on that Indigenous issues concerned all continents and crossed regimes. Indigenous Peoples from the Soviet Union and Africa started coming to the UN in 1989. In Cold War politics among states, the idea was that by accentuating Indigenous Peoples' rights, the countries mostly exposed would mainly be Western countries. Cuba demonstrated a strong interest in the WGIP, albeit declaring there are no Indigenous Peoples in Cuba. Although Indigenous leaders in later years defied this position of Cuba by pointing out the existence of Taino people on the island, Cuba has continued supporting Indigenous issues at the UN throughout.

Miguel Alfonso Martínez, the Cuban expert of the Sub-Commission on Prevention of Discrimination and Protection of Minorities, became a member of the WGIP for many years and its Chairman during the final years (2002–2005). Alfonso Martínez wrote the 1999 "Study on Treaties, Agreements and Other Constructive Arrangements between States and Indigenous Populations."[12] In that context he opined that the term "indigenous" does not apply to "ethnic groups, minorities, peoples or autochthonous groups" in the Asian and African contexts.[13] This view was met with protests by Indigenous representatives from those regions and has not been followed in the practice of the United Nations – namely, in the way the UNPFII and the EMRIP operate; those bodies accredit Indigenous participants also from Africa and Asia.[14]

China has been a cautious supporter of Indigenous issues over the years, while always stressing that there are no Indigenous Peoples in China. China

---

12 The final report appears in UN Doc. E/CN.4/Sub.2/1999/20 (22 June 1999). Miguel Alfonso Martinez, the Special Rapporteur, had presented one preliminary report and three progress reports before his final report.

13 UN Doc. E/CN.4/Sub.2/1999/20, para. 91.

14 Around the year 2005, Indigenous representatives from Ethiopia participated at a session of the UNPFII and complained about their situation in the country. The state diplomats of Ethiopia were not present at that meeting. As was explained to me, their understanding from discussions with Cuban delegates was that the Permanent Forum was about Western countries mainly. The Ethiopian diplomats had therefore decided not to follow the proceedings.

voted in favor of the adoption of the UNDRIP and also nominated experts as members of the UNPFII: Ms. Qin Xiaomei (2002–2007), wife of then Foreign Minister of China; Ms. Zhang Xiaoan (2017–2022); and Ms. Li Nan (2023–2025). It is a humanitarian spirit that mostly characterizes the participation of Chinese members at the Permanent Forum, one of understanding for the plight of Indigenous communities around the world. Representatives of the Chinese government have, at the same time, tried to avert references to China in Indigenous-related official UN documentation or the participation of persons identifying themselves as Indigenous coming from China.[15] China has demonstrated its support for the Permanent Forum by hosting the Forum's presessional meeting in Beijing in the spring of 2006. In preparation of the International Year of Indigenous Languages in 2019, China also organized, together with UNESCO, the international conference Role of Linguistic Diversity in Building a Global Community with Shared Future in Changsha, in September 2018. The agenda of that conference included a component on Indigenous languages, and the Outcome Document is a positive and significant contribution to international policy pronouncements on Indigenous languages.[16] Within the context of international politics, it is quite significant for powerful, important countries, such as China, to demonstrate interest in Indigenous issues that may be viewed as marginal by many. This increases the profile of the issue. At the same time, this is not without risks, as countries can use – and sometimes do use – Indigenous issues for political purposes in their international relations.

There is clearly a diversity in the politics of states in Indigenous affairs. At the same time, we observe that the question of definition of Indigenous Peoples is often interwoven with the diverse politics. Countries that were placing persistent obstacles to the formulation and adoption of the UNDRIP had also insisted on adopting a definition of "Indigenous Peoples" first. When this proved to be extremely difficult or not desirable, these countries suggested an indefinite postponement of any work on the substance of the Declaration. To "demystify" the lack of formal UN definition of "Indigenous Peoples," one should recall that formal UN definitions are clearly not a condition of policy and action. In its long history, the UN has still not defined "minorities" or "peoples" or "family" or "terrorism," among other terms. The lack of formal definition often signifies the lack of adequate political consensus among

---

15 For example, in 2010, China prevented the participation of a person from Inner Mongolia whose travel had been funded by the UN Voluntary Fund for Indigenous Peoples, alleging that the person had broken Chinese law and was thus arrested at the airport in Beijing before departing for the UN in New York.

16 UNESCO, *Protection and Promotion of Linguistic Diversity of the World, Yuelu Proclamation*, Role of Linguistic Diversity in Building a Global Community with Shared Future international conference (UNESCO 2018), https://en.unesco.org/sites/default/files/yuelu_proclamation_en.pdf.

states and others about the elements of a definition, but it does not imply that international and national public policies do not address these areas.

What were the positions of Indigenous leaders on the issue of definition? What did they advocate for? During several years of debate at the WGIP, Indigenous representatives developed a common position and rejected the idea of a formal definition of Indigenous Peoples that would be adopted by states and the UN. They expressed regret that colonizing states had assumed the power of defining who the Indigenous Peoples were, when they existed, and when they were extinct. Indigenous representatives did not wish the UN to assume such a paternalistic role by adopting a formal definition. An example of the eloquent and clear position of Indigenous representatives is quoted in the 1996 report of the Working Group as follows:

> We, the Indigenous Peoples present at the Indigenous Peoples Preparatory Meeting on Saturday, 27 July 1996, at the World Council of Churches, have reached a consensus on the issue of defining Indigenous Peoples and have unanimously endorsed Sub-Commission resolution 1995/32. We categorically reject any attempts that Governments define Indigenous Peoples. We further endorse the Martínez Cobo report (E/CN.4/ Sub.2/1986/Add.4) in regard to the concept of "indigenous." Also, we acknowledge the conclusions and recommendations by Chairperson-Rapporteur Madame Erica Daes in her working paper on the concept of indigenous peoples.
>
> *(E/CN.4/Sub.2/AC.4/1996/2)*[17]

During our interview, Claire Charters referred to the complexity of states recognizing Indigenous Peoples, a complexity that is linked to the negotiation of the legitimacy of the state:[18]

> *Recognizing Indigenous Peoples means potentially recognizing the illegitimacy of the state. That idea, that fundamental conflict, is probably at play, or will be at play if Indigenous Peoples have greater participation.*

The link between definition, recognition, and participation of Indigenous Peoples and the repercussions of this link, that Charters brings out, is crucial

---

17 UN Sub-Commission on Prevention of Discrimination and Protection of Minorities, Report of the Working Group on Indigenous Populations on Its Fourteenth Session, UN Doc. E/ CN.4/Sub.2/1996/21 (16 August 1996), para. 31.

18 Charters interviewed by the author, 2 November 2018. The list of persons with whom discussions were held appears in Annex 1. The questions discussed with interviewees are listed in the introduction.

in these debates. In recent times, after the 2014 World Conference on Indigenous Peoples, this point came to the surface again. The World Conference had asked for consultations to take place regarding enhanced Indigenous Peoples' participation. During the various consultations on this under the aegis of the President of the General Assembly, there have been some impressive moments where recognition, definition, and participation were intertwined.[19] One such moment was to see that the President of the General Assembly had two Indigenous representatives on one side and two state representatives on the other side of the podium, symbolizing the effort of constructive dialogue that should take place between the parties. This was an interesting moment until China and Russia made their comments. China commented on the idea of expanding the consultation to include an online consultation and expressed skepticism saying words to the effect of, "[W]e don't know about this online consultation, because maybe some Indigenous people don't have internet access." Then, Russia reflected a typical position of their delegation, resonating what the Soviet Union was saying in 1983.[20] They said words to the effect of, "[W]e cannot do any of this [enhance the participation of Indigenous Peoples at the UN] because in international law there is no definition of Indigenous."

Indigenous representatives have expressed their views about the concept of Indigenous Peoples from various angles. One of those is the difference with the concept of "minorities." Linking their plight, history, and struggles to anticolonialism and antidiscrimination, among other causes, over the decades, Indigenous Peoples have stressed the difference of the concept "Indigenous Peoples" from that of "minorities."[21] They have pointed out that Indigenous Peoples are majorities in some countries, or in any case, they are majorities in their traditional lands where they live.

As the years progressed, the distinction between Indigenous Peoples and minorities was gradually reflected in international fora and documents. This distinction was also accepted by the expert of the UN Sub-Commission on Prevention of Discrimination and Protection of Minorities, the Canadian judge Jules Deschênes, who presented a proposal on the term "minority" in 1985.[22]

---

19 The author has attended the various consultations on this topic following the 2014 World Conference on Indigenous Peoples. More discussion on the vision of enhanced participation appears at the end of Chapter 4.
20 The author was present on both occasions of these statements.
21 See also Chapter 1, Section F, "Indigenous Peoples Are Not Minorities."
22 UN Sub-Commission on Prevention of Discrimination and Protection of Minorities, Proposal Concerning a Definition of the Term "Minority," submitted by Mr. Jules Deschênes, UN Doc. E/CN.4/Sub.2/1985/31 (14 May 1985).

In addition, the 1989 UN Seminar on the Effects of Racism and Racial Discrimination on the Social and Economic Relations between Indigenous Peoples and States also made important pronouncements in that regard:

(k) Indigenous peoples are not racial, ethnic, religious and linguistic minorities;

(l) In certain states the indigenous peoples constitute the majority of the population, and in certain states indigenous peoples constitute the majority in their own territories.[23]

On 24 October 1991, the Home Rule Parliament of Greenland adopted a resolution reiterating the distinction between Indigenous Peoples and minorities:

It is important that the world's indigenous peoples have fundamental human rights of a collective and individual nature. Indigenous peoples are not, and do not consider themselves, minorities. The rights of indigenous peoples are derived from their own history, culture, traditions, laws and special relationship to their lands, resources and environment. Their basic rights must be addressed within their values and perspectives.[24]

Since those early debates, Indigenous delegates were stressing that they are "peoples," not merely "populations" or "groups," and that as peoples, they have the right to self-determination. They were pointing out that, in the past, states had concluded treaties with many Indigenous Peoples viewing them as sovereign nations. They also used the terms "native," "indigenous," "aboriginal," "tribal," or "Indian" interchangeably, pointing out that all these terms had the imperfection of having been created by outsiders. Indigenous delegates put forward the names they call themselves (Yanomami, Sioux, Penang, etc.), and in many of their languages, these words mean "human being."[25] At the end of these debates, the term "Indigenous Peoples" was selected as a generic term. The term can also be viewed as a political construct that has by

---

23 UN Commission on Human Rights, Report on the United Nations Seminar on the Effects of Racism and Racial Discrimination on the Social and Economic Relations between Indigenous Peoples and States, UN Doc. E/CN.4/1989/22 (8 February 1989), para. 40, p. 11. This also happened to be the first UN Indigenous-related meeting, where the bureau was held by one state representative and one Indigenous representative: the Chairperson was Ndary Toure of Senegal, and the Rapporteur was Ted Moses of the Grand Council of the Crees of Quebec; UN Doc. E/CN.4/1989/22, para. 12.

24 Quoted in "Status and Rights of the James Bay Crees in the context of Quebec's Secession from Canada," submission to the UN Commission on Human Rights, February 1992, p. 63; part of author's archives.

25 Elsa Stamatopoulou, "Indigenous Peoples and the United Nations: Human Rights as a Developing Dynamic," *Human Rights Quarterly* 16, no. 1 (February 1994): 73.

now become a concept and category of international law, especially after the adoption of the UNDRIP.

Many state delegations over time expressed the view that it was neither desirable nor necessary to elaborate a universal definition of Indigenous Peoples. Finally, at its fifteenth session, in 1997, the WGIP concluded that a definition of Indigenous Peoples at the global level was not possible at that time, and certainly not necessary for the adoption of the Draft Declaration on the Rights of Indigenous Peoples.[26]

The intense and complex discussions over the question of definition were obviously taken into account during the more than two decades of drafting the UNDRIP. The Declaration addresses the issue of definition indirectly by affirming the principle of self-identification and the right of Indigenous Peoples to determine their identity and membership. Article 9 of UNDRIP states that

> Indigenous peoples and individuals have the right to belong to an indigenous community or nation, in accordance with the traditions and customs of the community or nation concerned. No discrimination of any kind may arise from the exercise of such a right.[27]

Article 33, paragraph 1 states that

> Indigenous peoples have the right to determine their own identity or membership in accordance with their customs and traditions. This does not impair the right of indigenous individuals to obtain citizenship of the States in which they live.[28]

Already since 1989, Article 1 of ILO Convention No. 169 on Indigenous and Tribal Peoples, adopted that year, contains a statement of coverage rather than a definition, indicating that the Convention applies to

> a) tribal peoples in independent countries whose social, cultural and economic conditions distinguish them from other sections of the national community and whose status is regulated wholly or

---

26 UN Sub-Commission on Prevention of Discrimination and Protection of Minorities, Report of the Working Group on Indigenous Populations on Its Fifteenth Session, UN Doc. E/CN.4/Sub.2/1997/14 (13 August 1997), para.129. See also Report of the Working Group on Indigenous Populations on Its Fourteenth Session, UN Doc. E/CN.4/Sub.2/1996/21 (16 August 1996), para. 153–154.

27 www.un.org/development/desa/indigenouspeoples/wp-content/uploads/sites/19/2018/11/UNDRIP_E_web.pdf, accessed 11 January 2024.

28 Idem.

partially by their own customs or traditions or by special laws or regulations;

b) peoples in independent countries who are regarded as indigenous on account of their descent from the populations which inhabited the country, or a geographical region to which the country belongs, at the time of conquest or colonization or the establishment of present state boundaries and who, irrespective of their legal status, retain some or all of their own social, economic, cultural and political institutions.[29]

Article 1 also indicates that "self-identification as indigenous or tribal shall be regarded as a fundamental criterion for determining the groups to which the provisions of this Convention apply."

The two terms "Indigenous Peoples" and "tribal peoples" are used by the ILO. There are tribal peoples who are not necessarily "indigenous" in the literal sense in the countries in which they live, but who nevertheless live in similar situations – an example would be Afro-descendant tribal peoples in Central America or tribal peoples in Africa such as the San or Maasai who may not have lived in the region they currently inhabit longer than other population groups. Many of these peoples self-identify as "Indigenous" and participate in the relevant international discussions taking place at the United Nations. For practical purposes, the terms "Indigenous" and "tribal" are used as synonyms in the UN system when the peoples concerned identify themselves under the Indigenous agenda.[30] In some parts of Asia and Africa the term "ethnic groups" or "ethnic minorities" is used by governments, although some of these groups have identified themselves as "Indigenous." One of the useful approaches has been that of the "human rights concept of Indigenous Peoples" put forward by the African Commission on Human and Peoples' Rights and in particular its Working Group on Indigenous Populations/Communities.[31]

Another important element to the concept of "Indigenous Peoples" was added early on, especially as Indigenous delegates from Asia started coming to WGIP. Indigenous representatives stressed that the concept of "Indigenous Peoples" does not require "the blue water principle," indicating that colonizers from across the oceans – namely, the Europeans – came to Indigenous lands and colonized or exploited them. Indigenous delegates pointed out that

---

29 www.ilo.org/dyn/normlex/en/f?p=NORMLEXPUB:12100:0::NO::P12100_ILO_CODE:C169, accessed 11 January 2024.

30 Secretariat of the Permanent Forum on Indigenous Issues, The Concept of Indigenous Peoples, background paper PFII/2004/WS.1/3, prepared for the Workshop on Data Collection and Disaggregation for Indigenous Peoples, New York, 19–21 January 2004.

31 The 2005 report of the ACHPR Working Group is a seminal document; it can be accessed here: www.iwgia.org/images/publications/African_Commission_book.pdf.

exploitation, marginalization, and systemic discrimination of Indigenous Peoples is also perpetrated by states from within their own continents, and, therefore, the human rights concept of "Indigenous Peoples" must apply in those situations as well if the people concerned self-identify under this category. This position of Indigenous Peoples was significant since the UN's decolonization process did not include them. The doctrine of decolonization by the 1950s was that only overseas territories noncontiguous to the colonial power were eligible for decolonization and self-determination, understood at that time as statehood.[32]

In conclusion, regarding the concept of "Indigenous Peoples" as an international legal and political concept, the prevailing view today is that no formal universal definition of the term is necessary. For practical purposes, the understanding of the term commonly accepted and used is the one provided in the Martínez Cobo Study mentioned earlier. The consensus prevailing is that the most fruitful approach is to identify, rather than define, Indigenous Peoples in a specific context, most importantly, based on the fundamental criterion of self-identification as underlined in a number of international human rights documents.

The significance of self-identification is considerable also regarding Indigenous Peoples' direct participation and accreditation at the UN and other interstate meetings. This is the criterion applied – namely, that an organization or an entity considers itself Indigenous. The UN Secretariat has to follow the practice established and followed solidly for years by the WGIP, the UNPFII, and others to accept open and direct participation of Indigenous Peoples.

One good example of recognition of Indigenous Peoples' external self-determination through participation is the Arctic Council, in which six Indigenous organizations are permanent participants and are integrated into all areas of the Council's work. Similarly, the Barents Euro-Arctic Council includes the participation of most Indigenous Peoples in that region.[33]

The question of a definition of "Indigenous Peoples" has come back in an indirect way during recent efforts for enhanced participation of Indigenous Peoples in the General Assembly and other UN fora following the World Conference on Indigenous Peoples in 2014. This will be discussed in Chapter 4.

While it has been an achievement for the Indigenous Peoples' movement at the international level to not have states or the interstate system (UN and

---

32 Sheryl Lightfoot, *Global Indigenous Politics: A Subtle Revolution* (London: Routledge, 2016), 7–8.
33 Expert Mechanism on the Rights of Indigenous Peoples, Efforts to Implement the United Nations Declaration on the Rights of Indigenous Peoples: Recognition, Reparation and Reconciliation, UN Doc. A/HRC/EMRIP/2019/3/Rev.1 (2 September 2019), para. 37.

others) define the term "Indigenous Peoples," it has been made clear by various pronouncements that recognition of the existence of Indigenous Peoples at country level is closely linked to the implementation of their rights. In a 2019 study on Efforts to Implement the United Nations Declaration on the Rights of Indigenous Peoples: Recognition, Reparation and Reconciliation, the EMRIP made the connection of how recognition is linked with respect of Indigenous self-determination and participation rights:

> The Declaration has several provisions relating to the recognition of indigenous peoples as such and to the recognition of individual and collective rights that are integral to their very existence as distinct peoples. In particular, the Declaration upholds indigenous peoples' right to self-determination (art. 3); their right to maintain their distinct political, legal, economic, social and cultural institutions while retaining their right to participate fully in the life of the State (art. 5); their collective right to live in freedom, peace and security as distinct peoples (art. 7); their right to belong to an indigenous community or nation, in accordance with the traditions and customs of the community or nation concerned (art. 9); their right to determine their own identity or membership in accordance with their customs and traditions (art. 33); and their right to participate in decision-making and the States' duty to obtain their free, prior and informed consent before adopting measures that may affect them (arts. 18–19).[34]

The EMRIP report goes on to note examples of resistance to and codification of this recognition:

> Recognition of Indigenous Peoples is still a challenge in several regions. In Asia for example, they are often not recognized as "peoples" but referred to as cultural communities, national minorities or tribal groups, which can be interpreted as assimilationist language. In Africa, several states have long denied the existence of Indigenous Peoples as distinct peoples, sometimes referring to them using derogatory terminology. In the Russian Federation, although Indigenous Peoples are constitutionally recognized, legislation establishes a numerical barrier: communities with more than 50,000 people in total cannot be enrolled in the list of Indigenous small-numbered peoples that entitles them to the corresponding legal protection, despite having otherwise similar characteristics as those enrolled.[35]
>
> Constitutional recognition is afforded to indigenous peoples and their rights in several countries and is a practice that should be encouraged. This is particularly the case in Latin America, where the jurisprudential

34 UN Doc. A/HRC/EMRIP/2019/3/Rev.1, para. 9.
35 UN Doc. A/HRC/EMRIP/2019/3/Rev.1, para. 16.

developments of the Inter-American system and the use of the International Labour Organization (ILO) Indigenous and Tribal Peoples Convention, 1989 (No. 169) have played an important role.[36]

The report also emphasizes the importance of this recognition to addressing historical injustice:

> Indigenous peoples also see recognition, reparation and reconciliation as a means of addressing colonization and its long-term effects and of overcoming challenges with deep historical roots. In this regard, recognition of indigenous peoples' claims to their lands, the decolonization of education systems and the recognition of indigenous juridical systems and customary laws should be considered an essential part of recognition, reparation and reconciliation.[37]

In concluding this section, it should be pointed out that the ethic of decolonization that has been cultivated at the UN for a few decades already has had concrete results with many newly independent countries and has resulted in new ideas joining the international arena. This trend has helped the international Indigenous Peoples' movement, at least in its early years in the 1970s. Although Indigenous Peoples have had and still have decolonization as one of the inspirations for their struggles, states continue to be quite sensitive in connecting the Indigenous cause with decolonization. An indication of this reticence could be observed, for example, in 2013 when the Māori member of the UNPFII, legal scholar Valmaine Toki, presented her Study on Decolonization of the Pacific Region.[38] Some states reacted with surprising criticism, including the United States and New Zealand, while Indigenous representatives supported the analysis contained in the study.[39] Similarly, in the negotiations of the Outcome Document of the High-Level Plenary Meeting of the General Assembly Known as the World Conference on Indigenous Peoples at the UN General Assembly in 2014, no reference to decolonization was accepted by states.[40] In the introduction prepared by the Co-Chairs of the Indigenous Youth Caucus in 2019 for the book *Global Indigenous Youth: Through Their Eyes*,[41] one clearly sees that the young leadership of the

---

36 UN Doc. A/HRC/EMRIP/2019/3/Rev.1, para. 18.
37 UN Doc. A/HRC/EMRIP/2019/3/Rev.1, para. 14.
38 Valerie Toki and UN Permanent Forum on Indigenous Issues, Study on Decolonization of the Pacific Region, UN Doc. E/C.19/2013/12 (20 February 2013).
39 The author was present during these discussions at the UNPFII.
40 The Outcome Document was adopted by UN General Assembly Resolution 69/2, UN Doc. A/RES/69/2.
41 *Global Indigenous Youth: Through Their Eyes*, Institute for the Study of Human Rights (New York: Columbia University, 2019), xv–xxvii, https://doi.org/10.7916/d8-1bnv-z868.

Indigenous movement also has decolonization in their mind. The authors of the introduction write, "We ask you to challenge the colonial past, to see past the mere illusionary idea of indigeneity. We also invite you to embrace our truth – the truth is that we are alive, and our roots are strong."[42] Later, they add, "Decolonization, for Indigenous Youth, is the act of taking back our humanity."[43]

The politics of states regarding decolonization could probably be understood in at least two ways. Colonial countries would not wish their colonial legacy to be remembered and underlined constantly by the continuing marginalization of Indigenous Peoples in the present. The rest of the countries would not wish decolonization to be linked to their names either. States feel an existential threat since they identify decolonization with secession, the creation of new states. What states have probably not paid enough attention to is the conceptual contribution of Indigenous Peoples to the understanding of colonialism and neighboring concepts. This contribution has been made during the twenty-five years of preparing the UNDRIP and after that, especially through the discussions on the right to self-determination, nondiscrimination, the doctrine of discovery, borders, and similar areas. It seems to be one of the most catalytic tasks for Indigenous leadership today – political, academic, and cultural – to continue to stress and inform the world about concepts that are fundamental to the well-being of communities, nations, states, and individuals.

Words matter. The Indigenous Peoples' movement has always been careful about the background, subtle meanings, and results of certain terminologies. The negotiation of the UNDRIP that took twenty-five years to complete was itself proof of this careful crafting of words. In July 2023, a statement was issued by the three Indigenous-related UN mechanisms on the occasion of the one hundredth anniversary of the visit to Geneva of Haudenosaunee Chief Deskaheh, in his effort to be heard by the League of Nations.[44] The statement points out that

> in many conventions and processes, the term Indigenous Peoples has been used in conjunction with other ambiguous terms and groups such

---

The authors of the introduction are Qivioq Nivi Løvstrøm (Inuk, Greenland), Kibett Carson Kiburo (Endorois, Kenya), and Q"apaj Conde (Aymara, Plurinational State of Bolivia), Co-Chairs of the Global Indigenous Youth Caucus, 2018–2019. This book is entirely written by Indigenous youth, with two authors from each of the seven Indigenous sociocultural regions.

42 *Global Indigenous Youth*, xv.

43 *Global Indigenous Youth*, xxi.

44 See Joint Statement by the United Nations Permanent Forum on Indigenous Issues, Special Rapporteur on the Rights of Indigenous Peoples, and the Expert Mechanism on the Rights of Indigenous Peoples (Geneva, July 2023), https://social.desa.un.org/issues/indigenous-peoples/news/joint-statement-by-the-un-mechanisms-of-indigenous-peoples.

as "local communities." In fact, the characteristics, nature, and ori-
gins of the rights of Indigenous Peoples are very different from other
groups. Therefore, Indigenous Peoples should not be grouped with an
undefined set of communities that may have very different rights and
interests.

. . . We, the UN mechanisms of Indigenous Peoples urge all UN entities
in their methods of work to refrain from conflating, associating, combin-
ing, or equating Indigenous Peoples with non-indigenous entities, such as
minorities, vulnerable groups, or "local communities."

This statement, after many decades of dynamic presence of Indigenous Peoples at the international level, shows the challenges that continue to be posed
by states and the vigilance and attentiveness that Indigenous Peoples must
continue to demonstrate.

Direct Indigenous participation is clearly an achievement of the Indigenous
Peoples' movement and opens further possibilities for Indigenous voices to
be heard in more international fora. Direct participation at the international
level is a specific demonstration of external self-determination of Indigenous
Peoples. At the same time, it is not without challenges and limitations, as we
discuss in the following chapters. States, some more than others, have largely
accepted direct Indigenous participation, finding creative ways for exceptions
that are positive for Indigenous Peoples. These are expressions of corrective
exceptionalism on the part of states, exceptions that will hopefully help mend
historical injustices toward Indigenous Peoples.

The case of the Palestinians' participation at Indigenous-related UN human
rights fora is presented next, as it brings out several of the most intricate
points in the discussions of the term "Indigenous Peoples" internationally.

B. What Is at Stake in a Definition? Palestinian Participation in the UN's Indigenous-Related Bodies

A discussion of Palestinian participation in the UN's Indigenous-related bodies shows what can be at stake in a definition. Palestinians have followed the
"Indigenous trail" at the international level for decades, sometimes closely
and other times from afar, especially when this trail started becoming visible
in international affairs. Already in 1977, the Palestinian Liberation Organization (PLO) was registered to participate as an observer at the historic Conference on Discrimination against Indigenous Populations in the Americas
that took place in Geneva that year.[45]

---

45 See International Indian Treaty Council, *International NGO Conference on Discrimination
against Indigenous Populations in the Americas* (New York: IITC, 1977), https://ipdpow-
wow.org/%201977_conference%20ITTC%20Report%20copy.pdf.

It is also known that Palestinian expatriates consulted with Greenlanders over the years on Greenland's relations with Denmark and the home rule
arrangements for Greenland. Consultations of Palestinians with Greenlanders,
however, stopped when Greenland clearly opted for the Indigenous trail.[46] The
1970s saw a strong movement by Greenland toward self-determination, and,
as a result, a consultative referendum on home rule was held in Greenland on
17 January 1979. Over 70.1 percent of voters voted in favor of greater autonomy from Denmark and the establishment of a Home Rule Government.[47]
In 1977, a pivotal year for the Indigenous Peoples' movements around the
world, the Inuit from Alaska, Canada, Russia, and Greenland met in Barrow,
Alaska, and established the Inuit Circumpolar Conference (now called Inuit
Circumpolar Council). The Greenlanders, representing the largest number of
Inuit, joined the organization, which was clearly identifying as an Indigenous
Peoples' organization. By comparison, another island people of Denmark
with a distinct population and history, the Faroe Islanders, did not pursue the
Indigenous trail as they were seeking self-determination and statehood.[48] It
seems then that when Palestinians saw that the Greenlanders identified with
the international Indigenous Peoples' agenda, that process was not of interest
for Palestinians to pursue at that time, and therefore the Palestinians stopped
their consultations with Greenlanders.

Once the WGIP was established, the PLO registered as an observer participant at its first session in 1982.[49] The WGIP report mentioned various

46 Discussions of the author with Greenlanders involved in public affairs in the country and at
the United Nations.
47 For a background on Greenland's realities and self-determination struggles see Jens Boel and
Søren T. Thuesen, "Greenland and the World: The Impact of WWII on Danish-Greenlandic
Relations," in *Cultural and Social Research in Greenland: Selected Essays 1992–2010*,
ed. Karen Langgård et al. (Nuuk, Ilisimatusafik/Forlaget Atuagkat, 2010); Kuupik Kleist,
"Statement by Mr. Kuupik Kleist, Premier of Greenland, 2nd Session of the Expert Mecha-
nism on the Rights of Indigenous Peoples, Geneva, 10–14 August 2009," in *Making the
Declaration Work*, ed. Claire Charters and Rodolfo Stavenhagen (Copenhagen: IWGIA,
2010), www.iwgia.org/iwgia_files_publications_files/making_the_declaration_work.pdf.
Regarding the agreement on self-government of Greenland, see UN Permanent Forum on
Indigenous Issues, Information Received from Governments: Denmark and Greenland, UN
Doc. E/C.19/2009/4/Add.4 (3 March 2009), www.un.org/esa/socdev/unpfii/documents/
E_C_19_2009_4_Add_4_en.pdf. See also Gudmundur Alfredsson, "Greenland under Chap-
ter XI of the United Nations Charter. A Continuing International Law Dispute," in *The
Right to National Self- Determination: The Faroe Islands and Greenland*, ed. Sjúrður Skaale
(Leiden: Martinus Nijhoff, 2004); and Alfredsson, "The Greenlanders and their Human
Rights Choices," in *Human Rights and Criminal Justice for the Downtrodden: Essays in
Honour of Asbjørn Eide*, ed. Morten Bergsmo (Leiden: Martinus Nijhoff, 2003).
48 See "The Political and Legal Status of the Faroes," Government of the Faroe Islands website,
www.government.fo/en/foreign-relations/the-political-and-legal-status-of-the-faroe-islands/,
accessed 17 December 2020.
49 See UN Sub-Commission on Prevention of Discrimination and Protection of Minorities,
Report of the Working Group on Indigenous Populations on Its First Session, UN Doc. E/
CN.4/Sub.2/1982/33 (25 August 1982).

categories of observers: member states, UN agencies, Indigenous Peoples' NGOs, other NGOs, and other Indigenous organizations and groups. Given its special status at the UN, the PLO was its own category, mentioned in a separate paragraph after "member states."[50] That same year, the International Movement for Fraternal Union among Races and Peoples – a human rights organization of solidarity with anticolonial liberation movements – was also a registered observer. I mention this to say that, in those times of enthusiasm for decolonization, and given its own decolonization struggles, the PLO could not well be absent from political fora like the WGIP was, even if the PLO did not intend to be an active participant. It is possible that the PLO wanted to explore options available via this Working Group, although we do not know what the internal discussions were within the PLO regarding the nature and potential of this new forum. We should add, however, that, given the birth of the WGIP on the heels of the major decolonization process, with many new states having been created, the political atmosphere at WGIP was impacted by the question of statehood that was hovering, even if unuttered.

At the second session of the Working Group in 1983, there was a lot at stake in the evolving procedures that the WGIP would be following. Political pressure from states was extremely high on various fronts, especially since it was known that the WGIP was about to announce its decision to accept open and direct participation of Indigenous representatives at its meetings. A few minutes before 10 a.m. on 8 August 1983, as our team from the UN Secretariat of the Working Group entered the buzzing conference room carrying thick folders, one more issue revealed itself. The Palestinians, represented by the PLO, had again come to attend the Working Group. The start of the meeting was delayed.

Though the Palestinian cause had resonance and sympathy within the UN, the Palestinians' presence was highly politicized and controversial. Augusto Willemsen Díaz, the head of the UN Secretariat team from the then Center for Human Rights, who, as mentioned earlier, had devoted his life's work to opening up the UN to Indigenous Peoples, including through the establishment of the Working Group, started consulting with the PLO representatives. So did the Chairman of the Working Group, Asbjørn Eide from Norway. There was concern that, given the extensive politicization of Palestinian issues at the UN, once they were on the agenda of the Working Group, the Palestinian question might absorb this new and quite fragile body, overshadowing the other issues for which it had originally been created. Some Indigenous leaders, especially those from Latin America, approached the Palestinians. They explained to them first that they viewed the Palestinian cause with great solidarity, as the Palestinians faced similar issues as the rest of the Indigenous

50 UN Doc. E/CN.4/Sub.2/1982/33, para. 5.

Peoples, also suffering from colonization and dispossession of their lands, as well as other issues. At the same time, they pointed out that Palestinian issues were discussed at various other UN fora, while this Working Group was the only UN venue that Indigenous Peoples of the Americas and other parts of the world had. These discussions took place in a spirit of solidarity and mutual understanding. The PLO agreed not to pursue an active participation at the Working Group and did not register as an observer participant at the 1983 session. This discussion between the Palestinians and other Indigenous leaders was in the form of consultations and not in public deliberations of the Working Group. I witnessed some of these consultations, and Augusto Willemsen Díaz described the rest to me in those rushed and compact moments between and after WGIP meetings in the corridors of the Palais des Nations or in his office, moments that were precious in creating understandings and team spirit among us. Again, we do not know the internal discussion in the PLO that led them to agree not to pursue active participation in the WGIP. It could be the feeling of solidarity that was created between them and the Indigenous delegates who approached them. That is, they may have been convinced to leave this new and fragile body, low in the UN hierarchy, to those that did not have any other forum to voice their issues internationally, since the Palestine question was discussed in various UN bodies and, in 1975, the UN General Assembly had established the Committee on the Exercise of the Inalienable Rights of the Palestinian People.[51]

The first meeting of the second session of the Working Group started with some delay at around 11 a.m. on 8 August 1983, without the PLO.

Over the years, Palestinians, especially through Palestinian-related NGOs, attended Working Group meetings and, later, meetings of the UNPFII and the EMRIP. They did not and do not overwhelm these bodies with their issues, whether they were addressing human rights issues of all Palestinians or of Palestinian Bedouins specifically.[52] The participation of Bedouin Palestinians at the UNPFII since 2006 has had a high political profile. This has raised various other complex questions, including whether the choice of self-identification as "Indigenous" at the international level was made by the Bedouins themselves

---

51 UN General Assembly, Resolution 3376, Question of Palestine, UN Doc. A/RES/3376 (XXX) (10 November 1975).
52 Examples include a statement at WGIP in 1999 by LAW-The Palestinian Society for the Protection of Human Rights and the Environment (on the Bedouins); statements at UNPFII and EMRIP in 2006 by the Negev Coexistence Forum for Civil Equality (on the Bedouins); a statement at EMRIP in 2010 by the Badil Resource Center for Palestinian Residency and Refugee Rights (on the Palestinians); and a statement at EMRIP and the Universal Periodic Review of the Human Rights Council in 2016 by the Palestinian Return Center (on Indigenous Palestinians). For these statements, see the online archives of DOCIP, the Indigenous Peoples' Center for Documentation, Research and Information, www.docip.org/en/. In recent times, also the Bedouins from Area C in the West Bank occasionally participate in the UNPFII and make claims to indigeneity (discussion of the author with Lana Tatour).

through their own self-determined governance structures, with full cognizance of the significance this would have within the Palestinian movement.[53] This is discussed at greater length later.

At the same time, the feeling of solidarity toward Palestinians on the part of the Indigenous world has been indisputable. For example, when some Jewish NGOs from Israel attended the UNPFII in 2010 claiming indigeneity, they were met with resistance by the Indigenous caucus. They could not be seen as "Indigenous" in the international law and human rights understanding of the term. They were told that, actually, it is the Palestinians who fall under the category of "Indigenous Peoples" in this case because it is the Palestinians whose territories are occupied and settled, and it is the Palestinian population that is marginalized by the state of Israel.[54]

Within the context of the discussion of the concept of indigeneity in this book, it should be added that, over the years, the Indigenous caucus at UN meetings has, in rare cases, played a role of an informal vetter, in that the Indigenous delegates will not cooperate or will, in various ways, show that they do not consider some participating groups as "Indigenous" in the human rights sense of the term. This is a way the Indigenous movement preserves its legitimacy – a moral and political legitimacy that is fundamental in its continuing impact internationally. This role of the Indigenous caucus, even if rare and almost invisible, is also important in ensuring that the official UN Secretariat is not pushed (by states or others) to enter into a process of refusing accreditation to the Permanent Forum for groups self-identifying as Indigenous, something which is a great victory of the Indigenous Peoples' movement since the time of the WGIP.

It should be kept in mind that although Palestinian NGOs sporadically participated in the indigenous-related UN bodies, the more formal Palestinian representation – first via the PLO, then as the Palestinian Authority, and later, as Palestine, the name recognized now by the UN – did not participate in discussions to formally claim indigeneity at the international level. As previously mentioned, the PLO did participate as an observer at the beginning of the WGIP in 1982, and they allowed themselves to be convinced not to take an active part later on. Based on the author's observations over the decades, the PLO or Palestine, as the name is now recognized, sporadically appeared

---

53 Lana Tatour, "The Culturalisation of Indigeneity: The Palestinian-Bedouin of the Naqab and Indigenous Rights," *International Journal of Human Rights* 23, no. 10 (2019), https://doi.org/10.1080/13642987.2019.1609454.

54 From the author's discussions with those Jewish groups and other participants at the UNPFII in 2010. The Jewish groups seemed to be led by an academic in Israel and supported by some Jewish groups in the United States but did not seem to have political support in the Israeli or US political establishments. The author had several meetings with the groups to explain why they would not be seen as "indigenous" in the international law and human rights understanding of the term.

in the margins of Indigenous-related meetings at the UN, but they did not actively participate.

The question remains, however, of why the Palestinians did not consistently or formally pursue the "Indigenous trail" at the UN. This could be explained through a combination of factors. What would Indigenous status add to their cause that their international recognition had not provided already? Would their identification with what they may have seen as disempowered Indigenous populations in the Americas take away from the sense of their own strength, the strength of their issue internationally? Are the Palestinians "too big an issue" to call themselves "Indigenous"? Would the Palestinians' self-identification as Indigenous People at the UN somehow subtract from their claim to nationhood and statehood, since few Indigenous Peoples, if any, are pursuing self-determination and sovereignty via statehood? Or might the Indigenous Peoples' claim and later legally recognized right to self-determination also benefit the Palestinian cause, bringing it into the fold of a broader postcolonial social justice movement with high moral legitimacy? Might the human rights angle of self-determination that is centrally recognized for Indigenous Peoples in some fifteen articles of the UNDRIP bring new light to the suffering and vision of the Palestinian people for the future? It should be mentioned here that the deepest and most extensive international discussions on the right to self-determination after the main era of decolonization in the 1970s took place within the context of drafting the UNDRIP. Through their practices, that have been enhanced in recent years, Indigenous Peoples demonstrate their self-determination in multiple ways.[55] Is it possible that this human rights angle has sometimes been overshadowed by the overpoliticization and instrumentalization of the Palestinian issue by various states?

Shortly before he died in 2004, Yasir Arafat declared: "We are not red Indians."[56] It is unclear, Joseph Massad comments, whether Arafat meant that "the struggle of the Red Indians has been defeated while the Palestinians continue to resist" or that "the Palestinian struggle and resistance is not unlike the ongoing struggles in the Americas, Oceania, and South Africa, even if the forms and intensity of resistance may vary."[57] This statement and analysis show that the Palestinian political movement, even if ambivalent,

55 See Jens Dahl et al., *Building Autonomies* (Copenhagen: IWGIA, 2020), www.iwgia.org/en/resources/publications/3815-building-autonomies.html.

56 Kareem Fahim, "Yasir Arafat, 1929–2004," *Village Voice*, 9 November 2004, www.villagevoice.com/2004/11/09/yasir-arafat-19292004/.

57 Joseph Massad, "Against Self-Determination," *Humanity Journal* 9, no. 2 (11 September 2018), https://humanityjournal.org/issue9-2/against-self-determination/. The interview referred to by Fahim and Massad was "Not Red Indians," interview with Yasir Arafat conducted in October 2004 by Graham Usher, *Al-Ahram Weekly*, 4 November 2004, www.masress.com/en/ahramweekly/18801.

did feel itself part of the decolonization movement and that its advocates and politicians considered the pros and cons of using the "Indigenous trail" internationally at different times and had mixed feelings and results in that sense.

When it comes to the presentation of the Bedouin Palestinians as an Indigenous People at the international level, another set of complexities arises. Could one claim that the Bedouins, in exercise of their right to self-determination and self-identification as Indigenous Peoples, actually decided to proclaim themselves as Indigenous Peoples by coming to the UN? The right to self-determination is one of the three pillars of the UNDRIP, along with the right to land, territories and resources, and cultural rights. Some fifteen articles of the Declaration refer to the right to self-determination, including free, prior, and informed consent (FPIC). The Declaration is imbued with this right. From an international political and legal point of view, nobody could impose the label of "Indigenous People" on a people without their free, prior, and informed consent, meaning that any such effort would not be accepted under international norms. Under the right to self-determination, when it comes to strategies at international fora regarding a people, who decides the strategy? The academic experts and NGOs or the Bedouins themselves? The response is obvious, that this has to be the self-determined decision of the Bedouins themselves.

A critique has also been raised that Bedouins have been overculturalized, largely by outsiders, in order to fit under the international category of "Indigenous Peoples."[58] It is obvious now, especially under the UNDRIP, that people do not stop being Indigenous as they take on other lifestyles. Cultures are not ossified; they constantly change, and Indigenous Peoples are the first to stress this in UN fora. Here, again, we need to underline that international actors, especially the UN, do not distribute "certificates of indigeneity." The right to self-determination entails the right to self-identification. This is so, especially as there is no formal definition of the term "Indigenous Peoples," and most Indigenous Peoples resist it because they fear the exploitation from settler-colonial or other oppressive, disenfranchising states.

The concept or political construct of "Indigenous Peoples" continues to be highly political, a fact that is raised throughout this book. The right to self-determination is highly political as well. It implies that the peoples concerned must be in the front seat and have the determining role in self-identifying as such and in deciding their self-identification through their own governance structures. Obviously here, the opinion of individual advocates or experts is irrelevant, even if it may influence the eventual decision of the people. If the people concerned decide to follow the political and legal category

---

58 Tatour, *Culturalisation of Indigeneity.*

"Indigenous Peoples," then that is what counts according to international law, which, in this case, is epitomized by UNDRIP, the most comprehensive international normative instrument in this field. If there are cases of settler populations claiming indigeneity internationally at UN bodies, they are vetted by the Indigenous public opinion and caucus, and they are delegitimized and eventually stop coming and/or claiming this. Self-identification is what Indigenous Peoples advocated to include in the Declaration precisely because Indigenous Peoples did not want to be essentialized. Of course some states still use the essentialization argument to recognize or not recognize Indigenous Peoples and their land rights and other rights (e.g., Norway and Finland regarding the Sámi). But many Indigenous Peoples contest, before national and international bodies, that the state has the power to define them. There is interesting case law on Sámi cases created by the Human Rights Committee under the International Covenant on Civil and Political Rights. As for outsiders who essentialize or "overculturalize" Indigenous Peoples, their number is decreasing; they are the "old-fashioned" ones, if I can use this word.

When we come to the specific political situation of the Bedouins and the rest of the Palestinians, Lana Tatour brings out a crucial point: the impact of the claims of Indigenous legal status internationally on behalf of the Bedouins and the effects this creates for the rest of the Palestinians as a whole. In addition to how genuine the consent of the Bedouins was to being internationally characterized as "Indigenous," the political questions here are as follows: To what extent could that have been avoided and how? Whether and how can this be corrected for the future? Or should this be "corrected" at all? Tatour points to some new paths now emerging:

> This new generation of activists insists instead on centering demands for self-determination and sovereignty, framing the Bedouin struggle as integral to and inseparable from the wider Palestinian struggle for decolonisation.
> . . . It is, rather, about developing Bedouin life and culture on their own terms, not on terms imposed by others. . . .
> . . . Bedouin activists formulate their indigeneity in political and historical terms of contention between settlers and natives, not between "rivaling cultures."[59]

Nobody in the first two years of the WGIP could have imagined that this body "for the marginalized," low in the UN's hierarchy and with a weak status, would evolve into the carrier of one of the most robust global social movements of our times. It would have been hard to predict at that time that the Indigenous Peoples' movement would have scored so many

---

59 Tatour, *Culturalisation of Indigeneity*, 1585. The author is grateful to Lana Tatour for the insights she provided regarding the Bedouin case and the question of indigeneity.

normative and institutional achievements internationally in a span of a few decades, with self-determination and land rights as central human rights. Perhaps the most important role of the WGIP has been that it changed the narrative, where "the marginalized" became themselves the principal narrators and protagonists of their histories and visions. Year in and year out, Indigenous representatives did just that. When Edward Said was writing "Permission to Narrate" in 1984,[60] he was relating and interpreting the events around the massacre of Palestinians of Sabra and Shatila in 1982, the year that also happened to be the first year of the Working Group. He was stressing the crucial significance of narrative, "the narrative of their present actuality – which stems directly from the story of their existence."[61] In analyzing diplomatic work at the UN around that crisis, Said insightfully noted that there was no Palestinian narrative, "Palestine yes, Palestinians no."[62] The overpoliticization of the Palestine agenda internationally has often "dehumanized" Palestinians, hiding their painful human experiences behind strategic policy statements with geopolitical flavor. In retrospect, what Palestinians may have missed most by taking a back seat in the Indigenous rights-related UN bodies is precisely an organic opportunity to influence perceptions, to articulate and shape a narrative around their realities in human terms, in human rights terms, that typical political debates often do not offer.

This chapter discussed the linkages between the understanding of the term "Indigenous Peoples," decolonization, and self-determination. By stressing this link as well as the right to self-identification, Indigenous Peoples insisted on and achieved not being defined formally by the United Nations while also claiming all their human rights. By critiquing the doctrine of discovery and other concepts of colonization, Indigenous Peoples created an understanding of indigeneity that goes beyond the "blue water principle." "Indigenous Peoples" became a global, political, human rights, and legal category, valid for all continents. The discussion of the specific case of Palestinian participation in the UN's Indigenous-related bodies brought into relief the various questions that underlie the definition as well as self-identification.

If we look at the international paths of the Indigenous Peoples' movement through the long lens of time, we can see some crucial achievements that this chapter has brought out: the extraordinary and exceptional establishment of direct Indigenous participation, the recognition of Indigenous Peoples' right to self-determination and self-identification, and the acceptance of nondefinition of the term "Indigenous Peoples" by the UN. If we

---

60 Edward W. Said, "Permission to Narrate," in *The Edward Said Reader*, ed. Moustafa Bayoumi and Andrew Rubin (New York: Vintage Books, 2000).

61 Said, "Permission to Narrate," 247.

62 Said, "Permission to Narrate," 250.

link these achievements with a conceptual thread and make one entity out of them, we can appreciate even more the tremendous and positive weight of Indigenous Peoples internationally. If we were writing a book like this in the 1980s or 1990s, we would not have been able to use this conceptual thread. Now we can.

Bibliography

African Commission on Human and Peoples' Rights (ACHPR). *Report of the African Commission's Working Group of Experts on Indigenous Populations/Communities: Submitted in Accordance with the "Resolution on the Rights of Indigenous Populations/Communities in Africa."* Banjul, The Gambia: ACHPR; Copenhagen: IWGIA, 2005. www.iwgia.org/images/publications/African_Commission_book.pdf.

Alfredsson, Gudmundur. "Greenland Under Chapter XI of the United Nations Charter. A Continuing International Law Dispute." In *The Right to National Self-Determination: The Faroe Islands and Greenland*, edited by Sjúrður Skaale, 49–94. Leiden: Martinus Nijhoff, 2004.

Alfredsson, Gudmundur. "The Greenlanders and Their Human Rights Choices." In *Human Rights and Criminal Justice for the Downtrodden: Essays in Honour of Asbjørn Eide*, edited by Morten Bergsmo, 453–459. Leiden: Martinus Nijhoff, 2003.

Arafat, Yasir. "Not Red Indians." Interview by Graham Usher. *Al-Ahram Weekly*, 4 November 2004. www.masress.com/en/ahramweekly/18801.

Barume, Albert Kwokwo. *Land Rights of Indigenous Peoples in Africa: With Special Focus on Central, Eastern and Southern Africa*. 2nd ed. IWGIA Document 128. Copenhagen: IWGIA, 2014. www.iwgia.org/images/documents/popular-publications/land-rights-of-indigenous-peoples-in-africa.pdf.

Boel, Jens, and Søren T. Thuesen. "Greenland and the World: The Impact of WWII on Danish-Greenlandic Relations." In *Cultural and Social Research in Greenland: Selected Essays 1992–2010*, edited by Karen Langgård, Flemming Nielsen, Birgit Kleist Pedersen, Kennet Pedersen, and Jette Rygaard, 9–35. Nuuk: Ilisimatusafik/Forlaget Atuagkat, 2010.

Dahl, Jens, Victoria Tauli-Corpuz, Shapion Noningo Sesen, Shankar Limbu, and Sara Olsvig. *Building Autonomies*. Copenhagen: IWGIA, 2020. www.iwgia.org/en/resources/publications/3815-building-autonomies.html.

Fahim, Kareem. "Yasir Arafat, 1929–2004." *Village Voice*, 9 November 2004. www.villagevoice.com/2004/11/09/yasir-arafat-19292004/.

Institute for the Study of Human Rights. *Global Indigenous Youth: Through Their Eyes*. New York: ISHR, Columbia University, 2019. https://doi.org/10.7916/d8-dh2w-rz29.

International Indian Treaty Council. *International NGO Conference on Discrimination against Indigenous Populations in the Americas*. New York: IITC, 1977. https://ipdpowwow.org/%201977_conference%20IITC%20Report%20copy.pdf.

International Labor Organization. *Convention No. 169: Indigenous and Tribal Peoples Convention*. ILO, 1989. https://www.ilo.org/dyn/normlex/en/f?p=NORMLEXPUB:12100:0::NO::P12100_ILO_CODE:C169.

Joint Statement by the United Nations Permanent Forum on Indigenous Issues, Special Rapporteur on the Rights of Indigenous Peoples, and the Expert Mechanism on the Rights of Indigenous Peoples, Geneva, July 2023. https://social.desa. un.org/issues/indigenous-peoples/news/joint-statement-by-the-un-mechanisms-of-indigenous-peoples.

Kleist, Kuupik. "Statement by Mr. Kuupik Kleist, Premier of Greenland, 2nd Session of the Expert Mechanism on the Rights of Indigenous Peoples, Geneva, 10–14 August 2009." In *Making the Declaration Work: The United Nations Declaration on the Rights of Indigenous Peoples*, edited by Claire Charters and Rodolfo Stavenhagen, 248–251. Copenhagen: IWGIA, 2009. www.iwgia.org/images/ publications/making_the_declaration_work.pdf.

Lightfoot, Sheryl. *Global Indigenous Politics: A Subtle Revolution*. London: Routledge, 2016.

Lightfoot, Sheryl, and Elsa Stamatopoulou, eds. *Indigenous Peoples and Borders*. Durham, NC: Duke University Press, 2024.

Mamo, Dwayne, ed. *Indigenous World 2022*. Copenhagen: International Work Group for Indigenous Affairs, 2022. www.iwgia.org/en/resources/indigenous-world.

Martínez Cobo, José R. *Study of the Problem of Discrimination against Indigenous Populations*. Volume V: Conclusions, Proposals and Recommendations. Collected Edition. UN Doc. E/CN.4/Sub.2/1986/7/Add.4. New York: UN, 1987.

Massad, Joseph. "Against Self-Determination." *Humanity Journal* 9, no. 2 (11 September 2018). https://humanityjournal.org/issue9-2/against-self-determination/.

Nichols, Robert. *Theft Is Property! Dispossession and Critical Theory*. Durham, NC: Duke University Press, 2020.

Said, Edward W. "Permission to Narrate." In *The Edward Said Reader*, edited by Moustafa Bayoumi and Andrew Rubin, 243–266. New York: Vintage Books, 2000.

Secretariat of the Permanent Forum on Indigenous Issues. The Concept of Indigenous Peoples. Background Paper PFII/2004/WS.1/3, Prepared for the Workshop on Data Collection and Disaggregation for Indigenous Peoples, New York, 19–21 January 2004.

Stamatopoulou, Elsa. "Indigenous Peoples and the United Nations: Human Rights as a Developing Dynamic." *Human Rights Quarterly* 16, no. 1 (February 1994): 58–81. https://doi.org/10.2307/762411.

"Status and Rights of the James Bay Crees in the Context of Quebec's Secession from Canada." Submission to the UN Commission on Human Rights, February 1992.

Tatour, Lana. "The Culturalisation of Indigeneity: The Palestinian-Bedouin of the Naqab and Indigenous Rights." *International Journal of Human Rights* 23, no. 10 (2019): 1569–1593. https://doi.org/10.1080/13642987.2019.1609454.

Toki, Valerie, and UN Permanent Forum on Indigenous Issues. Study on Decolonization of the Pacific Region. UN Doc. E/C.19/2013/12, 20 February 2013.

UN Commission on Human Rights. Report on the United Nations Seminar on the Effects of Racism and Racial Discrimination on the Social and Economic Relations between Indigenous Peoples and States, Geneva, 16–20 January 1989. UN Doc. E/ CN.4/1989/22, 8 February 1989.

UN Expert Mechanism on the Rights of Indigenous Peoples (EMRIP). Efforts to Implement the United Nations Declaration on the Rights of Indigenous Peoples: Recognition, Reparation and Reconciliation. UN Doc. A/HRC/EMRIP/2019/3/ Rev.1, 2 September 2019.

UN General Assembly. Resolution 3376, Question of Palestine. UN Doc. A/RES/3376 (XXX), 10 November 1975.

UN General Assembly. Resolution 61/295, United Nations Declaration on the Rights of Indigenous Peoples. UN Doc. A/RES/61/295, 13 September 2007. www.un.org/development/desa/indigenouspeoples/wp-content/uploads/sites/19/2018/11/UNDRIP_E_web.pdf.

UN Permanent Forum on Indigenous Issues. Information Received from Governments: Denmark and Greenland. UN Doc. E/C.19/2009/4/Add.4, 3 March 2009. www.un.org/esa/socdev/unpfii/documents/E_C_19_2009_4_Add_4_en.pdf.

UN Sub-Commission on Prevention of Discrimination and Protection of Minorities. Proposal Concerning a Definition of the Term "Minority," Submitted by Mr. Jules Deschênes. UN Doc. E/CN.4/Sub.2/1985/31, 14 May 1985.

UN Sub-Commission on Prevention of Discrimination and Protection of Minorities. Study on Treaties, Agreements and Other Constructive Arrangements between States and Indigenous Populations. Final Report by Miguel Alfonso Martínez, Special Rapporteur. UN Doc. E/CN.4/Sub.2/1999/20, 22 June 1999.

UN Sub-Commission on Prevention of Discrimination and Protection of Minorities. Report of the Working Group on Indigenous Populations on Its Fifteenth Session. UN Doc. E/CN.4/Sub.2/1997/14, 13 August 1997.

UN Sub-Commission on Prevention of Discrimination and Protection of Minorities. Report of the Working Group on Indigenous Populations on Its First Session. UN Doc. E/CN.4/Sub.2/1982/33, 25 August 1982.

UN Sub-Commission on Prevention of Discrimination and Protection of Minorities. Report of the Working Group on Indigenous Populations on Its Fourteenth Session, Geneva, 29 July–2 August 1996. UN Doc. E/CN.4/Sub.2/1996/21, 16 August 1996.

UN Sub-Commission on Prevention of Discrimination and Protection of Minorities. Report of the Working Group on Indigenous Populations on Its Ninth Session. UN Doc. E/CN.4/Sub.2/1991/40/Rev. 1, 3 October 1991.

UNESCO. *Protection and Promotion of Linguistic Diversity of the World, Yuelu Proclamation*. Role of Linguistic Diversity in Building a Global Community with Shared Future: Protection, Access and Promotion of Language Resources, International Conference (Changsha, PRC, 19–21 September 2018). UNESCO, 2018. https://en.unesco.org/sites/default/files/yuelu_proclamation_en.pdf.

3
THE RISE OF CORRECTIVE EXCEPTIONALISM

The formative years, the 1970s and early 1980s, witnessed the increasing internationalization of Indigenous Peoples' issues. The rise of the international movement of Indigenous Peoples was organized and the movement set strategic, focused goals that it pursued actively and with positive effects already from the early days. Exceptions were approved by states at the UN in ways that proved positive for Indigenous Peoples. How did this exceptionalism develop as the years moved forward?

There was a feeling of great achievement at the end of the second session of the Working Group on Indigenous Populations (WGIP) in 1983. Indigenous Peoples' representatives could speak to the Working Group directly, and we had managed to include the development of international standards on Indigenous Peoples' rights in the agenda of the Working Group. However, the threat by some states, Peru and Brazil in particular, that they could "denounce" the opening of the Working Group for Indigenous delegates at the superior bodies, the "parent bodies," of the WGIP – namely, the Sub-Commission on Prevention on Discrimination and Protection of Minorities, the Commission on Human Rights (UNCHR), and, especially the Economic and Social Council (ECOSOC) – was hanging as a sword of Damocles above the WGIP. These threats never materialized. States never pushed these particular concerns to the higher bodies. We do not know what internal dialogues might have taken place on this matter in various permanent missions of states in Geneva or in foreign ministries in various capitals and how the arguments may have been formulated. In the end, states did not block the "out-of-the-ordinary" participation of Indigenous representatives at the Working Group. We can only try to interpret the attitude of states, especially as the same latitude or permissiveness repeated itself over the years, even well after the year 2000. I would

DOI: 10.4324/9781003464099-4

like to underline and analyze these nodal points of states' "permissiveness" at various moments of the Indigenous Peoples' interface with the UN as this research unfolds.

When the WGIP convened for its third session in 1984, the five members of the WGIP, most of them legal experts, the Secretariat staff, and other experts present, proclaimed that, by not objecting to this innovative practice of allowing Indigenous representatives to make statements at the Working Group, the higher bodies of the UN, especially the ECOSOC, had acquiesced to this, that these bodies had been in tacit agreement with this, giving it legitimacy. Acquiescence has implications in international law. It is the moment or moments where silence has a loud voice.

Some consideration of the international law concepts of acquiescence and protest is relevant to this discussion. In international law, the term "acquiescence" (from the Latin *quiescere*, to be still) denotes a specific kind of consent tacitly conveyed by a state,[1] "a silence that speaks," which has legal effects. In interstate relations, acquiescence or lack thereof (namely, consistent protest) is especially important when it comes to territorial claims. Protest itself

> has been described as "a formal objection by subjects of international law, usually a state, against a conduct or claim purported to be contrary to or unfounded in international law." The primary "function of a protest is the preservation of rights, or of making it known that the protestor does not acquiesce in . . . certain acts." Put another way, "a protest aims at rebutting any presumption of acquiescence in a particular claim or conduct."[2]

At the WGIP however, even adversarial states, were far from protesting consistently or did not protest before the higher competent UN bodies regarding Indigenous participation. Those higher bodies could have stopped the exceptions being practiced that facilitated Indigenous participation. Whatever protest states expressed was counterbalanced by the broad acceptance of direct Indigenous Peoples' participation.

This participation of Indigenous representatives continued over the years and gave birth to a new legal, well-established procedure of Indigenous Peoples' participation at the UN, primarily in Indigenous-focused processes. With time, after the establishment of the UN Permanent Forum on Indigenous Issues

---

1 *Oxford Public International Law*, s.v. "Acquiescence," entry by Nuno Sérgio Marques Antunes, last modified September 2006, https://opil.ouplaw.com/display/10.1093/law:epil/9780199231690/law-9780199231690-e1373?prd=OPIL.
2 Dustin A. Lewis, Naz K. Modirzadeh, and Gabriella Blum, "Quantum of Silence: Inaction and *Jus ad Bellum*" (Harvard Law School Program on International Law and Armed Conflict, 2019), part 2, "What We Mean by Silence," section A.3, https://pilac.law.harvard.edu/quantum-of-silence-web-version; citing Christophe Eick, "Protest," in *Max Planck Encyclopedia of Public International Law*, ed. Rüdiger Wolfrum (Oxford: Oxford University Press, 2006).

(UNPFII), its sessions in New York, following the same procedure, eventually gather more than one thousand Indigenous representatives annually. The Permanent Forum's mandate under ECOSOC resolution 2000/22 now formally recognizes that organizations of Indigenous Peoples may equally participate at the Forum as observers "in accordance with the procedures which have been applied in the Working Group on Indigenous Populations of the Sub-Commission on the Promotion and Protection of Human Rights."[3]

The story of Indigenous Peoples' participation at the international level continues to be written, as Indigenous Peoples have been asking to participate at the meetings of all United Nations bodies of interest to them. I will discuss this further in Chapter 4.

Indigenous Peoples' direct voices heard in the UN halls in 1982 and 1983 were powerful and had already left their mark. Rigoberta Menchú spoke in the Working Group before an audience in shock as she related the atrocities sustained by her people in Guatemala. The UN interpreters could hardly utter the words into the other five UN languages, their voices were breaking, one of them just had to pause.

The year 1983 was the last year that Asbjørn Eide, the Norwegian expert, served as member of the Sub-Commission on Prevention of Discrimination and Protection of Minorities and consequently as Chairman-Rapporteur of the WGIP. And 1984 was the last year that Augusto Willemsen Díaz served as the UN official focal point on Indigenous rights. He departed on retirement at age sixty, back to his native Guatemala. Erica-Irene Daes, a jurist and Sub-Commission member from Greece, took the position of Chairman-Rapporteur in 1984, a position she kept for twenty years.

A. Indigenous Peoples Are Not Nongovernmental Organizations (NGOs)

The status of NGOs at the UN is regulated by specific rules put together by states. What happens when it comes to Indigenous Peoples is an elastic interpretation of such rules. This is the topic of this first section of Chapter 3.

There were and are specific and strict rules about how NGOs can participate at the UN. There are various categories of NGOs that have been created by the UN, and each category has specific privileges and limitations. Having NGO status at the UN formally means receiving passes to access UN buildings and meetings, making oral or written statements at meetings of subsidiary bodies of the ECOSOC, organizing events on UN premises, and similar actions. In order to have such privileges, NGOs must have

---

3 UN Economic and Social Council, *Establishment of a Permanent Forum on Indigenous Issues*, UN Doc. E/RES/2000/22 (28 July 2000), para. 1, www.un.org/esa/socdev/unpfii/documents/about-us/E-RES-2000-22.pdf.

consultative status with the ECOSOC. The Committee on NGOs, a subsidiary body of ECOSOC established in 1946, screens NGO applications and makes decisions. There are three classes of consultative status defined by ECOSOC resolution 1996/31: General, Special, and Roster.[4] These three categories grant different rights for participation in ECOSOC and its subsidiary bodies – principally ECOSOC's Functional Commissions – including rights to United Nations passes, to speak at designated meetings, and to have documents translated and circulated as official UN documents.

Over many years, I followed the work of the Committee on NGOs at UN Headquarters in New York on behalf of the UN human rights office.[5] It was clear that human rights NGOs were always given a hard time to get through and be approved for "consultative status with ECOSOC." Countries with poor human rights records are especially likely to place obstacles before the Committee approving those organizations. The status of NGOs at the UN has been the topic of discussion within the UN Secretariat and among states several times over the decades. Depending on the international politics of specific periods and the balance of power among states, the interpretation and the rules of NGO status changes. The UN is sometimes more open to such participation, as was the case in the time of decolonization and the time of the global conferences of the 1990s, or more restrictive, as was the case subsequently.

When the UN Secretariat was preparing background documents for the review of NGO status that resulted in ECOSOC resolution 1996/31 previously mentioned, the Office of the UN High Commissioner for Human Rights (OHCHR) was also asked for its input. I was working at OHCHR's New York Office at the time and representing the office in the interdepartmental working group led by the Office of the Secretary-General. We consulted among colleagues in the UN human rights office, whether we should explain the exceptional procedure followed for years, since 1983, at the WGIP regarding participation of Indigenous organizations and nations. On the one hand, we felt that this was a procedure that allowed for people's voices to be heard by the UN in a much more direct way; we were proud of it and imagined that this example could perhaps be an inspiration for opening up the UN to more civil society opinions. On the other hand, we were aware that the circumstances

---

4 UN Economic and Social Council, Consultative Relationship between the United Nations and Non-governmental Organizations, UN Doc. E/RES/1996/31 (25 July 1996), www.unov.org/documents/NGO/NGO_Resolution_1996_31.pdf. Resolution 1996/31 is the most recent one adopted on NGO status at the UN after long debates in the early 1990s. The three classes indicated in UN Doc. E/RES/1996/31 are the equivalent of Category I, Category II, and Roster status that had been defined in the earlier ECOSOC resolution 1296 (XLIV) of 1968.

5 For the sake of brevity, I sometimes use the generic term "UN human rights office" since, what is now the Office of the High Commissioner for Human Rights had various other names before: Division of Human Rights until 1982, Center for Human Rights until 1993, and Office of the High Commissioner for Human Rights subsequently.

of Indigenous Peoples were special, with a professed decolonization ethos in the background. One could hardly consider that the tremendous diversity and great number of Indigenous Peoples from all continents could only be represented by the very few Indigenous NGOs that had obtained consultative status with ECOSOC. Those few were active hard-working organizations. The International Indian Treaty Council was the first Indigenous organization to receive consultative status in 1977. Most Indigenous representatives that were participating at the WGIP were representing Indigenous Peoples and their communities directly, and those could obviously not come under the category of NGOs. The feeling among OHCHR colleagues was also that the WGIP model of participation was working well for Indigenous participation and that it had become an accepted practice through acquiescence by the WGIP's higher bodies, including ECOSOC, even if there were no explicit UN rules that allowed such exceptional participation. In those consultations within OHCHR, we concluded that we did not need to draw attention to the WGIP Indigenous participation process, in order also to protect it from any undue political intervention by states in the intense intergovernmental politics at UN Headquarters in New York. OHCHR therefore did not bring up the WGIP participation practice for Indigenous representatives.

It was a victory for special Indigenous participation at the UN when the ECOSOC established the UNPFII in the year 2000. The Council unequivocally and formally recognized the participation procedures of the Working Group and decided these should be followed by the Permanent Forum. Council resolution 2000/22, entitled "Establishment of a Permanent Forum on Indigenous Issues," in paragraph 1, includes the following:

> States, United Nations bodies and organs, intergovernmental organizations and non-governmental organizations in consultative status with the Council may participate as observers; organizations of indigenous people may equally participate as observers in accordance with the procedures which have been applied in the Working Group on Indigenous Populations of the Sub-Commission on the Promotion and Protection of Human Rights.[6]

In fact, this particular point of the resolution went through smoothly in the negotiated resolution and was not the object of any controversy in the discussions for the establishment of the Permanent Forum. It seemed by then well agreed by states that direct Indigenous participation at the UN's Indigenous-related bodies was self-evident and formed an established international practice, and that this practice was now an explicit UN rule that is here to stay.

6 www.un.org/development/desa/indigenouspeoples/about-us/resolution-e200022.html, accessed 11 January 2024.

This practice is clearly not related to UN procedures for accrediting NGOs. When, in the summer of 2010, a small number of Asian countries, especially India, tried to raise some question about Indigenous participation at informal consultations of the ECOSOC, there was no resonance in the Council to give any follow-up to such an idea.[7]

By this point, and even before, it was clear that Indigenous direct participation at specific UN fora was no longer only a matter of international law acquiescence to a certain practice but a matter of explicit political will expressed by states in formal UN procedures and documents, in the UN resolution that established the Permanent Forum in particular.

Reflecting back and analyzing the phenomenon of "corrective exceptionalism," the reasons for states allowing such direct participation of Indigenous representatives, leaders shared some of their thoughts during our discussions.[8] They provided a time angle and global perspective as well. Rodion Sulyandziga, well-known Udege leader in the Russian Federation, founder and director of the Center for Support of Indigenous Peoples of the North\Russian Indigenous Training Center (CSIPN/RITC), and member of UN EMRIP pointed out that

> *It was a very long process. Even if you look back at the history, in terms of colonization and decolonization, it's the whole history of the UN and development, which came to the Declaration [on the Rights of Indigenous Peoples], which came to the Permanent Forum [on Indigenous Issues], and the Expert Mechanism [on the Rights of Indigenous People] creation. So [Indigenous participation is] already quite a strong institution established under the UN. Also it's a part of democracy development, it's a part of human rights development. Of course it's a part of political findings, political negotiations, and so far we see a lot of strong Indigenous institutions or governments around the world. We are working together.[9]*

On the same question, Chhing Lamu Sherpa, the respected senior Indigenous leader in Nepal, Founder and member of Mountain Spirit, explained that for development and long-term peace, states need to consult with Indigenous Peoples.[10] Moreover, it is also international pressure that counts.

> *I think our government has begun to incorporate and has welcomed Indigenous Peoples' issues without threatening and without feeling threatened.*

7 Based on the author's work at the UN.
8 The list of persons with whom discussions were held appears in Annex 1. The questions discussed with interviewees are listed in the introduction.
9 Sulyandziga interviewed by the author, 30 January 2017.
10 Sherpa interviewed by the author, 21 November 2016.

Because in the long run it will benefit the non-Indigenous people, and also the State. From the image point of view internationally, it is good for them, and also for long-term peace, because if they don't incorporate our rights and they use violence, this is really bad for our country's economics.

Antonella Cordone, senior official at the International Fund for Agricultural Development (IFAD), also mentioned various reasons she sees as to why states have allowed exceptional procedures for Indigenous Peoples' participation:[11]

I think that one of the reasons would be to diminish conflict at local and national levels; another is the public opinion, the international public opinion; the other is that probably the human rights agenda in general is still strong and it cannot be denied like that. Another [reason] is because Indigenous Peoples have become more organized and powerful, also through the international processes. . . . Looking from [IFAD's perspective] where we work in 3 regions, I can see that in Latin America, where you have – and where you had – strong organizations since the beginning, or strong constituencies since the beginning, you had to [deal with the issue of participation], I mean you cannot deny it. The capacity of Indigenous Peoples and the ability to negotiate also with government has improved through the years. Probably even states are starting to understand that maybe Indigenous Peoples are not only a threat, are not only a menace in many ways, but they can dialogue with Indigenous Peoples to find solutions. . . .

If we look at the historic perspective, the impact in the last twenty years has been huge. . . . We have a UN Declaration [on the Rights of Indigenous Peoples], and many are using the principles of the Declaration very seriously, so this is a big impact. Look at free, prior, and informed consent. At the beginning, it looked like a strange principle, now it's a principle that everybody is using. . . . And to me these are immense achievements that the [Indigenous] movement has brought in. I always go back and think when at IFAD we could not even mention the word "Indigenous", and this was less than ten years ago. At the Inter-Agency Support Group on Indigenous Peoples' Issues that we held in 2006, we didn't [yet] have a [an interagency UN] policy [on Indigenous issues]. We started the process of [preparing] the policy in 2007. Even the words free, prior, and informed consent were unimaginable then. Now it is a mandatory principle in the social and environmental assessment procedures.

11 Cordone interviewed by the author, 7 May 2016.

Aehshatou Manu, Mbororo in Cameroon, National Women Coordinator of the Mbororo Social and Cultural Development Association, explained why states allowed these special-exceptional participation procedures for Indigenous Peoples at the UN level by saying,

> *They did it because they felt that what the Indigenous were asking is right. It's just right, and they are organized, and they are strong in their movement. It's not just one country, it's the whole world coming together with the same issues, the same vision. So, states had to just say, okay, we have to do something for these people, because Indigenous Peoples had also convinced states to adopt the UN Declaration on the Rights of Indigenous Peoples.*[12]

Commenting on the question why states allow Indigenous Peoples direct participation at the UN, Mikaela Jade, an Indigenous leader from Australia said:

> *I think it provides governments an opportunity to promote what they're doing with Indigenous Peoples, I think [the UNPFII is] not really a forum that you come to have meaningful discussion with states necessarily. . . . I think, from the states' perspective, it's probably an opportunity to grand stand and show everyone in the world how they're interacting with Indigenous Peoples, when I know, when I get home, I'm probably not going to have the same opportunities to speak to people in the government. [While here at the UN, I have such opportunities]. . . . Obviously states have mandates that they need to abide by and one of the things is [to engage in] dialogue. So it's an opportunity [for states] to say that they are opening a space for dialogue [with Indigenous Peoples].*[13]

B. UN Commission on Human Rights Working Group on the Draft Declaration

Another moment of the UN considering and approving special participation rights for Indigenous Peoples was in 1995, when the UNCHR, by means of resolution 1995/32, established an open-ended intersessional working group to examine the text of the then Draft Declaration on the Rights of Indigenous Peoples adopted by the Sub-Commission on Prevention of Discrimination and Protection of Minorities.[14] The Commission's working group was

---

12 Manu interviewed by the author, 29 November 2016.
13 Jade interviewed by the author, 16 May 2016.
14 UN Commission on Human Rights, Establishment of a Working Group of the Commission on Human Rights to Elaborate a Draft Declaration in Accordance with Paragraph 5 of the General Assembly Resolution 49/214, UN Doc. E/CN.4/RES/1995/32 (3 March 1995).

named Working Group on the Draft Declaration (WGDD); states avoided continuing the title with the words "on the Rights of Indigenous Peoples" because the "s" in "Peoples" was still under contention. It was another positive exception for Indigenous Peoples that "specific consultative status was established for Indigenous representatives in the WGDD, thus becoming formally less open than the WGIP, although it must be noted that this status was not denied to any organization that requested it."[15]

It was a slightly different approach that states followed to accredit Indigenous Peoples to the UNCHR's Working Group on the Draft Declaration. I was working on the New York side of the UN human rights office following this. The process did not take place in the Committee on NGOs. The conditions arranged instead for the participation in the Commission's Working Group were not the same conditions as for the WGIP and were not the same as at the UNPFII, much later. This became a more controlled process. It did go through states under a special *ad hoc* working group of states that looked at Indigenous applications and did so quite liberally, I have to add, as I witnessed it in the room where negotiations were taking place. States were approving those applications – there were only one hundred or fewer Indigenous entities (institutions or organizations) that had put in their applications and were interested in following the drafting of the Declaration at the level of the UNCHR. I remember distinctly that there was an application by the Sovereign Nation of Hawaii; they had applied to participate in the Commission's Working Group; they were not present during the discussion of their application. It was just a paper application, and it was being considered by an interstate body. Interestingly, the United States said that they had absolutely no problem allowing the Sovereign Nation of Hawaii to participate, and it was with a little smile that this was said, perhaps to show that the United States did not feel threatened by this and so that the others could admire their generosity or courage. The working group of states considering the Indigenous applications in the mid-1990s approved the participation of almost everybody who applied and was interested to participate in the Working Group of the Commission on Human Rights on the Draft Declaration. States did that even if they did not believe the Declaration would be adopted. For example, in 2005, I was told by a Canadian state delegate that "this is it; look, after ten years, only two articles have passed at the Working Group of the UNCHR, meaning that this declaration doesn't pass; it is respectable to shelve it." But the draft was not shelved.

---

15 Augusto Willemsen Díaz, "How Indigenous Peoples' Rights Reached the UN," in *Making the Declaration Work: The United Nations Declaration on the Rights of Indigenous Peoples*, ed. Claire Charters and Rodolfo Stavenhagen (Copenhagen: IWGIA, 2010), 28, www.iwgia. org/iwgia_files_publications_files/making_the_declaration_work.pdf.

Lola Garcia-Alix of IWGIA recalled, during our interview, that the process of participation was not always smooth at the Commission's Working Group.[16] Indigenous representatives pushed hard for a level of equality in the discussions, and this ended in a procedure that had not been used before: the meetings were informal meetings where Indigenous Peoples and states were at the same level, and only after they had reached a decision, an agreement, could the meeting be officially opened for the formal adoption of the text by states.

On 13 September 2007, with the negotiation obstacles between Indigenous Peoples and states resolved, the UN Declaration on the Rights of Indigenous Peoples (UNDRIP) was finally adopted by the General Assembly.

Numerous formal and informal efforts of all kinds contributed to this result after a process of twenty-five years. One of those efforts, closer to the date of UNDRIP's adoption, was a meeting from 26 to 30 September 2005, that the government of Mexico had organized in Pátzcuaro, Michoacán, to build a closer spirit of cooperation among the parties.[17]

According to Māori advocate and scholar Claire Charters during our interview,

The Pátzcuaro meeting was about relationship building. It built a level of trust and camaraderie and was a real tipping point; Indigenous representatives were treated like states and were brought there as equals – it was a breakdown of all animosity.[18]

To the question of how Indigenous international participation changes the relations of the Indigenous community vis-à-vis the state, Charters pointed out that it gives even more authority or confidence to speak from a government-to-government position.

So it gives certain confidence or political clout, and the government [of New Zealand] doesn't know how to do that, because in a domestic setting, they would just assume authority, but because we are presenting to an [international] expert mechanism, . . . they trust us probably more. . . . We have more power I think, or not more power, but at least power to assert that we go in as equals, and whatever this document says has to be agreed by both of us.

---

16 Garcia-Alix interviewed by the author, 29 April 2016.
17 A documentary on the Pátzcuaro workshop is kept in the UN archives and can be accessed here: *The Spirit of Pátzcuaro: Seeking Consensus for a Strong Declaration on the Rights of Indigenous Peoples*, dir. Devasish Wangza and ed. Subrata Chakma (Tamaza Productions: Rangamati, Bangladesh, 2006), 31 min., www.youtube.com/watch?v=cfPswCSsmFg.
18 Charters interviewed by the author, 2 November 2018.

Victoria Tauli-Corpuz, senior Igorot leader, underlined Indigenous Peoples' visions of equality as they pursued their participation in UN fora.[19]

> *I remember very well how we asserted that we have to be part of the discussions, we have to be equally involved in the discussions. And then [at one point in negotiations] there was a long, half-day delay because they [states] wanted to consult the UN [Office of Legal Affairs] in New York about the procedures, the rules of procedure, whether Indigenous participation is allowed. . . . Indigenous Peoples managed to assert that they have to have an equal say with the states. That was when working groups were established, when states and Indigenous Peoples were together drafting, and bringing the draft to the plenary. That kind of participation I think again is path-breaking because it changed the rules, and I think that is the idea. You start challenging the rules which are supposed to be cast in stone, and in the process you can actually change these rules. That was what happened with this intergovernmental Working Group [of the Commission on Human Rights on the Draft Declaration]. . . . But after the Declaration was adopted at the level of the Commission, then of course you have to think which body is going to inherit this Declaration and operationalize it. There was no idea about that, and that's how the Permanent Forum idea also came about.*[20]

Understanding such initiatives and the value of even little, on the surface almost invisible, incidents is about unveiling what can catalyze change in international affairs. It is the approach of constructivism that is helpful here, as is explained in Chapter 4. It can be the spirit of engagement, generosity, and respect offered and cultivated by hosts of meetings and others that will have significant political implications and be the decisive factor to bring the much-desired consensus at the right moment. The adoption of UNDRIP in 2007 was such a moment, a moment that Indigenous Peoples and also the whole of humanity deserved, after so many years of efforts committed to its negotiation by so many and after many centuries of discrimination and atrocities against Indigenous Peoples.

C. Moments of Making History

People who were participating at the WGIP, especially in those early years of the 1980s, felt that they were shaping history or that history was in the

---

19 Tauli-Corpuz interviewed by the author, 18 October 2016.

20 Article 42 of the Declaration specifically mentions the Permanent Forum: "The United Nations, its bodies, including the Permanent Forum on Indigenous Issues, and specialized agencies, including at the country level, and States shall promote respect for and full application of the provisions of this Declaration and follow up the effectiveness of this Declaration."

making before their very eyes. Some moments of those times witnessed by the author are analyzed here to highlight this point.

Indigenous Peoples' direct voices heard in the UN halls in 1982 and 1983 were powerful and had already left their mark. The Working Group's 1984 session was special since we were expecting many new Indigenous delegates after the 1983 decision to open the Working Group to direct participation. It is not impossible to imagine that some states that did not see this decision favorably decided not to oppose it formally for reasons of their public image, given the decolonization and human rights environment prevalent at the time. They would have tried to block Indigenous participation in other indirect ways – for example, by attempting to influence high UN officials. Be that as it may, and we do not know details of this backstage scenario, some Indigenous delegates who traveled to Geneva for the Working Group in 1984 were hindered from entering UN premises. This obviously created commotion and concern in the Working Group, as the procedure of open participation was too new and fragile and needed to be protected and reaffirmed so it would "stick."

Tonya Gonnella Frichner of the Onondaga Nation and Ingrid Washinawatok of the Menominee Nation were two strong young Indigenous women leaders whose presence was visible in the Working Group. They were "working the room" fervently, consulting with many people and preparing and delivering statements. They were tall, with an impressive physical presence, their hair braided and their traditional clothes shining. They were to become major beloved leaders of the Indigenous movement over the decades, only too young and too soon to lose their lives, but inspiring and remembered for generations to come.[21]

On the second day of the 1984 WGIP, after its morning meeting, Ingrid Washinawatok and Tonya Gonnella Frichner went up to the podium to Erica-Irene Daes, the new Chairperson-Rapporteur. I was present then as Secretary of WGIP and witnessed the conversation. They told Daes with determination and in no uncertain terms that if the authorities in the Geneva Office of the UN did not allow Indigenous representatives access to the UN building, they would protest at the highest level and make declarations to the press. Daes, a seasoned diplomat as well, understood that statement fully and took it upon herself to make sure that access would be given. Contacts were made with Raymonde Martineau, the UN official from Canada, who was the Liaison Officer in charge of relations with NGOs and other civil society at the United Nations Office in Geneva (UNOG). Martineau

---

21 "Ingrid Washinawatok," Wisconsin Women Making History, https://womeninwisconsin.org/profile/ingrid-washinawatok/, accessed 6 July 2022; "In Memoriam: Tonya Gonella Frichner," American Indian Law Alliance, https://aila.ngo/about/in-memoriam-tonya-gonnella-frichner/, accessed 6 July 2022.

was sensitive to Indigenous Peoples issues; she had been the representative at the UN for the International Movement for Fraternal Union among Races and Peoples (UFER) and had worked at the UN in Geneva during the historic 1977 International NGO Conference on Discrimination against Indigenous Populations in the Americas, when many Indigenous leaders had participated. Daes and Martineau brokered a meeting of the Director-General of the UNOG with Ingrid Washinawatok and Tonya Gonnella Frichner. The matter of the Indigenous delegates whose access had been denied was resolved.[22]

This episode is one of many that created an irresistible wave for direct Indigenous participation at the UN. I can see how this played out as if it were yesterday, how Ingrid and Tonya approached Erica with force and extraordinary conviction that they were right and that what they were requesting was just. They were determined and eloquent and refused to take no for an answer; they sought to see the highest UN authority in Geneva and make their case. They were speaking for others who were excluded from access to UN grounds. Daes listened carefully. She definitely would not want her first year of chairing the Working Group to be diverted by negative protests. She was a solid diplomat and networker and of course knew Martineau and the Director-General of UNOG. She could place her mediation skills in the service of Indigenous participation. The contacts bore fruit, and Daes' mediation was successful.

Erica Daes's path accompanied Indigenous Peoples' challenges and achievements at the United Nations. She exercised unique leadership and embraced their struggles. This happened at a particular moment in history when the international Indigenous movement was new and when Daes, a diplomat and academic, happened to hold a mandate as a member at the UN Sub-Commission on Prevention of Discrimination and Protection of Minorities. Daes became a strong vehicle that brought forward the cause of Indigenous Peoples' human rights at the international level. She was the Chairperson-Rapporteur of the WGIP for almost twenty years, from 1984 to 2001. I accompanied Erica to the first session she chaired in 1984, as a junior officer then and Secretary of the WGIP. We walked together down the Salle des pas perdues corridor in the Palais des Nations, at the UN in Geneva. I had the chance, in a rush during this walk, to mention to Erica how this was not a working group like others she had chaired. We were all nervous, secretariat, NGOs, governments. How would this new chairperson be? I think the only person who was not nervous was Erica – at least she did not show it. Very

---

22 See Raymonde Martineau, interview by James S. Sutterlin, 7 July 1998, Geneva, transcript in UN Dag Hammarskjöld Library, https://digitallibrary.un.org/record/503509?ln=en. Martineau was one of the few women to be part of the UN Mission to support Namibia's first elections.

soon after she became the Chairperson, Erica established herself as a most unique leader, one that knew how to listen – with her mind and her heart, and I stress both – one that knew how to build bridges and understandings between Indigenous Peoples and states on some of the most difficult issues, one who was not afraid to be strict on both parties, with respect, if circumstances required. Many of us recall her strong and bold interventions. Her UN studies on the Protection of the Heritage of Indigenous People,[23] Indigenous Peoples and Their Relationship to Land,[24] and Indigenous Peoples' Permanent Sovereignty over Natural Resources,[25] as well as other papers, still remain works of reference. She helped create the legal arguments on various aspects of Indigenous Peoples rights.[26]

In her speech at the commemoration of the International Year of the World's Indigenous People – the "s" was not added to "people" then – in 1993, in the General Assembly Hall – the first time Indigenous leaders from around the world spoke there – Erica Daes said,

> I believe that Indigenous Peoples have reached a critical turning point, and that their long-neglected rights will soon emerge from the shadow of history into the light of contemporary recognition and implementation. I look forward to the day when Indigenous Peoples everywhere will be heard in the councils of the world, speaking in all their languages.[27]

In their presentations and other actions at UN fora, Indigenous representatives have shown continuing adaptability to the politics of the international bodies they are trying to influence. Two testimonies are eloquent in that regard. They were given at the twentieth anniversary online conference for the mandate of the UN Special Rapporteur on the Rights of Indigenous Peoples, organized by the University of Arizona College of Law, on 6 October 2021,

23 UN Doc. E/CN.4/Sub.2/1995/26 (21 June 1995).

24 UN Doc. E/CN.4/Sub.2/2000/25 (30 June 2000).

25 UN Doc. E/CN.4/Sub.2/2004/30/Add.1 (12 July 2004).

26 On 22 May 2009, Flying Eagle Woman Foundation, founded in memory of the late beloved Ingrid Washinawatok El-Issa, held an event in New York City to honor Erica-Irene Daes, or Erica, as thousands of her friends liked to call her. (*O'Peqtaw-Metamoh*, Flying Eagle Woman, was Ingrid's Menominee name.) Many leaders were there, including Bill Means and Oren Lyons who addressed words to Erica. I had also been invited to share thoughts about Erica, a fellow Greek, since our walks through the UN had coincided for so many years through our common commitment to the cause of Indigenous Peoples – whether in numerous UN meetings, in missions, in report writing, or simply in endless discussions in New York, Geneva, or Athens, analyzing, comparing notes, or strategizing "about our issues," as we used to say.

27 See "In Memory of Erica-Irene Daes," *IWGIA website*, 22 February 2017, www.iwgia.org/en/global-governance-cat/2487-in-memory-of-ericairene-daes.html. The quotation is taken from the author's copy of Daes's speech from the commemoration event.

and attended by the author.[28] Mario Ibarra, Mapuche and a human rights advocate from Chile, remembered discussions with Indigenous friends and states at the Palais des Nations in Geneva:

> We thought we should have an ombudsman for Indigenous Peoples, some-body much higher than a special rapporteur. We went to the Serpent Bar [at the UN Office in Geneva] to draft the first version of the resolution. We wanted an effective mechanism, that would also protect Indigenous women and children and that would prevent atrocities. . . .
>
> Guatemala's contribution was so important. Mrs. Carlita Rodriguez was so committed. They were supporting the new mandate and ended up signing the draft resolution by themselves. Vote on the resolution was post-poned for a year. We continued to fight for the proposal. Next year we had more cosponsors. . . . Mexico took over the resolution – they had more influence on the European countries, who then also supported the resolution. It was adopted twenty years ago [in 2001]. . . . At the Indigenous Caucus we realized that the resolution was the result of an agreement of the Indigenous Peoples of Guatemala with their government. . . . We all fought these battles and each made their contribution at the international level.

At the same conference, Chief Willie Littlechild of the Cree recalled that in the reform process of the UNCHR in the late 1990s, Indigenous issues were being ignored, so Indigenous Peoples proposed an alternative mechanism.

> I was a delegate with Chief Victor Buffalo. We took the floor and invited Rodolfo Stavenhagen and invited him to our land.[29] Some immediately put up an obstacle that only states can invite a rapporteur. . . .
>
> There is no parliamentary process in Canada to follow up on UN reports. . . . We hear the Special Rapporteur's reports as our own govern-ments and use them in our claims in lawsuits. We need to use the Special Rapporteur's recommendations in our own courts and resolutions, we, as governments and nations . . . [we need to] have a direct visit of the Spe-cial Rapporteur to our territories. [When the Special Rapporteur visited Canada] the James Bay Cree took the Special Rapporteur in a helicopter to

---

28 The conference was titled "20 Years of Indigenous Advocacy: A Celebration of the 20th Anniversary of the UN Special Rapporteur on the Rights of Indigenous Peoples." The author received written copies of the remarks from Ibarra and Littlechild that follow.

29 Rodolfo Stavenhagen was the first UN Special Rapporteur on the Rights of Indigenous Peoples from 2001 to 2008. He visited Canada in 2004, and his report appears here: UN Commission on Human Rights, Human Rights and Indigenous Issues: Report of the Special Rapporteur on the Situation of Human Rights and Fundamental Freedoms of Indigenous Peoples, Rodolfo Stavenhagen: Addendum, UN Doc. E/CN.4/2005/88/Add.3 (2 December 2004).

visit their land and visit the Indigenous Peoples themselves, because Canada was totally controlling the Special Rapporteur's agenda. . . . We need to be more assertive and invite the Special Rapporteur for official mission.

The Indigenous-state tension is not limited to face-to-face confrontation in interstate organizations. It has often been expressed in the interactions between Indigenous Peoples – pushing for changes on their own terms – and people working in the institutional machinery of interstate organizations. Employees in secretariats of the UN and other such organizations find themselves in the middle, between rules made by states and the lofty aims of the UN Charter, including the just cause of Indigenous Peoples. There have been several UN workers that have espoused this cause over the decades and have facilitated Indigenous Peoples' efforts within the institutions, sometimes at personal cost. There have been some harsh experiences shared among focal points on Indigenous issues in various interstate organizations at the Inter-Agency Support Group on Indigenous Peoples' Issues (IASG).[30] IASG has also functioned as a support and solidarity group of those international workers who have faced marginalization because of their work on Indigenous Peoples' rights.

During our discussion, Les Malezer recalled the challenges to Indigenous participation originally experienced in the process of preparation for the 2014 World Conference on Indigenous Peoples and how they were resolved:[31]

> *The process [in preparation of the World Conference] was done as much as possible to enhance Indigenous Peoples' participation, both in the room and in the agenda, to have people at the podium in a way that respected Indigenous Peoples. I think that might have been done by the Chair of the Permanent Forum. The agenda was basically worked out to be as respectful as it possibly could be to the Indigenous Peoples and not to be a hierarchical process. We had encouraged states to have Indigenous Peoples sitting in with them in their seats [seating area of the states], if possible. I actually worked on Australia in doing that, but I don't think I got a yes on that. I actually went and talked to the Minister for Foreign Affairs who represented Australia, and the other delegates before, during, and after the whole event, so they were quite respectful in that sense. But they couldn't answer the question about whether we could sit in the [state]seats. They said, "Oh, we don't know if there's a rule about all this." I said, "Well, Denmark does it with Greenland, you know. It's is not like there's no precedent."*

30 Some forty interstate organizations, UN and others, are part of the IASG. More discussion of the IASG is presented in Chapter 5.

31 Malezer interviewed by the author, 8 April 2016.

By trying to bend the machinery that represents the state symbolically or substantively, Indigenous representatives try to redefine state power, their relation to the state, and the content of self-determination. The machinery of interstate institutions is also transformed into trenches, where Indigenous struggles are fought. The rules, written and unwritten, appear at every step. They have a reason, and, most of the time, it is a political reason. Therefore, when Indigenous delegates tread those UN corridors, the road is often treacherous, trapped with mines that people cannot even imagine. It is states that have basically created the UN and its culture. So Indigenous Peoples analyze and learn to find or create the openings and ruptures of these systems through reinterpretation of rules, customs, and ways of these international institutions. They take initiatives based on these analyses. Indigenous delegates do that, through many painstaking, sometimes seemingly small acts that, over time, over the years, bend resistance and revise customs and rules. Indigenous representatives are sometimes strongly supported by UN workers and other persons and organizations of solidarity. In this way, they are able to make more of a home at the UN and other interstate organizations and slowly turn those organizations into entities that can understand them and their demands better. In those international arenas, they create spaces, friendly spaces at times, where they can pursue outcomes that respond to their rights and visions of the world.

D.   Building Documentation

1.   *Reporting Human Rights Abuses*

As we have described already, Indigenous representatives did get participation and speaking rights at the WGIP. However, it was quite another struggle to have their statements reflected in the WGIP's official annual report to its parent body, the Sub-Commission on Prevention of Discrimination and Protection of Minorities. I was writing the draft report in 1984, as I had been permitted to formally assist Augusto Willemsen Díaz as the WGIP Secretary. The Working Group told us, the Secretariat, that there could not be a reflection of country-specific information in the report nor a mention of who had made specific statements. The report had to reflect thematic issues and use phrases that would hide who delivered the statement – for example, phrases like "reference was made" or "some delegates stated" – so that the names of countries critiqued would not appear; the idea was that we had to tread delicately around the political sensitivities of states.

The WGIP's reports had obvious parameters. In summarizing discussions, the reports did not mention countries – except for rare exceptions – but issues. In the 1983 WGIP report, for example, apart from specific references to Guatemala and genocidal practices, there was no mention of country names.[32] A typical way of using language so as not to identify countries would be a sentence like this: "Observers further alleged that many indigenous populations still continue to be subject to systematic destruction of their cultures and distinct identity." States behind the scenes were imposing the preparation of reports in this manner, in order to avoid the WGIP being "a chamber of complaints," as was repeatedly stated in the public meetings by the Chairperson of the Working Group.

Years later, the UNPFII, clearly a hierarchically higher body than the WGIP, still cannot have a narrative report at all, even if it wished to have one. This is not because there is discrimination against this body, but because these are the rules of the ECOSOC that UNPFII has to follow as a subsidiary to the Council. No ECOSOC subsidiary bodies have a narrative report, nor do they have summary records, as per the UN rules. So where are Indigenous Peoples statements recorded? Indigenous Peoples make extraordinary efforts to come to UNPFII and hope they can make a statement if time allows, and their turn comes on the very long list of speakers. Where is the narrative trace of their public interventions?

The impact of Indigenous representatives' interventions is there because UNPFII members, states, and also the media and UN agencies are informed by, react to, and respond to some of these statements. Indigenous media also report these statements, and statements are often filmed and reported on social media. But where is the record of what is said? A written record can be found in the press releases issued twice a day during UNPFII sessions by the UN Department of Global Communications (formerly the Department of Public Information). According to UN practice, press releases include summaries of statements and are issued in English and French, the two working languages of the UN. Press releases are meant primarily for the press and are not necessarily read and used by advocates or researchers.[33] In a helpful practice established by the Secretariat of the UNPFII at some point, press releases and video coverage of UNPFII meetings are placed on its website.[34]

The Indigenous Peoples' Center for Documentation, Research and Information (DOCIP), based in Geneva, meticulously keeps the most extensive collection of statements in its publicly accessible archives.[35] DOCIP volunteers

---

32 UN Sub-Commission on Prevention of Discrimination and Protection of Minorities, Report of the Working Group on Indigenous Populations on Its Second Session, UN Doc. E/CN.4/Sub.2/1983/22 (23 August 1983).

33 See, for example, the results of a search under "Permanent Forum on Indigenous Issues" on the United Nations Meetings Coverage and Press Releases website, https://press.un.org/en.

34 See, for example, coverage of the 18th session (22 April–3 May 2019) of the UNPFII, www.un.org/development/desa/indigenouspeoples/news/2019/05/un-meetings-coverage-of-18th-unpfii/.

35 For a description of and access to what is available in DOCIP's documentation center, see www.docip.org/en/our-services-solutions/documentation-center/.

roam the conference rooms during UNPFII sessions as well as sessions of the UN Expert Mechanism on the Rights of Indigenous Peoples (EMRIP) to collect statements made by Indigenous, state, and other representatives.

Indigenous Peoples' statements at the international level and the written records mentioned earlier describe their situations and demands over the decades, in their own voices and their own words. These records, especially in the medium- and long-term, are crucial for each Indigenous nation that needs to trace its own itinerary in international oral history and politics, as well as for historians and other researchers. They can potentially be useful for political negotiations between states and Indigenous Peoples. They are also important for national or international criminal justice procedures, if, for example, International Criminal Court institutions wish to trace testimonies of imprescriptible international crimes.

Given the challenges and limitations of written records at the UN previously described, it remains a question how Indigenous delegates attempt to impact the narrative on Indigenous issues that comes out of the UN. Narrative is beyond just what is written. Indigenous Peoples leave their marks in many other ways, some tangible and others intangible, and have a significant impact on the narrative that results from their international participation. These methods and strategies are described in Chapter 4.

2. *Saving Papers from the Fire*

In the long process of preparation of the monumental Study of the Problem of Discrimination against Indigenous Populations, Augusto Willemsen Díaz had gathered rich documentation from Indigenous Peoples for the thirty-seven monographs that created the base of the Study. A lot of this documentation was describing atrocities against Indigenous Peoples, including those in Guatemala, his home country. *Don* Augusto's spacious office could hardly hold the documents, as they were piled up almost to the ceiling in his space at the old UN building in the Palais des Nations. In 1982, when the first parts of the final Study on the Problem of Discrimination against Indigenous Populations started being published, *Don* Augusto had already tried to send the documents to UN archives. They were too important for Indigenous Peoples who wanted them secured, for history and for future reference, in the UN's safe hands. Many people had placed themselves in danger putting testimonies together. Years later, the world was to pay attention to witness protection and to relive and admire the commitment of the Maya Ixil women of Guatemala, who exhibited extraordinary courage in testifying at the trial for genocide against the dictator Efraín Ríos Montt. But UN archives in the 1980s could no longer accept the documents *Don* Augusto was sending to them. *Don* Augusto whispered this sad news when we spoke in his office one day. It was not just the volume of the documentation but also the content, he thought, and he confided this in a low voice. It was a matter of principle to convince UN archives to keep the documents, but this became impossible at the end.

The documents were saved by the reputable NGO, the DOCIP, which was not just any organization. It had been created in Geneva at the initiative of the Indigenous Peoples' delegations at the UN at the 1977 antiracism conference, and Augusto Willemsen Díaz was DOCIP's first Chair. The documentation Indigenous Peoples were bringing to the UN in written or oral form was precious in creating the archive of Indigenous Peoples' own voices about what they had experienced as part of colonization, domination, and marginalization. It is a surge of history – writing from below, year in and year out, as more and more Indigenous delegates have been coming to the UN to tell their own story.

It is no surprise that states have tried to create limitations on documentation provided to the UN by Indigenous Peoples. Testifying to this is the very first report of the WGIP, in a section entitled "Sources of Information," where the Working Group was trying to include words that would somehow appease states' concerns, setting some parameters.[36] The report stated that the sources of information would include

> governments, [UN] specialized agencies, regional intergovernmental organizations and non-governmental organizations, particularly those of Indigenous Peoples . . . plus other indigenous organizations and groups, as well as experts and recognized authorities in the field of "the rights of indigenous populations," who would submit information with the consent of the Working Group. It was stated, however, that written material submitted and oral statements made with the consent of the Group must be relevant, not abusive in its expressions or contents and not too voluminous.[37]

The report also stated that in the case of the "organizations of indigenous populations," the Chairman

> might request that copies of information supplied by them be made available . . . to those attending the session of the Working Group. However, such documents should not be distributed, neither in full nor in summary, with a United Nations symbol.[38]

---

36 UN Sub-Commission on Prevention of Discrimination and Protection of Minorities, Report of the Working Group on Indigenous Populations on Its First Session, UN Doc. E/CN.4/Sub.2/1982/33 (25 August 1982), para. 21–24.

37 UN Doc. E/CN.4/Sub.2/1982/33, para. 21.

38 UN Doc. E/CN.4/Sub.2/1982/33, para. 23 (ii).

Such procedural limitations, pushed by the political reticence of states, could not stifle the voices of Indigenous Peoples, as the number of Indigenous representatives was expanding over the years and their human rights concerns were resonating in the UN conference rooms. Other ways had to be found, and were found, for those voices to be recorded.

The value of DOCIP meticulously collecting the statements at the WGIP became clear early on. Indigenous Peoples created the identity of DOCIP. The organization does not work "on" or "for" but "with" Indigenous Peoples, and this is the spirit that inspires DOCIP to this day.[39]

In 1986, there was no session of the WGIP. The fragility of this new body became apparent when the so-called "financial crisis of the UN," politically prompted by the United States, provided an excuse to this country and some others to select the WGIP as part of the budget cuts in the human rights program. After all, the Working Group had ruffled some feathers through its innovative approaches. Amnesty International offered to cover the costs of the WGIP session that year but that proved politically unacceptable.[40]

Then 1987 came. A dramatic fire broke out in the offices of DOCIP between 1 and 2 August. By that point, DOCIP was holding the archives of the Study. The fire destroyed the small building where DOCIP was then housed in Geneva, the annex to Palais Wilson, which today hosts the headquarters of the Office of the UN High Commissioner for Human Rights.

Pierrette Birraux, the long-time director of DOCIP, remembers very well when she was informed about the fire. She was in São Paulo that day, in the CEDI (Centro Ecumênico de Documentação e Informação), which was then being integrated into ISA (Instituto Socioambiental), the major resource about Indigenous Peoples in Brazil. She received the information about the fire from René Fuerst (founding member of DOCIP), and while she was trying to realize what it meant, she saw the director of CEDI (Carlo Alberto "Beto" Ricardo) scanning the shelves, supporting and protecting with his gesture CEDI's documents, with terror.[41] Such was the realization of the preciousness of documentation at that critical moment.

In the summer of 1987, the session of WGIP did take place, as it had been "saved" from the UN's financial and political mayhem. DOCIP invited the Indigenous delegates and supporters to a small, friendly reception one evening, after the meeting of the Working Group. We gathered under the Geneva sky at the yard where the "annex," the burned building, was. We were walking on the gravel, feeling the precarity, the sadness, awe, and solidarity after

---

39 Author's correspondence with Pierrette Birraux, June 2020. Birraux was the Director of DOCIP for twenty years and a member of its Founding Council.
40 Information provided to the author by NGO sources.
41 Author's correspondence with Birraux, June 2020.

what had happened. I recall the whispers among Indigenous representatives during that gathering, fearing that this happened because the documentation that perished included information about atrocities and crimes against humanity. Fortunately, DOCIP was later able to restore all the documents lost in the fire.

In 2017, UNESCO decided to include in its International Memory of the World Register the DOCIP archives with the speeches of representatives of Indigenous Peoples at the UN between 1982 and 2015. These are more than twenty-two thousand texts, most of which have been digitized and are therefore widely accessible.[42] DOCIP is the manager of this documentation, not the owner. The noncommercial use of the online material is free as long as the source is mentioned. The "physical" preservation of documents is ensured by the City of Geneva,[43] a city whose authorities have had a long tradition of friendship with Indigenous Peoples since the time of Deskaheh's travel to Geneva to address the League of Nations in 1923.

DOCIP continues its work with Indigenous Peoples providing secretariat services to the Indigenous delegates who come to the UNPFII in New York and the EMRIP in Geneva. Copies of the statements made by Indigenous delegates are always meticulously gathered by DOCIP.

The discussion about documentation is linked to a more fundamental issue: Who controls the narrative, states or Indigenous Peoples? How is the narrative conveyed? How is it divulged? This was and is a continuing question for Indigenous Peoples' issues, at national or international levels.

E. The UN Voluntary Fund for Indigenous Populations: Winning Financial Support

From 1982 to 1985, the number of Indigenous leaders attending the Working Group was rising and the circle was broadening, with new people joining in and new voices being heard. The intention on the part of Indigenous leaders to spread the word about that new WGIP and to encourage others to join was clear. The question that was equally clear and tough was how Indigenous representatives would pay for the travel expenses to Geneva and how they could afford spending a week there during the WGIP's session. The networks of support in Geneva for Indigenous representatives started expanding, including through DOCIP. The spirit of solidarity that Chief Deskaheh had built during the time he spent in Geneva in 1923 and 1924 had left its

---

42 See the DOCIP archive, "Main and legal documents, conferences and training events," https://cendoc.docip.org/cgi-bin/library.cgi/&l=en.

43 "La parole des Peuples autochtones au 'Registre de la Mémoire du Monde,'" by Bernard Comoli, *Les Blogs*, 23 November 2017, archived 8 August 2020 at the Internet Archive, http://bcomoli.blog.tdg.ch/archive/2017/11/23/la-parole-des-peules-autochtones-au-registre-de-la-memoire-d-287953.html.

legacy on Geneva's society and municipal authorities. Many stories have been told of people hosted in private homes that opened their doors – Indigenous people sharing tiny budgets with others who had less, sometimes staying outside during the night in the summer weather of Geneva, when they could not ensure an affordable room, and some having little to eat during the week of WGIP's sessions. We regularly heard stories of whole Indigenous communities gathering funds, little by little throughout the year, so they could send their representative to the Working Group. It was similar later on, in the challenging metropolis of New York, when Indigenous representatives started coming in 2002 for the annual sessions of the UNPFII.

This desire of Indigenous Peoples to participate and be heard at the international level led to a strategy to establish the Voluntary Fund for Indigenous Populations. Already at the first session of the WGIP in 1982, there was a recommendation for such a fund. The parent body of the WGIP, the Sub-Commission on Prevention of Discrimination and Protection of Minorities, made a recommendation to that effect to its higher body, the Commission on Human Rights. In 1983, the WGIP reverted to a fuller discussion and a strong recommendation on this, stressing the importance of direct Indigenous participation at the Working Group.[44]

These deliberations led to their desired result in 1985, when the Voluntary Fund for Indigenous Populations was established by UN General Assembly resolution 40/131 and started being operational in 1988.[45] It is the second voluntary fund in the history of the UN's human rights work after the Voluntary Fund for Victims of Torture, established in 1981, to focus global attention on the needs of torture victims.

The purpose of the Voluntary Fund for Indigenous Populations, later renamed the Voluntary Fund for Indigenous Peoples, was to assist representatives of Indigenous Peoples' communities and organizations to participate in the deliberations of the WGIP by providing them with financial assistance, funded by means of voluntary contributions from state governments, NGOs, and other private or public entities.[46] The General Assembly expanded the mandate of the Voluntary Fund in its resolution 56/140 in 2001 by deciding that the fund should also be used to assist representatives of Indigenous Peoples' communities and organizations in attending, as observers, the sessions of the UNPFII.[47] In its 2008 resolution 63/161, the General Assembly again adjusted the mandate of the fund so as to facilitate the participation of

---

44 UN Doc. E/CN.4/Sub.2/1983/22.
45 UN General Assembly, Resolution 40/131, United Nations Voluntary Fund for Indigenous Populations, UN Doc. A/RES/40/131 (27 February 1986).
46 For information about the fund, see www.ohchr.org/en/issues/ipeoples/ipeoplesfund/pages/ipeoplesfundindex.aspx.
47 UN General Assembly, Resolution 56/140, International Decade of the World's Indigenous People, UN Doc. A/RES/56/140 (15 February 2002).

representatives of Indigenous Peoples' representatives in the EMRIP established in 2007 in accordance with Human Rights Council resolution 6/36.[48] In its resolution 65/198 of 21 December 2010, the General Assembly further expanded the mandate of the Voluntary Fund in order to facilitate the participation of representatives of Indigenous Peoples' organizations in sessions of the Human Rights Council and of human rights treaty bodies.[49] In 2015, the mandate of the fund was again expanded to support representatives of Indigenous Peoples' organizations and institutions to participate in the consultation process on steps to enable the participation of Indigenous Peoples' representatives and institutions in meetings of relevant United Nations bodies on issues affecting them (General Assembly resolution A/RES/70/232)[50]; this is the process known as "enhanced participation" of Indigenous Peoples, discussed further in Chapter 4.

Augusto Willemsen Díaz became member of the first Board of Trustees of the Voluntary Fund, from 1988 to 1996, and kept coming to Geneva after his retirement, back from his native Guatemala, where he would live until his passing in 2014, after having been a political refugee for a very long time. By the end of his tenure as Chair of the fund, all members of the Voluntary Fund were Indigenous persons, and its Chairperson was the well-known Igorot leader Victoria Tauli-Corpuz.

In 2013, DOCIP organized a meeting at the UN in Geneva and brought together Indigenous leaders who had participated at the historic 1977 and 1981 conferences with younger generations of Indigenous leadership. The meeting took place in the same room where the historic 1977 conference had been held. A documentary around the meeting, *Bridge to the Future*, was produced by DOCIP together with Indigenous youth.[51]

One of the Haudenosaunee representatives, the well-known Mohawk leader Kenneth Deer, gave this advice to the younger generation of Indigenous leaders: "Remember, never lose the moral high ground."[52] George Manuel, the late founder of the World Council of Indigenous Peoples in 1975, once stated, in the 1970s, that "Aboriginal people can only argue the morality of their case."[53]

---

48 UN General Assembly, Resolution 63/161, Indigenous Issues, UN Doc. A/RES/63/161 (13 February 2009); UN Human Rights Council, Resolution 6/36, Expert Mechanism on the Rights of Indigenous Peoples, UN Doc. A/HRC/RES/6/36 (14 April 2008).
49 UN General Assembly, Resolution 65/198, Indigenous Issues, UN Doc. A/RES/65/198 (3 March 2011).
50 UN General Assembly, Resolution 70/232, Rights of Indigenous Peoples, UN Doc. A/RES/70/232 (16 February 2016).
51 *Bridge to the Future: Indigenous Youth Document the Achievements of the First Indigenous Peoples' Delegates at the United Nations*, dir. Wayanay Mamani et al. (DOCIP, 2014), 39 min., www.youtube.com/watch?v=KqtyUrPqQDs.
52 The author witnessed the 2013 meeting in Geneva.
53 Quoted in Robin M. Wright, "Anthropological Presuppositions of Indigenous Advocacy," *Annual Review of Anthropology* 17 (1988): 376.

During our discussions, Indigenous leaders reflected on how the quality of participation has been positively affected through the continuous presence of Indigenous representatives at the UN and how some states have also changed their positions. Claire Charters pointed out, regarding the Māori:

Now we're a lot more savvy, we're a lot more efficient. We pick our battles, we coalesce around which places and spaces to raise which issues. It's not a scatter gather, for some particular groups it might be, but for those of us working in the area, it's very calculated. It's coordinated, it's very strategic. We can do it efficiently, in a way by which we have our everyday jobs or domestic issues, and we can pick when we're going to work in the international fora and when we're not. That's not to say there aren't new groups coming through, which then learn their own way. But I think it depends a lot on the individuals and the knowledge there is in their community or communities. But certainly I see a lot more, at least in the area in which I work with, that it is much more strategic. The quality is quite better. For example, to participate in the UPR [Universal Periodic Review, at the UN Human Rights Council] we had the independent monitoring mechanism to prepare our report, we already had background information, it took us maybe a day to prepare for the presentation. We know that we might not go to Geneva [to the Human Rights Council], because we think going to the preparatory process [for the UPR] is enough, and we think handing in our documents the day of [the discussion in Geneva] is not worth the money [for the travel], so we've made that strategic choice. We've had our power or our moment, expressing what we think. We know the [state] delegates [involved in the UPR], we can ring up and explain why we want to ask those questions [during the UPR]. I think it's different for each people and it depends on one's institutional knowledge.[54]

Myrna Cunningham, senior Indigenous leader in Nicaragua, also discussed how Indigenous participation at international level has evolved:[55]

When we first came to the UN, we were only heard, we were not writing the recommendations – let's say it that way. And, I would say that in the last thirty-five years . . . things have changed a lot. Indigenous Peoples have become visible at the international level. There are ILO Convention 169, the UNDRIP, but I would say that, more than only those two instruments that are related to Indigenous Peoples, we see more and more the position of Indigenous Peoples in different spaces. For example, in the Commission on the Status of Women; even in CEDAW [Committee on the Elimination of All Forms of Discrimination against Women], the fact that they are

---

54 Charters interviewed by the author, 2 November 2018.
55 Cunningham interviewed by the author, 17 May 2016.

discussing the possibility of a General Comment of CEDAW on Indigenous women and girls,[56] *or the Convention on the Rights of the Child also wrote a General Comment;*[57] *and CERD [Committee on the Elimination of All Forms of Racial Discrimination] has already been chaired by an Indigenous person. So I would say in general, not only in the field of human rights, but also in the field of policy definition and development here [at the UN] in New York, I think we have seen changes. . . . States have [also] changed. For example, in Latin America, at least twenty states have changed their constitution and included Indigenous Peoples. . . . So I would say we have gained a lot as recognition, as legislative changes in the majority of the countries in Latin America. The problem is that there is still a gap between what is being recognized and what we can do at a practical level, but it gives us an opportunity to continue pushing, hard. . . . I think that the States have opened the door because they really believe that Indigenous Peoples have something to offer. I think a lot that States really understand that. . . .*

In terms of the impact of international Indigenous participation at home? The first impact is that what we have done at the international level opens the possibility to really influence and promote changes in our countries. The second big impact is related with Indigenous Peoples as such. If you come to this international space, you learn a lot. For the ones that come for the first time, it's like a school, a big school, where they come and learn every day from what they are hearing, from what they are seeing. So, with a developing capacity of Indigenous Peoples – women, youth, and everybody really goes back empowered to their community. They go back and share that. We have been able to influence, for example, traditional leaders in our communities that maybe were implementing negative practices. For example, we have done that with the women's movements. We bring the international legislation to the community, and we say, "This is what is happening." And that has changed the administration of justice in our communities. Two years ago, all of the judges, the communal judges in our communities, agreed that they are not going to apply the negative practices of customary administration of justice system when it is related with women's rights, for example. So that's another impact.

56 The General Recommendation was adopted by CEDAW in 2022. UN Committee on the Elimination of Discrimination against Women, General Recommendation No. 39 (2022) on the Rights of Indigenous Women and Girls, UN Doc. CEDAW/C/GC/39 (31 October 2022), www.ohchr.org/en/documents/general-comments-and-recommendations/general-recommendation-no39-2022-rights-indigenous.
57 UN Committee on the Rights of the Child, General Comment No. 11 (2009), Indigenous Children and Their Rights under the Convention [on the Rights of the Child], UN Doc. CRC/C/GC/11 (12 February 2009).

We have been able to build this Indigenous movement that is very important. This is the space where all of us come together, and we may have different points of view, but you can see the strength of the Indigenous movement. And this is something that governments can see, and that other institutions can see. This global strength of the Indigenous movement, is what keeps opening more and more doors.

In terms of how Indigenous participation has changed over time, Aehshatou Manu, Indigenous leader from Cameroon, said:

It has changed . . . maybe we were having two or three people [attending] in the beginning. And then it became ten, twenty, thirty. And maybe at the beginning they were not getting what the UN itself was, the mechanism, how it goes. Then they started getting it, understanding, going to school to even get more knowledge they need. . . . Then issues like climate change, where we also have the issue of free, prior, and informed consent [became part of the discussions]. . . . Now, Indigenous communities, when you go to them, they will say, "You need to consult us before you apply anything." So it's already a good and strong movement, and people are getting more and more knowledge about their own issues, and the technical themes, even though most Indigenous, like in my community, most Indigenous people are still not highly educated.[58]

Through their intense participation and expression of self-determination at international fora over decades, Indigenous Peoples have realized both the challenges and the possible benefits of being active at that level. Tensions in international bodies can be politically productive if strategies and subtle gestures are well thought out and implemented.[59]

The establishment of the Voluntary Fund on Indigenous Populations (now "Peoples") in 1985 could certainly be seen, from the beginning, as a benign, positive step and as a facilitator of Indigenous Peoples' participation at the UN. By the time of this writing, in 2023 – one hundred years after Chief Deskaheh of the Haudenosaunee tried to be heard by the League of Nations – the world had acquired a deeper understanding and historical perspective and can appreciate the extraordinary effects of this participation.

Looking at the 1985 decision to establish the Voluntary Fund from this perspective, it is impressive that this happened so fast, just two years after the launch of the unprecedented and, for some states, uneasy practice of

---

58 Manu interviewed by the author, 29 November 2016.
59 See the discussion of publicness and the public sphere in Toby Lee, *The Public Life of Cinema: Conflict and Collectivity in Austerity Greece* (Oakland: University of California Press, 2020).

open Indigenous participation at WGIP in 1983. I am thinking here of Brazil and Peru, for example, who had informally threatened to "close down" the Working Group at the beginning of this new practice. For many people who were working with the WGIP closely, it was clear that this new body was still fragile and low in the hierarchy of UN bodies. Therefore, the initiative to draw attention to the WGIP's innovative procedure of direct Indigenous participation could be seen as bold and risky.

Yet when the idea of establishing the Voluntary Fund came to the UN General Assembly (UNGA), the political atmosphere of the Assembly in New York was more "global" than that of the UN in Geneva. The majority of the vote at the UNGA is held by developing countries, certainly sensitive and sympathetic to issues of decolonization and to struggles against racial discrimination. This broad political constituency of states present at the UNGA could not compare with that of the Working Group in Geneva that was not widely attended by states. Twelve states attended the WGIP in 1982 and thirteen in 1983, and, in later years, about thirty-five states at best would attend the Working Group's annual sessions. The presence of many newly independent African and other states at the UNGA in New York gave the new decolonization ethic strength in the early 1980s. The decision to establish the Voluntary Fund firmed up a political understanding among states that Indigenous Peoples' direct participation in international deliberations that affect their lives was and is of high moral and political value and is required in order to give legitimacy to any Indigenous-related UN debates and actions.

F. Confirming Direct Participation: The UN Permanent Forum on Indigenous Issues

The dynamics that shaped Indigenous Peoples' practices in the WGIP were different from what they are today. At WGIP, the "review of developments" part of its mandate focused on Indigenous representatives presenting their situations, their problems and complaints vis-à-vis states, while it was repeatedly stressed by the Chairperson of the WGIP that the Working Group "is not a chamber of complaints." In reality, the Working Group was an international town hall, where Indigenous Peoples complaints could be heard but, technically, not be adjudicated. The only "judge" at the WGIP was international public opinion. That was an important judge for Indigenous Peoples, and it continues to be, as Indigenous Peoples continue to dialogue with and build bridges to the global public opinion.

Once the UNPFII was created and its first session took place in 2002, there was a change in the rhetoric expected from Indigenous Peoples on the part of states. The idea was that the Forum is a permanent high-level body of the UN, with a unique membership – eight indigenous-nominated and eight state-nominated members. The stakes were high, politically speaking, given also the Forum's significant visibility at UN Headquarters in New York. However, this high-level perception of the Permanent Forum was also accompanied by special expectations on the part of states. Many states hoped and hope to tone down the constant references to the dire human rights situation that Indigenous Peoples face. They clearly wanted and want the Permanent Forum to be more "development-oriented" than "human rights-oriented," something they also pursued by moving the secretariat of the UNPFII from the Office of the High Commissioner for Human Rights in Geneva to the Department of Economic and Social Affairs in New York.

Indigenous Peoples' organizations were not displeased with that decision, for their own reasons – namely because they appreciated the political visibility that the placement of the secretariat at UN Headquarters brings. The Indigenous movement was and is well aware that it is through the human rights angle that Indigenous issues received international attention. Human rights bring out a political edge that catches states' attention – and often their annoyance or sensitivity – because of the critique of their practices. Other approaches do not necessarily do that. In fact, the women's movement realized this around the end of the 1980s – about two decades after the Indigenous movement had started doing so – and launched a strong and successful campaign at the 1993 World Conference on Human Rights in Vienna under the slogan "Women's rights are human rights." By the time of the establishment of the Permanent Forum, for Indigenous Peoples, the UN human rights bodies had already become both a site of channeling their complaints of human rights violations and also for articulating their aspirations for a just future as Indigenous Peoples. The UN had already become a public space through which a global Indigenous Peoples' identity was born, especially as Indigenous Peoples from all continents were joining this movement. Indigenous leaders were, and are, fully aware of the significance of the human rights agenda for their issues and have actively pursued the strengthening of international human rights work, including through the establishment of the UN Special Rapporteur on the Rights of Indigenous Peoples in 2001 and of the UN EMRIP in 2007.

In the first years of the Permanent Forum, some states were saying that the UNPFII "should not become another Working Group," by which they really meant that it should not hear the long presentations of human rights complaints from Indigenous representatives. States wanted to avoid politically sensitive issues for them. After all, they pointed out, the broad mandate of the Permanent Forum covers environment, development, health, education, and culture, in addition to human rights. The emphasis at the UNPFII has been on formulating policy recommendations and proposals for solutions on all the aforementioned areas, addressed mainly to the UN system. While this may sound limiting, there have been many creative ways in which the Permanent Forum has interpreted its mandate and broadened its field of influence.

The Permanent Forum created a new situation in terms of how it hears Indigenous representatives' statements at its public meetings. While attendance at the UNPFII has been high, as have been Indigenous representatives' requests to speak, the time limit for statements is quite short, down to three minutes. Obviously, many of those on the list of speakers never get to speak, which was the case also at the WGIP. In these three minutes, people who get to speak have to be able to both expose their situation and make relevant recommendations. This has led to a common practice, where speakers start with their recommendations, enumerating them briefly, and then go to the narrative explanation of the situations that make these recommendations necessary. This approach relies heavily on the written word, becomes strict or mechanical sometimes, and often detracts from the force of a narrative that can convey the realities of Indigenous lives on the ground in a "human" way. Some Indigenous delegates, new to this "surgical" UN procedure, have barely started their statement when their three minutes are up and their microphone is automatically cut off. Others achieve to convey very strong statements in this very short time. The three-minute time limitation to UNPFII observers' statements is also implemented for states.

The issue is not that Indigenous delegates cannot adapt to these procedures – they can and do, and often times, the three-minute rhetoric works and is even quite effective. It is understandably hard to accommodate so many requests for the floor, and the Permanent Forum has a challenge in this area. The list of speakers when it comes to the human rights item on the agenda of the Forum can be three times as long as for other items, a continuing indication that this is the area that Indigenous Peoples have much to convey and much to demand.

Given the large number of Indigenous Peoples' organizations and institutions that participate in the Permanent Forum, the UNPFII has devised approaches to facilitate its cooperation with Indigenous Peoples. Its annual sessions are the second largest meeting at UN Headquarters. Over the years, observers from Indigenous Peoples and their organizations and other NGOs have come in large numbers, spanning from some 1,300 to 2,200, (one year some 3,100 persons preregistered to attend). They have created diverse ways of making their participation substantive and visible, even if the time limitations do not always allow them to speak at the public, plenary meetings of the Permanent Forum.

Indigenous Peoples have organized themselves in regional caucuses as well as thematic ones, including the one of Indigenous Women and the caucus of the Global Indigenous Youth, in order to better promote their representation at the annual session of the Permanent Forum. Before the sessions, Indigenous organizations from certain regions hold preparatory meetings and submit their results to the Permanent Forum. They also submit other presessional documents. On the Sunday before the start of the annual session, the

Permanent Forum's Chair and other members as well as the Secretariat of the Permanent Forum brief the Indigenous representatives that have gathered in New York. At the outset of the annual sessions of the Permanent Forum, an opening ceremony is held by the spiritual leader of the Indigenous Peoples of the land. Given the large number of Indigenous organizations wishing to speak during the sessions, the Permanent Forum had, at one point, devised a system, whereby the floor was given first to the regional and thematic caucuses, then to group statements, and then, if time permits, to statements by individual organizations. Indigenous representatives also consult informally with Permanent Forum members during the session regarding their concerns and the formulation of recommendations. Many of the recommendations made by Indigenous representatives find their way into the Permanent Forum's annual reports. Indigenous Peoples also organize numerous side events during the session of the Forum, where people participate actively, share experiences and lessons, and put forward policy proposals that they hope will be included in Permanent Forum's report. They also participate actively in the public debates on the special theme of every Forum session, in the region-specific and country-specific discussions and in the dialogue with the Special Rapporteur on the Rights of Indigenous Peoples. Regarding the latter, Indigenous representatives also have the opportunity to hold private pre-scheduled meetings with the Special Rapporteur.

The Permanent Forum, in order to further strengthen Indigenous participation, has decided to separately accredit Indigenous parliamentarians to its sessions and also to give them the floor individually. In a similar gesture, and following UN practice at the Human Rights Council, the Permanent Forum has decided to separately accredit national human rights institutions that wish to attend its sessions.

Between sessions, Permanent Forum members participate at national, regional, and international meetings and conferences especially at the invitation of Indigenous Peoples and their organizations, thus expanding their contacts with Indigenous Peoples. Given the composition of the Permanent Forum and the representation on it of Indigenous experts from the seven Indigenous sociocultural regions, it would be accurate to say that the Permanent Forum's connection with Indigenous Peoples is an organic one. This, however, does not mean that the Permanent Forum members, appointed as "independent experts" by the ECOSOC President, *represent* Indigenous Peoples in the strict sense of the word. Permanent Forum members, as UN independent experts, are there to pursue the fulfillment of the UNPFII's broad mandate, keeping in mind especially their expertise of their region. This is also the case with state-nominated members of the Permanent Forum – that is, they do not *represent* a national state government but are to pursue the fulfillment of the UNPFII's mandate, keeping in mind especially their expertise and knowledge of the region they come from.

The exceptional aspects of the UNPFII – namely its broad mandate and, especially, its membership that conveys parity (eight state-nominated members and eight Indigenous-nominated members) – are definitely a point of analysis by many, including people working in different fields. What we should add to these impressive characteristics of this committee, the Permanent Forum, is the extraordinary number of participants from around the world at the Forum's annual sessions. Despite weaknesses that the Permanent Forum may have, as all human constructs have, the aforementioned special elements lift it to a deeply significant forum for Indigenous issues. I have spoken with a large number of people over the years, and we all agree that that Permanent Forum would not have the profile and strength it has if large numbers of Indigenous representatives were not there annually to participate actively, raise their voices, and demand measures to promote equality and justice. Indigenous leaders do just that. They participate at the UNPFII, year in and year out, also ensuring the intergenerational transmission of the Indigenous movement as well.

The moral high ground Indigenous Peoples have been holding internationally has created a new normal. This has had strong and broad resonance and can help explain, to a considerable extent, positive exceptions made by the interstate system not only to accept but also to foster direct Indigenous participation at the UN, as this chapter explained. The ongoing efforts at the General Assembly to enhance Indigenous Peoples' participation open new visions and possibilities, as Chapter 4 discusses.

Political realities, at the same time, continue to be harsh for Indigenous Peoples, and their struggles continue. The drama of the confrontation between Indigenous Peoples and states has played out visibly in the international arena, and this has often been virulent, including resistance of states to documenting their abuses against Indigenous Peoples. Yet it is a welcome paradox that states either acquiesced or proactively cultivated direct Indigenous participation at the UN. Corrective exceptionalism has had ever-increasing reverberations regarding political visibility and normative and institutional achievements of the Indigenous Peoples' movement. This positive exceptionalism has occurred for so long that we can hope it also has a future.

Bibliography

Daes, Erica-Irene A. Special Rapporteur on Protection of the Heritage of the Indigenous People. Protection of the Heritage of Indigenous People. UN Doc. E/CN.4/Sub.2/1995/26, 21 June 1995.

Daes, Erica-Irene A. Special Rapporteur on Protection of the Heritage of the Indigenous People. Indigenous Peoples and Their Relationship to Land. UN Doc. E/CN.4/Sub.2/2000/25, 30 June 2000.

Daes, Erica-Irene A. Special Rapporteur on Protection of the Heritage of the Indigenous People. Indigenous Peoples' Permanent Sovereignty Over Natural Resources. UN Doc. E/CN.4/Sub.2/2004/30/Add.1, 12 July 2004.

Lee, Toby. *The Public Life of Cinema: Conflict and Collectivity in Austerity Greece.* Oakland, CA: University of California Press, 2020.

Lewis, Dustin A., Naz K. Modirzadeh, and Gabriella Blum. "Quantum of Silence: Inaction and Jus ad Bellum." *Harvard Law School Program on International Law and Armed Conflict,* 2019. https://pilac.law.harvard.edu/quantum-of-silence-web-version.

Mamani, Wayanay, Judy Kipkenda Jemutai, Haydee Banasen, Morgan Catlett, Jacquelynn Lambert, Sharni Maree Hooper, and Alancay Morales, dirs. *Bridge to the Future: Indigenous Youth Document the Achievements of the First Indigenous Peoples' Delegates at the United Nations.* DOCIP, 2014. 39 min. www.youtube.com/watch?v=KqtyUrPqQDs.

Martineau, Raymonde. Interview by James S. Sutterlin, 7 July 1998, Geneva. Transcript in UN Dag Hammarskjöld Library. https://digitallibrary.un.org/record/503509?ln=en.

UN Commission on Human Rights. Establishment of a Working Group of the Commission on Human Rights to Elaborate a Draft Declaration in Accordance with Paragraph 5 of the General Assembly Resolution 49/214. UN Doc. E/CN.4/RES/1995/32, 3 March 1995.

UN Commission on Human Rights. Human Rights and Indigenous Issues: Report of the Special Rapporteur on the Situation of Human Rights and Fundamental Freedoms of Indigenous Peoples, Rodolfo Stavenhagen: Addendum. UN Doc. E/CN.4/2005/88/Add.3, 2 December 2004.

UN Committee on the Elimination of Discrimination against Women. General Recommendation No. 39 (2022) on the Rights of Indigenous Women and Girls. UN Doc. CEDAW/C/GC/39, 31 October 2022. www.ohchr.org/en/documents/general-comments-and-recommendations/general-recommendation-no39-2022-rights-indigeneous.

UN Committee on the Rights of the Child, General Comment No. 11 (2009): Indigenous Children and Their Rights under the Convention [on the Rights of the Child]. UN Doc. CRC/C/GC/11, 12 February 2009.

UN Economic and Social Council. Consultative Relationship between the United Nations and Non-governmental Organizations. UN Doc. E/RES/1996/31, 25 July 1996. www.unov.org/documents/NGO/NGO_Resolution_1996_31.pdf.

UN Economic and Social Council. Establishment of a Permanent Forum on Indigenous Issues. E/RES/2000/22, 28 July 2000. www.un.org/esa/socdev/unpfii/documents/about-us/E-RES-2000-22.pdf.

UN General Assembly. Resolution 40/131, United Nations Voluntary Fund for Indigenous Populations. UN Doc. A/RES/40/131, 27 February 1986.

UN General Assembly. Resolution 56/140, International Decade of the World's Indigenous People. UN Doc. A/RES/56/140, 15 February 2002.

UN General Assembly. Resolution 61/295, United Nations Declaration on the Rights of Indigenous Peoples. UN Doc. A/RES/61/295, 13 September 2007. www.un.org/development/desa/indigenouspeoples/wp-content/uploads/sites/19/2018/11/UNDRIP_E_web.pdf.

UN General Assembly. Resolution 63/161, Indigenous Issues. UN Doc. A/RES/63/161, 13 February 2009.

UN General Assembly. Resolution 65/198, Indigenous Issues. UN Doc. A/RES/65/198, 3 March 2011.

UN General Assembly. Resolution 70/232, Rights of Indigenous Peoples. UN Doc. A/RES/70/232, 16 February 2016.

UN Human Rights Council. Resolution 6/36, Expert Mechanism on the Rights of Indigenous Peoples. UN Doc. A/HRC/RES/6/36, 14 April 2008.

UN Sub-Commission on Prevention of Discrimination and Protection of Minorities. Report of the Working Group on Indigenous Populations on Its First Session. UN Doc. E/CN.4/Sub.2/1982/33, 25 August 1982.

UN Sub-Commission on Prevention of Discrimination and Protection of Minorities. Report of the Working Group on Indigenous Populations on Its Second Session. UN Doc. E/CN.4/Sub.2/1983/22, 23 August 1983.

Wangza, Devasish, dir. *The Spirit of Pátzcuaro: Seeking Consensus for a Strong Declaration on the Rights of Indigenous Peoples*. Subrata Chakma, ed. Tamaza Productions: Rangamati, Bangladesh, 2006. 31 min. www.youtube.com/watch?v=cfPswCSsmFg.

Willemsen Díaz, Augusto. "How Indigenous Peoples' Rights Reached the UN." In *Making the Declaration Work: The United Nations Declaration on the Rights of Indigenous Peoples*, edited by Claire Charters and Rodolfo Stavenhagen, 16–31. Copenhagen: International Work Group on Indigenous Affairs, 2009.

Wright, Robin M. "Anthropological Presuppositions of Indigenous Advocacy." *Annual Review of Anthropology* 17 (1988): 365–390.

4

SELF-REPRESENTATIONS AND DEMANDS OF INDIGENOUS PEOPLES

This book is about Indigenous Peoples' participation and external self-determination, especially as expressed at international fora over the decades. Chapter 4 goes deeper into specific methodologies of the Indigenous Peoples' movement, both those already developed over time and newer ones in the process of dynamic development. It is important to discover and shed light on such approaches in order to help explain the various successes of the Indigenous movement, as well as the possible relevance of these approaches for younger generations of Indigenous leaders and for other sociopolitical movements.

The UN Expert Mechanism on the Rights of Indigenous Peoples (EMRIP) stated, in its 2019 study on recognition, reparation, and reconciliation, that in "attempts at reparation and reconciliation, indigenous peoples and States should take into consideration that the process is as important as the outcome" – that is, that "indigenous perspectives need to be incorporated at all stages, and indigenous peoples' full and effective participation is essential if the outcomes of such processes are to be successful and, indeed, legitimate."[1] This should also be followed in transitional justice processes, with the

---

1 UN Expert Mechanism on the Rights of Indigenous Peoples, Efforts to Implement the United Nations Declaration on the Rights of Indigenous Peoples: Recognition, Reparation and Reconciliation, UN Doc. A/HRC/EMRIP/2019/3/Rev.1 (2 September 2019), para. 40. See also EMRIP's studies in the issue of participation, Final Report of the Study on Indigenous Peoples and the Right to Participate in Decision-Making, UN Doc. A/HRC/18/42 (17 August 2011); and Report of the Expert Mechanism on the Rights of Indigenous Peoples on Its Fourth Session, Geneva, 11–15 July 2011, UN Doc. A/HRC/18/43 (19 August 2011).

DOI: 10.4324/9781003464099-5

participation of the victims themselves throughout the process.[2] The report continues:

> Indigenous representatives, chosen by indigenous peoples themselves, must participate at all levels and stages. Particular attention should be given to hearing the voices of Indigenous elders, women, children and persons with disabilities. Full participation also nurtures an environment of trust, which is a crucial factor in the success of any truth and reconciliation commission.[3]

Indigenous Peoples have indeed been advocating for these points for years so that such elements of participation actually become public policies. The UN Declaration on the Rights of Indigenous Peoples (UNDRIP) is imbued with the principle of participation, and, in Articles 18 and 41, refers to the right of Indigenous Peoples to participate in matters that concern them.

International law experts have explored links of international law to constructivism. Several of these links are relevant to the Indigenous Peoples' movement. Constructivism "sees the world and what we can know about the world, as socially constructed."[4] Constructivists

> go beyond the material reality by including the effect of ideas and beliefs on world politics. This also entails that reality is always under construction, which opens the prospect for change. In other words, meanings are not fixed but can change over time depending on the ideas and beliefs that actors hold.[5]

International lawyers, like constructivists, must pay close attention to nonstate actors: NGOs, corporations, informal intergovernmental expert networks, and a variety of other groups who are actively engaged in the creation of shared understandings and the promotion of learning among states.[6] Although states remain formally dominant within the interstate system, they are influenced (admittedly in different ways and to different extents) by the persuasive activities of less obviously powerful actors.[7] Enhancing the knowledge of actors is central to constructivism and legal interactionism; humans are viewed as active agents constantly making choices about present and

---

2 UN Doc. A/HRC/EMRIP/2019/3/Rev.1, para. 44.
3 UN Doc. A/HRC/EMRIP/2019/3/Rev.1, para. 83.
4 Sarina Theys, "Introducing Constructivism in International Relations Theory," *E-International Relations*, 23 February 2018, www.e-ir.info/2018/02/23/introducing-constructivism-in-international-relations-theory/.
5 Theys, "Introducing Constructivism in International Relations Theory."
6 Brunnée and Toope, "International Law and Constructivism," p. 69.
7 Brunnée and Toope, "International Law and Constructivism," p. 69.

future conduct; these choices can be influenced by knowledge, and knowledge can include so-called "rhetorical knowledge" – that is, knowledge offered or created in dialogue and employed in practical reasoning.[8] "Basic understandings among parties in dialogue can, however, be fostered through pre-legal mutual interaction in informal and formal institutions, through the work of norm entrepreneurs, through the engagement of epistemic communities and issue networks, and through the processes of socialization affecting the self-perception and identity of actors; these processes include conditions of membership in organizations, the desire for esteem and good reputation, the need for aid, confidence-building measures, and identification with 'prominent' actors within a system."[9]

The exceptions to regular UN protocols or rules that Indigenous Peoples have sought become struggles that have to be fought one by one by various actors and be won one by one. The other strategic point is that, through the various Indigenous protocols that are advocated and incorporated in interstate processes, Indigenous Peoples are able to express themselves more fully, get their points across, and possibly convince more people. Such strategies have led to concrete, substantive successes at international and, slowly, national levels. Indigenous protocols, in other words, are beyond formality and become vehicles for political achievements.

A. Special Features of the International Indigenous Peoples' Movement

In modern times, Indigenous Peoples were part of social struggles in many parts of the world before they raised their voices *as* Indigenous Peoples. Many mobilized together with other actors – for example, in Latin America they became part of peasants' movements in the early 1970s.[10] However, as the years progressed and the global Indigenous movement was shaping itself and taking hold, Indigenous Peoples became more aware of their distinctiveness in terms of problems and cultures and of their identity and their visions that could not be contained or were largely ignored in other social justice movements. Through the international connections among Indigenous Peoples, a new international Indigenous identity was created, and Indigenous Peoples were giving content to this Indigenous identity in human rights language. This continues today.

---

8 Brunnée and Toope, "International Law and Constructivism," p. 70.
9 Brunnée and Toope, "International Law and Constructivism," p. 71.
10 Courtney Jung, *The Moral Force of Indigenous Politics: Critical Liberalism and the Zapatistas* (Cambridge: Cambridge University Press, 2008); Kay B. Warren, *Indigenous Movements and Their Critics: Pan-Maya Activism in Guatemala* (Princeton, NJ: Princeton University Press, 1998).

An important meeting was organized by Indigenous Peoples' Center for Documentation, Research and Information (DOCIP) at the UN in Geneva, Switzerland, in September 2013, to commemorate the first conference of Indigenous leaders at the UN in 1977, discussed earlier in the book. The meeting gathered those historic first delegates still surviving, together with Indigenous young people. The Elders were explaining what made them come to the UN, what they were expecting, what they had achieved and how. One of the Elders, Kenneth Deer (Mohawk), said a phrase that stuck in my mind: "Never drop the moral high ground."[11] These words actually evoked what we understand as underlying the human rights agenda. Believing and struggling under the umbrella of a moral high ground is also an antidote to frustration and cynicism that are often present in politics. People complain of the failure to implement international human rights norms, and they are disappointed and indignant that human rights language is often abused by states or is used rhetorically to promote unrelated political aims and geopolitics of specific states or regions of states. The issue is how to keep up hope and a struggle that upholds the moral high ground.

The questions we can raise in response to disappointment include the following: Can people be robbed of the tremendous significance of the human rights paradigm and its moral high ground because states abuse the human rights language for their own purposes? Are people to abandon their pursuit of human rights that are actually meant to be a protective moral and legal system *against* the state? Are we to believe that human rights, the result of bottom-up efforts and of social movements in the first place, are now just a tool in the hands of the state?

Charles Tilly, the famous sociologist, defined social movements as a series of contentious performances, displays, and campaigns by which ordinary people make collective claims on others.[12]

Approaching the question of social movements from a human rights perspective, we could suggest a typology of social movements, relevant also for Indigenous Peoples, based on the following reflections:

1. Not all social justice and human rights causes have a social movement behind them, worthwhile as they may be. They may have advocates behind them but not necessarily a movement. For example, the protection of the homeless is a human rights cause, but it does not have a visible social movement behind it.

---

11 The author attended the conference and witnessed this statement. For the Declaration adopted at the 2013 conference, see Declaration of the International Symposium, "Indigenous Peoples at the United Nations: From the Experience of the First Delegates to the Empowerment of the Younger Generations," 13 September 2013, http://cendoc.docip.org/collect/cendocdo/index/assoc/HASH017a/4a4a35f7.dir/DeclSymposium2013_final_en.pdf.
12 Charles Tilly, *Social Movements, 1768–2004* (Boulder, CO: Paradigm, 2004).

2. Not all social movements are international and thus not all of them have the same force to engage with states at state and interstate levels and to push for their cause. Some social movements are at local, national, or regional levels. For example, the protests against the Keystone XL Pipeline, or the protests of the Idle No More movement were national or regional in nature.

3. Not all social international movements have engaged with the human rights paradigm – for example, "new social movements," those represented at the Porto Alegre series of global conferences. And even if they did engage, not all of those who engaged with the international human rights system did so in a sustained, methodical manner over a long period of time; for example, the environmentalists engaged with the human rights system in the 1980s and then interrupted their human rights efforts there for many years.

The two major social movements that are both international and engaged with human rights are the international women's movement(s) and the international Indigenous Peoples movement(s). We can note at least four similarities between them: (a) they both saw and see the moral force of human rights; (b) they use the political edge of human rights to draw focused attention of states to their issues; (c) they take the UN seriously as the most global ground to debate ideas and policies that impact on people's lives on the ground; and (d) they spent and are spending energy and resources consistently over a long period of time to plan, strategize, pressure, and influence states and others over the years in an effort to bring about results on the ground.

B.   Who Are the Indigenous Representatives at International Fora?

Cayuga Chief Deskaheh, Levi General, the representative of the Haudenosaunee who went to the League of Nations in Geneva in 1923 to plead the cause of his people, presented himself in these words in a letter to the Secretary-General of the League, Sir James Eric Drummond, on 6 August 1923, entitled "The Red Man's Appeal for Justice."[13] This excerpt demonstrates the profound sense of self-determined international representation of the Iroquois.

Sir,

Under the authority vested in the undersigned, the Speaker of the Council and the sole Deputy by choice of the Council composed of forty-two chiefs, of the Six Nations of the Iroquois, being a state within the purview and meaning of Article 17 of the Covenant of the League of Nations, but

---

13 For the full letter, see DOCIP archives, http://cendoc.docip.org/collect/deskaheh/index/assoc/
HASH0102/5e23c4be.dir/R612-11-28075-30626-8.pdf.

not being at present a member of the League, I, the undersigned, pursuant to the said authority, do hereby bring to the notice of the League of Nations that a dispute and disturbance of peace has arisen between the State of the Six Nations of the Iroquois on the one hand and the British Empire and Canada, being Members of the League, on the other . . .

3. The constituent members of the State of the Six Nations of the Iroquois, that is to say, the Mohawk, the Oneida, the Onondaga, the Cayuga, the Seneca and the Tuscarora, now are, and have been for many centuries, organised and self-governing peoples, respectively, within domains of their own, and united in the oldest League of Nations, the League of the Iroquois, for the maintenance of mutual peace; and that status has been recognised by Great Britain, France and the Netherlands, being European States which established colonies in North America; by the States successor to the British colonies therein, being the United States of America, and by the Dominion of Canada, with whom the Six nations have in turn treated, they being justly entitled to the same recognition as all other peoples.

Deskaheh signed the letter with his title as "Sole Deputy and Speaker of the Six Nations Council." He waited one year working for recognition by the League, was not received, and came back to North America. A few months before his death in 1925, he made a speech by radio in Rochester, New York. The following is an excerpt:

This is the story of the Mohawks, the story of the Oneidas, of the Cayugas – [I am a Cayuga –] of the Onondagas, the Senecas, and the Tuscaroras. They are the Iroquois. Tell it to those who have not been listening. Maybe I will be stopped from telling it. But if I am prevented from telling it over, as I hope I do, the story will not be lost. I have already told it to thousands of listeners in Europe. It has gone into the records where your children can find it when I may be dead or be in jail for daring to tell the truth. I have told this story in Switzerland. They have free speech in little Switzerland. One can tell the truth over there in public, even if it is uncomfortable for some great people.

. . . I am the speaker of the Six Nations, the oldest League of Nations now existing. . . . It is a League which is still alive and intends, as best it can, to defend the rights of the Iroquois to live under their own laws in their own little countries now left to them, to worship their Great Spirit in their own way, and to enjoy the rights which are as surely theirs as the white man's rights are his own.[14]

14 Deskaheh, "An Iroquois Patriot's Fight for International Recognition," 53.

A similar journey was made by Māori religious leader T. W. Ratana. He decided to protest the breaking of the Treaty of Waitangi, concluded with the Māori in New Zealand in 1840, that gave Māori ownership of their lands. He first traveled to London with a large delegation to petition King George V, but he was denied access. He then sent part of his delegation to the League of Nations in Geneva, with Hine Aka Tioke, a Māori woman, as part of the delegation.[15] He arrived there later himself, in 1925, but was also denied access.

A less discussed case is that of the 1924–1925 uprising of Indigenous people in Siberia and the Far East, known as the "Tungus uprising" in the Okhotsk district of the Yakut region. The Tungus people was an old common name for the Okhotsk region's Evenki people. They reacted to violence they experienced from the government of the Soviet Union and sought the establishment of a Tungus Republic. In 1924, there was an all-Tungus nation congress in Nelkan, which proclaimed the independence of the Tungus people and established a national sovereign state – the Tungus Republic. The congress of the Tungus also declared the inviolability of its maritime, forest, mountain, and natural resources. The leaders of the movement appealed to foreign countries and to the League of Nations to protect them. The Tungus Republic had state symbols, such as a flag and an anthem. As in the other two cases discussed earlier, there was no help from the League of Nations.[16]

There is a long history of Indigenous Peoples seeking participation in the institutions of the international community of nations. Indigenous Peoples' sense of themselves as sovereign nations, in parity with the other nations of the world, has always been very strong. The fact that states, the colonizing or discriminating powers, concluded treaties with many Indigenous Peoples is a testimony that Indigenous Peoples were viewed as sovereign, not only by themselves but also by those who actually invented international law.

In one of the historic pictures of the 1977 international antiracism conference in Geneva,[17] the late Audrey Shenandoah, Onondaga Nation Clan

---

15 The author was told about the participation of Hine Aka Tioke in the Māori delegation to the League of Nations by the late Māori leader Moana Jackson (interviewed 16 May 2017, in Vancouver, Canada).

16 In 1928 this protest was suppressed, and the separatist leaders were killed. Sources: "Tunguska Uprising," archival documents, *Ilin Cultural and Historical Magazine*, no. 1 [13] (1998) [in Russian], https://ilin-yakutsk.narod.ru/1998-1/17-6.htm; Yaroslav Butakov, "The Tungus Uprising in 1924: How It Ended," *Russian Seven*, 2021 [in Russian], https://russian7.ru/post/vosstanie-tungusov-v-1924-godu-chem-ono-zav/; National Archives of the Republic of Sakha (Yakutia), "Tunguska Uprising, May 1924–August 1925," [in Russian], archived 15 February 2020 at the Internet Archive, https://web.archive.org/web/20200215013910/http://archivesakha.ru/?page_id=5919. The author expresses her appreciation to Dr. Vera Solovyeva for making relevant material available.

17 Jean-François Graugnard, Photographic report of the "International Conference against Discrimination against Indigenous Populations of the Americas," United Nations, Geneva, 1977.

Mother, displayed her Haudenosaunee passport, a continuing testimony to the words and actions of Deskaheh and a continuing testimony of Indigenous sovereignty.

The thread of history through their own eyes has been carefully woven by Indigenous Peoples in their representations at the UN. Indigenous traditional authorities, Elders, Indigenous authorities elected according to state systems, Indigenous mayors, Indigenous parliamentarians, Indigenous NGOs, and Indigenous academics have participated over the decades, playing various roles. Upon its establishment in early 2003, the Secretariat of the UN Permanent Forum on Indigenous Issues (UNPFII) also prepared a website. The Secretariat considered it quite significant to include the aforementioned stories of the two leaders who went to the League of Nations in the 1920s so that this history would not be lost for succeeding generations of people involved in international Indigenous issues.

The mark that the UN Working Group on Indigenous Populations (WGIP) was clearly leaving from the start in the 1980s was that Indigenous participation was indispensable. The demand of Indigenous representatives that it would be unthinkable to have a UN body dealing with Indigenous issues without the participation of Indigenous Peoples themselves had clear resonance. The first report of the WGIP mentioned that "the Working Group should be open and accessible to representatives of indigenous populations, as well as to non-governmental organizations with consultative status, to intergovernmental agencies and to Governments," and that it "should encourage wide participation by representatives of indigenous peoples and encourage the establishment of a fund to make such participation possible."[18] That very first report of the WGIP mentioned the participation of nine Indigenous Peoples organizations with the consent of the Working Group: Haudenosaunee-Six Nations Iroquois Confederacy, Oglala Lakota Legal Rights Fund, Lakota Treaty Council, Nishaniwbe-Aski Nation (Grand Council Treaty No. 9), Native Council of Canada, Standing Rock Sioux Tribal Council, Santeioi Maoaiomi Mikmaoei (Grand Council Mikmaq Nation), Indian Council of South America (CISA), and the National Federation of Land Councils (Australia). In addition, three "Indigenous Peoples NGOs in consultative status" are mentioned as participants: the International Indian Treaty Council, the World Council of Indigenous Peoples, and the Indian Law Resource Center.[19] This small number of institutions and organizations at the beginning was to multiply by hundreds over the years after the adoption of the new exceptional UN procedures

18 UN Sub-Commission on Prevention of Discrimination and Protection of Minorities, Report of the Working Group on Indigenous Populations on Its First Session, UN Doc. E/CN.4/Sub.2/1982/33 (25 August 1982), para. 111–112.
19 UN Doc. E/CN.4/Sub.2/1982/33, para. 7 (a).

discussed throughout this book; the number of Indigenous representatives at the WGIP and at the UNPFII reached more than a thousand at the annual meetings. The numerous Indigenous organizations and Peoples from around the world designate their own representatives to such international meetings, with a variety of profiles and institutional affiliations, whether they are community-level authorities, tribal authorities, representatives of Indigenous institutions, or NGOs, including Indigenous women and youth representatives. Indigenous academics also participate at the international level, sometimes invited as experts at international meetings organized by UN bodies and organizations.

C. The Drafting of the United Nations Declaration on the Rights of Indigenous Peoples

The UNDRIP was adopted on 13 September 2007, twenty-five years after the first session of the UN Working Group on Indigenous Populations. It felt almost like a "miracle," an extraordinary achievement. This book analyzes reasons and processes that made this possible. Before and after the vote at the UN General Assembly (UNGA), the excitement was palpable, as was a sense of what a historical moment this was. Once the result of the vote became visible on the electronic board of the General Assembly Hall and it was clear that the Declaration was adopted, an Indigenous leader from the Arctic, who had devoted many years of his life in the efforts of negotiating the Declaration, stood up from his seat and said: "Is that it?" He could only be heard by those around him as he was capturing, with his few words, the astonishment and admiration of this moment.

1. Role of the UN Working Group on Indigenous Populations

The WGIP was mandated under Economic and Social Council (ECOSOC) resolution 1982/34 of 7 May 1982. The Council authorized the Sub-Commission on Prevention of Discrimination and Protection of Minorities to establish an annual Working Group on Indigenous Populations to meet for a maximum of five working days prior to the Sub-Commission with the aims of (a) reviewing developments pertaining to protecting and promoting Indigenous populations' human rights and freedoms and (b) giving special attention to the evolution of standards concerning the rights of Indigenous populations.[20]

The beginning of the WGIP is discussed in some detail in Chapter 1. The five members of the WGIP came from the five regional groups that states

---

20 UN Economic and Social Council, Resolution 1982/34, Study of the Problem of Discrimination against Indigenous Populations, UN Doc. E/RES/1982/34 (7 May 1982).

divide themselves into.[21] Experts that made a consistent long contribution to the WGIP came from Greece (through the late Erica-Irene Daes), Cuba (through the late Miguel Alfonso Martínez), and the former Yugoslavia (through the late Ivan Tosevski, and also Danilo Türk, who later also served as President of Slovenia). Daes was Chair for twenty years and Alfonso Martínez for two years. In addition, China and Japan were alternating with expert members of the WGIP from Asia for several years. The WGIP was ended in 2005, when there was an institutional change and the UN Commission on Human Rights (UNCHR), reporting to ECOSOC, was changed into the UN Human Rights Council, reporting to the General Assembly. The UN Expert Mechanism on the Rights of Indigenous Peoples (EMRIP) became a sort of successor mechanism within the UN human rights system.

The interpretation of the WGIP's mandate, its methods of work and long-term visions, were developed through a creative and at times robust dialogue with Indigenous Peoples. It is important for such analysis to factor in the very active participation of Indigenous Peoples and the unprecedented facilitating procedures that were developed in the WGIP.

The WGIP adopted a multipronged approach in carrying out its mandate and creating an active space for Indigenous Peoples. First, Indigenous Peoples continued to bring up the situation of their human rights. Although the WGIP was not a court and could not adjudicate cases (not a "chamber of complaints," as the Chairperson used to say), countries felt obliged to respond in public and they did so, often sending delegations from the capitals. Although not formally a court, the WGIP was a "court of public opinion." Through their advocacy and reports on their situations, Indigenous Peoples established the fact that specific action and specific mechanisms were needed by the UN so that their human rights would be respected.

Second, Indigenous Peoples pursued the education of the UN and of states about their histories, cultures, and *cosmovisiones* (worldviews) in many ways:

1. They wore their traditional clothes at the UN meetings.
2. They spoke their languages in the WGIP.
3. They used Indigenous protocols that will be described later; for example, the Māori would sing before their leader would speak.
4. The UN has accepted and established the protocol of the "opening ceremony" of Indigenous-related meetings that is given by "the Indigenous people of the land."
5. Indigenous Peoples have been explaining at length and for many years their relation to their traditional land – that is, their spiritual, cultural,

---

21 African States, Asian and Pacific States, Eastern European States, Latin American and Caribbean States, and Western European and Other States.

and material relationship, which is a condition for their survival as Indigenous Peoples. They explained the concept of collective ownership of the land, which is different from private property.

6. They spoke about their existence as peoples since time immemorial until the colonizers and settlers came; they explained their own governance systems.

7. They accompanied their Elders and medicine men or women to WGIP, who spoke like oracles about their philosophies, their relation with Mother Earth, and their visions for the future.

We can therefore say that the WGIP, in its formative years, was a space where Indigenous cultures and systems were actively conversing with dominant cultures and systems of states through the intermediary of the UN. In this way, Indigenous Peoples established the idea that their human rights could not be adequately covered by already existing human rights treaties and declarations but that specific international standards and procedures were needed; a new declaration on the rights of Indigenous Peoples was needed. At the same time, Indigenous Peoples were winning the hearts and minds of people – specifically, members of the WGIP and of the Sub-Commission, officials of states and of international organizations, NGOs, and the media. In other words, at the same time, a pro-Indigenous solidarity movement was being created.

A third element of the WGIP's multipronged approach was that strategy meetings among Indigenous Peoples were systematically taking place before each session of the Working Group. During those meetings, efforts were made to galvanize common positions among Indigenous Peoples from different regions on specific articles of the Declaration. These positions were then announced during the formal meetings of the Working Group and carried particular weight, as was to be expected. During the long drafting process for the Declaration, it would not be uncommon to hear some state diplomats almost rejoicing and saying that Indigenous Peoples were just too diverse and had too many different positions; states would not be able to agree on a text either. However, over time, Indigenous Peoples, having observed the techniques of states in establishing global policies, used similar techniques plus their own techniques to unite and to push their positions forward.

Additionally, trainings were also taking place before the sessions of the WGIP about how the UN and its human rights system work, so that the Indigenous representatives could use this specialized knowledge and language with increasing effectiveness.

Finally, studies were requested and conducted by WGIP members to shed light on specific complex issues, such as studies by Daes on lands, territories, and resources and studies by Alfonso Martinez on safeguarding treaties between Indigenous Peoples and states. The studies' analyses helped solidify several draft articles in the Declaration.

The aforementioned methodologies sent the message clearly and crystal-lized the awareness that new standards were needed regarding Indigenous Peoples' rights and bent the original resistance of some states (e.g., the former Yugoslavia) against such standards. Thus, in 1992, the WGIP completed its draft of the UNDRIP and, in 1993, submitted it to the Sub-Commission, which in turn submitted it to the UNCHR. The Commission established its own working group to negotiate the text.

The years 1992 and 1993 were a watershed for the Indigenous Peoples' movement. Apart from the completion of UNDRIP by the WGIP, 1992 was the five hundredth anniversary of the "discovery" of the Americas, and efforts took place to declare the year as an international year of Indigenous Peoples. These efforts did not succeed due to opposition of several states, especially from Africa, that resisted any possible glorification of colonization. Finally, 1993 was the year that became the International Year of the World's Indig-enous People; again, no "s" was added to "People" in the title of the Year because states were still debating this issue: the meaning of using "Peoples," which would also imply recognition of the right to self-determination under international law. At the Rio de Janeiro Conference on Environment and Development in 1992, Indigenous Peoples got deeply involved and achieved high political profile as well as special language in the conference's final docu-ment on Indigenous traditional knowledge and the need for its protection. The WGIP passed on the Draft Declaration on the Rights of Indigenous Peo-ples to the Sub-Commission in 1993. At the World Conference on Human Rights, in 1993, in Vienna, Indigenous Peoples again tried to add the "s" to "Indigenous People," but this was again not accepted by states. What was accepted, however, was the call on the UN to adopt the UNDRIP, to establish a permanent forum on Indigenous issues, and to have a Decade of the World's Indigenous People. All three calls were indeed implemented by the UN: the first Decade of the World's Indigenous People was from 1995 to 2004, the UNDRIP was adopted in 2007, and the UNPFII was established in 2000. As the years were progressing, the high international visibility and achievements of the Indigenous movement were becoming a phenomenon, later to be followed by the 2014 World Conference on Indigenous Peoples, the 2019 International Year of Indigenous Languages, and the International Decade of Indigenous Languages that began in 2022.

2. Role of the UN Commission on Human Rights and Its Working Group on the Draft Declaration (1996–2005)

In order to contextualize the process of adoption of the UNDRIP, it is impor-tant to recall how the UN adopts international human rights instruments. Human rights standard-setting has been one of the basic roles of the Com-mission on Human Rights since the 1940s. The Commission was replaced by the Human Rights Council in 2006, so this role is now part of the Council's work. Some one hundred human rights instruments, both treaties and declarations, have by now been prepared by the UN. Human rights treaties include the Convention on the Elimination of All Forms of Racial Discrimination, the International Covenant on Civil and Political Rights, the International Covenant on Economic, Social and Cultural Rights, the Convention against Torture and Other Cruel, Inhuman or Degrading Treatment or Punishment, the Convention on the Elimination of All Forms of Discrimination against Women, the Convention on the Rights of the Child, the Convention on the Protection of the Rights of All Migrant Workers and Members of Their Families, and the Convention on the Rights of Persons with Disabilities. The UNCHR elaborated some important international human rights declarations as well, starting with the most famous one, the Universal Declaration of Human Rights (UDHR) in 1948, and another famous one about sixty years later, the UNDRIP in 2007.

If we ask why the UN continues to elaborate human rights instruments, we should recall that international law, including human rights law, is dynamic and develops with time. It develops based on politics and possibilities for broad consensus on new areas of interest at the international level. For example, the right to self-determination was not included in the UDHR but became a cornerstone right later, in the time of decolonization, and was included as common Article 1 of the two International Covenants on human rights: the International Covenant of Economic, Social and Cultural Rights and the International Covenant on Civil and Political Rights. Similarly, the rights of children; the rights of Indigenous Peoples; the rights of persons with disabilities; the rights of human rights defenders; the rights of persons belonging to national or ethnic, religious, and linguistic minorities; and other areas of human rights were elaborated later, as ideas fermented and crystallized in the international community. Over the decades the UN has served as a kind of international parliament where these potential standards are debated and eventually adopted after years of elaboration.

The process for the elaboration of international human rights standards usually starts with a UN study. A UN study in this context is a comparative law analysis based on national experiences. NGO and other civil society participation generally provides input in the studies and in the debates. Once studies and working group negotiations are completed over time, eventually an international human rights instrument is expected to come for adoption to the UNGA. In recent decades, it generally takes about ten years to negotiate a human rights instrument at the UN, as it is important to formulate a text that, as much as possible, gathers the consensus of states. Such consensus is especially important for the country-level implementation of international human rights standards, as countries need to feel ownership of the international human rights standards so they promote their application.

The Commission on Human Rights Working Group on the Draft Declaration on the Rights of Indigenous Peoples, an interstate group, met from 1996–2005. Participation of Indigenous Peoples was not as broad as at the WGIP but quite good, as around one hundred Indigenous organizations and other Indigenous entities participated, with the Commission having facilitated the participation of organizations without consultative status with the UN's Economic and Social Council.[22] This was another demonstration of what I call "corrective exceptionalism" regarding Indigenous Peoples' issues at the UN, especially on the issue of Indigenous participation.

At the Commission's Working Group there was fear among Indigenous Peoples that the UNCHR would weaken the draft put forward by the WGIP, and this led Indigenous Peoples to adopt a strong "no-change" position on the Draft Declaration for some years. Later on, this position was modified through an initiative by states and Indigenous Peoples around the last session of the Commission on Human Rights, aimed at facilitating the adoption of the Draft Declaration. A few months later, the Human Rights Council, at its first session in June 2006, adopted the UNDRIP by a vote, with thirty in favor, two against, and twelve abstentions.

3. Role of the UN Permanent Forum on Indigenous Issues

At its session in May 2006, the Permanent Forum had done its own policy advocacy work and recommended the adoption of the UNDRIP by the Human Rights Council at its first session.[23] Given the high political profile of the Forum and the location of its sessions at UN Headquarters in New York, this action was a significant push for the Declaration. Moreover, due to the Forum's bipartisan composition – eight state-nominated and eight Indigenous-nominated members – the UNPFII's pronouncements have a special weight and political impact. It is no wonder that 2006 was the year when a great number of people, more than two thousand, had registered to attend the Forum, showing their strong support for the Declaration as well. Around eighteen hundred people ultimately attended the Forum's session, and this impressive participation had an impact on how negotiations evolved soon after that at the UNGA.

22 UN Commission on Human Rights, Leaflet No. 5: The Draft United Nations Declaration on the Rights of Indigenous Peoples, Office of the UN High Commissioner for Human Rights website, www.ohchr.org/sites/default/files/Documents/Publications/GuideIPleaflet5en.pdf, accessed 16 May 2022. See also report of the Secretary-General on Improving Indigenous Participation at the UN, Ways and Means of Promoting Participation at the United Nations of Indigenous Peoples' Representatives on Issues Affecting Them, UN Doc. A/HRC/21/24 (2 July 2012), pp. 3, 4, 10–12.

23 UN Permanent Forum on Indigenous Issues, Report on the Fifth Session (15–26 May 2006), UN Doc. E/2006/43 (2006), para. 68.

4. *Role of the General Assembly*

The UNDRIP came to the UN General Assembly for action and hopefully adoption in the fall of 2006. However, this did not happen. A number of reasons and actors contributed to this temporary yet dramatic pausing of the Declaration for a few months.

Although African states had barely participated in the processes toward the Draft Declaration for twenty-four years in Geneva, at the 2006 watershed moment in New York, they appeared at the UNGA bringing out various difficulties and disagreements they had. The African Group insisted they could only support the Draft Declaration if thirty-five amendments they proposed could be accepted. This created shockwaves in the international diplomatic environment. From the fall of 2006 to September 2007, Indigenous Peoples undertook an intensive diplomatic campaign to negotiate with members of the African Group. They clarified issues around concerns of the African Group, particularly regarding the right to self-determination and the reasoning for not defining "Indigenous Peoples" in the Declaration. The African Group appeared particularly worried about ethnic conflicts or the breakdown of territorial integrity of sovereign African states, many of which had only recently managed to unify their countries internally, despite tribal conflicts. The General Assembly resolution of 2006, upon the proposal of Namibia, deferred the vote on the Declaration in order to give time to African states to consider their position. The relevant resolution was carried at the UNGA's Third Committee with eighty-two votes in favor, sixty-seven against, and twenty-five abstentions.

The role of Africa has to be understood due to the aforementioned issues. That role subsequently ended up being quite positive and supportive of the Declaration. There was high political level in the involvement of African states: African heads of state were following the negotiations around the Declaration from the beginning of 2007. The constructive and crucial role of the African Commission on Human and Peoples' Rights (ACHPR) and its honoring of its own Working Group of Experts on Indigenous Populations/Communities has to be underlined. In the summer of 2007, the ACHPR issued a Response to the African Group's Draft Aide Memoire on the Declaration.[24] The African Group of Experts also responded to the Draft Aide Memoire:

> In Africa, the term "indigenous peoples or communities" is not aimed at protecting the rights of "first inhabitants that were invaded by foreigners."

---

24 African Group, Draft Aide Memoire, 9 November 2006, http://cendoc.docip.org/collect/cendocdo/index/assoc/HASH0110/1b549795.dir/draft_africangroup.pdf; African Commission on Human and Peoples' Rights, *Advisory Opinion of the African Commission on Human and Peoples' Rights on the United Nations Declaration on the Rights of Indigenous Peoples:*

Nor does the concept aim to create hierarchy among national communities or set aside special rights for certain people. On the contrary, within the African context the term "indigenous peoples" aims to guarantee equal enjoyment of rights and freedoms to some communities that have been left behind. This particular feature of the African continent explains why the term "indigenous peoples" cannot be at the root of the ethnic conflicts or of any breakdown of the Nation State.[25]

It is also very clear that African states did not wish to bear the brunt of blocking the adoption of a human rights instrument, the UNDRIP, that was also part of the decolonization effort. The amendment that made the major difference in the turn of the African Group's position was a specific reference to territorial integrity inserted in the last article, Article 46, of the UNDRIP. In exchange, the African Group dropped most of its requested revisions. Thus the African Group as a whole supported the anticolonial message of UNDRIP.

Article 46, paragraph 1, of the UNDRIP reads:

> 1. Nothing in this Declaration may be interpreted as implying for any State, people, group or person any right to engage in any activity or to perform any act contrary to the Charter of the United Nations or construed as authorizing or encouraging any action which would dismember or impair, totally or in part, the territorial integrity or political unity of sovereign and independent States.

The more general political subtext and context of these last few months of negotiations on the Declaration are also important to take into account in the analysis. For example, the role of Canada was broadly discussed in the UN corridors. Canadian civil society was criticizing the government for its position of resisting the adoption of the Declaration and for trying to convince African states to do the same.

The role of the Group of 77 (G77) and its position toward the new Human Rights Council in 2006 is also important to take into account. Established in 1964 and by now composed of 134 countries, the G77 was created to

---

Adopted by the African Commission on Human and Peoples' Rights at Its 41st Ordinary Session Held in May 2007 in Accra, Ghana (Banjul: The Gambia, 2007), archived 11 October 2022 at the Internet Archive, www.achpr.org/public/Document/file/Any/un_advisory_opinion_idp_eng.pdf.
25 Response Note to the Draft Aide Memoire of the African Group on the UN Declaration on the Rights of Indigenous Peoples, presented by an African group of experts, 21 March 2007, www.iwgia.org/es/documents-and-publications/documents/publications-pdfs/english-publications/138-response-note-to-african-group-final-eng/file.html.

promote the collective interests of developing countries. The Group wanted to assert the authority of the UNGA over the new Human Rights Council, instead of accepting a strong autonomy of this new body. In other words, there was some opposition to the Human Rights Council that the G77 expressed by asserting the role and authority of the UNGA *over* the Human Rights Council; such authority would be exercised by having the UNGA get involved in the substance of UNDRIP at this late stage. This point of the G77 was unrelated to the UNDRIP as such or not fully related to UNDRIP.

The role of Indigenous Peoples' diplomacy was extraordinary in this last phase. Regional representatives of the Global Indigenous Caucus and other senior Indigenous leaders were sent to New York in the summer of 2007 and actively advocated for the Declaration. An important role was played by Native American representatives in the diplomatic efforts to convince African and other states. The diplomacy of a number of states was also important. In the last few months before the adoption of the Declaration a positive role was played by the Philippines, Mexico, and Guatemala. In closed consultations among delegations in the summer of 2007, it was interesting to learn that some countries with well-known negative positions, such as Canada, the United States, and Russia, were not accepted in the room by other delegations. Passions were running high on various sides, but the conclusion of efforts from many people in many quarters were positive when, on 13 September 2007, the UN General Assembly finally adopted the UN Declaration on the Rights of Indigenous Peoples,[26] with 144 votes in favor, 4 against (Australia, Canada, New Zealand, and the United States), and 11 abstentions. The four countries that voted against as well as Colombia and Samoa, who had abstained, have since declared their support for the Declaration.

To convey some of the atmosphere in the General Assembly Hall on the historic day of the adoption of UNDRIP on 13 September 2007, I will share some moments I witnessed. Many Indigenous leaders from around the world were there. When the moment came for the actual adoption of the Declaration, people were holding their breath and their tears. When the voting result appeared on the electronic screen on the wall, people could not even wait for the General Assembly President to actually announce the result. A cry came out of peoples' mouths spontaneously, and people clapped – both Indigenous delegates and state delegates clapped. There was exhilaration in realizing the meaning of this moment. The media was incredibly responsive. The news spread around the world, and messages of congratulations continued to be exchanged around the clock. It had taken twenty-five years of negotiation. Now, the UNDRIP is here.

---

26 UN General Assembly, Resolution 61/295, UN Declaration on the Rights of Indigenous Peoples, UN Doc. A/RES/61/295 (13 September 2007), www.un.org/development/desa/indigenouspeoples/wp-content/uploads/sites/19/2018/11/UNDRIP_E_web.pdf.

D. Conceptual Contributions of Indigenous Peoples to Human Rights Norms

During the twenty-five years of drafting of the UNDRIP, Indigenous representatives put forward a number of concepts that were not yet accepted as part of human rights and were eventually included in the text of the Declaration. Most or all of them were interpretations of already proclaimed human rights, indicating how such human rights apply to Indigenous Peoples. This was not necessarily a predictable result but a victory of the Indigenous Peoples' movement, of the ways in which Indigenous Peoples represented themselves and participated at the international fora. They took the time, made the sustained efforts, and adopted educational and convincing strategies to counterbalance the power inequality between them and states at the UN.

More specifically, through their involvement at the international level, Indigenous Peoples contributed at least five conceptual areas to international human rights norms applicable to them, which actually revolutionized these norms.

The first new concept introduced by Indigenous leaders in international human rights doctrine is that land rights for Indigenous Peoples are beyond individual property rights. They are in fact collective human rights of Indigenous Peoples, given the primordial spiritual, cultural, and material relations of Indigenous Peoples to their lands and territories for their survival *as* peoples.

The second concept Indigenous leaders introduced is that the right to self-determination is fundamental for Indigenous Peoples as a human right, including respect for their own governance systems and their right to free, prior, and informed consent.

The third concept Indigenous leaders introduced is spiritual rights as human rights. Spiritual rights include but also go beyond freedom of religion. One could say that spiritual rights reinterpret freedom of religion. They also include the recognition of Indigenous Peoples' spiritual relation to the land. Indigenous Peoples have repeatedly explained that their ways of seeing the world do not necessarily all fit under the term "religion" and have insisted that "spirituality" be included in UNDRIP, which became the case.

The fourth new conceptual contribution of Indigenous Peoples is the articulation of a rich body of cultural rights, as a response to systemic discrimination against their cultures and even ethnocide that many Indigenous Peoples have suffered – that is, the attempted erasure of groups through the destruction of their cultures.[27]

---

27 Elsa Stamatopoulou, "Taking Cultural Rights Seriously: The Vision of the UN Declaration on the Rights of Indigenous Peoples," in *Reflections on the UN Declaration on the Rights of Indigenous Peoples*, ed. Stephen Allen and Alexandra Xanthaki (Oxford: Hart Publishing, 2011).

1. The Controversy Over Collective Rights

The fifth new conceptual innovation is that collective rights are human rights and that a precondition for the individual rights and dignity of Indigenous persons is the respect of the rights of the Indigenous collectivity. This point created a controversy over time, not only within the context of the binary *individual vs. collective rights* but also as an ideological, theoretical contestation of whether collective rights are human rights at all when they do not trample upon individual rights.

Indigenous Peoples have contributed various concepts to international human rights norms over the decades, and additional analysis is offered in the section on the role of research and academia in Indigenous affairs (Section J). If we ask the question, "What are the specific, innovative areas that Indigenous Peoples have made us think about in the field of human rights?", the most comprehensive answer that would group together many issues would probably be *breaking the taboo of the dominant – till recent times – human rights doctrine and recognizing collective human rights, in addition to individual human rights.*

The historic UNDRIP crystallized the recognition of collective human rights when it was adopted by the UN in 2007, after about twenty-five years of negotiations between Indigenous Peoples and states through the intermediary of the United Nations – a unique and unprecedented process.

The main human rights doctrine in the West has traditionally seen human rights as only individual, placing as the central and ultimate goal the protection of the most vulnerable entity in society, the individual human being. This is no doubt a laudable and indispensable human rights goal that continues to hold in the international human rights instruments and in the UN's practice of advocacy and monitoring. However, at the same time, there has been systematic refusal on the part of the West to recognize collective or group rights as part of human rights. This point has been highly politicized over the decades. Let us say immediately that the negation of collective rights as human rights has not been the case for other parts of the world, especially Africa, as expressed, for example, in the very title of the African Charter of Human and Peoples' Rights.

The seminal Universal Declaration of Human Rights negotiated within the UN and adopted in 1948 recognized only individual rights. However, in the time of decolonization that followed and swept the world with the creation of new states coming into being, the right to self-determination was added to the panoply of human rights: it became common Article 1 of the International Covenant on Economic, Social and Cultural Rights and of the International Covenant on Civil and Political Rights, both adopted in 1966. The right to self-determination is of course the collective right *par excellence*, although it has also expanded its normative impact to the individual, especially due to the advocacy of the Indigenous Peoples' rights movement and the women's movement.

If we go a bit back in time, we can expose some inconsistencies in the positions taken by states on this issue of individual vs. collective human rights. States do not tend to reveal, except rarely, their real reasons for their positions, but they use various, often lofty, arguments to which, especially the legal profession contributes.

A first inconsistency appears in 1948: the Convention on the Prevention and Punishment of the Crime of Genocide was adopted by the UN on 9 December 1948, one day before the Universal Declaration of Human Rights.[28] The Convention defined genocide in Article 2 as

> any of the following acts committed with intent to destroy, in whole or in part, a national, ethnical, racial or religious group, as such:
>
> (a) Killing members of the group;
> (b) Causing serious bodily or mental harm to members of the group;
> (c) Deliberately inflicting on the group conditions of life calculated to bring about its physical destruction in whole or in part;
> (d) Imposing measures intended to prevent births within the group;
> (e) Forcibly transferring children of the group to another group.

In other words, the very first human rights treaty of the UN era recognized the right of groups to survive as such and to be protected from genocide, the most odious crime. But somehow this was forgotten in the scheme of things by states when they embarked, after 1948, to codify human rights in what are now some one hundred international human rights instruments, both declarations and treaties.

The UNDRIP is the most recent addition to this code of international human rights. The exceptional processes that led to the contestation of a solely individual nature of human rights during the preparation of the UNDRIP are being discussed in this book, as is the special and extraordinary participation of Indigenous Peoples in the UN processes that led to UNDRIP.

Three major collective rights are recognized in the Declaration, and they also apply as individual rights: the right to self-determination; the right to lands, territories, and resources; and cultural human rights.

Will Kymlicka points out that a liberal democracy's most basic commitment is to the freedom and equality of its individual citizens regardless of their group membership. For some, "group-differentiated rights" (Kymlicka's

---

28 UN General Assembly, Resolution 260 A (III), Convention on the Prevention and Punishment of the Crime of Genocide (9 December 1948), www.ohchr.org/en/instruments-mechanisms/instruments/convention-prevention-and-punishment-crime-genocide.

term for collective rights) seem to reflect a collectivist or communitarian out-look rather than the liberal belief in individual freedom and equality, and this idea creates erroneous assumptions about the relationship between individual rights and group-differentiated rights or collective rights – the idea that these rights oppose each other or are in tension with each other.[29] This debate is sometimes known under the rubric of cultural relativism vs. universality regarding human rights.

Kymlicka makes an interesting distinction regarding collective rights: "external protections vs internal restrictions." This useful distinction can help clarify questions around collective rights. Kymlicka points out that we need to distinguish between two kinds of claims that an ethnic or national group might make. The first involves the claim of a group against its own members ("internal restrictions"), and the second involves the claim of the group against the larger society ("external protections"). Both of these, he points out, are labeled as or are known as "collective rights." External pro-tections, he says, such as land rights, language rights, and special represen-tation rights, are needed to put various groups on a more equal footing by reducing the extent to which the smaller group is vulnerable to the larger. Kymlicka proceeds to say that while external protections are acceptable, internal restrictions are not.[30]

In human rights language, we can say that if the internationally proclaimed human rights are curtailed by a group, this should not be accepted by the group's leadership or by the state. The UNDRIP says just that. However, one fundamental philosophical point needs to be added, apart from the debate of what libertarians think and what communitarians or collectivists think; and this point is the perspective that the human rights doctrine contributes to this question. First of all, the terminology "collective rights" will continue to be used, so it is important for us to analyze it from a human rights perspec-tive. Some collective rights are not *human* rights – for example, class action at courts, where many cases may be combined and heard together. There is a clear human rights aspect of collective rights for Indigenous Peoples, and in that sense, we should speak of collective *human* rights. Collective rights are human rights for Indigenous Peoples because they go to the core of their human dignity; they aim to promote their survival as human groups, as cul-tures, and often, even their physical survival. If their rights as a group are not protected, then individual rights of Indigenous persons are also threat-ened. For example, the recognition of land rights for Indigenous Peoples is a primordial condition for their survival, culturally, physically, and spiritu-ally. Their land, however, is vulnerable to external economic and political

29 Will Kymlicka, *Multicultural Citizenship: A Liberal Theory of Minority Rights* (Oxford: Clarendon Press, 1995), 34–35.
30 Kymlicka, *Multicultural Citizenship*, 35–36.

pressures; it must therefore be protected as a collective human right so that Indigenous Peoples as groups and as persons are not deprived of this fundamental element of their existence.

During the negotiations on the then Draft UNDRIP, the opposition to any recognition of collective rights as human rights was led intransigently for some time by the United Kingdom. Even at the final stages before the adoption of the Declaration, the United Kingdom at one point opined that since, in their view, collective rights are not human rights, references to human rights in the Declaration would need to be deleted.[31] The Declaration outlines the borders between individual and group rights by clearly placing its norms within the overall normative framework of internationally recognized human rights.

Article 34 of the Declaration states that

> Indigenous peoples have the right to promote, develop and maintain their institutional structures and their distinctive customs, traditions procedures and practices and, in the cases where they exist, juridical systems or customs, *in accordance with internationally recognized human rights standards.*[32]

Article 46 of the Declaration states

> 2. In the exercise of the rights enunciated in the present Declaration, human rights and fundamental freedoms of all shall be respected. The exercise of the rights set forth in this Declaration shall be subject only to such limitations as are determined by law and in accordance with international human rights obligations. Any such limitations shall be non-discriminatory and strictly necessary solely for the purpose of securing due recognition and respect for the rights and freedoms of others and for meeting the just and most compelling requirements of a democratic society.
> 3. The provisions set forth in this Declaration shall be interpreted *in accordance with the principles of justice, democracy, respect for human rights, equality, non-discrimination, good governance and good faith.*[33]

These articles indicate that an Indigenous people or community must respect the human rights of individuals within it. In addition, a group cannot oblige an individual within it to exercise his or her rights as an Indigenous person;

---

31 Author's personal information.
32 UN Doc. A/RES/61/295. Emphasis added.
33 Emphasis added.

in other words, a group cannot impose indigeneity on an individual. This is a matter of choice, with the repercussions that such a choice may have on membership or citizenship in an Indigenous community or nation. The duties that an Indigenous people's community would require of its members must comply with international human rights standards. It is well-known that Indigenous leaders who participated in the negotiations of the UNDRIP over the years were well aware of and agreed to this principle early on.

An excellent publication from the International Indigenous Women's Forum (FIMI), *Mairin Iwanka Raya: Indigenous Women Stand against Violence*, gives a clear vision and espouses the demand for respect of internationally recognized human rights of Indigenous women, while adding their collective human rights, including the rights to land and to self-determination.[34]

The UNDRIP confirms an *ad hoc* method of solving possible conflicts by insisting that Indigenous rights are firmly within the wider human rights system and, as such, they are subject to the same restrictions (no fewer restrictions, but no more either) as other human rights. Preambular paragraph 1 of the Declaration links the UNDRIP with the "purposes and principles of the Charter of the United Nations," while Article 1 links the text with the UN Charter, the Universal Declaration of Human Rights, and international human rights law.[35]

* * *

In other international areas of norm-creation and policy, such as that of development, Indigenous Peoples have also been making significant conceptual contributions, thanks to their continuing engagement to explain, educate, advocate, and convince the non-Indigenous world.

Each of the aforementioned five conceptual areas contributed to human rights doctrine by Indigenous Peoples could take volumes to discuss to the extent they deserve, and this would be beyond the purview of this book. After long debates over twenty-five years between states and Indigenous Peoples, these five conceptual areas, new to the then mainstream international human rights framework, were embedded in the UNDRIP adopted by the

---

34 International Indigenous Women's Forum, *Mairin Iwanka Raya: Indigenous Women Stand against Violence* (New York: FIMI/IIWF, 2006), www.fimi-iiwf.org/en/biblioteca-propias/mairin-iwanka-raya-indigenous-women-stand-against-violence/.

35 Alexandra Xanthaki, "Limitations to Indigenous Autonomy" (paper presented at the Expert Seminar on Indigenous Peoples' Languages and Cultures, Brunel Law School, Uxbridge, 8–9 March 2012). Preambular paragraph 1 of the Declaration reads: "The General Assembly, Guided by the purposes and principles of the Charter of the United Nations, and good faith in the fulfilment of the obligations assumed by States in accordance with the Charter." Article 1 of the UNDRIP reads: "Indigenous peoples have the right to the full enjoyment, as a collective or as individuals, of all human rights and fundamental freedoms as recognized in the Charter of the United Nations, the Universal Declaration of Human Rights and International Human Rights Law."

UNGA in 2007. These concepts opened new ways of defining Indigenous Peoples' rights and possibly enriching and reinterpreting the human rights of all, especially of other discriminated groups in society. Human rights advocates working in areas other than Indigenous Peoples' rights have been wondering and analyzing how Indigenous Peoples have achieved this normative enrichment in the international arena. Such analysis certainly continues to be useful. At the same time, it is crucial to keep in mind that the Indigenous Peoples' international movement is many decades long; it is global, methodical, committed, and sustainable in terms of the human and financial resources devoted to it. These and other characteristics are not always present in the struggles for justice in other areas. Human rights advocates can certainly learn from each other's experiences, and opportunities for exchange and mutual learning should continue to be organized at various levels.

E.   Significance and Content of the UNDRIP

The adoption of the Declaration displayed strong support for Indigenous Peoples' rights internationally and has important legal, moral, and political significance. The Declaration is a gesture of states and Indigenous Peoples trying to reconcile with their painful histories and resolving to move forward together on a path of human rights, justice, peace, and development for all. By adopting the Declaration, states admitted that their unjust regimes impacted Indigenous Peoples and that they wish to move forward in a spirit of cooperation. The political importance of the Declaration today is that it is on the basis of the Declaration that new, respectful relationships can be established.

More than 476 million Indigenous people live in some ninety countries in all continents, often facing marginalization and extreme poverty.[36] Legally, the Declaration is important because, at the normative level, it establishes the rule of equality and affirms the right to lands, territories, and resources; the right to self-determination; and cultural rights. It establishes how these rights are to be applied for Indigenous Peoples. Even though the Declaration is not a treaty, its language is that of a treaty (for example, using "shall" instead of "should" in the text). The Declaration outlaws discrimination; establishes significant measures that promote respect for Indigenous Peoples' lands and natural resources, including subsistence rights; and recognizes that peoples deprived of their means of subsistence and development are entitled to just and fair redress. The adoption of the Declaration requires the inclusion of culture in development policies and encourages the building of genuine partnerships with Indigenous Peoples in order to fight poverty and achieve a

---

36 International Labor Organization, *Implementing the ILO Indigenous and Tribal Peoples Convention No. 169*, www.ilo.org/wcmsp5/groups/public/–dgreports/–dcomm/–publ/documents/publication/wcms_735607.pdf.

truly inclusive development. The UNPFII and the other Indigenous-related UN mechanisms, as well as the whole UN system, are expected to play an important role in promoting the implementation of the Declaration alongside states and Indigenous Peoples.

The Chairperson of the UNPFII in 2007, Victoria Tauli-Corpuz, Igorot leader from the Philippines, shared her insights, marking the day of the adoption of the Declaration:[37]

> Through the adoption of the Declaration on the Rights of Indigenous Peoples, the United Nations marks a major victory in its long history towards developing and establishing international human rights standards.
>
> It marks a major victory for Indigenous Peoples who actively took part in crafting this Declaration. . . .
>
> The 13th of September 2007 will be remembered as an international human rights day for the Indigenous Peoples of the world, a day that the United Nations and its Member States, together with Indigenous Peoples, reconciled with past painful histories and decided to march into the future on the path of human rights. . . .
>
> I hail representatives of Indigenous Peoples who patiently exerted extraordinary efforts for more than two decades to draft and negotiate the Declaration. . . .
>
> . . . This magnificent endeavour which brought you to sit together with us, Indigenous Peoples, to listen to our cries and struggles and to hammer out words which will respond to these is unprecedented.
>
> The long time devoted to the drafting of the Declaration by the United Nations stemmed from the conviction that Indigenous Peoples have rights as distinct peoples and that a constructive dialogue among all would eventually lead to a better understanding of diverse worldviews and cultures, a realignment of positions and, finally, to the building of partnerships between states and Indigenous Peoples for a more just and sustainable world.
>
> For the UN Permanent Forum on Indigenous Issues, the Declaration will become the major foundation and framework in implementing its mandate . . . It will further enflesh and facilitate the operationalization of the human rights-based approach to development as it applies to Indigenous Peoples . . .
>
> The United Nations Permanent Forum on Indigenous Issues is explicitly asked in Article 42 of the Declaration to promote respect for and full

---

37 Statement of Victoria Tauli-Corpuz, Chair of the UN Permanent Forum on Indigenous Issues on the Occasion of the Adoption of the UN Declaration on the Rights of Indigenous Peoples, 61st session of the UN General Assembly (13 September 2007), www.un.org/esa/socdev/unpfii/documents/2016/Docs-updates/STATEMENT-VICTORIA-TAULI-CORPUZ-IDWIP-2007.pdf.

application of the provisions of the Declaration and follow-up the effectiveness of this Declaration . . .

This is a Declaration which sets the minimum international standards for the protection and promotion of the rights of Indigenous Peoples. Therefore, existing and future laws, policies, and programs on [Indigenous Peoples] will have to be redesigned and shaped to be consistent with this standard. . . .

I call on governments, the UN system, Indigenous Peoples and civil society at large to rise to the historic task before us and make the UN Declaration on the Rights of Indigenous Peoples a living document for the common future of humanity.

The ultimate test of the Declaration's impact will obviously be proven in practice, in terms of how states and Indigenous Peoples as well as the UN system, the rest of the international community, and nonstate actors, including corporations, use and implement it. But to those who say that the Declaration is difficult to implement because "It is just a Declaration and not a treaty," I would say that the manner in which the Declaration was adopted by the United Nations over a long period of time gives it a different status from that of other international declarations that are viewed as "soft law." Essentially, the Declaration was the result of negotiations between Indigenous Peoples and states under the mediation of the United Nations. The length of the negotiations, more than twenty years, the tremendous diplomatic efforts of states and Indigenous Peoples to reach agreement, and the goal of consensus that underpinned the negotiations until the very last minute illustrate the special status of this Declaration. The human rights contained in the Declaration are not new but are established in other preexisting sources of international law, whether normative instruments, jurisprudence, international practice and custom, or reputable academic writings. The Declaration sets high standards and has an ambitious vision in terms of what justice is in today's world – and so do the other international human rights instruments. The high standards of the preexisting international human rights instruments galvanize the efforts of all to strive toward the implementation of those standards. And the same, we expect, will be the case with the Declaration. As the UNPFII states in its General Comment on Article 42 of the Declaration, the purpose of the Declaration is to constitute the legal basis for all activities on Indigenous issues; the Declaration is the most universal, comprehensive, and fundamental instrument on Indigenous Peoples' rights.[38]

---

38 UN Permanent Forum on Indigenous Issues, Report on the Eighth Session (18–29 May 2009), UN Doc. E/2009/43 (2009), Annex, para. 1, 6, https://digitallibrary.un.org/record/54456?ln=en.
  See also para. 6–13, the section entitled "The Legal Character of the Declaration."

What the member states of the UN did not achieve in 1948, while preparing the Universal Declaration of Human Rights and the Convention on the Prevention and Punishment of the Crime of Genocide, they were able to accomplish in 2007 by adopting the UNDRIP and boldly recognizing Indigenous Peoples' rights, including cultural rights – namely, their human right to exist as peoples and as cultures. The Declaration is about building bridges among Indigenous and non-Indigenous communities and fostering inclusive, pluricultural, democratic societies.[39]

1. What Is the Declaration About?

This segment provides a brief reference to the content of the Declaration. Any detailed analysis of the Declaration would require a book or several volumes, and this is beyond the purview of this publication.[40] The Declaration does not establish new rights, but it is a detailing, an interpretation of existing rights as they apply to Indigenous individuals and collectivities. The Declaration addresses both individual and collective rights; land rights; cultural rights, including language and other aspects of identity; rights to education, health, and employment; and others. The text says Indigenous Peoples have the right to fully enjoy as collectivities or as individuals, all human rights and fundamental freedoms recognized in the UN Charter, the Universal Declaration of Human Rights, and human rights law overall. Indigenous Peoples and individuals are free and equal to all other peoples and individuals and have the right to be free from any kind of discrimination in the exercise of their rights, in particular that based on their origin or identity. Indigenous Peoples have the right to self-determination. They have the right to maintain and strengthen their distinct political, legal, economic, social, and cultural institutions, while retaining their rights to participate fully, if they choose to, in the political, economic, social, and cultural life of the state.

The Declaration has three pillars: the right to self-determination; the right to lands, territories, and resources; and cultural rights. A cluster of articles is devoted to each of these rights. These three pillars are interlinked and support each other; in fact, they support the continuing existence and well-being of Indigenous Peoples.

---

39 This paragraph is based on Stamatopoulou, "Taking Cultural Rights Seriously," 411–412.

40 See, for example, Mattias Åhrén, *Indigenous Peoples' Status in the International Legal System* (Oxford: Oxford University Press, 2016); Sheryl Lightfoot, *Global Indigenous Politics: A Subtle Revolution* (London: Routledge, 2016); Alexandra Xanthaki, *Indigenous Rights and United Nations Standards: Self-Determination, Culture and Land* (Cambridge: Cambridge University Press, 2007); S. James Anaya, *Indigenous Peoples in International Law*, 2nd ed. (Oxford: Oxford University Press, 2004).

a.   The Right to Self-Determination

Nine preambular and fifteen operative paragraphs of UNDRIP deal with consultation, partnership, and participation of Indigenous Peoples in a democratic polity. The text recognizes that Indigenous Peoples have the right to self-determination. By that right, they can freely determine their political status and pursue their economic, cultural, and social development. They have the right to maintain and strengthen their distinct political, legal, economic, social, and cultural institutions, while retaining their rights to participate fully, if they so choose, in the political, economic, social, and cultural life of the state.

Given the focus on self-determination in this research, it is useful to briefly recall the historical perspective of this right. The UN Charter, in Article 1 describes the purposes of the organization. Paragraph 2 of Article 1 states one of those purposes:

> To develop friendly relations among nations based on respect for the principle of equal rights and self-determination of peoples, and to take other appropriate measures to strengthen universal peace.[41]

Yet even before the UN Charter included the concept of self-determination, Indigenous nations were, and saw themselves as, sovereign and self-determining. In fact, colonizing states saw that as well, and while trying to conquer, marginalize, and destroy Indigenous Peoples, when they could not do so, those states were establishing government-to-government relations with them, through treaties and other arrangements.

The UN era saw the development of the concept of self-determination. It signaled the time of decolonization soon after the organization's creation. Self-determination and sovereignty became concepts much cherished by the newly independent countries.

The famous 1960 Declaration on the Granting of Independence to Colonial Countries and Peoples set the parameters of the concept of self-determination and linked it closely to human rights. It also proclaimed self-determination as a human right:[42]

> 1.   The subjection of peoples to alien subjugation, domination and exploitation constitutes a denial of fundamental human rights, is contrary to the Charter of the United Nations and is an impediment to the promotion of world peace and co-operation.

---

41 UN Charter, 26 June 1945, www.un.org/en/about-us/un-charter/.

42 UN General Assembly, Resolution 1514 (XV), Declaration on the Granting of Independence to Colonial Countries and Peoples, A/RES/1514(XV) (14 December 1960), www.ohchr.org/en/instruments-mechanisms/instruments/declaration-granting-independence-colonial-countries-and-peoples.

At the same time, it is interesting to remember that the 1948 Universal Declaration of Human Rights did not include the right to self-determination. It is clear that in 1948 states were not yet ready to recognize this right nor to decolonize the world.

International law, including human rights law, is dynamic. This allows for the continuing development and refinement of concepts. As the international society and international relations evolve, it becomes possible, through often robust debates, to establish new international human rights standards. It therefore became possible, in 1966, to establish the right to self-determination as a universal human right, as the collective right *par excellence*, as in common Article 1 of the International Covenant on Economic, Social and Cultural Rights and the International Covenant on Civil and Political Rights, which states that:

> 1. All peoples have the right to self-determination; by virtue of that right they freely determine their political status and freely pursue their economic, social and cultural development.[43]

Significantly, the 1966 International Covenants added one paragraph which is very important for Indigenous Peoples: it is about natural resources and subsistence rights. The paragraph reads:

> 2. All peoples may, for their own ends, freely dispose of their natural wealth and resources without prejudice to any obligations arising out of international economic co-operation, based upon the principle of mutual benefit, and international law. In no case may a people be deprived of its own means of subsistence.

Despite these innovative and significant treaty provisions, states' defensiveness has led to relatively limited discussions of the right to self-determination at the UN, limiting them over the years mostly to issues of foreign occupation. The 2021 study on the right to self-determination by the UN EMRIP calls this right the most controversial and contested right in international law.[44] The most (and only) comprehensive debates on self-determination at

---

43 UN General Assembly, Resolution 2200A (XXI), International Covenant on Economic, Social and Cultural Rights, UN Doc. A/RES/2200(XII) (16 December 1966), www.ohchr.org/en/instruments-mechanisms/instruments/international-covenant-economic-social-and-cultural-rights.

44 UN Expert Mechanism on the Rights of Indigenous Peoples, Efforts to Implement the Rights of Indigenous Peoples: Indigenous Peoples and the Right to Self-Determination, UN Doc. A/HRC/48/75 (4 August 2021), para. 7; for a brief history, see para. 3–7. The report also provides various examples of the exercise of the right to self-determination by Indigenous Peoples in different parts of the world, as well as the challenges Indigenous Peoples face in that regard.

the UN, after the 1950s/early 1960s discussions on decolonization, have been held in the context of the preparation of the UNDRIP.

Article 3 of UNDRIP uses the same words on the right to self-determination as the common Article 1 of the two International Covenants:

> Indigenous peoples have the right to self-determination. By virtue of that right they freely determine their political status and freely pursue their economic, social and cultural development.[45]

Articles 4 and 5 read:

> Indigenous peoples, in exercising their right to self-determination, have the right to autonomy or self-government in matters relating to their internal and local affairs, as well as ways and means for financing their autonomous functions.
>
> Indigenous peoples have the right to maintain and strengthen their distinct political, legal, economic, social and cultural institutions, while retaining their right to participate fully, if they so choose, in the political, economic, social and cultural life of the State.[46]

In fact, the whole text of the Declaration can be seen as imbued with the concept of self-determination, as interpreting it and stating how it applies to Indigenous Peoples in various ways: autonomy, including cultural autonomy; the education sector; self-identification; the requirement of free, prior, and informed consent for a number of issues; development; and other areas.

Manifestations of external self-determination include the right of Indigenous Peoples, "in particular those divided by international borders, to maintain and develop contacts, relations and cooperation, including activities for spiritual, cultural, political, economic and social purposes, with their own members as well as other peoples across borders."[47] External self-determination may also include Indigenous Peoples' "right to determine their place in the international community," to participate in the international Indigenous movement, and to participate at the United Nations and other international fora "where they can express their worldviews and perspectives on the international level, external to their own communities."[48]

---

45 www.un.org/development/desa/indigenouspeoples/wp-content/uploads/sites/19/2018/11/UNDRIP_E_web.pdf, accessed 11 January 2024.
46 Idem.
47 UN Doc. A/HRC/48/75, para. 16; UN Doc. A/RES/61/295, article 36 (1).
48 UN Doc. A/HRC/48/75, para. 17.

Among its recommendations in the aforementioned 2021 study on Indigenous Peoples' right to self-determination, EMRIP included the following, relevant to the focus of this book:

> 74. States should ensure the effective involvement of indigenous peoples in international forums, including in non-indigenous-specific bodies, such as the United Nations human rights treaty bodies. Indigenous peoples should be encouraged to participate actively in regional and international standard-setting bodies to litigate on the right to self-determination in order to contribute to the ongoing development of international human rights law. States should establish a process, with the equal participation of States and indigenous peoples, to consider ways to enhance the participation of indigenous peoples in the work of the Human Rights Council. . . .
>
> 76. Without prejudice to the ongoing consultative process referred to in General Assembly resolution 71/321, aimed at enhancing the participation of the representatives and institutions of indigenous peoples in United Nations meetings, States should support ongoing efforts to ensure the meaningful, effective and enhanced participation of indigenous peoples in the United Nations through their own representative institutions in all meetings relevant to them. In particular, it is important to include indigenous peoples in meetings of the Human Rights Council on issues affecting them.[49]

b. The Right to Lands, Territories, and Resources

The UNDRIP devotes many articles to the right to lands, territories, and resources: four preambular paragraphs (6, 7, 10, and 12), and nine operative paragraphs (8, 10, 25–30, and 32). Article 8 refers to the prohibition of forced assimilation and destruction of Indigenous cultures and links it to the effect of dispossessing Indigenous Peoples of their lands, territories, or resources. Article 10 is about the prohibition of forced removal from their lands or territories and provides that no relocation shall take place without the free, prior, and informed consent of the Indigenous Peoples concerned. Article 25 is about the preservation of the spiritual relationship of Indigenous Peoples to the land.

---

49 UN Doc. A/HRC/48/75.

Article 26 is the bold declaration of Indigenous Peoples' rights to land:

1. Indigenous peoples have the right to the lands, territories and resources which they have traditionally owned, occupied or otherwise used or acquired.
2. Indigenous peoples have the right to own, use, develop and control the lands, territories and resources that they possess by reason of traditional ownership or other traditional occupation or use, as well as those which they have otherwise acquired.
3. States shall give legal recognition and protection to these lands, territories and resources. Such recognition shall be conducted with due respect to the customs, traditions and land tenure systems of the indigenous peoples concerned.[50]

Article 27 is about the recognition of Indigenous land tenure systems, a demonstration of support for legal pluralism. Article 28 is about redress for land taken (restitution and compensation), and the article points out, in paragraph 2, that "unless otherwise freely agreed upon by the peoples concerned, compensation shall take the form of lands, territories and resources equal in quality, size and legal status or of monetary compensation or other appropriate redress." Article 29 is about the right to conservation and protection of the environment and the productive capacity of Indigenous Peoples' lands, territories, and resources – and protection from hazardous materials. Article 30 is about the prohibition of military action on Indigenous lands, unless the people concerned have been consulted through their representative institutions, prior to using their lands or territories for military activities. Article 32 is about the right of Indigenous Peoples to determine and develop priorities and strategies for the development and use of their lands, with the free, prior, and informed consent (FPIC) of their own representative institutions.

The Declaration, in Article 20, recognizes subsistence rights and recognizes that Indigenous Peoples "deprived of their means of subsistence and development are entitled to just and fair redress."

c. Cultural Rights

Seventeen of the forty-six articles of the Declaration deal with Indigenous cultures and how to protect and promote them, including by respecting Indigenous Peoples' direct inputs in decision-making and providing resources for education in Indigenous languages and other culture-related areas. The word "identity" is mentioned in Article 2 (the right to be free from any discrimination

---

50 www.un.org/development/desa/indigenouspeoples/wp-content/uploads/sites/19/2018/11/
   UNDRIP_E_web.pdf, accessed 11 January 2024.

based on Indigenous origin or identity) and Article 33 (the right of Indigenous Peoples to determine their own identity or membership in accordance with their customs and traditions). The word "culture" or "cultural" is mentioned no fewer than eight times in the preamble and sixteen times in the articles of the Declaration (Articles 3, 5, 7, 11, 12, 14, 15, 16, 31, 32, and 36). Significantly, around fifteen of the forty-six articles deal with governance and participation in a democratic polity; in other words, they are crucial process and substantive rights via which the culture and identity of Indigenous Peoples will have an impact in the public sphere, in relations with the state.[51]

One can find the cultural rights angle in each article of the Declaration: the right of Indigenous Peoples and individuals to be free from any kind of discrimination, in particular that based on Indigenous origin or identity (Art. 2); the right to self-determination, by virtue of which Indigenous Peoples should "freely determine their political status and freely pursue their economic, social and cultural development" (Art. 3); "the right to maintain and strengthen their distinct cultural institutions, while retaining their rights to participate fully, if they so choose, in the cultural life of the state" (Art. 5); the collective right to live as distinct peoples (Art. 7); the right "not to be subjected to forced assimilation or destruction of their culture," including mechanisms of prevention and redress (art. 8); the right to belong to an Indigenous community or nation "in accordance with the traditions and customs of the community or nation concerned" (Art. 9); the right to practice "and revitalize their cultural traditions and customs" and to receive redress for "cultural, intellectual, religious and spiritual property taken without their free, prior and informed consent" (Art. 11); the right "to manifest, practice, develop and teach their spiritual and religious traditions, customs and ceremonies; . . . to maintain, protect and have access to their religious and cultural sites; . . . to use and control their ceremonial objects" and to have their human remains repatriated (Art. 12); the right to revitalize and "transmit to future generations their histories, languages, oral traditions, philosophies" and to "designate their own names for communities, places and persons"; and the obligation of states to ensure that Indigenous Peoples "can understand and be understood in political, legal and administrative proceedings" (Art. 13); the right to "establish and control their education systems and institutions providing education in their own language, in a manner appropriate to their cultural methods of teaching and learning;" and the right "to have access, when possible, to an education in their own culture and provided in their own language" (Art. 14); the right to have "the dignity and diversity of their cultures . . . reflected in education and public information" (Art. 15); the right "to establish their own media in their own languages and

---

51 Stamatopoulou, "Taking Cultural Rights Seriously," 389.

have equal access to all forms of non-indigenous media" (Art. 16); the right to "their traditional medicines and to maintain their health practices" (Art. 24); the right to maintain, control, protect and develop their cultural heritage, traditional knowledge and traditional cultural expressions, as well as the manifestations of their sciences, technologies and cultures, including human and genetic resources, seeds, medicines, knowledge of the properties of fauna and flora, oral traditions, literatures, designs, sports and traditional games and visual and performing arts; they also have "the right to their intellectual property over such cultural heritage, traditional knowledge and traditional cultural expressions" (Art. 31); the right to "determine their own identity or membership in accordance with their customs and traditions" (Art. 33); the right to "their distinctive customs, spirituality, traditions, procedures, practices and, in the cases where they exist, juridical systems or customs, in accordance with international human rights standards" (Art. 34); and the right of Indigenous Peoples "divided by borders to maintain and develop contacts, relations and cooperation . . . across borders" (Art. 36).

Aspects of cultural rights additional to UNDRIP stem from other human rights instruments and the work of international human rights treaty bodies:

1. Education of the broader society about the cultures of minorities and Indigenous Peoples: the state has the obligation to take measures in this direction. This norm has emerged from the assumption that nondiscrimination policies must be supported by a participatory and informed civil society. The role of the media has been repeatedly stressed in combating racism and discrimination vis-à-vis Indigenous Peoples.
2. Protection of certain economic activities of Indigenous Peoples closely linked to their cultural preservation and development: the state must also respect special cultural rights of Indigenous Peoples related to the continuation of certain economic activities linked to the traditional use of land and natural resources, such as hunting and fishing.
3. The right to choose in which culture or cultures to participate (individual right and group right).

Cultural rights have for a long time been the most neglected category of human rights. Through the advocacy and meticulous work of Indigenous Peoples, the UNDRIP became the boldest international instrument to detail the content and parameters of cultural rights in international law. This achievement is positive not only for Indigenous Peoples but for other parts of our societies.

2. Unsettling and Resetting Relations with States

As is to be expected, conflicts can and do surge around the implementation of Indigenous Peoples' rights. Some of the conflicts have to do with foreign and domestic companies exploiting Indigenous natural resources. Military activities often take place on Indigenous lands. Land grabbing of Indigenous lands takes place, and Indigenous Peoples are obliged to leave their territories. Sometimes, states bring up their desire to use resources on Indigenous lands for the well-being of the whole population. They raise the question of how UNDRIP can help resolve complex issues. The prevailing idea and hope is that UNDRIP can guide societies toward peaceful solutions. The Declaration, for example, recognizes the right to lands, territories, and resources. It then gives us the methodology of dealing with conflicts: Indigenous Peoples must be consulted; they have to be represented by their own representative authorities; free, prior, and informed consent is required; redress must be provided; and there cannot be forced relocation and similar processes.

Essentially, the Declaration outlaws discrimination against Indigenous Peoples, promotes their full and effective participation in all matters that concern them, as well as the right to remain distinct and to pursue their own visions of economic and social development. The adoption of the Declaration requires new approaches to global issues, such as development, diversity, pluricultural democracy, and peace – and encourages the building of genuine partnerships with Indigenous Peoples. The adoption of the Declaration has shown that Indigenous Peoples and their issues are of global concern. The definition of development and well-being cannot be the prerogative of some groups of people, states, or corporations at the exclusion of others. This human rights Declaration provides the framework for more just and inclusive societies where Indigenous Peoples, along with others, will strive together for justice for all.

The Declaration resets the relationship between Indigenous Peoples and states, paving the path to the decolonization of Indigenous Peoples and "the reestablishment of the state," a phrase used by various Indigenous leaders during their statements at the UN. The Declaration represents the dynamic development of legal norms and reflects the commitment of states to move in certain directions, abiding by principles that respect the human rights of Indigenous Peoples.

F. Indigenous Philosophies, Protocols, Ceremonies, and Prophecies

1. Toward Legal Pluralism Through Indigenous Participation

Indigenous Elders spoke, especially in the early years of the WGIP, and have continued to come and speak in UN bodies today, to represent their peoples. The Elders' way of exposing the hard realities of their peoples and their discourse were often times spiritual, metaphorical, almost poetic. At least in the early days of the Indigenous Peoples' interface with UN bodies, in the early 1980s, such language could resonate as unusual and difficult to grasp within a UN context. Indigenous leaders, for example, would bring with them symbolic objects, such as a wampum belt,[52] to demonstrate how their ancestors had concluded treaties with states and how such agreements had been registered and depicted in a particular weaving or beading. There was, in other words, no piece of paper to signal the agreement for them; it was an object, such as a particular weaving.

The way Indigenous representatives spoke at the UN since the early days of contacting the Organization showed a long-term vision of their international involvement. They were conveying not only that the history of their nations came from far back but that they would be here for the long run and that their struggle for justice and equality had profound moral roots and would continue, with resistance, persistence, and resilience. They were seeking to educate others about their ways of seeing the world, their value systems, their relation to the land, their cultures, and their governance systems and to convince their non-Indigenous counterparts – states, UN agencies, NGOs, and the media. In terms of their political struggle, they have been seeking to "win hearts and minds."

Since the early days of the WGIP through to today's sessions of the UNPFII and of the EMRIP, Indigenous leaders have spent a considerable amount of time explaining to the world the specificities of their cultures, including their legal systems; customs; languages; spirituality; world views; concepts of economic, social, cultural, and political development; traditional knowledge systems; and other aspects of their ways of life that form the basis of their collective sense of who they are and what their vision is for the future. Year in and year out, during the drafting of the UNDRIP, Indigenous Elders and other Indigenous representatives from all parts of the world spared no effort to describe, for example, the special spiritual, moral, and material relationship of Indigenous Peoples to their ancestral land, the concept of community ownership of the land, and various traditional systems of governance. It has also been a common occurrence at UN meetings that Indigenous languages are spoken by the leaders at the beginning of their speeches to mark the significance of language to identity and that, following Indigenous cultural

---

52 Beaded belts, wampums, were used by Indigenous Peoples in North America to mark agreements and, later, when the colonists arrived to North America, to mark treaties between States (the British Crown) and the Indigenous Peoples. Wampum has a special significance to the Haudenosaunee (Iroquois) people. "Archaeological evidence shows that wampum was in use by the Haudenosaunee in the period before the Haudenosaunee Confederacy. But it was during the founding of the Confederacy that Aiionwatha (Hiawatha) introduced wampum in the way that it is currently being used by the Haudenosaunee. Wampum is used to signify the importance or the authority of the message associated with it. As such, treaties and other such agreements would have a large amount of wampum that had been loomed into a 'belt' for them." "What Is Wampum," *Ganondagan website*, www.ganondagan.org/Learning/Wampum; see also Wikipedia, s.v. "Wampum," last modified 20 October 2023, 20:38, https://en.wikipedia.org/wiki/Wampum.

protocol, recognition of the Indigenous Peoples of the land where the meeting is held is expressed. Indigenous Peoples have also come to the UN wearing traditional costume, exhibiting their art, and sharing music, dance, stories, film, and other aspects of their traditional and contemporary cultural expressions.

2. Conversing Symbolisms

Indigenous Peoples have sought to mark their presence at the UN in ways that are significant from the perspective of their own cultures. They have sought to inform but also reform UN protocols so they would make sense in terms of Indigenous protocols and convey mutual respect. Far from being claustrophobic and introverted, these Indigenous ways of participation have been at once performative to non-Indigenous audiences, assertive of self-defined cultural distinctiveness, cosmopolitan and highly political in those international spaces.[53]

Protocols and ceremonies are important both for Indigenous Peoples and for the UN. They are the ground rules that are indispensable so that sovereign entities can relate and discuss even the most controversial issues of interest to them. These underlying norms of behavior, often called diplomacy, develop over a long period of time, decades or centuries, and become international custom. In their interface with empires and states over time, Indigenous Peoples pursued protocols that would be meaningful to them, especially in conveying good faith from both sides. Upon contacting the UN, they pursued such protocols again, meaningful to them, at a global level this time, in order to establish ground rules of interface that would signify the mutual respect of sovereigns. The fundamental principle of good faith in international law is also captured in the very last sentence of the UNDRIP, where Article 46 states that the provisions set forth in the Declaration "shall be interpreted in accordance with the principles of justice, democracy, respect for human rights, equality, non-discrimination, good governance and good faith."

Indigenous Peoples, through constructing protocols new to the UN, also shaped new spaces for themselves, in what has also been called "place-making,"[54] seemingly only cultural at first, but with political and normative implications over time. The multitude of these new protocols have left a mark on the UN and have created new international customs. In this chapter, I discuss Indigenous protocols and how they impact interstate spaces.

---

53 Mary Lawlor, *Public Native America: Tribal Self-Representations in Museums, Powwows, and Casinos* (New Brunswick, NJ: Rutgers University Press, 2006). In *Public Native America*, Lawlor explores the process of tribal self-definition that the communities in her study make available to off-reservation audiences.

54 Andrea Muehlebach, " 'Making Place' at the United Nations: Indigenous Cultural Politics at the UN Working Group on Indigenous Populations," *Cultural Anthropology* 16, no. 3 (August 2001), https://doi.org/10.1525/can.2001.16.3.415.

3. Writing Letters

Indigenous Peoples have been writing letters to the UN for decades addressing the Secretary-General directly with their complaints against states and other matters, long before the establishment of the UN's Indigenous-related bodies and procedures. Like Deskaheh's letter to the Secretary-General of the League of Nations in 1923, the letters of other Indigenous leaders have been signed and sealed by formal authorities of Indigenous Peoples, and the tone of those letters is that of sovereigns addressing the UN. It is a language that assumes that the place of Indigenous Peoples is at the UN, in parity with other nations. I recall several of these letters arriving on my desk at the New York Office of the then Center for Human Rights (later, the Office of the High Commissioner for Human Rights) transmitted from the Office of the Secretary-General.[55] As the UN did not have ways of addressing such complaints early on, the human rights office seemed to be the most open entity to such voices. This gave UN staff the opportunity to prepare briefs on Indigenous issues with suggestions of possible follow-ups from the Office of the Secretary-General, ranging from a written response to the letter of the Indigenous authority; the offer of a meeting with the Secretary-General or somebody in his office or with some other UN department, such as the Department of Political Affairs and the New York human rights office; the undertaking of a humanitarian intervention of good offices vis-à-vis the state concerned by the Secretary-General; or the sending of a special mission to the country concerned. These letters from Indigenous authorities provide the opportunity to also inform, educate, and engage the high UN officials on Indigenous issues and create a favorable atmosphere and fertile ground for high-profile UN action on these issues.

A special kind of letter to the UN is recalled by Russel Barsh regarding the initiative of the Mi'kmaw.[56] Barsh mentions that

> the traditional confederacy council made more than a merely symbolic commitment to upholding the International Covenants of Human Rights through internal reforms and periodic reporting.
>
> It fell to me to deliver the instruments of ratification personally to the UN Treaty Office. I was treated with the utmost respect and solemnity until the director of the office began reading the "whereas" clauses. His face changed expression several times and then he smiled and said simply,

---

55 The author served in the New York Office of the Center for Human Rights and Office of the High Commissioner for Human Rights from 1984 to 2003.

56 Barsh, "The Inner Struggle of Indigenous Peoples," in *Indigenous Peoples' Rights in International Law*, ed. Roxanne Dunbar-Ortiz et al. (Kautokeino: Gáldu and Copenhagen: IWGIA, 2015), www.iwgia.org/en/documents-and-publications/documents/publications-pdfs/english-publications/126-indigenous-peoples-rights-in-international-law/file.html.

"This is good, this is really good" and accepted the documents. Our first periodic reports under the conventions were similarly received, with awareness that while the Mi'kmaw could not simply transform themselves into a state by adhering to international norms of human rights, they could set an example by which statehood implies internal responsibilities that are too often neglected in the rush to sovereignty. It was an example aimed as much at Mi'kmaw institutions as Canadian ones.

For Mi'kmaq, engaging the UN was a valuable element in a broad mobilization.[57]

We should add here that this initiative of the Mi'kmaw was an expression of their external self-determination.

4. The Hopi Prophecy and the "House of Mica"

The official website of the Hopi Tribe[58] informs the readers that the Hopi Tribe is a sovereign nation in northeastern Arizona and its reservation is more than 1.5 million acres and consists of twelve villages on three mesas. The website states,

> Since time immemorial the Hopi people have lived in Hopitutskwa and have maintained our sacred covenant with Maasaw, the ancient caretaker of the earth, to live as peaceful and humble farmers respectful of the land and its resources. Over the centuries we have survived as a tribe, and to this day have managed to retain our culture, language and religion despite influences from the outside world. We invite and encourage you to visit our Hopi lands. However, please be respectful of our laws, culture and way of life.

The Hopi people, active participants at international level, sent a delegation to the WGIP in Geneva already in the early 1980s. Between 1986 and 1987 they sent a delegation of Elders to the UN in New York, preceded by a letter to the Secretary-General.[59] As was often the practice of the Office of the Secretary-General, the New York Office of the then Center for Human Rights was asked to receive the delegation.

The Hopi delegation came to the thirty-sixth floor of the Secretariat building of UN Headquarters, where the human rights office was located then. Four people were part of the delegation, all Hopi Elders. Except for one

---

57 Barsh, "Inner Struggle of Indigenous Peoples," 94.
58 www.hopi-nsn.gov/.
59 I received the delegation in my capacity as Acting Chief of the New York Office of the then UN Center for Human Rights.

delegate, Thomas Banyacya, the others spoke only Hopi.[60] They were accompanied by a Diné Elder, Grace Smith, who explained how the traditional authorities of the two peoples, Diné and Hopi, were collaborating, as their lands were geographically intertwined and they faced grave issues, including the controversial Kayenta and Black Mesa coal mines.[61] The questions raised by the Elders were specific to the damage done to their traditional territories through the mines, and they also expressed broad concerns about impending catastrophic damage to the environment and the planet. They mentioned that an old Hopi prophecy predicted such a major disaster. Thomas Banyacya said that it was the duty of the Hopi to deliver their prophecy to the world, so it would change its route. He said that the prophecy spoke of the Great House of Mica where one day world leaders would gather to solve the world's problems without war. Thomas Banyacya said that the UN was the Great House of Mica and therefore that was the place where the prophecy had to be delivered. My capacity to assure the Elders that this would happen was weak, despite listening carefully and with understanding to what they were conveying. How could one imagine an occasion at the UN, where the conveying of the Hopi prophecy could take place, with a protocol that would be commensurate to the importance the Hopi ascribed to their prophecy? How could the UN rise to the occasion to converse with and be the interlocutor of this message that would be in the form of a prophecy? This was certainly not an approach or a language that the UN was used to in the political speeches of states. Years passed and the Hopi continued sending letters to the UN about the prophecy and their determination and urgency to deliver it to the UN.

The occasion presented itself around the proclamation of 1993 as the International Year of the World's Indigenous People. Following a proposal of the UNCHR, and originally coming from the WGIP, the Year was proclaimed by the United Nations General Assembly "to strengthen international cooperation for the solution of problems faced by indigenous communities in areas such as human rights, the environment, development, education and health."[62] The Year was requested by Indigenous Peoples and was the result

---

60 Hopi elder Thomas Banyacya (1909–1999) was selected as spokesman for traditional leaders in 1948, after atom bombs triggered Hopi awareness that the prophesized "gourd full of ashes" had finally appeared.

61 The word "Diné" is from the Navajo's own language and means "the people." *Cultural Survival* published a summary of the case: Enei Begaye, "The Black Mesa Controversy," *Cultural Survival*, 7 May 2010, www.culturalsurvival.org/publications/cultural-survival-quarterly/black-mesa-controversy.

62 International Year for the World's Indigenous People, UN Doc. A/RES/45/164 (18 December 1990), para. 1, http://undocs.org/A/RES/45/164. See also International Year for the World's Indigenous People, 1993, UN Doc. A/RES/47/75 (14 December 1992), http://undocs.org/A/RES/47/75. Note that the word "Peoples" with an "s" at the end had not yet been accepted at the UN; this became the case after the adoption of UNDRIP in 2007.

of their efforts to secure their cultural integrity and status into the twenty-first century. It aimed to encourage a new relationship between states and Indigenous Peoples, and between the international community and Indigenous Peoples – "a new partnership," as the motto of the Year indicated, based on mutual respect and understanding.

The year 1992 was one of preparation of the International Year, as well as a year of great mobilization by Indigenous Peoples. It was also the year that the Indigenous world was preparing its advocacy at the Rio de Janeiro Conference on Environment and Development that left its international mark through the impressive activities and the Kari-Oca Declaration adopted by some four hundred Indigenous delegates a week before the Earth Summit in May 1992. Indigenous Peoples were at the same time also organizing around the World Conference on Human Rights that was to take place in Vienna in 1993. In the meantime, the WGIP, in July 1992, completed its work on the Draft Declaration on the Rights of Indigenous Peoples and transmitted it to its higher bodies, the Sub-Commission and the UNCHR. Nineteen ninety-two was also a significant year for the Indigenous Peoples of the Americas, as it marked "five hundred years of resistance" since 1492, the beginning of colonization of the continent by Europeans. In fact, Indigenous Peoples had wanted the UN to proclaim 1992 as the International Year of the World's Indigenous Peoples, but the symbolism was too heavy for many states to bear, states that had been colonial powers from afar, as well as the settler-colonial states of the American continent. Therefore, 1993 was proclaimed as the International Year of Indigenous People instead of 1992.[63] The strong anticolonial mobilization in 1992 led to many Indigenous efforts and appeals to the Vatican to annul Papal Bull *Inter Caetera* of 1493 issued by Pope Alexander VI, which established the doctrine of discovery, a spiritual, political, and legal justification for colonization and seizure of land not inhabited by Christians.[64]

This global Indigenous mobilization, with which the UN Center for Human Rights was closely in touch, was informing our preparations for the International Year. The UN Center for Human Rights and the International Labor Organization (ILO) were coordinators of the Year. So the idea was born, in early 1992, to pursue the opening of the International Year on 10 December 1992 at the UNGA. Imagining Indigenous leaders speaking in the General Assembly Hall – the inner sanctum and most prestigious ceremonial

---

63 For a description of the General Assembly discussions see Roxanne Dunbar-Ortiz, *An Indigenous Peoples History of the United States* (Boston, MA: Beacon Press, 2014).

64 Tonya Gonnella Frichner, Preliminary Study of the Impact on Indigenous Peoples of the International Legal Construct Known as the Doctrine of Discovery, UN Doc. E/C.19/2010/13 (10 February 2010), www.un.org/esa/socdev/unpfii/documents/E.C.2010.13%20EN.pdf; Steven T. Newcomb, *Pagans in the Promised Land: Decoding the Doctrine of Christian Discovery* (Golden, CO: Fulcrum, 2008).

room at UN Headquarters – was exciting and meaningful. If we could get this room for the launch of the Year, the space would seem appropriate to represent the Great House of Mica where the Hopi wanted to deliver their prophecy.

It was an uphill battle and took about ten months. We had to convince the "gate keepers" who were guarding the very strict protocol of the UNGA. The Department of General Assembly Affairs were now my neighbors, on the twenty-ninth floor of the Secretariat building. I had to convince them in "UN speak." My heart was pounding as I walked into the offices of the high-level officials in the Department of General Assembly Affairs, having amassed all my documents and formality of a civil servant. The terms and arguments had to be convincing in words familiar to them, and while I would ask for something exceptional and outside the rules – that is, Indigenous representatives to speak at the UNGA – this would have to be presented in ways that would not raise fear of political controversy. At the same time, I had to appeal to my colleagues' sense of international morals, based on the high ideals the UN stands for, and convince them as human beings, as UN staff, that this was a good thing to do. The Department of General Assembly Affairs was in general skeptical and strict about anniversaries and publicity events in the General Assembly Hall. Any proposal has to be cleared first by the officials working in that department. Proposals then need to be brought to the attention of the President of the General Assembly, whose team and consultations with states bring out the political angle of things. We had to explain to UNGA officials the procedures of the WGIP in Geneva, where Indigenous representatives had participated directly for a decade already, and we had to assure them that the UN Center for Human Rights would be in a position to undertake the consultation process over who the Indigenous speakers would be at the UNGA. This sensitive process would be undertaken by my colleague Julian Burger, who was in charge of the Working Group in Geneva. Thomas Banyacya would need to be added to the speakers in order to deliver the Hopi prophecy. In New York, we would need to organize consultations with states to facilitate statements by each regional group – Western European and Other States, Eastern European States, Latin American and Caribbean States, African States, and Asian and Pacific States.

It was explained to me by the Department of General Assembly Affairs that, as I should know, only states' representatives and the UN Secretary-General speak at General Assembly meetings, with rare exceptions for other entities. The officials of the Department of General Assembly Affairs understood that the International Year of the World's Indigenous People would have no moral legitimacy without Indigenous Peoples' participation at the launch of the Year. And they volunteered a creative solution because, I believe, they were convinced about the substance of the matter "in their hearts and minds," so that they, as gatekeepers, would volunteer to facilitate an exception. The way to do this would be in the well-scripted, word-for-word notes prepared for the President of the General Assembly, who would conduct the meeting. On the day of the launch of the International Year, the states would speak first and then the Indigenous representatives would follow. Between the first group of speakers and the second, there would be a small bridge of words in the notes of the General Assembly President who would say something like, "Now we move to a briefing where we will hear statements of Indigenous representatives." The meeting would not be interrupted at all; it would continue seamlessly, the audience would remain seated, as Indigenous speakers would move to the UNGA lectern, one after the other, to deliver their speeches.

Preparations ahead of 10 December 1992 were intense. I was elated that we had finally invited Thomas Banyacya to deliver the Hopi prophecy. Aware of the special cultural and spiritual significance of this occasion for the Hopi and others, we felt it would be best for Thomas Banyacya to be the last speaker and close the event. Many states wanted to speak, as we were not able to limit the number of speeches to representatives of the five regional groups of states. After global consultations among Indigenous Peoples, twenty-two Indigenous leaders from around the world were designated to speak.

In the early morning of 10 December, also the International Human Rights Day of 1992, I was standing in the entrance of the UN building, after a sleepless night of anticipation, with a sense that I was about to partake in an event of political and also historic and symbolic significance, an event that was breaking some barriers of the past. Indigenous representatives were expected to enter through the General Assembly Lobby, or Visitors Lobby. The moment had come. I saw Thomas Banyacya among the people. I walked toward him and uttered a simple phrase that I had prepared for a long time. I welcomed him to the Great House of Mica on behalf of the UN Center for Human Rights. The moment was overwhelming.

The excitement was palpable among the Indigenous delegates as it was the first time that they would address the UN in the General Assembly Hall. This ceremonial and also political dialogue between Indigenous Peoples and the UN on that significant day included various other symbols as well. For the first time, again, other "gate keepers" in the UN services agreed to open the ceremonial stair to the General Assembly Hall, adjacent to the impressive Foucault pendulum given to the UN by the Netherlands in 1955. The Pendulum offers visual proof of the rotation of the Earth on its axis and consists of a two-hundred-pound gold-plated sphere suspended from the seventy-five-foot ceiling by a stainless-steel wire. As scores of Indigenous delegates, many in impressive traditional clothes, were walking up the ceremonial stair, it felt like the pendulum was readjusting the Earth's balance. At the UNGA meeting, speakers had been given a seven-minute limit to make their statements, but statements were longer. The last speaker, Thomas Banyacya, delivered the

Hopi prophecy in a speech of forty minutes. The General Assembly President did not interrupt.[65]

Whether states really listened to the substance of the speeches by Thomas Banyacya and the other leaders is questionable, as is whether they understood the significance of this precedent-setting event that took place in the General Assembly Hall, the most prestigious UN room. I do not know what Thomas Banyacya felt as he was speaking at the General Assembly when he saw that a limited number of states were attending. What certainly followed that day were many other similar events, where Indigenous Peoples spoke and continue to speak in that prestigious Hall. The meeting in the General Assembly Hall in December 1994 when the UN launched the International Decade of the World's Indigenous People was one of those occasions.

After the establishment of the UNPFII, it has by now become regular practice that the opening of every annual session of the Forum takes place in the General Assembly Hall. Hardly anybody, a state delegate or a UN official, would question this practice today. It is normal to see Indigenous delegates fill the space, no longer sitting in the gallery of the General Assembly Hall but in seats adjacent to states. At the end of these meetings, Indigenous representatives enjoy the space by taking pictures on the podium or at the lectern of the General Assembly Hall, appreciating the symbolic moment that they own, a moment that they have achieved over generations of advocacy at the UN, intertwining their protocols with those of the UN.

5. Opening of UN Meetings by "The People of the Land"

When the UN Permanent Forum started meeting at UN Headquarters in New York in 2002, it was the first time that a UN Indigenous-related body was formally meeting on Indigenous Peoples' traditional territories. This was obviously not the case with the WGIP in Geneva. An Indigenous protocol was soon welcomed at UN Headquarters, one that is still followed today: at the opening of the UNPFII's annual sessions, the first speaker is an Indigenous Elder "of the Indigenous Peoples of the land" who gives a ceremonial opening in his language (Onondaga of the Haudenosaunee), which is simultaneously interpreted into English and the other five official UN languages (Arabic, Chinese, French, Russian, and Spanish). Tadodaho Sid Hill opened the Forum's annual session for several years. For this to happen, a speaker of the Onondaga language sits in a UN interpreter's booth, renders the speech

---

65 See the blog post on Thomas Banyacya's speech, delivering the Hopi prophecy at the UN on 10 December 1992: "House of Mica: The Message of the Hopi at the United Nations," *UNPFIP Network blog*, 3 May 2013, http://unpfip.blogspot.com/2013/05/house-of-mica-message-of-hopi-at-united.html.

into English, and the interpreters of the other official languages follow. This practice of having a nonofficial UN language used and interpreted is followed at the UN in exceptional circumstances, as for heads of state or government or, occasionally, somebody at ministerial level, who wish to speak in their own language. In such situations, they usually bring their own interpreters who will interpret into an official UN language, as explained earlier for Onondaga. I remember the delight of so many when the Onondaga interpretation through UN interpreters' booths first happened around 2005. We felt that the very fact that the original language heard by all was an Indigenous language and that the interpreter of an Indigenous language was using a UN interpreter's booth to facilitate the official UN languages, had a special meaning. It did.

The cultural Indigenous protocol of an Onondaga spiritual leader speaking at the opening of the Permanent Forum has also had another protocol dimension – namely, that he speaks first, before even the Secretary-General of the United Nations or his representative. The regular UN protocol is that the Secretary-General or his representative speak first at a meeting hosted within and by the UN. In the case of the Indigenous Elder speaking first, the symbolism is that the original historic hosts, "the Indigenous People of the land," welcome the meeting. It is, in other words, a land recognition of the original owners of the land before colonization, a symbolic recognition of the moral significance of the traditional owners of these lands welcoming the participants.[66]

In 2004 Kofi Annan, who supported the UNPFII from the very beginning,[67] addressed the opening of the third session personally as the Secretary-General of the UN. He spoke after the ceremonial opening by the Onondaga Tadodaho.[68] Our office had to prepare a note to the Secretary-General's Office, sent through my superiors, explaining the protocol and why the Indigenous Elders would say welcoming words first. I was elated and grateful to find sincere understanding in the Office of the Secretary-General regarding this protocol that was accepted. That year, the Secretary-General made an impassioned speech at the Permanent Forum, a good part of which was later used

---

66 In my capacity as Acting Chief of the Secretariat of the UNPFII in 2003, I sent the first invitation to Tadodaho Sid Hill stating that "I am now writing to invite you to participate and offer words of welcome in the formal opening of the Permanent Forum that will take place at United Nations Headquarters, in Conference Room 2, at 10.00 a.m. on Monday, 12 May 2003." The Elder opened the second session of the UNPFII in 2003, preceding the Under-Secretary General for Economic and Social Affairs.

67 Kofi Annan had also addressed the closing meeting of the first session of the Permanent Forum in 2002.

68 The Tadodaho in New York State is the spiritual leader of the Haudenosaunee, the Six Nations, a confederacy that includes the Cayuga, Mohawk, Oneida, Onondaga, Seneca, and Tuscarora peoples. Wikipedia, s.v. "Tadodaho," last modified 16 April 2023, 20:41, https://en.wikipedia.org/wiki/Tadodaho.

in the UN film *Indigenous Peoples and the United Nations, Vol. 1.*[69] Annan recalled:

> Just over 80 years ago, Chief Deskaheh travelled from Canada to Geneva to tell the League of Nations about the right of his people to live on their own land, follow their own laws, and practice their own faiths. Chief Deskaheh was refused permission to speak and had to return home without accomplishing his mission. But his vision has inspired countless indigenous leaders since then to articulate and pursue the goals of their peoples.[70]

It was actually the first time that the Indigenous protocol of an Indigenous Elder welcoming a UN meeting *first*, before the Secretary-General, was followed at such high level. Kofi Annan was an exceptional Secretary-General and an exceptional leader. He was the most pro-human rights Secretary-General of recent times, a person of tremendous cultural sensitivity and humanitarian spirit, and he demonstrated these extraordinary qualities by supporting Indigenous Peoples as well. During his tenure, he also opened his offices and received Indigenous high-level delegations to hear from them directly.

An additional symbolism of the Onondaga Tadodaho opening the Permanent Forum meetings has to do with his Haudenosaunee ancestor Deskaheh, who appealed to the League of Nations, the UN's predecessor, in 1923. Keeping that thread of history alive is part of the intangible heritage of the Indigenous Peoples' global movement, and it continues to give strength and inspiration to younger generations of Indigenous leaders from around the world. It is not uncommon in recent times to hear Deskaheh's story integrated in speeches of Indigenous representatives from around the world at United Nations meetings.

In the spring of 2009, I received an email from a great-granddaughter of Chief Deskaheh. She had been following the developments and work of the UNPFII. We invited her, and she came to the May session of the Permanent Forum that year. At the opening, she gave a brief speech. Among other things she said,

> My name is Kim Morf, and I am here today to give thanks to those who have made the UNPFII possible. On behalf of my great-grandfather Levi

---

69 *Indigenous Peoples and the United Nations, Vol. 1*, produced by Rebecca Sommer for the Secretariat of the UN Permanent Forum on Indigenous Issues, YouTube videos, parts 1 and 3, 18 min., www.youtube.com/watch?v=8I8QgA1tQQ8 and www.youtube.com/watch?v=LlS6ANY1aDM.

70 Kofi Annan, speaking at UNPFII, 2004, audio presented *in Indigenous Peoples and the United Nations, Vol. 1*, part 1, at 5:07 min.

General, better known as Chief Deskaheh of the Haudenosaunee, I commend the Forum. . . . Chief Deskaheh was determined to preserve the treaty rights of the Haudenosaunee; he believed in the "Spirit of Geneva" and felt the League of Nations was the venue to give voice to the smaller nations of the world. I give thanks to the nations of Estonia, Ireland, Panama, Persia, and the Netherlands, who all supported my great-grandfather in Geneva at the League of Nations on his quest for peace and recognition of Indigenous political independence.

. . . My great grandfather would have been very proud . . . to know that this Forum exists so that we have a voice to express our concern.[71]

Two years later, in 2011, I met another great-granddaughter of Deskaheh, Karla General, at the Permanent Forum. She is a lawyer and has worked at the Indian Law Resource Center and as legal counsel of the Seneca Nation, one of the Six Nations.

The intangible cultural heritage of the Indigenous Peoples' movement is patiently and deliberately interwoven by many acts of political, spiritual, cultural, and other interventions across generations. These acts are threads that feed and keep alive the connections among Indigenous Peoples globally and strengthen solidarity as an organic element of the movement.

6. Saying a Prayer, Smoking a Peace Pipe, Exhibiting Indigenous Arts, and Protecting Sacred Staffs

Indigenous Elders' words of welcome at UN meetings are more often than not spiritual invocations or prayers, mostly in their own languages. With the exception of the opening of the Permanent Forum's session by an Onondaga Elder, there is no formal interpretation of these invocations. Prayer is not part of the protocol in official UN meetings. International Chief Wilton Littlechild, a Cree leader, respected Elder, and mentor to so many, has often expressed his amazement that Indigenous Peoples were told they could not pray at the UN. Now Indigenous people simply offer and say prayers, and this goes uncontested and is also appreciated as another exception to the UN's usual protocols. The program of the first meeting at the annual session of the Permanent Forum refers to "opening ceremony" instead of prayer or invocation, and this satisfies all parties in this constant dance of respect and mutuality in international metaprotocols inspired by Indigenous Peoples.

Indigenous protocols have hardly left any UN departments untouched, including Interpretation Services, UN Security and Building Management Services, or the Department of Global Communications (formerly the

---

71 Kim Morf, speech at the eighth session of the UN Permanent Forum on Indigenous Issues, New York, May 2009. The author received a copy of Morf's speech at the session.

Department of Public Information). After intense efforts to explain to them the special characteristics of Indigenous representation at the UN, most of these services have become friends of the Indigenous Peoples, or in any case, many people within those services have. UN officials work hard to prepare the various aspects of the annual session of the UNPFII, from arranging podiums and other infrastructure for cultural performances and exhibits, to offering registration stations and the preparation of documents. UN workers often express their support by small comments on the side – for example, by saying fleetingly, in a low voice at the end of a coordination meeting, things like, "You know, this is my favorite meeting of the year." There is something above their regular duty that they are responding to, something where the very purpose of the UN is tested. Seeing so many Indigenous People coming from all over the world and giving meaning to this UN gathering certainly appears compelling and can bend tendencies of cynicism rampant in this political organization. Some UN staff even organized an informal group of volunteers at some point to support Indigenous delegates who needed low-cost lodging or food. Solidarity was spreading. There was an urge to make the hundreds of Indigenous participants feel welcome to this "international house," a feeling that each UN staffer was a kind of host for the Indigenous people and had to make the UN "look good."

At the annual celebrations of Indigenous Peoples Day, 9 August, at UN Headquarters in New York since 1993, events have included the smoking of a peace pipe and other pipe ceremonies of Indigenous Peoples. Given that the ceremony takes place in the summer on the plaza outside the General Assembly Lobby, there has been no issue conducting the ceremony that included smoking of the pipe. In the late 1990s, however, for the first time we were confronted with the possibility of rain and had to have a backup plan to hold the opening ceremony inside the General Assembly Lobby. This created a lot of consternation in UN Security, who are mindful of fire regulations. The day came and so did the rain. In a typical UN compromise, the opening ceremony and smoking of the peace pipe were moved just outside the revolving doors of the entrance to the General Assembly Lobby – outside, but under the protective narrow awning. Most of the participants, who could not be covered by the awning, did not seem to mind experiencing the New York City rain for close to two hours.

The sacred staffs and other precious ceremonial objects Indigenous Peoples bring into the UN building have also raised some security-screening issues. Indigenous representatives complained at times that these items risked being damaged during security screening and had to be handled with special care and respect. Special treatment of such objects has by now become the practice, following annual meetings between the Secretariat of the UNPFII and the UN's Security Service that established the proper procedures.

One of the most difficult cultural conversations we had in the 1990s was with the Exhibits Committee, which has the task to screen proposals for exhibits on UN premises. The precious and limited UN Headquarters space ensures good exposure and publicity for whatever or whomever the exhibit represents. The General Assembly Lobby is a cherished space for that, and there is competition among states mostly and the requirement of long-term planning for the use of that space for exhibits. We, at the New York Office of the UN High Commissioner for Human Rights, were asked to prepare a folder about the Indigenous exhibit we were proposing, for the first time, in 1993 or 1994. The proposal would be closely examined by the Exhibits Committee. The crucial point communicated to us when we spoke about an Indigenous exhibit was a kind of defensive alert: that the items of the exhibit had to be "art" not "crafts." The underlying assumption that Indigenous objects would not be "art" clearly showed that we had a long way to go to raise awareness and educate that particular corner of the UN. There was no reference to such distinction in the guidelines of the Committee.[72] What was conveyed to us was simply people's prejudice. We had to make intense efforts to contain our surprise, sadness, and indignation at the idea that the UN's internal system would uphold the old-fashioned, elitist idea of "high culture," and we had to turn this into a diplomatic dialogue that would hopefully convince our colleagues. The Exhibits Committee officers did not seem to realize how they sounded in relation to the UN's decolonization and human rights nondiscrimination ethic. Would, for example, the items offered by Indigenous people for an exhibit be "less art" than the many objects offered as gifts to the UN by states that are permanently exhibited, and why? Be that as it may, we had to amass all the good arguments over a period of time. What became quite helpful was the information we fed the Committee that the Permanent Mission of Australia to the UN was supporting exhibits of famous Aboriginal artists in New York City.

By the end of the 1990s, the Indigenous Exhibit had become an annual practice at UN Headquarters around the International Day of the World's Indigenous Peoples. The active collaboration of the New York Office of the High Commissioner for Human Rights with the NGO Committee on Indigenous Peoples' Rights and the direct link with Indigenous artists and communities strengthened the effectiveness of this effort. Since the establishment of the UNPFII, the Indigenous exhibit takes place around the annual sessions of the Forum in the spring and is opened on the Tuesday of the first week of the Forum's session, also combined with a cultural event of music, song, poetry, and dance. The impressive visual collections, including paintings, weavings and other objects, and historic and contemporary photographs from around

---

72 The current UN Exhibits Committee Guidelines (accessed 5 October 2023) appear here: www.un.org/sites/un2.un.org/files/un_exhibits_committee_guidelines_2022_-_final_1.pdf.

the world, representing a wide diversity of Indigenous cultures, have now become a permanent feature that enrich the UN space in a distinct way.

The political force of Indigenous protocol and the push to equalize power dynamics between states and Indigenous Peoples also resulted in, on one occasion, a state requesting an Indigenous protocol that would trample upon UN protocol. When Aotearoa/New Zealand decided to endorse the UNDRIP in 2010 – after having been one of the four countries to vote against it in 2007, along with Australia, Canada, and the United States – the government prepared a special presentation following Māori custom.[73] On 20 April 2010, at the opening meeting of the UNPFII in the General Assembly Hall, the Minister of Māori Affairs, Sir Pita Sharples, was the first speaker, after some procedural points on the agenda. When his name was called by the Presiding Officer and he started walking toward the lectern, all of a sudden, other New Zealanders started walking along with him, Māori and non-Māori together, including the Minister of Māori Affairs, himself a Māori, the Permanent Representative of New Zealand in New York, and other diplomats. They formed a procession, and the room was shaken by a powerful *haka*, the Māori ceremonial dance with its vigorous movements, stamping of the feet, and the rhythmic shouted accompaniment, traditionally used on the battlefield as well as when groups came together in peace. It was only after the end of the *haka*, and after some confusion on the podium – where officials were not sure whether this was not a kind of activism or "disruption" from NGOs – that the Minister of Māori Affairs actually reached the lectern and delivered his speech of endorsement of the Declaration. It was a moment of elation, and the fact that the New Zealand government had kept confidential the intent for a *haka* performance and the impending endorsement of the UNDRIP by New Zealand only added to the uniqueness of the moment. The New Zealand government had wanted to keep the event confidential until its actual implementation so as to avoid any pressure, both internally and internationally. Of the four "no" votes of the CANZUS group at the adoption of the Declaration in 2007, Australia had been the first to endorse the Declaration, and New Zealand would be the second, thus leaving the pressure heavy on the two remaining, the United States and Canada. Canada and the United States finally endorsed the Declaration by the end of 2010.

7.   Evolving Protocols and Expectations

Indigenous protocols in global fora have not remained stagnant but are constantly renewed. What was described earlier is not exhaustive or final. Protocols are reinvented to respond to new needs, new technologies,

---

73 In UN meetings, especially those on Indigenous issues, diplomats from New Zealand often use the combined Māori and English name for the country, "Aotearoa/New Zealand."

changing cultures, and the desire to communicate with as broad an audience as possible. New practices are often created by Indigenous women and Indigenous youth in their organized global interventions. Some examples are presented next.

When collective Indigenous women's and Indigenous youth's statements are read out by a speaker at the UN, a large group will often stand behind them to indicate solidarity and support. Other participants who may not be part of the collective that prepared the statement will often walk from their seats and join the group behind the speaker, in solidarity. This act of togetherness and solidarity adds extraordinary dynamism to the speech being delivered, moves people, and is often followed by applause. At the same time, the image of the speaker and the group standing behind her or him is projected onto big screens of the conference rooms, thus presenting a great opportunity for all to see and for the image to be actively used in various social media. This practice has spread to other Indigenous participants, not just Indigenous women and youth.

Indigenous representatives have developed the custom, in addition to wearing traditional clothes and headdress, of using weavings of the particular area they come from as another way to demonstrate presence, resistance, and resilience. They place the weavings on the desk behind which they are speaking during the Permanent Forum or on the podium if they are having a side event. They create a cultural space that is specific to them, drawing strength from it, declaring their continuing existence and presence.

Global political fora, such as the UNPFII, function as global parliaments, where the most difficult issues can be raised, including many grave critiques against states, such as violations of human rights. This parliamentary character of discussions means that demonstrations and protests, such as those that take place on the streets, are not allowed on UN premises. In other words, whatever critiques Indigenous Peoples make against states must be expressed by taking the floor in a public meeting of the Permanent Forum and other ways available, such as side events, press conferences, or the circulation of written material.

Indigenous protocols and symbolisms at the international level obviously have their limits, as they do not translate into immediate or visible political victories with concrete results in Indigenous Peoples' lives. Yet it is indisputable that they matter because they create a cultural shift in those international spaces, a shift that will make these spaces into a more fertile ground for positive changes.

The exchange and flow of protocols and symbolisms between Indigenous Peoples and states at the United Nations, including at the highest levels, has also signified acceptance of legal pluralism coming from Indigenous Peoples' contributions, an aspirational equality that is being cultivated between "two parties." One party is the notional sum of the Indigenous Peoples of the world, and the other is the notional sum of states that the UN epitomizes. These two notional parties weave a web of symbols that matter in the struggles of Indigenous Peoples for equality, self-determination, and decolonization. Compounded symbols, ceremonies, and protocols have been making possible real political victories, as well as the phenomenon of "corrective exceptionalism" – namely, exceptions in UN system procedures and practices that were and are favorable for Indigenous Peoples. We could say that the thousands of Indigenous delegates that have participated at the UN since 1977 have engaged states, interstate agencies, and the global civil society in a notional *haka*, learning delicate and challenging steps together over the decades, and creating a unique landscape where Indigenous Peoples can be welcomed in the UN system, what the Hopi have called "the House of Mica."

G.   Participation of Indigenous Women

Indigenous women have been at the forefront of the Indigenous Peoples' movement at the international level from the very beginning. Names that come to mind from early on include Tonya Gonnella Frichner, Ingrid Washinawatok, Roxanne Dunbar-Ortiz, Victoria Tauli-Corpuz, Rigoberta Menchú, Myrna Cunnigham, Dalee Sambo Dorough, Sharon Venne, Audrey Shenandoah, Tarcila Rivera Zea, Lucy Mulenkei, Otilia Lux de Cotí, and many others.

One of the most recognized Indigenous advocates shared some of her own memories and perspectives in a brainstorming meeting of Indigenous women that I attended in 2021. Her words, as recorded in my notes, were approximately as follows:

> In the 1980s, we, Indigenous women, went to the UN Working Group on Indigenous Populations in Geneva to see what human rights mean for us as Indigenous Peoples, within our context. Later on, we also got involved in the women's movement. Then, we looked around and saw that we were invisible in both movements. So, in the mid-1990s we decided to raise our own voices, as Indigenous women. . . . My generation opened the door and now we are inside the room. The new generations will have to make their own impact. The struggle is not easy and is not fast.

Many questions are relevant to Indigenous women from a human rights standpoint: How does UNDRIP cover Indigenous women's rights? Regarding Indigenous women and equality, is the principle of nondiscrimination enough to solve their issues? What are the parameters of Indigenous women's individual human rights and collective human rights? How are conflicts to be resolved between Indigenous women's human rights and cultural affirmations of the collectivity, including some traditional practices and traditional justice systems? How can Indigenous women exercise and strengthen their human rights *through* culture, especially through the respect of their cultural human rights?[74]

Throughout the world, Indigenous women continue to be discriminated against and marginalized. The threefold discrimination they suffer (for being women, Indigenous, and often poor) marginalizes them further, compared with Indigenous men, regarding economic and political opportunities for employment, social services, access to justice, and more particularly, access to land and other productive resources.

Indigenous women tend to be overrepresented in the migratory cycles of agricultural workers, domestic service, and other ill-paid and poorly protected private jobs. They are also increasingly present in international migration, in the informal economy, and among the swelling ranks of urban poor. Even more alarming is the victimization of many Indigenous women and girls in drug trafficking, sex tourism, and prostitution in vast regions of the world. To date, there has been inadequate attention to these matters, and where there are social and welfare policies in place, they have not been effective in protecting Indigenous women.

In some countries globalization often results in new agreements between Indigenous Peoples and states to facilitate new economic development projects. This situation has a tendency to marginalize Indigenous women in a number of ways. It often neglects the socioeconomic and cultural implications that may disproportionately affect women in the form of disruption to family and social relations. More importantly, however, Indigenous women and their concerns are often left out of the negotiations. This is evident because land-use and occupancy agreements tend to focus on traditional male activities such as hunting, fishing, and trapping. There is a view that, in general, development has not benefited Indigenous women to any significant degree. Rather, it has contributed to the erosion of viable community economies and social structures, corroded the environment, and marginalized Indigenous women and children.

The effects of military rule and the establishment of military detachments in Indigenous communities continue to have a major effect on Indigenous women. It curtails their movement and economic activities, and it disrupts the entry of food supplies and basic social services including the education of Indigenous children. Rape of Indigenous women is used as a weapon to force displacement and demoralization of Indigenous communities.

---

74 The next five paragraphs draw from materials published by the UN Office of the Special Adviser on Gender Issues and the Advancement of Women (OSAGI) and the Secretariat of the UN Permanent Forum on Indigenous Issues (SPFII), *Gender and Indigenous Peoples: Briefing Notes* (New York: UN, 2010), www.un.org/development/desa/indigenouspeoples/publications/2009/06/briefing-notes-gender-and-indigenous-women/.

See also the sources listed on UNPFII's summary page, "Publications on Indigenous Women," www.un.org/development/desa/indigenouspeoples/mandated-areas1/indigenous-women/publications-on-indigenous-women.html, accessed 5 October 2023.

At the same time however, Indigenous women do not see themselves as passive victims. In many instances, Indigenous women have bravely taken up the roles of mediators and peace builders. Indigenous women have sought to address these issues at the local, national, and international levels. At the United Nations, Indigenous women have been advocates and leaders since the very first year of the WGIP, in 1982. They were active participants and contributors during the more than two decades of negotiations regarding the UNDRIP.

It has been pointed out that the current focus on Indigenous-state relations is too limited in scope to convey the full meaning of "self-determination" for Indigenous Peoples. Rauna Kuokkanen considers that self-determination "seeks to restructure all relations of domination," not only hegemonic relations with the state. Importantly, it challenges the opposition between "self-determination" and "gender" created and maintained by international law, Indigenous political discourse, and Indigenous institutions. Kuokkanen states that restructuring relations of domination further entails examining the gender regimes present in existing Indigenous self-government institutions, interrogating the relationship between Indigenous self-determination and gender violence, and considering future visions of Indigenous self-determination.[75]

Special attention to Indigenous women's issues is now evident within the United Nations. The special theme of the third session of the UNPFII in 2004 was Indigenous women. At that session the Permanent Forum took note of the fact that the United Nations Convention for the Elimination of All Forms of Discrimination against Women (CEDAW) does not make reference to Indigenous women and the specific nature of the gender dimension of racial discrimination. The UNPFII recommended that "special attention" should be paid "to the issues related to maintaining the integrity of indigenous women and the gender dimension of racial discrimination against indigenous peoples."[76] Moreover, in 2022, CEDAW adopted the excellent General Recommendation 39 on Indigenous Women and Girls that was for a long time advocated for by the Indigenous women's movement.[77] The UNPFII has also been monitoring the implementation of its recommendations regarding Indigenous women.[78]

---

75 Rauna Kuokkanen, *Restructuring Relations: Indigenous Self-Determination, Governance, and Gender* (Oxford: Oxford University Press, 2019).

76 UN Permanent Forum on Indigenous Issues, Report on the Third Session (10–21 May 2004), UN Doc. E/2004/43, para. 6 (a). The recommendations on Indigenous women are contained in para. 3–15.

77 UN Committee on the Elimination of Discrimination against Women, General Recommendation No. 39 on the Rights of Indigenous Women and Girls, UN Doc. CEDAW/C/GC/39 (31 October 2022).

78 See for example an update prepared in 2017: Secretariat of the Permanent Forum on Indigenous Issues, Update on the Implementation of the Recommendations of the Permanent Forum, UN Doc. E/C.19/2017/3 (6 February 2017).

In March 2005, thanks to Indigenous women's mobilization, a resolution on Indigenous women was adopted at the forty-ninth Session of the UN Commission on the Status of Women (CSW), which was the first ever resolution on Indigenous women by this body.[79] This moment can also be viewed as a moment of relative rapprochement between the global women's movement and the Indigenous women's movement. In 2012, thanks to the efforts of the International Indigenous Women's Forum (FIMI), a second resolution was adopted by CSW entitled "Indigenous women: key actors in poverty and hunger eradication" and supported by Australia, Argentina, Bolivia, Ecuador, El Salvador, Guatemala, Mexico, and Nicaragua.[80]

Indigenous women have indeed participated in the global mobilization of the women of the world. At the first UN women's conference in Mexico City in 1975, the only visible Indigenous woman present was the Bolivian Domitila Chungara, who raised her voice to say that what was being discussed was not about her.[81] Indigenous women feel that the colonial system gave them a role, that they have to serve other people; they want to be very clear about the important role they have in the world.[82] More Indigenous women participated at the 1985 UN conference on women in Nairobi.[83] The issue of discrimination was raised by Indigenous women at the Fourth World Conference on Women (held in Beijing in 1995), and Indigenous women also participated at the tenth and twentieth anniversaries of the Beijing conference.[84]

At the Permanent Forum on Indigenous Issues, Indigenous women participate in great numbers; many have their own organizations and have a strong voice. Indigenous women's issues constitute a perennial item on the Forum's agenda. The annual expert meeting of the UNPFII in 2012 was devoted to violence against Indigenous women, a topic of great international interest, an

---

79 Resolution 49/7, "Indigenous women: beyond the ten-year review of the Beijing Declaration and Platform for Action." See UN Commission on the Status of Women, Report on the Forty-Ninth Session (28 February–11 and 22 March 2005), UN Doc. E/CN.6/2005/11 (2005), 23–24. See also the website of the Secretariat of the CSW, www.unwomen.org/en/csw.

80 Resolution 56/4. See UN Commission on the Status of Women, Report on the Fifty-Sixth Session (14 March 2011, 27 February–9 March and 15 March 2016), UN Doc. E/CN.6/2012/16 (2016), 22–25.

81 Presentation of Tarcila Rivera Zea, the Indigenous leader from Peru, to an unidentified seminar organized by FIMI and Columbia University's Institute for the Study of Human Rights in 2021.

82 Tarcila Rivera Zea, 2021 seminar presentation. For more on the debates and frictions within the women's caucus at the Mexico conference, see Jocelyn Olcott, " 'We Are Our Sister's Keeper': US Feminists at the 1975 International Women's Year Conference," United Nations History Project, Image of the Month, June 2017, www.histecon.magd.cam.ac.uk/unhist/image-of-the_month/image_of_the_month_June17.html.

83 Tarcila Rivera Zea, 2021 seminar presentation.

84 See Secretariat of the Permanent Forum on Indigenous Issues, Twenty-Year Review of the Beijing Declaration and Platform for Action and Beyond: A Framework to Advance Indigenous Women's Issues, UN Doc. E/C.19/2015/2 (4 February 2015).

overarching issue, and also a topic of intense advocacy by Indigenous women.[85][86] Indigenous women also gather among themselves at global and regional levels to strategize and issue important policy statements.[87]

At the high-level plenary meeting of the General Assembly in 2014 known as the "World Conference on Indigenous Peoples," the UNGA invited the CSW to consider the issue of the empowerment of Indigenous women at a future session.[88] The Permanent Forum, at its fourteenth session, recommended that the CSW consider the empowerment of Indigenous women as a priority theme of its sixty-first session, in 2017, on the occasion of the tenth anniversary of the adoption of the UNDRIP.[89] The Commission decided to consider the empowerment of Indigenous women as a *focus area/emerging issue* at its session. The focus area was covered in a half-day session held during the high-level week of the Commission. Indigenous women, members of the Forum, and the Special Rapporteur on the rights of Indigenous Peoples were invited to attend. The Commission Chair's summary of the discussion may have not gathered high enthusiasm among Indigenous women's organizations by comparison to what comes out of the UNPFII and the other Indigenous-specific UN mechanisms, but it was a reflection of Indigenous women's success in making their issues visible in other relevant international bodies, whose policies may affect their lives and certainly are expected to affect the behavior of states.[90]

85 Report of the International Expert Group Meeting on Combating Violence against Indigenous Women and Girls: Article 22 of the United Nations Declaration on the Rights of Indigenous Peoples, UN Doc. E/C.19/2012/6 (28 February 2012); International Work Group on Indigenous Affairs, *IWGIA Gender Strategy 2021–2025* (IWGIA, 2021), 4, https://iwgia.org/en/about/organisation.html.

86 See also International Indigenous Women's Forum (FIMI), *Global Study on the Situation of Indigenous Women And Girls* (FIMI, 2020), https://fimi-iiwf.org/en/biblioteca-propias/the-global-study-on-the-situation-of-indigenous-women-and-girls/; and Summer Rain Bentham, Hilla Kerner, and Lisa Steacy, "Sisterhood on the Frontiers: The Truth as We Hear It from Indigenous Women," in *Forever Loved: Exposing the Hidden Crisis of Missing and Murdered Indigenous Women and Girls in Canada*, ed. D. Memee Lavell-Harvard and Jennifer Brant (Bradford, ON: Demeter Press, 2016).

87 For example, World Conference of Indigenous Women: Progress and Challenges Regarding the Future We Want, *Lima Declaration*, 30 October 2013, www.culturalsurvival.org/sites/default/files/lima_declaration1.pdf; and Second World Conference of Indigenous Women: Together for Wellbeing and Mother Earth, *Global Political Declaration of Indigenous Women*, 2 September 2021, www.asianindigenouswomen.org/files/Global_Political_Declaration_of_Indigenous_Women_2WCIW.pdf.

88 UN General Assembly, Resolution 69/2, Outcome Document of the High-Level Plenary Meeting of the General Assembly Known as the World Conference on Indigenous Peoples, UN Doc. A/RES/69/2 (25 September 2014), https://documents-dds-ny.un.org/doc/UNDOC/GEN/N14/468/28/PDF/N1446828.pdf.

89 UN Permanent Forum on Indigenous Issues, Report on the Fourteenth Session (20 April–1 May 2015), UN Doc. E/2015/43-E/C.19/2015/10 (2015), para. 43, https://documents-dds-ny.un.org/doc/UNDOC/GEN/N15/143/74/PDF/N1514374.pdf.

90 UN Commission on the Status of Women, Interactive Dialogue on the Focus Area: Empowerment of Indigenous Women, UN Doc. E/CN.6/2017/12 (20 March 2017), https://documents-dds-ny.un.org/doc/UNDOC/GEN/N17/073/17/PDF/N1707317.pdf.

The particular issues of Indigenous women pose some special concerns. Indigenous women have to challenge "patriarchy within Native communities, but also white supremacy and colonialism within mainstream white feminism."[91] Also, there have been on occasion differences in the viewpoints and in the agendas of feminist movements and Indigenous women's movements. For example, the Fourth World Conference of Women in Beijing in 1995 saw "a contradictory and often conflictual relationship between feminist organisations and female indigenous representatives," as Indigenous women were pushing for a different agenda to that of feminists.[92] Some scholars stress that sex-based oppression does not relate to tribal cultures but derives from Western colonial influences and stems from the hierarchical nature of Western society.[93] The historical context cannot and should not be overlooked when discussing such issues.[94] Indigenous women scholars have discussed such matters,[95] and various international human rights mechanisms have continued to issue reports on Indigenous women's human rights.[96] Some of the previous questions are discussed in this section.

1. How Does UNDRIP Cover Indigenous Women?

Every article of the Declaration is relevant for Indigenous women, both as individuals and as collectivities, including land rights, the right to self-determination, and cultural human rights. In fact, Indigenous women have the right to enjoy all human rights and fundamental freedoms recognized in all international human rights instruments, from the Universal Declaration of Human Rights to the Convention on the Elimination of all Forms of Discrimination against Women to various other instruments. Articles 21 and 22 of UNDRIP make special reference to Indigenous women:

---

91 Andrea Smith, "Indigenous Feminism without Apology," *New Socialist*, no. 58 (September – October 2006): 16.

92 Sarah A. Radcliffe, "Indigenous Women, Rights and the Nation-State in the Andes," in *Gender and the Politics of Rights and Democracy in Latin America*, ed. Nikki Craske and Maxine Molyneux (New York: Palgrave, 2002), 164.

93 Madhavi Sunder, "Piercing the Veil," *Yale Law Journal* 112, no. 6 (March 2003): 1430; see also Andrea Smith, *Conquest: Sexual Violence and American Indian Genocide* (New York: South End Press, 2005), 139.

94 Xanthaki, "Limitations to Indigenous Autonomy."

95 See, for example, Kuokkanen, *Restructuring Relations*, 1–21.

96 For example, Secretariat of the Permanent Forum on Indigenous Issues, Study on the Extent of Violence against Indigenous Women and Girls in Terms of Article 22 (2) of the United Nations Declaration on the Rights of Indigenous Peoples, UN Doc. E/C.19/2013/9 (12 February 2013); UN Human Rights Council, Report of the Special Rapporteur on the Rights of Indigenous Peoples, Victoria Tauli-Corpuz, UN Doc. A/HRC/30/41 (6 August 2015); Inter-American Commission on Human Rights, *Indigenous Women and their Human Rights in the Americas*, OEA/Ser.L/V/II., Doc. 44/17 (IACHR, 2017).

Article 21

1. Indigenous peoples have the right, without discrimination, to the improvement of their economic and social conditions, including, inter alia, in the areas of education, employment, vocational training and retraining, housing, sanitation, health and social security.

2. *States shall take effective measures and, where appropriate, special measures to ensure continuing improvement of their economic and social conditions. Particular attention shall be paid to the rights and special needs of* indigenous elders, *women*, youth, children and persons with disabilities.[97]

Article 22

1. *Particular attention shall be paid to the rights and special needs of* indigenous elders, *women*, youth, children and persons with disabilities *in the implementation of this Declaration.*

2. *States shall take measures, in conjunction with indigenous peoples, to ensure that indigenous women and children enjoy the full protection and guarantees against all forms of violence and discrimination.*[98]

An analytical explanation of these provisions, and a detailing of the measures that the wording implies, follows next.

2. Indigenous Women and Equality: Is the Principle of Nondiscrimination Enough?

According to the UN Permanent Forum on Indigenous Issues (UNPFII), the dominant gender-neutral conception of equality prevailing in countries where Indigenous Peoples live has not been adequate in addressing the multiple disadvantages of Indigenous women.[99] It has become a daunting task in each country to repeal policies and practices that perpetuate sexual objectification of Indigenous women, their disempowerment, and victimization. In other words, the view of separate but equal, as expressed by Radhika

---

97 www.un.org/development/desa/indigenouspeoples/wp-content/uploads/sites/19/2018/11/ UNDRIP_E_web.pdf, accessed 11 January 2024.

98 Idem. Emphasis added.

99 UN Permanent Forum on Indigenous Issues, Report on the Third Session (10–21 May 2004), UN Doc. E/2004/43 (2004), para. 3. The concerns and recommendations on Indigenous women are contained in paragraphs 3–15.

Coomaraswamy, the first UN Special Rapporteur on Violence against Women, is what has prevailed.[100]

In addition, what is also part of the UN human rights norms explicitly, as in UNDRIP, or via interpretation, is that positive targeted measures are required by the state in order to address the inequality and discrimination faced by Indigenous women. For example, such special measures are required to overcome the hurdles in educational, health, vocational/economic, and political disadvantages of Indigenous women.

In the sessions of the UNPFII over the years, various speakers have pointed out the challenges of demolishing structural barriers to eliminate complex oppressions experienced by Indigenous women and to achieve a multicultural democracy and gender equality throughout the world. Yet nondiscrimination and equality continue to be complex principles to put into practice, having also to do with issues of forced assimilation, cultural specificity, agency, and self-determination of Indigenous women.

3. Parameters of Indigenous Women's Rights

Indigenous women have been at the forefront of their peoples' struggles. They have been fighting for their peoples' survival and for their peoples' collective rights. They have often placed on the backburner the problems they have faced as individuals within their communities, including violence and discrimination. The black women in South Africa during apartheid and the Palestinian women have often done the same – that is, they have placed priority on the struggle of their peoples for survival and freedom.

Indigenous women became even stronger leaders along with the growth of the international Indigenous movement. Gradually, they also approached the global women's movement more actively, while maintaining their Indigenous rights demands. As mentioned earlier, they participated at the Beijing Conference in 1995, and at the Beijing+5 Conference in 2000, they created the FIMI. In 2005, they marked their special arrival to the global women's movement: they actively participated in Beijing+10 and achieved the adoption of the first ever resolution on Indigenous women by the UN Commission on the Status of Women.

---

100 See, for example, Ms. Coomaraswamy's statement at the UN Commission on Human Rights on 9 April 2003, where she stated, among other things, that "Strategies must therefore be sensitive to cultural realities and, most importantly, we must listen to the voices of the women from those cultures. When we fight for human rights of women, we must always do so by respecting the dignity of the very women whose rights we are defending." Integration of the Human Rights of Women and the Gender Perspective: Violence against Women, www.ohchr.org/en/statements/2009/10/integration-human-rights-women-and-gender-perspective-violence-against-women.

With different degrees of persistence and different strategies, Indigenous women in different countries started to fight for nondiscrimination also *within* their countries and communities. It is the Indigenous women themselves, as agents of their own destinies, who will tell outsiders whether they, the women, want to accept certain cultural roles in the community or not. Indigenous women, like most human beings, do not just copy cultural patterns. They constantly change and create culture as well, especially since, in today's world, Indigenous women contribute to and receive ideas from other cultures, from within their country, or from outside their country, including the United Nations and the global women's and human rights movements.

Since Indigenous women should be respected as agents of their own destiny, the question is, what should be the human rights response in case of violations of Indigenous women's human rights within the community? Here the UNDRIP is clear. It outlines the borders between individual and group cultural rights by clearly placing its norms within the overall normative framework of internationally recognized human rights. Article 34 states:

> Indigenous peoples have the right to promote, develop and maintain their institutional structures and their distinctive customs, spirituality, traditions procedures, practices and, in the cases where they exist, juridical systems or customs, *in accordance with international human rights standards.*[101]

Article 46, paragraphs 2–3, state:

> 2. In the exercise of the rights enunciated in the present Declaration, human rights and fundamental freedoms of all shall be respected. The exercise of the rights set forth in this Declaration shall be subject only to such limitations as are determined by law and *in accordance with international human rights obligations.* Any such limitations shall be non-discriminatory and strictly necessary solely for the purpose of securing due recognition and respect for the rights and freedoms of others and for meeting the just and most compelling requirements of a democratic society.
> 3. *The provisions set forth in this Declaration shall be interpreted in accordance with the principles of justice, democracy, respect for human rights, equality, non-discrimination, good governance and good faith.*[102]

---

101 www.un.org/development/desa/indigenouspeoples/wp-content/uploads/sites/19/2018/11/ UNDRIP_E_web.pdf, accessed 11 January 2024. Emphasis added.
102 www.un.org/development/desa/indigenouspeoples/wp-content/uploads/sites/19/2018/11/ UNDRIP_E_web.pdf, accessed 11 January 2024. Emphasis added.

These provisions mean that an Indigenous people or community must respect the human rights of individuals within it. The duties that an Indigenous community would require of its members must comply with international human rights standards. It is well-known that Indigenous leaders who participated in the negotiations of the UNDRIP over the years were well aware of and agreed to this principle early on.

Of course the question remains, as to how the state should intervene within an Indigenous community to protect Indigenous women's human rights if they are violated. This is a question that begs a multipronged response: legislative, judicial, and educational measures, as well as restorative justice. There may be a possibility of a creative interface between traditional justice and state justice systems, and such efforts are being made in recent times in a number of countries.[103]

The debate around women's human rights and traditional justice or traditional law is a long one regarding several ethnic or religious communities, not only regarding Indigenous Peoples. As mentioned earlier, due to the fact that UNDRIP is clear on the requirement of respect for universal human rights by all, Indigenous women leaders may well have felt that this clarity for the prevalence of international human rights norms has been adequate for now to cover their own internal efforts and voices within their communities and countries. As cultures, politics, and peoples' initiatives evolve constantly, it is up to Indigenous women themselves to choose what further options to follow internationally, nationally, regionally, and locally on such issues. The excellent publication of FIMI, *Mairin Iwanka Raya: Indigenous Women Against Violence*, gives a clear vision on many of these responses and espouses the demand for respect of internationally recognized human rights of Indigenous women, while adding the collective human rights, including the right to land and to self-determination.

4. *Exercising Cultural Human Rights*

Because of inadequate general understanding of cultural rights,[104] the subject of cultural rights and women commonly brings up the issue of women and culture. It is the oversimplified view of how culture has negative effects on women's human rights. One thinks in particular about the role of the woman in the family, where the woman is traditionally seen in her reproductive and

103 For example, among the Igorot people in the Philippines, the penalty against a rapist was permanent expulsion from the community as the whole community is considered attacked by this crime. Today the state imposes its own laws on the crime of rape. (Author's discussion with Victoria Tauli-Corpuz in 2010).

104 Elsa Stamatopoulou, *Cultural Rights in International Law: Article 27 of the Universal Declaration of Human Rights and Beyond* (Leiden: Martinus Nijhoff, 2007).

family-caring role, or in the community, with the woman's traditional role as keeper of culture, and in the state, where the woman is dealt with in the legal sphere, with her life regulated in a traditional way. While the negative effects of aspects of culture on women's human rights have been discussed for years, there has been little exploration on the positive aspects of culture and its potential for changing women's lives toward gender equality, with women themselves in the front seat.

What people often fail to see, blinded at times by a concept of culture as a static "thing," is the empowering aspect that culture has or can have for Indigenous women, who play a very important role in the culture of their communities. In fact, gender, women's human rights, cultural human rights, and Indigenous Peoples' rights are interlinked.

The promotion of women's full and effective participation in a democratic polity and in all aspects of civil society has special significance in terms of cultural rights, so that women can have the opportunity to assert their agency, to interpret and reinterpret culture in the light of new elements they have gathered, to amend or eliminate, in their way, cultural specificities that are negative for them, and to exercise their cultural rights.[105]

A briefing note prepared by the United Nations Office of the Special Adviser on Gender Issues and the Advancement of Women (OSAGI) and the Secretariat of the UNPFII sums up Indigenous women's role in cultural practices very well:

> In many cultural and religious traditions, women have primary responsibility for transmitting cultural and spiritual knowledge and practices, and group identity more generally, to succeeding generations. Because culture exists and is generated through the lived experiences of people, the role of women in transmitting culture also situates them as creators and custodians of culture. For this reason, people across a diverse range of communities view women's adherence to and promulgation of cultural norms as integral to cultural survival. In many instances, this relationship between gender and culture is used as a basis for justifying violations of women's human rights. For example, in many cultures, religions, and state systems, the rights of individual women are subordinated to upholding women's role as the carriers of group identity. Thus, women are often denied the right to make autonomous decisions regarding their own sexuality, child-bearing, and marriage; and their children's nationality, religion, and citizenship. These violations of basic rights are rationalized as necessary to

---

105 Gayatri Chakravorty Spivak has said that "Destruction of cultural specificity is part of good globalization." Spivak, Statement at the First Planning Meeting for the Women Leaders Intercultural Forum, New York, 11 October 2005. The author was present at that meeting.

ensure cultural preservation and other collective identities, which women are thought to embody.

On the other hand, women's primary role in transmitting and creating culture can serve as a basis for protecting and enhancing women's status within their families and communities. For example, the international indigenous women's movement has demonstrated that among many indigenous peoples, women's roles as spiritual guides, midwives, healers, and political leaders – all forms of cultural expression – are a central basis of women's power and status among their peoples. Indeed, women's cultural practices are important not only for the spiritual health of their communities but also for their communities' overall well-being. In most communities around the world, women are the primary providers of food, water, and healthcare for their families. Women fulfill these roles in culturally specific ways, highlighting the relationship between women's gender-based human rights, cultural rights, and economic and social rights.[106]

The question then is how a human rights approach to culture, including the cultural human rights of women, can promote gender equality by various means, including through strengthening women's agency. First, it is clear that a change of culture, whether traditional or not, that violates the human rights of women will be the result of change from within, so it can be sustainable, with women as agents of change. Indigenous women's increasing visibility in the public sphere, locally, nationally, and internationally will support this agency of change. Strategic cooperation among Indigenous women and non-Indigenous women leaders in different social positions can be productive. Young Indigenous women leaders have to be brought into this struggle, and spaces for dialogue have to be created with progressive and other men, including young men. The Indigenous movement, the women's movement, the human rights movement, labor, and new social movements for social justice are important entry points for such cultural interventions.

Another useful strategy would be for Indigenous women to share their experiences and perspectives on the supportive elements of their traditional cultural contexts that empowered them to become leaders and dynamic agents of change, as well as on the obstacles generated by traditional norms or values that limit social, economic, and political participation of women and curb their leadership potential. The world has heard more about the obstacles but not enough about the supportive elements of various cultural contexts, as women have interpreted, reinterpreted, and used them for their empowerment and the well-being of their communities.

106 OSAGI and SPFII, *Gender and Indigenous Peoples*, 20.

Conceptual clarification in the discussion on "culture of a group vs. the human rights of women" is crucial for the following reasons: (a) because human rights, cultural rights, and group rights are used in the discourse we are dealing with, and each provokes profound emotions and political reverberations; (b) because we need this clarity so as not to appear to discredit all cultures at all times when we deal with women's issues, and thus create unnuanced, wrong, unnecessary, or absolute confrontations; and (c) because we need to positively assert the need for respect for the cultural rights of Indigenous women in this debate.

The UNDRIP views the Indigenous individual as an individual, a member of the Indigenous group, a member of the national society, a member of other categories (women, children, older persons), and of course, as a member of the world community.[107] The individual will manage and prioritize these different identities at any decision (s)he takes.[108] The beliefs that underpin a human rights framework do find their origin in a wide range of cultures – whether we call them traditional or not is not important – that put forward notions of human rights and dignity upon which to condemn oppression and discrimination. This is the case with Indigenous cultures as well.

A multilateral, multiagency initiative at the UN sprang out of the dynamism of Indigenous women themselves at the Permanent Forum. In 2004, a group of agencies took the initiative to form a Task Force on Indigenous Women under the Inter-Agency Network on Women and Gender Equality. The Group worked for three years and completed a survey of how Indigenous women's issues are addressed by the UN system; they also issued a collection of good practices and lessons learned in the work of UN agencies with Indigenous women.[109] The substantive participation of Indigenous women was a major focus in the findings and was highlighted as a criterion for successful results.

Chhing Lamu Sherpa, Indigenous leader in Nepal, in a discussion with the author,[110] reflected on the solidarity and inspiration she felt during her participation at the UNPFII and how this participation helped her organize important Indigenous women's events in her country that increased women's

---

107 For more on this model, see Alexandra Xanthaki, "Multiculturalism and International Law: Discussing Universal Standards," *Human Rights Quarterly* 32, no. 1 (February 2010): 40, https://doi.org/10.1353/hrq.0.0139.

108 Xanthaki, "Limitations to Indigenous Autonomy."

109 Secretariat of the Permanent Forum on Indigenous Issues and Inter-Agency Network on Women and Gender Equality Task Force on Indigenous Women, *Indigenous Women and the United Nations System: Good Practices and Lessons Learned* (New York: UN, 2007), www.un.org/esa/socdev/publications/Indigenous/indwomen07.htm.

110 Sherpa interviewed by the author, 21 November 2016. The list of persons with whom discussions were held appears in Annex 1. The questions discussed with interviewees are listed in the introduction.

profiles and numbers in such events. Looking into the future, she pointed out that for such progress to happen and be consolidated, academics with resources are needed from the backside, and advocates and defenders are needed as well. Sherpa also referred to intergenerational transmission of knowledge and said that all possible opportunities should be given to young people, while "at the same time, we should also make sure who has the history, the oral history."

Taking a long-term historical perspective within the decades of the international Indigenous Peoples' movement, one can certainly see that Indigenous women have increased their voice and profile so that it would be impossible in contemporary times to imagine relevant international debates without their presence and participation. Indigenous women have organized, strategized, theorized, advocated, and extended solidarity and political advice to each other and to the Indigenous movement overall. They have clearly gained special respect and admiration within the movement and also among international agencies that systematically seek their cooperation. The intergenerational transmission of knowledge and mutual wisdom shared between the older and younger Indigenous women leaders is visible, and the strengthening of the international profile of the Indigenous Peoples' movement continues as a result. These trends create the expectation that new achievements of and for the Indigenous women of the world will be possible.

H. Participation of Indigenous Youth

There is something fundamental when it comes to Indigenous Peoples' participation at the UN, especially in Indigenous-related fora. It is surrounded by the ethic of decolonization, which has deep historical roots and impacts and is therefore intergenerational. The reversal of historic injustices, even at a symbolic level in the UN, creates the expectation that there should be space for Indigenous ways and Indigenous concerns that are beyond the UN's practices and agendas. Indigenous Peoples' lives cannot be straightjacketed by states' ways, and this is a fundamental part of the right of Indigenous Peoples to self-determination. Indigenous participation at the UN requires creativity on the part of all concerned.

Some new ways of participation have been emerging, especially through the Global Indigenous Youth Caucus (GIYC) at the UNPFII. The Caucus was formally recognized as a working caucus at the Permanent Forum in 2008.[111]

111 The GIYC provides a link between Indigenous youth and other organizations. Currently, the area of work of the GIYC covers UNPFII, EMRIP, the Special Rapporteur on the Rights of Indigenous Peoples, the Sustainable Development Goals of Agenda 2030, and the UN Food and Agriculture Organization (FAO). See Qivioq Nivi Løvstrøm, Kibett Carson Kiburo, and Qhapaj Conde, introduction to *Global Indigenous Youth: Through Their Eyes*, ed. Dali Angel Pérez, Victor Arthur Lopez-Carmen, and Elsa Stamatopoulou (New

Their well-crafted statements convey vision and the conviction that the new generation of leaders will strengthen the Indigenous Peoples' movement even further. When representatives of the GIYC speak, other youth from diverse parts of the world stand behind them, making this practice moving and compelling. The image of the speaker surrounded by other Indigenous youth is also projected onto the two big screens of the UN conference room, and many participants film it while it is being delivered, spreading it through social media. Indigenous women and others are also using this way of amplifying their statements at the Permanent Forum.

Inspiring Indigenous Peoples and others around them was and continues to be a fundamental approach in the statements of Indigenous representatives, Indigenous youth included. As the Coordinators of the GIYC wrote in 2019,

> We, Indigenous Youth, have listened to the stories of our elders, and we remember that we are the guardians of the forest. We are the protesters that stand for water rights, the sisters who demand environmental change in a world that is simultaneously melting and drowning, the brothers who advocate for policy change in a world that is plagued by droughts and floods, the communities who combat hunger and corruption. We are the survivors who are healing after the rape of our peoples and our lands, who, to this day, are fighting the people and corporations who want us gone for the sake of profit.
>
> We, Indigenous Peoples, have been mowed down and burned, frozen and drowned, but our roots remained strong; we are sprouting and growing and we want you to witness our hybrid flowers blossoming. We demand the acknowledgement of our space in the contemporary world as Young, Indigenous and Living.
>
> Indigenous Youth are not a relic of the past; rather, we are a promise of a better future.[112]

The challenges for Indigenous youth, both inside and outside their communities, are complex. Some Indigenous leaders, more mature in age, see that contemporary Indigenous youth, having been raised with Indigenous rights already proclaimed, do not always feel the urge to engage with the movement or with "being Indigenous."[113] While intergenerational dialogue

---

York: Institute for the Study of Human Rights, Columbia University, 2019), https://doi.org/10.7916/d8-dh2w-rz29.

112 Løvstrøm, Kiburo, and Conde, introduction, xxvii. The authors were the Co-Chairs of Global Indigenous Youth Caucus 2018–2019.

113 This phenomenon was noted in the women's movement as well. The achievements of the movement in the past decades have led many younger women to often feel too comfortable

among Indigenous leaders can have tensions, it is clear that Indigenous youth have increased their political profile within the movement and more broadly. Indigenous youth are able to rely on many achievements of previous generations in terms of human rights norms, especially the Declaration, as well as international institutions devoted to Indigenous issues or open to Indigenous Peoples. At the same time, Indigenous youth have compounded their own education, contemporary skills, and savvy, also opening dialogues for new areas for policy intervention, including issues of integration in the job market, entrepreneurship, and sexual orientation.[114] The Cree Nation in Canada, for example, started offering a community college course on the UNDRIP, another course on the OAS Declaration on the Rights of Indigenous Peoples, a course on the Convention on the Rights of the Child, the Convention on Biological Diversity, and other international human rights instruments. And a few times, the community leaders took students from that class to Geneva, to the sessions of the WGIP.[115]

We note that the Indigenous movement, including or especially the youth, adapts both to new methods of work brought before it, such as the time limit on speakers at UNPFII, and to the new ways available for affecting world public opinion, such as visual technologies and social media. In recent times, it would be no exaggeration to say that when the Global Indigenous Youth Caucus takes the floor at the UN, the attention of the room is focused on their messages, visions, and demands. The enthusiasm, support, and warmth expressed toward Indigenous youth reverberates the deep satisfaction that hope brings to social struggles.

I. The First Indigenous Leader to Meet with a UN Secretary-General: The Yanomami Case

Indigenous Peoples have valued, pursued, and achieved various types of participation in international affairs, often outside specific processes mandated by states. Over time, various Indigenous delegations have sought to meet with the UN Secretary-General, symbolizing the head of the world Organization and giving high political profile to Indigenous interlocutors.[116] While Indigenous leaders pursued meeting with the UN Secretary-General on various occasions since the establishment of the WGIP, it was not until 1991 that this became possible, when Davi Kopenawa Yanomami became the first

---

and not engage with women's issues, creating retraction of positive measures in some cases, such as in the issue of abortion and others.

114 Løvstrøm, Kiburo, and Conde, introduction, xxvii.

115 Insights into the Cree experience were given to the author in an interview with Grand Chief Wilton Littlechild, conducted 28 January 2017.

116 The author headed the New York Office of the then UN Center for Human Rights in the mid-1980s and witnessed several such efforts, including by the Hopi and Diné Peoples.

Indigenous leader to be received by the UN Secretary-General, Javier Pérez de Cuéllar, at the time.

A unique humanitarian intervention in the name of the UN Secretary-General took place at the end of 1990 regarding the Yanomami people in Brazil. The Yanomami were experiencing a critical situation and massive loss of life threatening them with extinction due to the influx of wildcat gold diggers (*garimpeiros*) in their territories. Numbering some thirty-five thousand, the Yanomami live across the border areas in Brazil and Venezuela, with some twelve thousand estimated to live in Brazil. Diseases, especially a new type of malaria, mercury contamination of the waters that entered the food chain, and outright killings were leading several Yanomami settlements in Brazil to perish. About 20 percent of the population died in seven years. The word genocide was used by many to describe the gravity of the situation. Between 1987 and 1990 some forty thousand gold-miners, several times more than all the Yanomami in Brazil, entered Yanomami lands, encouraged by then President of Brazil José Sarney's rhetoric on economic ventures.[117]

An Indigenous organization in the United States, the Indian Law Resource Center, was following the situation closely in collaboration with the Brazilian Commission for the Creation of the Yanomami Park (CCPY – *Comissão pela Criação do Parque Yanomami*) and wrote to the UN Secretary-General to ask for his good offices and his humanitarian intervention with the Brazilian government to address this critical situation.

Brazil, a harsh country on Indigenous matters since the early days of the WGIP, accepted a UN mission to visit the country, headed by the Chairperson of the WGIP, Erica-Irene Daes. It was the first international mission on Indigenous issues that Brazil had accepted, despite previous requests by the International Labor Organization for such a visit. The government preferred the seemingly "softer" approach of humanitarianism – that was the frame of the Daes visit – rather than the shaming and finger-pointing approach of the UN's human rights monitoring procedures.[118] Daes had convinced the Brazilian government to accept her visit, which, despite the humanitarian

---

117 "The Yanomami," Survival International, www.survivalinternational.org/tribes/yanomami, accessed 7 June 2022. Survival International has actively advocated on the Yanomami case for years.

118 For a discussion of the Secretary-General's humanitarian intervention of good offices, see Elsa Stamatopoulou, "The Good Offices of the Secretary-General in Human Rights Issues: Past Practice and Future Challenges," in *Justice Pending: Indigenous Peoples and Other Good Causes, Essays in Honour of Erica-Irene A. Daes*, ed. Gudmundur Alfredsson and Maria Stavropoulou (The Hague: Martinus Nijhoff, 2002). The chapter includes a discussion of the intervention for the Yanomami people and of a mission in which the author participated. The Indian Law Resource Center was closely involved in the appeal to the Secretary-General.

frame of "good offices of the Secretary-General," was nevertheless a human rights visit.

Once the Daes mission, in which the author participated, arrived in Yanomami land in Roraima, Brazil, the first meeting Daes held was with Davi Kopenawa Yanomami and Levi Yanomami, spokesmen, elders, and shamans of the Yanomami. The meeting took place in a Brazilian army base in the heart of the Amazon rainforest. In the long meeting, Davi and Levi described the dire situation. The diseases brought in by the illegal gold diggers were so different from what the Yanomami had experienced before that their traditional medicine could not deal with them. In one of their villages, Davi said, all children under two had perished due to diseases. At the same time, the government was neither preventing the illegal gold diggers from coming in nor taking care of this health crisis, but they were also not allowing humanitarian medical assistance to be offered by UN agencies, such as the UN Children's Fund (UNICEF) or by Brazilian civil society organizations. Moreover, the powerful army establishment was claiming that the Brazil-Venezuela border was supposedly threatened by the Yanomami who inhabited both sides of the border. Having created military governments in Brazil from 1964 to 1985, it was hard for the military to give up some narratives, including one offensive to common intelligence, that people with bows and arrows would be a threat to the country's border with Venezuela. The Yanomami case was clearly a human rights case as it displayed the negative political will of a government that, through actions and inactions, actually fostered this situation, endangering the existence of the Yanomami. Daes's outspoken declarations to the Brazilian media subsequently clearly underlined that.

The Brazilian government was trying to take away with one hand what it had given with the other, in an effort to temper the human rights critique that they saw coming from the UN.

An episode during the mission was indicative of the deep concern and indignation felt by this UN mission. The Government was telling the mission that in an effort to stop the *garimpeiros*, they were from time to time bombing the illegal airstrips. Our UN mission was staying for a few nights in a military base in Roraima, and as part of our official program, one morning we were to use a military small plane to visit a deeply affected community in the rainforest. However, once we were ready to leave for that community early in the morning, we were suddenly informed that the plane was "busy," as it was needed to drop some bombs to destroy an airstrip. I had never seen Erica Daes so angry at what she saw as a "diplomatic" excuse for us not to be taken to that community. She asked to speak to the military commander. She told him in no uncertain terms that she had a specific agreement with the Foreign Minister for the program of this mission. The visit to the affected community was part of the official mission, and it had to take place. She could not believe the "coincidence" that the plane assigned for her specific visit was supposedly busy keeping the gold diggers out that particular morning at 8 a.m. She demanded to speak to the Foreign Minister immediately. Daes's intervention was effective: we could use the military plane immediately, and we did go and visit the community. We saw many people sick in their *malocas*, their big family huts. At one point, as I walked on my own separately from the mission group, a number of community members approached me. A man who looked like a grandfather was holding a child in his arms. The child seemed very ill. The people started talking to me in Yanomami and showing me the child. They probably didn't know what the UN was but imagined that we were there to see the situation and help. So, in Greek, in a moment of deep human communication beyond just language, I assured them we would do all we could.

A few months after the mission took place, the renowned spokesman and shaman of the Yanomami, Davi Kopenawa Yanomami traveled to New York and was received by the UN Secretary-General Pérez de Cuéllar in March 1991.[119] Davi became the first Indigenous leader to meet with the leader of the UN. He explained the grave danger faced by his people. He left a gift with the Secretary-General, a bouquet from the Amazon, three long red feathers combined with short white and black ones – Yanomami men wear these around their arms. During that visit in the United States, Davi also met with then Senator Al Gore and visited the Onondaga Nation.

The report of the UN mission to Brazil went directly to the Secretary-General, and since the mission was taking place under his humanitarian good offices, it remained confidential. Following the mission, the Brazilian government allowed some medical assistance to be delivered to the Yanomami by UNICEF. The lands of the Yanomami were demarcated in 1992–9.6 million hectares, twice the size of Switzerland – and the gold-miners were expelled. However, the difficulties of implementing this demarcation in the long-term through protection of the lands by the state soon started to appear, and the struggle of the Yanomami has continued. In June 1992 Davi participated at the Earth Summit in Rio de Janeiro, and in December 1992, Davi was one of the speakers at the opening of the International Year of the World's Indigenous People at the UN General Assembly in New York.

The UN remains vigilant about the situation of the Yanomami and generally about the situation of the Indigenous Peoples in Brazil.[120] After all,

---

119 Survival International's website has a biographical sketch of Davi Kopenawa, "Selected Chronology of Davi Kopenawa's Life," www.survivalinternational.org/articles/3638-davi-kopenawa-biography, accessed 7 June 2022.
120 The UN Special Rapporteurs on the Rights of Indigenous Peoples have visited Brazil repeatedly and presented reports; see UN Human Rights Council, Report of the

they were described as the largest relatively isolated tribe, and the idea was that if the Yanomami, who are also well-known outside Brazil, cannot have their lands and livelihoods respected in Brazil, what can one expect for other Indigenous Peoples in Brazil? In 1993, there was another intervention by the UN Secretary-General toward the Brazilian government. This time it concerned a massacre in Haximu of sixteen Yanomami in a clash with *garimpeiros*.[121]

Davi Yanomami has continued to advocate and defend his peoples at all fora that appear useful, galvanizing international public opinion in solidarity. Since Jair Bolsonaro became President of Brazil in 2019, and following his anti-Indigenous rhetoric, some twenty thousand *garimpeiros* invaded Yanomami land. Agencies responsible for law enforcement in the Amazon were defunded by that government.[122]

The Yanomami struggle to defend their land rights, their livelihoods, and their cultures continues in a constant interface of strategies between the local, national, and international levels. There is video footage of Davi that graphically tells this story in a film produced for the Secretariat of the UNPFII in 2005.[123] We see some Yanomami gathered in a *maloca* getting information about the UN. There are various graphs on a board with the names of the UNPFII, the Economic and Social Council, and the General Assembly, in Portuguese. In another graph, the acronym "ONU" (United Nations) appears in the middle of a circle with arrows pointing to it, with names of various states and sketches of *malocas* to show that both states and Indigenous Peoples have their input in the UN. The other visual aid of Davi's seminar is the glossy folder/poster produced by the UN for the International Decade of the World's Indigenous People, depicting various Indigenous faces from around the world. Davi points to an Indigenous person's image and says "Sámi," and then he points to another image, from North America, and says "Americano." Davi then points to a map of the world showing where these different peoples live. He is explaining geography, the UN system, and

Special Rapporteur on the Rights of Indigenous Peoples on Her Mission to Brazil: Note by the Secretariat, UN Doc. A/HRC/33/42/Add.1 (8 August 2016); and Report of the Special Rapporteur on the Situation of Human Rights and Fundamental Freedoms of Indigenous People, James Anaya: Addendum, UN Doc. A/HRC/12/34/Add.2 (26 August 2009).

121 "Remembering the Haximu Massacre 20 Years On," Survival International website, www. survivalinternational.org/articles/3298-haximu-survivors, accessed 24 November 2023.

122 Sue Branford, "Yanomami Amazon Reserve Invaded by 20,000 Miners; Bolsonaro Fails to Act," *Mongabay*, 12 July 2019, https://news.mongabay.com/2019/07/yanomami-amazon-reserve-invaded-by-20000-miners-bolsonaro-fails-to-act/.

123 *Indigenous Peoples and the United Nations, Vol. 1*, part 3, at 7:10 min., www.youtube.com/watch?v=LlS6ANY1aDM.

international solidarity, implying that the Yanomami are not isolated but are part of all this.

Davi Kopenawa Yanomami expresses his people's philosophy and vision of a better world in a rich book that appeared in 2013:[124]

I have never stopped talking to the white people. My heart has stopped beating too fast when they look at me and my mouth has lost its shame. My chest has become stronger and my tongue has lost its stiffness. If the words had gotten tangled up in my throat and I spoke in a needy, hesitant voice, those who came to hear me would have told themselves: "Why does this Indian want to make speeches to us? We were expecting words of wisdom from him, but he isn't saying anything! He is far too scared!" This is why I always try to talk with courage. . . . Then I continue: "You are other people. You do not hold *reahu* feasts. You do not know how to make the *xapiri* dance. We are the few inhabitants of the forest who survived your fathers' and grandfathers' epidemic fumes. This is why I want to speak to you. Do not be deaf to my words! Stop your people from ravaging our land and making us die too!" . . .

In the past, the white people used to talk about us without our knowledge, and our true words remained hidden in the forest. No one other than us could listen to them. So I started traveling to make the city people hear them. . . . even if we eventually disappear, they will continue to exist far from the forest. No one will be able to erase them. Many white people know them now . . .

When I was younger, I often asked myself: "Do the white people possess words of truth? Can they become our friends?" Since then, I have often traveled to them to defend the forest, and I have learned to know a little of what they call politics. It really made me become more suspicious! Their politics is nothing but mixed-up talk. These are the words of those who want our death and to seize our land.[125]

He continues:

If your minds were not so closed, you would chase the earth eaters out of our forest! You claim that we want to cut out a piece of Brazil to live there alone. These are lies to steal our land and confine us to it in little pens like chickens . . . You only know how to cut down and burn its [the forest] trees, to dig holes in its floor and soil its watercourses. Yet it does not belong to you and none of you created it!

124 Davi Kopenawa and Bruce Albert, *The Falling Sky: Words of a Yanomami Shaman*, trans. Nicholas Elliott and Alison Dundy (Cambridge, MA: The Belknap Press of Harvard University Press, 2013).
125 Kopenawa and Albert, *The Falling Sky*, 311–312.

I know that their [the white people's] elders will not easily listen to my talk because their thought has been set on minerals and merchandise for too long. Yet the people who were born after them and will replace them one day may understand me. They will hear my words or see their drawing while they are still young. These words will enter into their mind and they will have far more friendship for the forest. This is why I want to speak to the white people![126]

During his visit to the UN to see the Secretary-General in March 1991, we sat with Davi in the UN staff cafeteria in the UN Secretariat building in New York, next to some planters dividing rows of tables. Davi observed the strangeness of enclosing plants in buildings and said that the opposite would be good, enclosing building in the forest.

The UN Secretary-General's intervention in the Yanomami case was exceptional – in other words, it was not repeated again in other cases. It was a coincidence of various facilitating factors at once that made this action possible. They included the looming word "genocide" that characterized the dramatic developments of the case and the fact that the Peruvian Secretary-General, Pérez de Cuéllar, was willing to take a political risk. The decisive, systematic collaboration of Yanomami leaders with the Brazilian organization CCPY and with the Indian Law Resource Center, as well as the creative intervention of the Chairperson of the WGIP and her team, also facilitated this process. We should also recall that when the case was unfolding in the late 1980s, there was not yet a High Commissioner for Human Rights, nor a Special Rapporteur on the Rights of Indigenous Peoples, nor a Special Adviser of the Secretary-General on the Prevention of Genocide to create high level interventions. In 1991 the only available international actor for such an intervention was the UN Secretary-General, and he did decide to act on the case. There were indeed some positive results following this good-offices intervention.

What did this case demonstrate in retrospect? There was almost an ideal alignment of circumstances to prompt such political intervention of the UN at the highest level. The case also demonstrated that the combination of the obvious and well-known injustices suffered by the Yanomami that were morally compelling, the systematic feeding of information to the UN, and the strategic use of all available international routes can produce results and strengthen the struggles of Indigenous Peoples on the ground. The long struggles of the Yanomami at all levels also show that even if there are some positive results on the way, there must always be continuing vigilance, strategy, political action, and participation because positive results may be reversed and new challenges added by state and nonstate actors.

126 Kopenawa and Albert, *The Falling Sky*, 314–315.

J. The Role of Researchers and Academics

A few academics spoke in the first three years at the WGIP, in a way lending their expertise to mediate philosophical, legal, social, and other concepts between cultures. Later on, by the late 1980s, academics stopped making statements at the WGIP. The ground was exclusively available to Indigenous leaders themselves, who were dynamically conveying their own knowledge systems, aspirations, and demands in terms that the mainstream diplomatic audiences could comprehend – that is, the mediation of non-Indigenous expert academics was no longer needed. There is a clear feeling among Indigenous representatives that nobody will speak on their behalf unless they explicitly allow it and that the time that others spoke for Indigenous Peoples is over.[127] Many academics have of course kept their interest in Indigenous affairs, also working in solidarity with Indigenous Peoples. Over the years and quite soon after the Indigenous Peoples' movement contacted the UN, Indigenous experts in international law and other relevant areas started coming to the UN Indigenous-related meetings, and they continued the cultural mediation of concepts over the long period of negotiations on the UNDRIP until its adoption in 2007. Training sessions of Indigenous leaders in international law, especially in human rights, were conducted by Indigenous organizations or by NGOs in cooperation with them, timed around the sessions of the WGIP. These continue today in connection with the annual sessions of the UNPFII and the EMRIP and in other settings. Academia is also supporting these efforts. Already by the 1990s, considerable literature had been produced on the reshaping of ideas and norms on human rights through Indigenous Peoples' own representation.[128]

How significant has been the theoretical mediating role of researchers and academics in "translating" Indigenous Peoples' aspirations into international law language and human rights norms?[129]

It is clear that during the formative years of the Indigenous Peoples' movement, two academic disciplines played a special role: anthropology and international law, especially human rights law. Academics and researchers from those two areas accompanied and teamed up with Indigenous leaders at the WGIP. This is where the role of academics came in during the early days, bridging the language and cultural gap, interpreting Indigenous

---

127 Author's discussion with Rune Fjellheim, Director General, Sámi Parliament, Norway, 15 April 2020.
128 Linda Tuhiwai Smith, *Decolonizing Methodologies: Research and Indigenous Peoples*, 2nd ed. (London: Zed Books, 2012).
129 Elsa Stamatopoulou, "The Role of Research and Academia in Indigenous Peoples' Issues: Interculturality in the Making," in *Unsettling Discourses: The Theory and Practice of Indigenous Studies*, Proceedings of the 2013 International Seminar-Workshop on Indigenous Studies (Baguio City: Cordillera Studies Center, University of the Philippines Baguio, and Tebtebba Foundation, 2014).

concerns in mainstream language, and promoting intercultural dialogue on concepts, where agreement between states and Indigenous Peoples was crucial. Academics sometimes spoke, not on behalf of Indigenous leaders but on their own behalf, as "expert witnesses," one could say, and in the process of addressing international law theory, they were also progressively developing and expanding that theory to include concerns that Indigenous Peoples had as well as conveying Indigenous philosophies. I recall, for example, crucial discussions on the concepts of sovereignty and self-determination, in which academics explained, in detail and by using legal precedent and theory, why Indigenous Peoples are sovereign, how they implement their own governance systems, and why it is a human rights issue to respect these systems, so that Indigenous Peoples will survive as peoples, as cultures. Many discussions were also held about colonization, ethnocide, and genocide during those formative years and are also held today. Indigenous leaders and academics, each using their own language and means, were and are explaining and advocating that such situations must be remedied and prevented by the international human rights legal system.

Relatively soon, a good number of Indigenous leaders specialized in the fields of international law, human rights, anthropology, political science, and other areas and, since the late 1980s, were making their contributions to the WGIP. Being Indigenous persons themselves, they were in a good position to translate the concerns of their peoples into international law and human rights terms and to draft the articles they wanted to see included in a UNDRIP. The increase in the number of Indigenous-advocate academics and researchers in decolonizing international law and participating in UN debates accelerated the opening of theoretical, conceptual, and political spaces for Indigenous Peoples.

The phenomenon that we could observe through the 1980s at the WGIP was that the intense intercultural discussion between Indigenous Peoples and states was gradually winning "hearts and minds" of a number of state delegates, despite official government views the delegates would have to defend. The value of such change in government bureaucracies over the years cannot be underestimated in the eventual adoption of the UNDRIP. The Indigenous movement had made those "subtle" allies, who would work "from within" to change governmental positions. We were aware, for example, that some state delegates who had instructions to take hard positions in the debates were able to moderate their statements but also to send reports back to their home ministries in the capitals that were aiming to change those hard positions. This was and is also true for officials of UN agencies. The contribution of Indigenous experts and academics to this change was significant; one could call it spectacular.

Indigenous Peoples' activism and movement clearly contributed to the impact that Indigenous academics had in changing concepts and policies – in fact, it is easy to imagine that without the movement, the impact of Indigenous researchers and academics could have been less visible.

Indigenous Peoples had been for centuries the object of study by researchers who often applied positivist theories, based on the rationality of some Western traditions, that reflected dominant and colonial paradigms and power structures. Social justice and social transformation activism in the 1960s and 1970s pushed for a change in the approach to research and its link to power. Anthropology, which largely made its own discipline via studying and describing Indigenous Peoples, had for a long time studied Indigenous Peoples without taking into account their own voices and allowing their agency to be expressed or making space for their knowledge systems, without returning the results of research to the communities so they would benefit, and without adequately weighing the negative effects of their presence among Indigenous Peoples. By comparison to other disciplines, such as history, law, or political science, anthropology is the discipline that has since critiqued its methodologies the most. Its self-critique eventually resulted in a radical shift of its approaches. Researchers in the social justice area, in the critical research tradition, have established that it is crucial for research to pay particular attention to matters that affect the integrity of research and of the researcher, continuously develop their understandings of ethics and community sensibilities, and critically examine their research practices.[130]

In the past twenty years considerable literature on Indigenous topics has been published by Indigenous researchers around the world. This is creating not only a shift in methodologies but also a shift in the topics of research such that they respond more to the Indigenous Peoples' own interests and visions for transformation. Indigenous communities started having an input in shaping the research agenda. In the second edition of her classic book *Decolonizing Methodologies: Research and Indigenous Peoples*, Linda Tuhiwai Smith describes twenty-five cases of community driven research that has led to important results.[131] This resetting of the research agenda was not unrelated to the international Indigenous Peoples' movement advocating for Indigenous rights. The Indigenous research agenda is now clearly

---

130 Smith, *Decolonizing Methodologies*, 204. The author refers to the following works on this topic: Norman K. Denzin and Yvonna S. Lincoln, "Introduction: The Discipline and Practice of Qualitative Research," in *Handbook of Qualitative Research*, 2nd ed., ed. Norman K. Denzin and Yvonna S. Lincoln (Thousand Oaks, CA: Sage Publications, 2000); Lester-Irabinna Rigney, "Internationalization of an Indigenous Anticolonial Cultural Critique of Research Methodologies: A Guide to Indigenist Research Methodology and Its Principles," *Wicaso Sa Review* 14, no. 2 (Autumn 1999), https://doi.org/10.2307/1409555; Fiona Cram, "Rangahau Māori: Tona Tika, Tona Pono – The Validity and Integrity of Māori Research," in *Research Ethics in Aotearoa New Zealand: Concepts, Practice, Critique*, ed. Martin Tolich (Auckland: Pearson Education, 2001).
131 Smith, *Decolonizing Methodologies*, 111–164.

reflected also in the subjects of studies selected by the UN Indigenous-related mechanisms, the EMRIP, the Special Rapporteur on the Rights of Indigenous Peoples, and the UNPFII. The Permanent Forum, which enjoys flexibility in selecting and conducting studies has, since its inception in 2002, identified more than 120 topics of Indigenous-related research. One of the topics the Permanent Forum recommended but has not yet been conducted is a study toward guidelines for culturally sensitive and objective survey instruments for academia.[132]

Indigenous Peoples' successes in resetting the research agenda and bringing forward their own contributions is also reflected in other areas of international action – for example, the Intergovernmental Science-Policy Platform on Biodiversity and Ecosystem Services (IPBES) has agreed that there are diverse knowledge systems, which are equally important, especially in the conservation and sustainable use of biodiversity.[133]

Similarly, there has been significant focus on Indigenous traditional knowledge in international climate change discussions and research.[134] At a pivotal session on the topic in 2008, the UNPFII focused on the theme "Climate Change, Biocultural Diversity and Livelihoods: The Stewardship Role of Indigenous Peoples and New Challenges," and reflecting Indigenous views, set the parameters of climate action as it concerns Indigenous Peoples, including Indigenous traditional knowledge.[135] President Evo Morales Ayma of Bolivia participated at the session and so did some 1,700 Indigenous representatives, the highest number recorded at the Forum, bringing their stories of challenges, adaptation, and mitigation actions. Indigenous Peoples from the Arctic shared stories about how reindeer could no longer find the soft and nutritious greens that were now unreachable under the ice; women from a northern village in Siberia told us that their village was sinking into the Arctic Sea; Elders spoke of the clearly changing patterns of flora and fauna they had

132 The Permanent Forum, reflecting the expressed wishes of Indigenous Peoples, identifies topics for study. It conducts research by designating rapporteurs among its members to do so. The Forum has at times also recommended conducting certain research to other parts of the UN system. Sometimes the Forum recommends the convening of international expert meetings that will gather the most updated research and thinking on a specific complex topic. Although much research has already been produced, due to resource constraints, the research mandated by the UNPFII is sometimes delayed, partly implemented, or postponed.

133 See "Indigenous and Local Knowledge in IPBES," *IPBES website*, accessed 21 August 2021, https://ipbes.net/indigenous-local-knowledge.

134 See, for example, Sala Elise Patterson, "First-Ever Compendium of Indigenous Technologies Provides a Powerful Toolkit for Climate-Resilient Design," *Harvard University Graduate School of Design website*, 3 February 2020, www.gsd.harvard.edu/2020/02/first-ever-compendium-of-indigenous-technologies-provides-a-powerful-toolkit-for-climate-resilient-design/.

135 Permanent Forum on Indigenous Issues, Report on the Seventh Session (21 April–2 May 2008), UN Doc. E/2008/43 (2008), para. 4–47.

observed in the past several years; and Pacific islanders described their sinking islands, displacement, conflicts, and plans to evacuate whole islands, with dramatic effects on the prospects of their survival as peoples. The UNPFII made many bold recommendations and affirmed that

> as stewards of the world's biodiversity and cultural diversity, Indigenous Peoples' traditional livelihoods and ecological knowledge can significantly contribute to designing and implementing appropriate and sustainable mitigation and adaptation measures. Indigenous peoples can also assist in crafting the path towards developing low-carbon release and sustainable communities.[136]

After the 2015 Paris Agreement on climate change, the Local Communities and Indigenous Peoples Platform (LCIPP) was established as an open and inclusive space to bring together people and their knowledge systems to build a climate-resilient world for all.[137] Indigenous Peoples nominate their own expert representatives to this platform, which

> promotes the exchange of experiences and best practices with a view to applying, strengthening, protecting and preserving traditional knowledge, knowledge of indigenous peoples and local knowledge systems, as well as technologies, practices and efforts of local communities and indigenous peoples related to addressing and responding to climate change, taking into account the free, prior and informed consent of the holders of such knowledge, innovations and practices.[138]

The Platform also "facilitates the integration of diverse knowledge systems, practices and innovations in designing and implementing international and national actions, programmes and policies in a manner that respects and promotes the rights and interests of local communities and indigenous peoples."[139]

Thus, a dialogue is underway between those who know and are practicing traditional knowledge systems and scientists to discuss various issues,

---

136 UN Doc. E/2008/43, para. 4.
137 See UN Framework Convention on Climate Change (UNFCCC) web portal for LCIPP, https://unfccc.int/LCIPP; and the announcement about the portal, "The Engagement of Indigenous Peoples and Local Communities Crucial to Tackling Climate Crisis," https://www4.unfccc.int/sites/NWPStaging/News/Pages/LCIPP-Webportal.aspx, accessed 21 August 2021.
138 "Functions of the LCIPP," *LCIPP web portal*, https://lcipp.unfccc.int/about-lcipp/functions-lcipp, accessed 21 August 2021.
139 "Functions of the LCIPP."

such as validation or peer review, coproduction of knowledge, and documentation.[140] These encouraging examples of intercultural collaboration of knowledge systems, established at the international level in IPBES and LCIPP, despite tensions between states and Indigenous Peoples, can presumably also inspire academia's further contributions to Indigenous issues.

While not devoid of tensions and challenges, Indigenous Peoples' relations with academia and researchers continues to be strengthened. The Indigenous-related UN mechanisms have asked and received the support of academic institutions, and this is a relationship that will continue to grow. UNPFII has addressed academia in some recommendations. The EMRIP and the UNPFII have created groups of academic friends for EMRIP's and UNPFII's work, so that academia can contribute research to the studies by those bodies.[141]

K. Impacts, Potential, and Limits of Indigenous Peoples' Participation

This book is deeply focused on the multiple impacts and achievements of the Indigenous Peoples' movement in the international arena, the complex and creative methods used, and of course, the constant struggles to overcome state opposition on the way. This section is intended to enrich our understanding by listening to some leaders' voices directly and also to address the limits and potential of Indigenous participation.

1. Impacts

Claire Charters, Māori Senior Lecturer in Law at Victoria University of Auckland, Aotearoa/New Zealand, has pointed out that Indigenous Peoples indeed use different approaches at international fora in order to have an

---

140 "Indigenous and Local Knowledge in IPBES & Traditional Knowledge in the CBD: Approaches and Synergies for Biodiversity and People," *SwedBio (website)*, Stockholm Resilience Centre at Stockholm University, 1 July 2016, https://swed.bio/news/indigenous-and-local-knowledge-in-ipbes-traditional-knowledge-in-the-cbd/.

141 Columbia University's Institute for the Study of Human Rights has joined EMRIP's and UNPFII's academic friends. In support of the work of those bodies, in February 2013, the Institute hosted an international expert seminar on Indigenous Peoples' Access to Justice, including Truth and Reconciliation Processes; in 2016, an International Seminar on Indigenous Peoples' Rights and Unreported Struggles: Conflict and Peace; and in 2019, an International Symposium Indigenous Peoples and Borders: Decolonization, Contestation, Trans-border Practices. Books were published following these three international seminars. See also the interesting 2013 study conducted by UNPFII-members Myrna Cunningham and Álvaro Pop: Cunningham, Pop, Study on How the Knowledge, History and Contemporary Social Circumstances of Indigenous Peoples Are Embedded in the Curricula of Education Systems, UN Doc. E/C.19/2013/17 (20 February 2013).

impact on states: sometimes they use very formal, legalistic language, and other times they use a language outside the states' diplomatic formulas, a less formalistic and more emotive language, and their arguments are based on justice in a sense.[142]

The impacts of Indigenous international participation at the national level have been important, according to Kenneth Deer of the Haudenosaunee.[143] For example, in Canada, Indigenous participation has affected decisions of the Supreme Court on the question of "extinguishment," making it clear that Canada cannot extinguish Aboriginal rights.

Cree Grand Chief Wilton Littlechild considers the impact of Indigenous participation at national level impressive.[144] For example, seeing the government of Canada embracing the UNDRIP and making public commitments to implement it. Grand Chief Littlechild says,

> *I think a large push came from the Truth and Reconciliation Commission, because we called on Canada and the provinces to use the Declaration as the framework for reconciliation going forward. . . . Little did I know that way back when we started, thirty-eight, thirty-nine, forty years later that we were going to be here. And I think it's because of the continued trust that our Elders had in the system. The continued encouragement to keep advocating for our rights, the respect they wanted to see, the justice they wanted to fuel.*

Aehshatou Manu of MBOSCUDA (Mbororo Social and Cultural Development Association) voiced similar positive impacts in her country, Cameroon.[145] Vicky Tauli-Corpuz, Igorot leader and former UN Special Rapporteur on the Rights of Indigenous Peoples, also sees the positive impact at the national level, although, as she points out, implementation of international norms and policies still remains a gap.[146]

2. *Achievements*

It is clear that Indigenous Peoples have achieved a considerable political and moral profile internationally through their massive and strategic participation at interstate bodies, especially at the UN, but also in the Inter-American system, the system of the African Union, and at the Arctic Council. They have achieved the proclamation of their rights, through the UNDRIP in 2007, the

---

142 Charters interviewed by the author, 2 November 2018.
143 Deer interviewed by the author, 6 April 2016.
144 Littlechild interviewed by the author, 28 January 2017.
145 Manu interviewed by the author, 29 November 2016.
146 Tauli-Corpuz interviewed by the author, 18 October 2016.

American Declaration on the Rights of Indigenous Peoples in 2016, and before that, the ILO Convention No. 169 on Indigenous and Tribal Peoples in 1989.[147] They have also achieved the establishment of international bodies and other mandates that focus on their issues and rights, including the UN Special Rapporteur on the Rights of Indigenous Peoples, the UNPFII, and the EMRIP, two International Decades on Indigenous Peoples, the International Day of Indigenous Peoples, the World Conference on Indigenous Peoples, the International Year of Indigenous Languages, and the International Decade of Indigenous Languages. Indigenous Peoples have also achieved the pronouncement of positive decisions regarding their cases on the part of international human rights tribunals and committees, especially the Inter-American Commission and Court of Human Rights and the African Commission and Court on Human and Peoples' Rights, and a number of human rights treaty monitoring bodies, including the Human Rights Committee, the Committee on the Elimination on All Forms of Racial Discrimination (CERD), the Committee on the Rights of the Child (CRC) and the Committee on the Elimination of Discrimination against Women (CEDAW). The aforementioned is not an exhaustive list of achievements, yet it is indicative of the successes of the Indigenous Peoples' movement through its intensive and sustained participation over the decades that this book attempts to analyze. The very processes of participation, often exceptional in the interstate system, what I call "corrective exceptionalism," have been crucial in carrying out and enhancing a strong and effective impact of Indigenous Peoples at the international level.

On the achievements of Indigenous Peoples, Lola Garcia-Alix of the International Work Group on Indigenous Affairs (IWGIA) considers that the global movement has developed some very strong advocates, and she believes that some use the same tools that the states and their diplomats use.[148]

Maintaining this Indigenous voice, but at the same time being able to argue with the same words that the governments have . . . I have a lot of respect for these Indigenous leaders, experts, their persistence in advocating for their case in the UN.

Antonella Cordone of the International Fund for Agricultural Development (IFAD) referred to the successes of the international Indigenous Peoples' movement and pointed out that coalitions formed at the regional level are key and that it is crucial for the critical mass of Indigenous Peoples of

---

147 The 1957 ILO Convention No. 107 on Indigenous and Tribal Populations was heavily criticized in the 1980s by the Indigenous Peoples' movement as assimilationist; Indigenous representatives had hardly any say in the drafting of this convention.
148 Garcia-Alix interviewed by the author, 29 April 2016.

a region to be included.[149] Cordone also underlined the milestones in Indigenous international participation that she has witnessed; for her, the issue of climate change has given a new push and a new wave to the movement. The other uplifting moment she saw was the 2014 World Conference on Indigenous Peoples.

3. Challenges

Howard Thompson of the Haudenosaunee reflects on the intergenerational challenges.[150] To the question of what caused young Indigenous people to become more inquisitive, Chief Thompson sees that education did that; at one point, it was tolerated to educate your children about the culture, while for many years this was not tolerated.

> *The priests and the nuns that ruled over our communities became more lax, and they started, I suppose, Catholic schools started leaving. So we were able to get in there and educate the children. And a lot of times now, we get to educate the people outside of our communities, of our ways and the way we should be thinking as Native Peoples.*

Reflecting on the challenges to Indigenous participation at international fora, Chhing Lamu Sherpa, Founder of Mountain Spirit in Nepal, agrees with other leaders and points out that one challenge is that Indigenous people do not get information on time.[151] Because most of the people are in the mountains and rural areas, there is not much access to the internet, "so we need to also bring more internet facilities to our village." Another challenge is obtaining funding to attend international meetings. Another challenge, according to Sherpa, is for people who have gone to international meetings to find the time to organize and brief their communities when they return, and for everybody "to manage the calendar." It is also crucial, she says, to reach out to individuals with different perspectives and to create strong monitoring of the implementation of international norms and policy recommendations regarding Indigenous Peoples.

On the challenges of participation, Lola Garcia-Alix of IWGIA referred to the diversification of international meetings and the technical knowledge required for effective participation and how this creates challenges, especially for newcomer Indigenous representatives. Indigenous Peoples have been very successful in opening doors and legitimizing the right to participate, and in some cases the "participation also has huge demands, because participants have to give inputs, they have to comment on several documents."

---

149 Cordone interviewed by the author, 7 May 2016.
150 Thompson interviewed by the author, January 2018.
151 Sherpa interviewed by the author, 21 November 2016.

Carson Kiburo, Endorois in Kenya, Executive Director of the Jamii Asilia Centre, stated in response to questions I raised that among the challenges Indigenous representatives face through their international participation are reprisals after they call out their countries at the UN level for human rights violations.

4. Expectations

In terms of the expectations at the level of Indigenous communities, Antonella Cordone of IFAD sees them as focusing on autonomy over their territories and resources because the main menace today is that the rich environments that Indigenous Peoples have maintained for millennia are under pressure by the greedy interests in the world. According to her, the UN system's role is to open ways and find systems to bring the private sector and Indigenous Peoples to the table, to discuss the issues at a level of equality. Indigenous Peoples have to enhance their unity at national and local levels as well as their capacities to engage with the system, particularly to enhance the capacities of young people.

As Carson Kiburo has stated, at the United Nations, Indigenous Peoples utilize the space(s) to advocate about their issues as they face member states, who often times do not recognize their self-determination. The basic rule book is what Indigenous Peoples advocated for and was included in the UNDRIP. Kiburo also pointed out that among the most significant years in the international Indigenous Peoples' movement in Africa were 1986, when the African Charter on Human and Peoples Rights entered into force, and 2000, when the African Commission's Working Group on Indigenous Populations/Communities was established.

On the question of the expectations of Indigenous Peoples from the international participation of their delegates, Claire Charters pointed out that they sort of expect them "to change the world," and they feel disappointed when they hear that it may take many years to make the change. Charters thinks there is also an appreciation that you are bringing attention from the outside into the specific local situation. Indigenous communities often feel that if you go to the state, at the national level, you meet with a dead end and you feel helpless; but when you go to the international stage, you feel that there is hope, even if it is a long-term project, the system might actually change. "But it is a mixed bag," Charters says. "There is a lot of disappointment because you cannot make immediate change, but there is also hope because it might lead to a fundamental systemic change."

5. Limits in the Midst of Achievements

It comes as no surprise that, despite significant achievements, limits to Indigenous Peoples' participation at the international, and also national, level are quite visible at the same time. Indigenous Peoples see such international participation as part of expressing an external aspect of their right to self-determination as well as a requirement of the principle of equality.[152] Even at the UN Human Rights Council, difficulties in terms of participation continue and obstacles have not been resolved, despite some good efforts. In 2019, for example, the current Chief Deskaheh of the Haudenosaunee, Steven Jacobs, had travelled to Geneva to deliver a statement to the Human Rights Council and was denied the right to speak as a Chief of his people, as had his famous ancestor Chief Deskaheh, Levi General, in 1924 at the League of Nations. At a 2021 roundtable on the topic of international participation, Kenneth Deer, Co-Chair of the meeting, challenged the Council to resolve that issue by 2024, one hundred years after the League of Nations first refused to allow Chief Deskaheh to speak.[153]

Looking at Indigenous Peoples' often very hard realities on the ground, it is indispensable to be aware of the limits of Indigenous Peoples' international participation, what those limits are, who can set them, and whether and how they could be overcome. Such limits can also be called obstacles, some of which could perhaps be overcome as conditions, politics, and history are in constant motion. Limits or obstacles can be set (a) by states and the systems they establish and monitor in interstate bodies, and (b) by adverse conditions faced by Indigenous Peoples, such as lack of adequate information or lack of resources to attend crucial meetings. These two broad categories are not absolute, and they often interject, as several of the items under each category are relational. They are discussed further next.

a. States

It is obvious that states are the main actors in interstate systems, such as the UN, and that they set the rules and processes to protect and pursue what they define as state interests. The defense of the existence of the state is a paramount aim for them, and, as has been explained throughout the book, actors and actions that states may see as threatening are kept at a distance. Tools for that have been, among others, the participation rules of nongovernmental actors at the UN, NGOs, and others. Although Indigenous Peoples have achieved special participation rights in some international bodies and processes, certain states continue to feel uncomfortable as they perceive such participation as menacing to state authority. They have expressed such

---

152 UN Doc. A/HRC/48/75, para. 17; see also UN Office of the High Commissioner for Human Rights, Intersessional Round Table on Ways to Enhance the Participation of Indigenous Peoples' Representatives and Institutions in Meetings of the Human Rights Council on Issues Affecting Them, UN Doc. A/HRC/49/69 (11 January 2022), para. 50.

153 UN Doc. A/HRC/49/69, para. 70.

skepticism periodically at the UN, but such skepticism was never strong enough to bend the existing positive Indigenous participation practices. One can see the resistance of some states having some impact on the issue of enhanced Indigenous participation discussed in the following section. One could explain the delay of positive outcomes through such resistance.

At the same time, it is important to explore and evaluate to what extent some states would be willing to stand out as relentless deniers of enhanced Indigenous participation, a participation described by its advocates as respectful and constructive and actually representing the voices and ideals of anticolonialism, antioccupation, antidiscrimination, justice, human rights, and inclusion. From the experience in international organizations until now, it appears that very few states would choose to stand out internationally in such a way and spend precious political capital to create coalitions for this purpose. In practical terms, this means that giving more time, enough time, to international negotiations on enhanced participation of Indigenous Peoples can help create common understandings of such participation, smooth out difficulties, and create consensus and procedures that will implement such enhanced participation.

When we deal with human rights, and other issues for that matter, the question of imbalance of power needs to be brought into relief. In the case under discussion, it is clear that states have state power in their hands, with the tools of state law, budget, and policy and their claim of the monopoly of state violence. Indigenous Peoples have the moral power of having survived and resisted colonialism and other forms of violence and discrimination, which unfortunately continue in many countries. It would be a challenge in international politics and geopolitics for even a powerful country to appear to defend, in interstate bodies, the injustices that Indigenous Peoples are suffering because in fact many of the states that have come out of colonialism support similar principles as those of Indigenous Peoples.

There is one more question that needs analysis through the angle of Indigenous participation internationally. It is actually a question relevant to many social movements around the world. If an Indigenous-friendly government has been brought to the helm of a state by the Indigenous movement – as was the case in Bolivia, for example – what are the limitations to which such a government is subjected in the global economic and political system? And what is the role of Indigenous participation in such cases? The Bolivian government headed for the first time by an Indigenous President, Juan Evo Morales Ayma, in 2006, reverberated with the language and visions of the strong Indigenous Peoples' movement of the country, including on self-determination, climate change, the rights of Mother Earth, antiextractivism, the concepts of "living well" or *vivir bien*, and other issues. For defending these ideas, the Bolivian government often stood out at the UN and attracted attention and interest from other states and actors, such as corporations with investments in Bolivia. Such attention was not necessarily positive for Bolivia at a diplomatic level since it was sometimes accompanied by fears that these ideas might "spill over" to other countries.

While the Bolivian government gathered the sympathy and wishes of many for success and its ideas had an international impact, Bolivia *as a state* had/has to function, survive, and pursue its interests in an international political and economic environment of states and of economic globalization. For example, land-locked Bolivia wishes to have the access to the Pacific that it lost in the war of 1884 with Chile. Entering into a constructive dialogue with Chile for such a high goal would certainly require Bolivia to "behave as a state" in the international arena, to practice diplomatic, political, and economic cooperation with Chile and other states of the region, even if Bolivia disagreed with various of their positions. Similarly, the interests of Brazil in creating a road through the TIPNIS (Isiboro Sécure National Park and Indigenous Territory) area of Bolivia, led the Bolivian government to pursue the building of such a road despite major repeated protests, the need for protection of Indigenous Peoples in voluntary isolation in that area, and other issues. The protracted TIPNIS conflict led to violence against protesters and tremendous political tension, and it has resulted in the suspension of the project. Situations such as these send various messages to social movements, including Indigenous Peoples' movements. It is clear that, even if a government has been brought to power by Indigenous Peoples, once in power, it is expected to represent the state with its strengths, weaknesses, and limitations as an actor internally and internationally.

This means that social movements need to be vigilant, to take critical distance, and continue to advocate their positions through active participation. Since such participation may have various limits at national level or even be suppressed, ensuring the international participation of Indigenous Peoples is important in such cases. The limitations of the state as a structure internally and internationally, in other words, have to be recognized and taken into account in strategies of Indigenous Peoples at all levels.

b.   Indigenous Peoples

The harsh Indigenous Peoples' realities that range from the struggle to overcome poverty and survive, to the efforts to defend Indigenous lands and resources as well as culture, to deal with discrimination in various areas and even with outright persecution, all these common circumstances often constitute limitations for Indigenous participation at the international level. Added to these challenges are lack of adequate information about the time and agendas of meetings of interstate bodies, lack of adequate understanding of how to strategically use such bodies, and also, lack of adequate financial resources needed for travel. Especially for people who may wish to travel to UN fora for the first time, it is important to have briefings or trainings before they attend, so that they understand in a more analytical way the mandate, role, and possibilities offered by each body and so that they prepare and strategize about the goals of their participation, including through networking. In other words, harsh material conditions of Indigenous Peoples, combined with lack of adequate information and training, can pose additional limitations to Indigenous participation. As discussed elsewhere in this book, such limitations are partially softened through the availability of travel resources under various UN voluntary funds, such as the UN Voluntary Fund for Indigenous Peoples, as well as through training programs organized by various actors, before meetings of Indigenous-related bodies.[154] Trainings also take place based on Indigenous Peoples' initiatives and collaborations at regional or local levels.[155] It should be added that capacity-building on Indigenous issues based on UNDRIP is certainly also needed for state and UN officials, and opportunities are periodically created by the UN to attend such trainings. However, the often fast pace of thematic or geographical movement of such officials makes the available number of training opportunities until now inadequate.[156] The extent to which such limitations can be overcome depends upon a combination of financial resources and policy initiatives; meaning that if increased travel funds are raised for Indigenous representatives to travel to international meetings and participate and training initiatives are available for all who wish to attend such training, better results can be pursued and achieved in the field of Indigenous Peoples' rights.

One more limitation is occasionally set by approaches or methodologies of some Indigenous Peoples based on ways of seeing their relation to states and hence to the UN as an interstate organization. Due to a profound sense of sovereignty and self-determination as well as the critique of colonialism and its harsh impacts on Indigenous Peoples, some Indigenous nations and their representatives do not wish to seek negotiations with states. They therefore do not always wish to participate in international bodies and negotiations, which of course is their right. Although this position, expressed mostly in

---

154 Training programs for Indigenous leaders are, for example, organized before the annual session of the UNPFII by the FIMI in cooperation with Columbia University's Institute for the Study of Human Rights, and by Tribal Link Foundation.

155 One example is the Indigenous Intercultural University in Latin America, a project of the Fondo para el Desarrollo de los Pueblos Indígenas de América Latina y El Caribe (FILAC), headquartered in La Paz, Bolivia; see profiles of Indigenous Intercultural University at the UpSocial website, https://upsocial.org/en/sic/soluciones/indigenous-intercultural-university; and at the GIZ website, www.giz.de/en/worldwide/22779.html, accessed 27 June 2022. See also UN Doc. E/C.19/2013/17.

156 Considerable material for training has been prepared by the UN for some time now. It can be found on the website of the Secretariat of the UNPFII, www.un.org/development/desa/indigenouspeoples/declaration-on-the-rights-of-indigenous-peoples/training-materials.html.

North America, is not necessarily easily visible to outsiders, given the great numbers of Indigenous participants at several international fora, it has been shown in recent times during discussions on climate change at the UNPFII and during preparations of the 2014 World Conference on Indigenous Peoples at the UN General Assembly. The expression of the right to self-determination, including its external aspects, by Indigenous Peoples certainly includes their own decisions about who they will dialogue, negotiate, or collaborate with, and when and on what topic they may engage.

One of the most interesting and exciting developments in recent years is the sharing of knowledge about the various ways that Indigenous Peoples around the world exercise their right to self-determination, the variety of approaches they use in their autonomy and self-government, and the positive outcomes as well as obstacles. In some cases, they pursue recognition by the state and in others not. A rich bibliography has been collected and published by the IWGIA.[157]

A more recent publication is the report on the *Right to Self-determination of Indigenous and Tribal Peoples* by IWGIA and the Inter-American Commission on Human Rights (IACHR), facilitated by the IACHR's Rapporteurship on the Rights of Indigenous Peoples and supported by IWGIA.[158] As the report highlights, Indigenous and tribal peoples of the Americas have the fundamental right to self-determination, which encompasses the right to freely determine their political status and freely pursue their economic, social, and cultural development; from the historical and cultural perspectives of these peoples, self-determination is a right that exists before the creation of the current American States; therefore, it is a fundamental right for the effective enjoyment of other rights. The report also analyzes the standards and jurisprudence of the Inter-American Human Rights System in relation to the various constituent elements of self-determination, the recognition of this right in the domestic legal systems of various states, and the practices and experiences of these peoples in the exercise of self-determination as well as the obstacles they face in exercising it. In addition, the report addresses the reparative nature of this right and the understanding of the right from a crosscutting, gender, intergenerational solidarity, and intercultural approach.

What this richness of positive Indigenous efforts for survival and well-being shows is that, despite limitations and obstacles, historic and

---

157 Many of these sources can be found by searching on "self-determination" at IWGIA's website, https://iwgia.org/en/search.
158 *Right to Self-determination of Indigenous and Tribal Peoples* (Inter-American Commission on Human Rights and IWGIA, 2021), www.iwgia.org/en/resources/publications/4592-iachr-presents-the-report-right-to-self-determination-of-indigenous-and-tribal-peoples.html.

contemporary, Indigenous Peoples have been finding solutions, at national and local levels, to express one of their most fundamental human rights, the right to self-determination, with which the UNDRIP is imbued. It would therefore be logical to assume that Indigenous self-determination through participation at the international level would be able to help overcome some of the obstacles described earlier. Indigenous methodologies and strategies developed at the international level, and analyzed in this book, have already given many positive results over the decades, and one can expect that they can produce more.

L.   The Vision of Enhanced Participation

When a state initiative, originally launched by Bolivia, landed the proposal of a World Conference on Indigenous Peoples at the UN, Indigenous Peoples started organizing strategically for what such a high-level political occasion could offer for the implementation of their rights and the improvement of their situation. Participation was again a central issue. The Indigenous preparatory conference in Alta, Norway, became the global forum for this preparation in June 2013, and the Alta Declaration adopted became the collective vision for Indigenous advocacy at the World Conference and beyond.[159]

The World Conference on Indigenous Peoples (WCIP) or "the high level plenary meeting (HLPM) of the General Assembly known as the World Conference on Indigenous Peoples," as it was also called, took place at UN Headquarters in New York on 22–23 September 2014. It became another ground for reaffirming Indigenous Peoples' meaningful participation in the process of the conference and also in all international bodies relevant to their lives and interests. Going to the World Conference, the message from Indigenous Peoples was that the Alta Outcome Document should be the base document for the final Outcome Document of the UN Conference, and indeed, this became the case, as Les Malezer said in an interview with the author of this book.[160] His only criticism was that the process of the final drafting of the document at the conference excluded Indigenous Peoples from the room; but the Indigenous delegates were waiting outside the conference room, and several state delegates were taking messages out to them and asking for their advice during the process of negotiation.

---

159 The conference was hosted by the Sámi Parliament of Norway. See Alta Outcome Document, Global Indigenous Preparatory Conference for the United Nations High Level Plenary Meeting of the General Assembly to Be Known as the World Conference on Indigenous Peoples, Alta, Norway, 10–12 June 2013, www.un.org/esa/socdev/unpfii/documents/wc/AdoptedAlta_outcomedoc_EN.pdf. The Alta Outcome Document is also reproduced in UN Doc. A/67/994, annex.
160 Malezer interviewed by the author, 8 April 2016.

The Preamble of the Alta Outcome Document (OD) includes, among other things, the following points:

> As the original and distinct Peoples and Nations of our territories we abide by natural laws and have our own laws, spirituality and world views. We have our own governance structures, knowledge systems, values and the love, respect and lifeways, which form the basis of our identity as Indigenous Peoples and our relationship with the natural world. . . .
>
> The provisions of the Declaration that affirm the inherent rights of Indigenous Peoples to participate fully in decision-making that affects us, will continue to guide and frame our work for the HLPM/WCIP. . . .
>
> We affirm that the inherent and inalienable right of self determination [*sic*] is preeminent and is a prerequisite for the realization of all rights. We Indigenous Peoples, have the right of self determination and permanent sovereignty over our lands, territories, resources, air, ice, oceans and waters, mountains and forests.[161]

A major recommendation of Indigenous Peoples in the Alta document was the following:

> *Pursuant* to the universal application of the right of self determination for all Peoples, [the conference] recommends that the UN recognize Indigenous Peoples and Nations based on our original free existence, inherent sovereignty and the right of self determination in international law. We call for, at a minimum, permanent observer status within the UN system enabling our direct participation through our own governments and parliaments. Our own governments include *inter alia* our traditional councils and authorities.[162]

Similarly, the Outcome Document of the 2014 UN World Conference on Indigenous Peoples includes a recommendation of states along the following lines:[163]

> 33. We commit ourselves to considering, at the seventieth session of the General Assembly, ways to enable the participation of indigenous peoples' representatives and institutions in meetings of relevant United Nations bodies on issues affecting them,

---

161 Alta Outcome Document, 1–2.
162 Alta Outcome Document, 5.
163 UN Doc. A/RES/69/2.

including any specific proposals made by the Secretary-General in response to the request made in paragraph 40 below. . . .

40. We request the Secretary-General, in consultation with the Inter-Agency Support Group on Indigenous Peoples' Issues and Member States, taking into account the views expressed by indigenous peoples, to report to the General Assembly at its seventieth session on the implementation of the present outcome document, and to submit at the same session, through the Economic and Social Council, recommendations regarding how to use, modify and improve existing United Nations mechanisms to achieve the ends of the United Nations Declaration on the Rights of Indigenous Peoples, ways to enhance a coherent, system-wide approach to achieving the ends of the Declaration and specific proposals to enable the participation of indigenous peoples' representatives and institutions, building on the report of the Secretary-General on ways and means of promoting participation at the United Nations of indigenous peoples' representatives on the issues affecting them.[164]

The Outcome Document of the World Conference, adopted by the UNGA by consensus, included several paragraphs directly linked to Indigenous Peoples' participation.[165] Of the forty operative paragraphs in the document, sixteen make reference to participation in various fields:[166] the preparatory process of the WCIP; the implementation of UNDRIP; the development of national action plans; collaboration with Indigenous People with disabilities; empowerment of Indigenous youth; dialogue with Indigenous justice institutions; participation of Indigenous women; free, prior, and informed consent regarding Indigenous lands, territories, and resources; major projects and extractive industries; Indigenous Peoples' occupations, traditional subsistence activities, economies, livelihoods, food security, and nutrition; and enhanced participation of Indigenous Peoples at the UN on issues affecting their lives – that is, not only at the UN Indigenous-related mechanisms. At that historical moment of the WCIP, the OD is imbued with the principle of Indigenous participation at almost every step and field. It also reverberates the respect required for Indigenous Peoples' own governance systems, even though the OD omits explicit reference to Indigenous Peoples' right to

---

164 The report referred to in this paragraph is contained in this report: UN Secretary-General, Ways and Means of Promoting Participation at the United Nations of Indigenous Peoples' Representatives on Issues Affecting Them, UN Doc. A/HRC/21/24 (2 July 2012).

165 UN Doc. A/RES/69/2.

166 Paragraphs 2, 3, 7–9, 15–17, 19–23, 25, 28, and 40.

self-determination, indicating the continuing existential fear of some states. The OD also omits any reference to colonialism that Indigenous Peoples wished to include but that was resisted by states.

Although a detailed analysis of the OD of the WCIP is beyond the purview of this book, some reflections about its legal and political validity are relevant. Is the OD mandatory? Is it "just a General Assembly resolution"? Is it "soft law?" I am part of the school of thought that sees value and legal validity in the progressive development of international law through not only treaties but also declarations, UNGA, and other UN resolutions. This is even more so in the case of a high-level world conference, such as the WCIP. Based on experiences and lessons of the world conferences the UN held in the 1990s, we could say that (a) the world conferences unleash considerable political momentum at the international level for years to come; (b) they become an important point of reference at national and international levels; (c) they give rise to new international mechanisms and procedures; (d) they may stimulate more resources for a topic; (e) implementation of the outcome documents can take a long time, especially for the most contested recommendations; and (f) the resistance of some states to the sensitive points in the outcome documents manifests itself in the stages of implementation.

It is important to point out that the Outcome Document of the World Conference asked for the involvement of the UN Secretary-General in various policy actions. In paragraph 40 the Secretary-General was requested (a) to report to the General Assembly at its seventieth session in 2015 on the implementation of the Outcome Document and (b)

> To submit at the same session . . . recommendations regarding how to use, modify and improve existing United Nations mechanisms to achieve the ends of the United Nations Declaration on the Rights of Indigenous Peoples, ways to enhance a coherent, system-wide approach to achieving the ends of the Declaration and specific proposals to enable the participation of indigenous peoples' representatives and institutions, building on the report of the Secretary-General on ways and means of promoting participation at the United Nations of indigenous peoples' representatives on the issues affecting them.[167]

In UN political culture, these mandates to the Secretary-General are significant, as they require quite a high-profile engagement of the highest UN

---

167 UN Doc. A/RES/69/2. Another report on the topic was submitted by the Secretary-General to the General Assembly in 2020: Enhancing the Participation of Indigenous Peoples' Representatives and Institutions in Meetings of Relevant United Nations Bodies on Issues Affecting Them, UN Doc. A/75/255 (27 July 2020), https://documents-dds-ny.un.org/doc/UNDOC/GEN/N20/196/88/PDF/N2019688.pdf.

official. The words "coherence" and "system-wide" are buzz words for internal UN system committees, actions, and monitoring, provided of course that there is a group of dedicated officials behind the scenes to work diligently on this.

As a methodological point for the assessment of the results of the World Conference, it is important to ask to what extent the OD marks progress by comparison to what existed before the World Conference in terms of standards, policies, and budgets.

The World Conference OD has enhanced the political profile of Indigenous issues at the UNGA. There are many concrete positive outcomes in terms of policies and new mechanisms as well, such as the System-Wide Action Plan on the Rights of Indigenous Peoples, adopted by UN agencies in 2016.[168] There are also missing points in the OD, given the numerous parties to this negotiation at the World Conference; a comparison between the Alta Outcome Document and the World Conference Outcome Document demonstrates that.

A major positive result of the World Conference is the call in the OD regarding enhanced participation of Indigenous representatives and institutions at UN fora. Consultations started in February 2016 under the aegis of the President of the General Assembly (PGA) and continued through to 2019. Reflecting the spirit of the World Conference, the PGA appointed two Indigenous advisers and two advisers from states. As is indicated in the Secretary-General's 2020 report that describes the processes from 2016 to 2020,[169] Indigenous Peoples' representatives clearly put forward their view that a special process had to be created for the participation of representatives from their own institutions because the existing process of NGO accreditation was not applicable to them, since they were not NGOs. The issues that surfaced and are described in the aforementioned report of the Secretary-General included the definition of Indigenous Peoples by the UN, which does not exist (see Chapter 2 of this book), as well as the question of accreditation of Indigenous institutions and the process for it, including the need for a mixed committee comprised of Indigenous and state representatives to be created. The Secretary-General's report described some examples of Indigenous participation in the UN system besides the EMRIP and the UNPFII – namely, the UN Framework Convention on Climate Change; the World Intellectual Property Organization (WIPO); the IFAD; the UN Educational, Scientific and Cultural Organization (UNESCO); the Convention on Biological Diversity

---

168 *System-Wide Action Plan on the Rights of Indigenous Peoples* (UN Department of Information, 2016), www.un.org/esa/socdev/unpfii/documents/2016/Docs-updates/SWAP_Indigenous_Peoples_WEB.pdf.

169 UN Doc. A/75/255.

(CBD); and the High-Level Forum on Sustainable Development. Such participation varies and sometimes includes travel funding for Indigenous representatives and systematic opening to Indigenous participants over the years. The Indigenous movement has also held consultations of its own to prepare discussions at the UN – specifically, a meeting in 2016 in Bangkok, and one in 2020 in Quito. The latter decided to establish an Indigenous Peoples' coordination committee for this process. The pause of in-person meetings at the UN that the COVID-19 pandemic brought since 2020 also delayed the debates on enhanced Indigenous Peoples' participation at the UN. At the same time, it is clear that more discussions are needed so that all parties enjoy an adequate level of information before agreements can be reached.

Commenting on the push for enhanced Indigenous Peoples' participation at the UN, during a discussion with the author, Claire Charters, one of the two Indigenous advisers appointed by the PGA in 2016, pointed out that there was a momentum around self-determination of peoples and recognition that Indigenous Peoples are a unique entity in the international legal fora and that they are not just civil society, not just NGOs that had been recognized.[170] The natural kind of next step from that is that Indigenous Peoples have particular and specific representation at the UN that was not like civil society or human rights institutions; a way to mark that was by having particular participation in the General Assembly and across all UN entities. Charters thinks that for some Indigenous Peoples, particularly from North America, such recognition in UN processes was about another extension of the inherent sovereignty of Indigenous Peoples.

Charters sees several obstacles to Indigenous participation at the international level, the main one being that some states do not want to recognize certain groups in their territory as Indigenous and would of course not like to see them at international meetings. Being one of the advisors to the PGA during the participation negotiations, Charters was deeply surprised by the level of objection to Indigenous participation as Indigenous Peoples at the UN by some Asian states. She knew it was there but did not expect that these states would use considerable political capital to come together to prevent that. That happened because of domestic fear, in most cases, of recognizing Indigenous Peoples as sub-state groups that may be threatening to the state. Charters does hold hope that this issue will be well resolved at the UN in the future.

On the issue of enhanced Indigenous participation, Antonella Cordone of IFAD underlined that Indigenous Peoples and their governance institutions cannot be considered as NGOs and that something in-between has to be formulated to recognize special status for Indigenous Peoples.[171]

170 Charters interviewed by the author, 2 November 2018.
171 Cordone interviewed by the author, 7 May 2016.

During our interview, Kenneth Deer of the Haudenosaunee said that the United Nations would be better if it did represent all of humanity, including Indigenous Peoples, and this is why Indigenous Peoples have been asking to have observer status at least.[172]

In the words of Aehshatou Manu, Mbororo leader from Cameroon, having representation at the UNGA

> *would be like a dream come true . . . It would really have a moral symbolic significance, for the community itself and the nation at large because these people are no more like outcasts, they are no more minorities, they are now capable to be at the UN and also express themselves.*[173]

According to Lola Garcia-Alix of the IWGIA, the general vision is that Indigenous Peoples can participate at the UN as rights holders, as peoples and not as NGOs; there is an opportunity to operationalize this vision despite challenges.[174]

Reflecting on possibilities for enhanced Indigenous Peoples' participation at the UN in the future, Binota Moy Dhamai, a Tripura Indigenous leader from Bangladesh and member of UN EMRIP, thinks that participation of Indigenous Peoples derives from three principles: inclusion, integration, and diversity. Over the years, these principles have been neglected, denied, and ignored by various state mechanisms. Thus, following the states' international commitments for the promotion, protection, and respect of human rights, Dhamai believes that an exceptional procedure of enhanced Indigenous participation at the UN is possible and should be created.[175]

Victoria Tauli-Corpuz, senior Igorot leader and former UN Special Rapporteur on the Rights of Indigenous Peoples, also reflected on the issue of enhanced Indigenous participation in UN processes that was requested in the Outcome Document of the World Conference on Indigenous Peoples, giving a deep time perspective and a long vision toward the future:[176]

> *I think the aspiration would be to be recognized as distinct peoples and not as NGOs. Because the participation in the UN is more shaped within the framework of nongovernment organizations, and Indigenous Peoples have consistently said they are not NGOS, they are Indigenous Peoples. So, I think that the idea behind this proposal for enhanced participation is to really push a new category of stakeholders, of participants within the*

172 Deer interviewed by the author, 6 April 2016.
173 Manu interviewed by the author, 29 November 2016.
174 Garcia-Alix interviewed by the author, 29 April 2016.
175 Dhamai interviewed by the author, March 2022.
176 Tauli-Corpuz interviewed by the author, 18 October 2016.

UN. Which reflects the demand of Indigenous Peoples to be recognized as distinct peoples and not as NGOs, and that they are peoples who are representing their own communities or organizations, and they cannot just be lumped together with the NGOs as such. This to an extent is also coming from some of the major groups within the Commission on Sustainable Development. You have the Indigenous Peoples, you have farmers, you have children and youth, you have labor unions. . . . And then you have NGOs – NGOs is just one category under the major groups structure. So it's just being consistent with that. I think that Indigenous Peoples also push for this kind of enhanced participation. I think what's significant about it is that at least we are trying to challenge the UN to develop other categories. . . . If Indigenous are able to participate not as NGOs, then to a certain extent that will affirm the assertion of Indigenous Peoples of the right to self-determination; they are indeed a group, they are peoples who should be engaged directly with the States in terms of pushing the States to respect their rights. I think that's the idea so you don't need to be identified as an NGO. Because being identified as such will of course lessen your stature, your status as a distinct people with distinct cultures and distinct rights.

As to why states allowed this exceptionalism for Indigenous Peoples' participation, well, it's because of the consistency of Indigenous Peoples in terms of really addressing this issue and pursuing the essence of what self-determination is all about. That's really operationalizing self-determination in the fullest sense because you are really saying that you are the ones who should freely determine your political status and freely pursue your own economic, social and cultural development. I think that's really where it's coming from. . . . I think also, to an extent, states also recognized the kind of mistakes that they have made in relation to how they have treated Indigenous Peoples. To a certain extent, I think they do recognize that Indigenous Peoples have been treated badly, therefore there may be some element of conscience there somehow, which sort of makes states more accommodating because they are guilty of creating all these problems that Indigenous Peoples face. I think to a certain extent, there is that element. But the other part of course is the persistence of Indigenous Peoples themselves. You know if we sort of just gave up and said we cannot go beyond what is there now, I think this wouldn't happen. But because Indigenous continued to participate . . . and then we got the Voluntary Fund for Indigenous Peoples, which at least helps bring Indigenous Peoples to come. And then Indigenous Peoples were also innovative enough, to raise money to be able to come to these meetings.

All those factors have helped, because it will always be the presence that makes a big difference. It's the physical presence in these arenas where these discussions are happening that can really bring about that change. Because if you are not there, they forget about you. . . . It's really that kind *of consistent and sustained participation that has also pushed states to accommodate those kinds of demands.*

Well, the quality of participation has improved significantly because of course Indigenous Peoples are now able to undertake research themselves, they are able to be more sophisticated in terms of bringing the evidence, the evidence to show that Indigenous Peoples are not just victims but also contributors, active agents of their own for change. And I think now this is more understood and cannot just be ignored. You can look at the results from different perspectives. You have results in terms of establishing the international standards, the global standards that should define the rights of Indigenous Peoples. And the existence of the UN Declaration on the Rights of Indigenous Peoples is a major accomplishment, because then you can go to different arenas and say that there is already this Declaration and therefore you should be able to conform to what that Declaration is saying in terms of respecting and protecting the rights of Indigenous Peoples.

Having attended the discussions on enhanced Indigenous Peoples' participation at the UN and having spoken with many other participants, it is clear to me that the aspiration of Indigenous Peoples for participation at all UN fora whose work and policies affect Indigenous communities is strong. Enhanced participation is one of the steps for inclusion of Indigenous Peoples and for strengthening Indigenous inputs in important decision-making internationally.[177] Even if this aspiration was not as clear at the beginning in all parts of the Indigenous world, the relevant information has by now spread enough so that enhanced participation can be viewed as a global Indigenous vision, a step toward a broader expression of Indigenous external self-determination at the international level. As stated in one report by the UN Secretary-General,

> Indigenous peoples are best placed to authoritatively advise on their situation and the most appropriate methods to tackle the challenges that they face. Issues relevant to indigenous peoples are often addressed in general United Nations fora, beyond the bodies specifically focused on indigenous peoples. The participation of indigenous peoples' organizations in the United Nations that has been possible to date has facilitated the strengthening of cooperation between States and indigenous peoples in a peaceful and constructive fashion.[178]

---

177 See also the 2012 and 2015 reports of the Secretary-General on the topic of Indigenous Peoples participation: UN Doc. A/HRC/21/24; and Progress Made in the Implementation of the Outcome Document of the High-Level Plenary Meeting of the General Assembly Known as the World Conference on Indigenous Peoples, UN Doc. A/70/84 (18 May 2015), issued following the 2014 World Conference on Indigenous Peoples.

178 UN Doc. A/HRC/21/24, para. 13.

Some of the challenges for enhanced participation of Indigenous Peoples include the complexities from the lack of an international definition of Indigenous Peoples and the accreditation process that would need to be created, as well as the question of who would be the members of an accreditation committee. Expressing this concern, in a 2016 statement regarding the General Assembly consultations on enhanced participation, the American Indian Law Alliance pointed out that "we, as indigenous peoples are to sit along side member states to determine who is and who isn't indigenous is the same divide and conquer mentality and systems we have been fighting since contact."[179] Perhaps the biggest challenge is the lack of political will of certain states to accept that they have Indigenous Peoples within their borders, to recognize who these peoples are, and to implement Indigenous Peoples' rights. The history of the international Indigenous Peoples' movement has, however, demonstrated that constant dialogue, more often than not facilitated by the United Nations, can help soften various disagreements and pave the road toward solutions that will be respectful for all. Far from being a formality, substantive Indigenous Peoples' participation creates new routes to peace, human rights, and well-being.

The discussions under the auspices of the President of the UN General Assembly regarding enhanced Indigenous Peoples' participation have not been easy, but efforts continue, and ideas are developed to facilitate the process. A Dialogue Meeting on Enhanced Indigenous Peoples' Participation at the UN took place in Quito, Ecuador, 27–30 January 2020,[180] and one of its decisions was to establish a Temporary Committee. The African member of the Committee, Dr. Mariam Wallet Aboubakrine, former Chairperson of the UNPFII, addressed the UNPFII at its 2021 session and shared some reflections on the approach and possible solutions.[181] She stressed that it is a mistake to think that the issue of enhanced participation started only in 2014 (when the WCIP referred to it); the enhanced participation is an almost one hundred-year process, and it can be traced back to the early 1920s when Deskaheh Levi General from the Haudenosaunee and Māori religious leader T. W. Ratana traveled to Geneva to the League of Nations to defend the rights of their peoples. As both were denied permission to speak, this denial fueled Indigenous Peoples' desire for justice and the advocacy

179 "AILA Statement: Consultations with Advisers to UNGA President – UNPFII 2016," UNPFIP Network website, 11 May 2016, http://unpfip.blogspot.com/2016/05/aila-statement-consultations-with.html.

180 Information about the meeting including its Outcome Document can be found on DOCIP's website: "Dialogue Meeting on Enhanced Indigenous Peoples' Participation at the UN," 28 April 2020, www.docip.org/en/our-services-solutions/news/single-news/article/dialogue-meeting-on-enhanced-indigenous-peoples-participation-at-the-un/.

181 The author obtained a copy of Dr Aboubakrine's speech directly from her and heard the speech while it was delivered.

for their rights under international law. Addressing some concerns of states, Dr. Aboubakrine said that (a) enhanced participation is for representative institutions, authorities, and governments of Indigenous Peoples; (b) participation of Indigenous Peoples' representative institutions would aim at contributing to the important work of the UN; and (c) an enhanced status for Indigenous Peoples is in line with their right to self-determination. She pointed out that the UNDRIP, which affirms the inherent right of Indigenous Peoples to participate in decision-making in matters that affect them, will continue to guide and frame the Indigenous work on enhanced participation, and she was heartened by the support for these goals found among some states and UN entities.

We see therefore that Indigenous Peoples' participation in international fora has been a move toward more equality, an affirmation of the right to self-determination, and also a move toward renegotiating the nature of the modern states in which Indigenous Peoples live.

This chapter explored how Indigenous Peoples present and represent themselves at the international level on their own terms, while laying out their demands on states. We saw how and why these self-presentations create a cultural, legal, and political space that impacts positively on political outcomes. The long negotiation process of the UNDRIP provided the basic ground for the analysis of these questions, including new concepts engrained in the Declaration as well as Indigenous protocols that represent Indigenous philosophies. The role of Indigenous women and Indigenous youth in the international arena was also analyzed. The early internationalization of the case of the Yanomami gave further insights of novel approaches promoted by Indigenous Peoples. The chapter reflected on the limits and possibilities of Indigenous Peoples' participation within the international interstate system, including an analysis of efforts to enhance Indigenous participation at the UN General Assembly and elsewhere.

Bibliography

African Commission on Human and Peoples' Rights (ACHPR). *Advisory Opinion of the African Commission on Human and Peoples' Rights on the United Nations Declaration on the Rights of Indigenous Peoples: Adopted by the African Commission on Human and Peoples' Rights at Its 41st Ordinary Session Held in May 2007 in Accra, Ghana*. Banjul: The Gambia, 2007. Archived 11 October 2022 at the Internet Archive. www.achpr.org/public/Document/file/Any/un_advisory_opinion_idp_eng.pdf.

African Group. Draft Aide Memoire [on] United Nation Declaration of the Rights of Indigenous Peoples, 9 November 2006. http://cendoc.docip.org/collect/cendocdo/index/assoc/HASH0110/1b549795.dir/draft_africangroup.pdf.

Åhrén, Mattias. *Indigenous Peoples' Status in the International Legal System*. Oxford: Oxford University Press, 2016.

Alta Outcome Document. Global Indigenous Preparatory Conference for the United Nations High Level Plenary Meeting of the General Assembly to Be Known as the World Conference on Indigenous Peoples, Alta, 10–12 June 2013. www.un.org/esa/socdev/unpfii/documents/wc/AdoptedAlta_outcomedoc_EN.pdf.

Anaya, S. James. *Indigenous Peoples in International Law*. 2nd ed. Oxford: Oxford University Press, 2004.

Barsh, Russel. "The Inner Struggle of Indigenous Peoples." In *Indigenous Peoples' Rights in International Law: Emergence and Application*, edited by Roxanne Dunbar-Ortiz, Dalee Sambo Dorough, Gudmundur Alfredsson, Lee Swepston, and Petter Wille, 88–97. Kautokeino: Gáldu; Copenhagen: IWGIA, 2015. www.iwgia.org/en/documents-and-publications/documents/publications-pdfs/english-publications/126-indigenous-peoples-rights-in-international-law/file.html.

Begaye, Enei. "The Black Mesa Controversy." *Cultural Survival*, 7 May 2010. www.culturalsurvival.org/publications/cultural-survival-quarterly/black-mesa-controversy.

Bentham, Summer Rain, Hilla Kerner, and Lisa Steacy. "Sisterhood on the Frontiers: The Truth as We Hear It from Indigenous Women." In *Forever Loved: Exposing the Hidden Crisis of Missing and Murdered Indigenous Women and Girls in Canada*, edited by D. Memee Lavell-Harvard and Jennifer Brant, 231–246. Bradford, ON: Demeter Press, 2016.

Branford, Sue. "Yanomami Amazon Reserve Invaded by 20,000 Miners; Bolsonaro Fails to Act." *Mongabay*, 12 July 2019. https://news.mongabay.com/2019/07/yanomami-amazon-reserve-invaded-by-20000-miners-bolsonaro-fails-to-act/.

Brunnée, Jutta, and Stephen J. Toope. "International Law and Constructivism: Elements of an Interactional Theory of International Law." *Columbia Journal of Transnational Law* 39, no. 1 (2000): 19–74.

Butakov, Yaroslav. "The Tungus Uprising in 1924: How It Ended." *Russian Seven*, 2021. [In Russian]. https://russian7.ru/post/vosstanie-tungusov-v-1924-godu-chem-ono-zav/.

Cram, Fiona. "Rangahau Māori: Tona Tika, Tona Pono – The Validity and Integrity of Māori Research." In *Research Ethics in Aotearoa New Zealand: Concepts, Practice, Critique*, edited by Martin Tolich, 35–52. Auckland: Pearson Education, 2001.

Cunningham, Myrna, Álvaro Pop, and Secretariat of the Permanent Forum on Indigenous Issues. Study on How the Knowledge, History and Contemporary Social Circumstances of Indigenous Peoples Are Embedded in the Curricula of Education Systems. UN Doc. E/C.19/2013/17, 20 February 2013.

Declaration of the International Symposium, "Indigenous Peoples at the United Nations: From the Experience of the First Delegates to the Empowerment of the Younger Generations," 13 September 2013. http://cendoc.docip.org/collect/cendocdo/index/assoc/HASH017a/4a4a35f7.dir/DeclSymposium2013_final_en.pdf.

Denzin, Norman K., and Yvonna S. Lincoln. "Introduction: The Discipline and Practice of Qualitative Research." In *Handbook of Qualitative Research*, 2nd ed., edited by Denzin and Lincoln, 1–28. Thousand Oaks, CA: Sage Publications, 2000.

Deskaheh. "An Iroquois Patriot's Fight for International Recognition: The Last Speech of Deskaheh." In *Basic Call to Consciousness*, edited by Akwesasne Notes, 41–54. Summertown, TN: Native Voices, 2005.

Dunbar-Ortiz, Roxanne. *An Indigenous Peoples History of the United States*. Boston, MA: Beacon Press, 2014.

Frichner, Tonya Gonnella. Preliminary Study of the Impact on Indigenous Peoples of the International Legal Construct Known as the Doctrine of Discovery, UN Doc. E/C.19/2010/13, 10 February 2010. www.un.org/esa/socdev/unpfii/documents/E.C.19.2010.13%20EN.pdf.

Graugnard, Jean-François. *Photographic report of the "International Conference against Discrimination against Indigenous Populations of the Americas."* Geneva: United Nations, 1977.

Indigenous Peoples and the United Nations, Vol. 1. Film produced by Rebecca Sommer for the Secretariat of the Permanent Forum on Indigenous Issues. YouTube videos, parts 1 and 3, 18 min. www.youtube.com/watch?v=8I8QgA1tQQ8 and www.youtube.com/watch?v=LlS6ANY1aDM.

Integration of the Human Rights of Women and the Gender Perspective: Violence against Women – Statement by Ms. Radhika Coomaraswamy, Special Rapporteur on Violence against Women. UN Commission on Human Rights, 59th session, 9 April 2003. www.ohchr.org/en/statements/2009/10/integration-human-rights-women-and-gender-perspective-violence-against-women.

Inter-American Commission on Human Rights. Indigenous Women and Their Human Rights in the Americas. OEA/Ser.L/V/II., Doc. 44/17. IACHR, 2017.

International Indigenous Women's Forum (FIMI). *Global Study on the Situation of Indigenous Women and Girls: In the Framework of the 25th Anniversary of the Beijing Declaration and Platform for Action*. FIMI, 2020. https://fimi-iiwf.org/en/biblioteca-propias/the-global-study-on-the-situation-of-indigenous-women-and-girls/?lang=en.

International Indigenous Women's Forum (FIMI). *Mairin Iwanka Raya: Indigenous Women Stand against Violence*. New York: FIMI/IIWF, 2006. www.fimi-iiwf.org/en/biblioteca-propias/mairin-iwanka-raya-indigenous-women-stand-against-violence/.

International Labor Organization. *Implementing the ILO Indigenous and Tribal Peoples Convention No. 169: Towards an Inclusive, Sustainable and Just Future*. Geneva: ILO, 2019. www.ilo.org/wcmsp5/groups/public/-dgreports/-dcomm/-publ/documents/publication/wcms_735607.pdf.

International Work Group on Indigenous Affairs. *IWGIA Gender Strategy 2021–2025*. IWGIA, 2021. https://iwgia.org/en/about/organisation.html.

Jung, Courtney. *The Moral Force of Indigenous Politics: Critical Liberalism and the Zapatistas*. Cambridge: Cambridge University Press, 2008.

Kopenawa, Davi, and Bruce Albert. *The Falling Sky: Words of a Yanomami Shaman*. Translated by Nicholas Elliott and Alison Dundy. Cambridge, MA: The Belknap Press of Harvard University Press, 2013.

Kuokkanen, Rauna. *Restructuring Relations: Indigenous Self-Determination, Governance, and Gender*. Oxford: Oxford University Press, 2019.

Kymlicka, Will. *Multicultural Citizenship: A Liberal Theory of Minority Rights*. Oxford: Clarendon Press, 1995.

Lawlor, Mary. *Public Native America: Tribal Self-Representations in Museums, Powwows, and Casinos*. New Brunswick, NJ: Rutgers University Press, 2006.

Lightfoot, Sheryl. *Global Indigenous Politics: A Subtle Revolution*. London: Routledge, 2016.

Løvstrøm, Qivioq Nivi, Kibett Carson Kiburo, and Qhapaj Conde, introduction to *Global Indigenous Youth: Through Their Eyes*, edited by Angel Pérez, Dali, Victor Anthony Lopez-Carmen, and Elsa Stamatopoulou, xv–xxvii. New York: Institute for the Study of Human Rights, Columbia University, 2019. https://doi.org/10.7916/d8-dh2w-rz29.

Muehlebach, Andrea. "'Making Place' at the United Nations: Indigenous Cultural Politics at the U.N. Working Group on Indigenous Populations." *Cultural Anthropology* 16, no. 3 (August 2001): 415–448. https://doi.org/10.1525/can.2001.16.3.415.

National Archives of the Republic of Sakha (Yakutia). "Tunguska Uprising, May 1924–August 1925." [In Russian]. Archived 15 February 2020 at the Internet Archive. https://web.archive.org/web/20200215013910/http://archivesakha.ru/?page_id=5919.

Newcomb, Steven T. *Pagans in the Promised Land: Decoding the Doctrine of Christian Discovery*. Golden, CO: Fulcrum, 2008.

Olcott, Jocelyn. "'We Are Our Sister's Keeper': US Feminists at the 1975 International Women's Year Conference." United Nations History Project, Image of the Month, June 2017. www.histecon.magd.cam.ac.uk/unhist/image-of-the_month/image_of_the_month_June17.html.

Radcliffe, Sarah A. "Indigenous Women, Rights and the Nation-State in the Andes." In *Gender and the Politics of Rights and Democracy in Latin America*, edited by Nikki Craske and Maxine Molyneux, 149–172. New York: Palgrave, 2002.

Report of the International Expert Group Meeting on Combating Violence against Indigenous Women and Girls: Article 22 of the United Nations Declaration on the Rights of Indigenous Peoples. UN Doc. E/C.19/2012/6, 28 February 2012.

Response Note to the Draft Aide Memoire of the African Group on the UN Declaration on the Rights of Indigenous Peoples, Presented by an African Group of Experts. Copenhagen: IWGIA, 21 March 2007. www.iwgia.org/es/documents-and-publications/documents/publications-pdfs/english-publications/138-response-note-to-african-group-final-eng/file.html.

Right to Self-determination of Indigenous and Tribal Peoples. Inter-American Commission on Human Rights and IWGIA, 2021. www.iwgia.org/en/resources/publications/4592-iachr-presents-the-report-right-to-self-determination-of-indigenous-and-tribal-peoples.html.

Rigney, Lester-Irabinna. "Internationalization of an Indigenous Anticolonial Cultural Critique of Research Methodologies: A Guide to Indigenist Research Methodology and Its Principles." *Wicazo Sa Review* 14, no. 2 (Autumn 1999): 109–121. https://doi.org/10.2307/1409555.

Second World Conference of Indigenous Women: Together for Wellbeing and Mother Earth. *Global Political Declaration of Indigenous Women*, 2 September 2021. www.asianindigenouswomen.org/files/Global_Political_Declaration_of_Indigenous_Women_2WCIW.pdf.

Secretariat of the Permanent Forum on Indigenous Issues. Study on the Extent of Violence against Indigenous Women and Girls in Terms of Article 22 (2) of the United Nations Declaration on the Rights of Indigenous Peoples. UN Doc. E/C.19/2013/9, 12 February 2013.

Secretariat of the Permanent Forum on Indigenous Issues. Twenty-Year Review of the Beijing Declaration and Platform for Action and Beyond: A Framework to Advance Indigenous Women's Issues. UN Doc. E/C.19/2015/2, 4 February 2015.

Secretariat of the Permanent Forum on Indigenous Issues. Update on the Implementation of the Recommendations of the Permanent Forum. UN Doc. E/C.19/2017/3, 6 February 2017.

Secretariat of the Permanent Forum on Indigenous Issues and Inter-Agency Network on Women and Gender Equality Task Force on Indigenous Women. *Indigenous Women and the United Nations System: Good Practices and Lessons Learned.* UN Doc. ST/ESA/307. New York: UN, 2007. www.un.org/esa/socdev/publications/Indigenous/indwomen07.htm.

Smith, Andrea. "Indigenous Feminism without Apology" *New Socialist*, no. 58 (September–October 2006): 16–17.

Smith, Andrea. *Conquest: Sexual Violence and American Indian Genocide.* New York: South End Press, 2005.

Smith, Linda Tuhiwai. *Decolonizing Methodologies: Research and Indigenous Peoples.* 2nd ed. London: Zed Books, 2012.

Stamatopoulou, Elsa. *Cultural Rights in International Law: Article 27 of the Universal Declaration of Human Rights and Beyond.* Leiden: Martinus Nijhoff, 2007.

Stamatopoulou, Elsa. "The Good Offices of the Secretary-General in Human Rights Issues: Past Practice and Future Challenges." In *Justice Pending: Indigenous Peoples and Other Good Causes, Essays in Honour of Erica-Irene A. Daes,* edited by Gudmundur Alfredsson and Maria Stavropoulou, 175–185. The Hague: Martinus Nijhoff, 2002.

Stamatopoulou, Elsa. "The Role of Research and Academia in Indigenous Peoples' Issues: Interculturality in the Making." In *Unsettling Discourses: The Theory and Practice of Indigenous Studies. Proceedings of the 2013 International Seminar-Workshop on Indigenous Studies,* 249–272. Baguio City: Cordillera Studies Center, University of the Philippines Baguio, and Tebtebba Foundation, 2014.

Stamatopoulou, Elsa. "Taking Cultural Rights Seriously: The Vision of the UN Declaration on the Rights of Indigenous Peoples." In *Reflections on the UN Declaration on the Rights of Indigenous Peoples,* edited by Stephen Allen and Alexandra Xanthaki, 387–412. Oxford: Hart Publishing, 2011.

Statement of Victoria Tauli-Corpuz, Chair of the UN Permanent Forum on Indigenous Issues on the Occasion of the Adoption of the UN Declaration on the Rights of Indigenous Peoples, 13 September 2007. www.un.org/esa/socdev/unpfii/documents/2016/Docs-updates/STATEMENT-VICTORIA-TAULI-CORPUZ-IDWIP-2007.pdf.

Sunder, Madhavi. "Piercing the Veil." *Yale Law Journal* 112, no. 6 (March 2003): 1399–1472.

System-Wide Action Plan on the Rights of Indigenous Peoples. UN Department of Information, 2016. www.un.org/esa/socdev/unpfii/documents/2016/Docs-updates/SWAP_Indigenous_Peoples_WEB.pdf.

Theys, Sarina. "Introducing Constructivism in International Relations Theory." *E-International Relations,* 23 February 2018. www.e-ir.info/2018/02/23/introducing-constructivism-in-international-relations-theory/.

Tilly, Charles. *Social Movements, 1768–2004.* Boulder, CO: Paradigm, 2004.

"Tunguska Uprising." Archival documents, *Ilin Cultural and Historical Magazine,* no. 1 [13], 1998. [In Russian]. https://ilin-yakutsk.narod.ru/1998-1/17-6.htm.

UN Charter, 26 June 1945. www.un.org/en/about-us/un-charter/.

UN Commission on Human Rights. Leaflet No. 5: The Draft United Nations Declaration on the Rights of Indigenous Peoples. Office of the UN High Commissioner for Human Rights. Accessed 16 May 2022. www.ohchr.org/sites/default/files/Documents/Publications/GuideIPleaflet5en.pdf.

UN Commission on the Status of Women. Interactive Dialogue on the Focus Area: Empowerment of Indigenous Women. UN Doc. E/CN.6/2017/12, 20 March 2017. https://documents-dds-ny.un.org/doc/UNDOC/GEN/N17/073/17/PDF/N1707317.pdf.

UN Commission on the Status of Women. Report on the Fifty-Sixth Session (14 March 2011, 27 February–9 March and 15 March 2016). UN Doc. E/CN.6/2012/16, 2016.

UN Commission on the Status of Women. Report on the Forty-Ninth Session (28 February–11 and 22 March 2005). UN Doc. E/CN.6/2005/11, 2005.

UN Committee on the Elimination of Discrimination against Women. General Recommendation No. 39 (2022) on the Rights of Indigenous Women and Girls. UN Doc. CEDAW/C/GC/39, 31 October 2022.

UN Economic and Social Council. Resolution 1982/34, Study of the Problem of Discrimination against Indigenous Populations. UN Doc. E/RES/1982/34, 7 May 1982.

UN Expert Mechanism on the Rights of Indigenous Peoples. Efforts to Implement the Rights of Indigenous Peoples: Indigenous Peoples and the Right to Self-Determination, UN Doc. A/HRC/48/75, 4 August 2021.

UN Expert Mechanism on the Rights of Indigenous Peoples. Efforts to Implement the United Nations Declaration on the Rights of Indigenous Peoples: Recognition, Reparation and Reconciliation, UN Doc. A/HRC/EMRIP/2019/3/Rev.1, 2 September 2019.

UN Expert Mechanism on the Rights of Indigenous Peoples. Final Report of the Study on Indigenous Peoples and the Right to Participate in Decision-Making, UN Doc. A/HRC/18/42, 17 August 2011.

UN Expert Mechanism on the Rights of Indigenous Peoples. Report of the Expert Mechanism on the Rights of Indigenous Peoples on Its Fourth Session, Geneva, 11–15 July 2011, UN Doc. A/HRC/18/43, 19 August 2011.

UN General Assembly. Resolution 45/164, International Year for the World's Indigenous People. UN Doc. A/RES/45/164, 18 December 1990. http://undocs.org/A/RES/45/164.

UN General Assembly. Resolution 47/75, International Year for the World's Indigenous People. 1993, UN Doc. A/RES/47/75, 14 December 1992. http://undocs.org/A/RES/47/75.

UN General Assembly. Resolution 61/295, United Nations Declaration on the Rights of Indigenous Peoples. UN Doc. A/RES/61/295, 13 September 2007. www.un.org/development/desa/indigenouspeoples/wp-content/uploads/sites/19/2018/11/UNDRIP_E_web.pdf.

UN General Assembly. Resolution 69/2, Outcome Document of the High-Level Plenary Meeting of the General Assembly Known as the World Conference on Indigenous Peoples. UN Doc. A/RES/69/2, 25 September 2014. https://documents-dds-ny.un.org/doc/UNDOC/GEN/N14/468/28/PDF/N1446828.pdf.

UN General Assembly. Resolution 260 A (III), Convention on the Prevention and Punishment of the Crime of Genocide, 9 December 1948. www.ohchr.org/en/instruments-mechanisms/instruments/convention-prevention-and-punishment-crime-genocide.

UN General Assembly. Resolution 1514 (XV), Declaration on the Granting of Independence to Colonial Countries and Peoples. UN Doc. A/RES/1514(XV), 14 December 1960. www.ohchr.org/en/instruments-mechanisms/instruments/declaration-granting-independence-colonial-countries-and-peoples.

UN General Assembly. Resolution 2200A (XXI), International Covenant on Economic, Social and Cultural Rights. UN Doc. A/RES/2200(XXI), 16 December 1966. www.ohchr.org/en/instruments-mechanisms/instruments/international-covenant-economic-social-and-cultural-rights.

UN Human Rights Council. Report of the Special Rapporteur on the Rights of Indigenous Peoples on Her Mission to Brazil: Note by the Secretariat. UN Doc. A/HRC/33/42/Add.1, 8 August 2016.

UN Human Rights Council. Report of the Special Rapporteur on the Rights of Indigenous Peoples, Victoria Tauli-Corpuz. UN Doc. A/HRC/30/41, 6 August 2015.

UN Human Rights Council. Report of the Special Rapporteur on the Situation of Human Rights and Fundamental Freedoms of Indigenous People, James Anaya: Addendum. UN Doc. A/HRC/12/34/Add.2, 26 August 2009.

UN Office of the High Commissioner for Human Rights. Intersessional Round Table on Ways to Enhance the Participation of Indigenous Peoples' Representatives and Institutions in Meetings of the Human Rights Council on Issues Affecting Them: Report of the Office of the United Nations High Commissioner for Human Rights. UN Doc. A/HRC/49/69, 11 January 2022.

UN Office of the Special Adviser on Gender Issues and the Advancement of Women and the Secretariat of the Permanent Forum on Indigenous Issues. *Gender and Indigenous Peoples: Briefing Notes.* New York: United Nations, 2010. www.un.org/development/desa/indigenouspeoples/publications/2009/06/briefing-notes-gender-and-indigenous-women/.

UN Permanent Forum on Indigenous Issues. Report on the Eighth Session (18–29 May 2009). UN Doc. E/2009/43, 2009.

UN Permanent Forum on Indigenous Issues. Report on the Fifth Session (15–26 May 2006). UN Doc. E/2006/43, 2006.

UN Permanent Forum on Indigenous Issues. Report on the Fourteenth Session (20 April–1 May 2015). UN Doc. E/2015/43-E/C.19/2015/10, 2015. https://documents-dds-ny.un.org/doc/UNDOC/GEN/N15/143/74/PDF/N1514374.pdf.

UN Permanent Forum on Indigenous Issues. Report on the Seventh Session (21 April–2 May 2008). UN Doc. E/2008/43, 2008.

UN Permanent Forum on Indigenous Issues. Report on the Third Session (10–21 May 2004). UN Doc. E/2004/43, 2004.

UN Secretary-General. Enhancing the Participation of Indigenous Peoples' Representatives and Institutions in Meetings of Relevant United Nations Bodies on Issues Affecting Them. UN Doc. A/75/255, 27 July 2020. https://documents-dds-ny.un.org/doc/UNDOC/GEN/N20/196/88/PDF/N2019688.pdf.

UN Secretary-General. Progress Made in the Implementation of the Outcome Document of the High-Level Plenary Meeting of the General Assembly Known as the World Conference on Indigenous Peoples. UN Doc. A/70/84, 18 May 2015.

UN Secretary-General. Ways and Means of Promoting Participation at the United Nations of Indigenous Peoples' Representatives on Issues Affecting Them. UN Doc. A/HRC/21/24, 2 July 2012.

UN Sub-Commission on Prevention of Discrimination and Protection of Minorities. Report of the Working Group on Indigenous Populations on Its First Session. UN Doc. E/CN.4/Sub.2/1982/33, 25 August 1982.

Warren, Kay B. *Indigenous Movements and Their Critics: Pan-Maya Activism in Guatemala*. Princeton, NJ: Princeton University Press, 1998.

World Conference of Indigenous Women: Progress and Challenges Regarding the Future We Want. *Lima Declaration*, 30 October 2013. www.culturalsurvival.org/sites/default/files/lima_declaration1.pdf.

Xanthaki, Alexandra. *Indigenous Rights and United Nations Standards: Self-Determination, Culture and Land*. Cambridge: Cambridge University Press, 2007.

Xanthaki, Alexandra. "Limitations to Indigenous Autonomy." Paper presented at the Expert Seminar on Indigenous Peoples' Languages and Cultures, Brunel Law School, Uxbridge, London, 8–9 March 2012.

Xanthaki, Alexandra. "Multiculturalism and International Law: Discussing Universal Standards." *Human Rights Quarterly* 32, no. 1 (February 2010): 21–48. https://doi.org/10.1353/hrq.0.0139.

5

THE RIGHT TO SELF-DETERMINED DEVELOPMENT

A. Introduction

The area of "development" spreads over many UN-system and other inter-state organizations, funds, and programs, and significant resources and politics are devoted to it. Its concept has evolved over time in international affairs after World War II. In broad terms, we can identify the following phases: the macroeconomic concept of development; sustainable development (which incorporated the idea of environmental sustainability) as of the early 1990s; human development (following Amartya Sen's concept that the well-being of the human being is at the center of development) as of the mid-1990s; human sustainable development (putting together the well-being of people and the environment) as of the end of the 1990s; human rights based approach to development (contributes the human rights normative framework to development: accountability, participation, nondiscrimination, and attention to the most vulnerable) as of the early 2000s; development with culture and identity (DCI), and *vivir bien* (Indigenous Peoples' perspectives, bringing together the idea that living well means that human beings are in harmony with nature and with community and also enjoy spiritual well-being) as of the 2010s.

Given the emphasis on development in the international system, and the involvement of Indigenous Peoples, this chapter will unveil additional opportunities but also challenges for Indigenous participation. The issues woven together under the concept of development, including environment, climate change, and traditional knowledge, also help us understand what self-determined development would mean for Indigenous Peoples.

DOI: 10.4324/9781003464099-6

The world of international intergovernmental organizations (IGOs), global or regional, can be seen as its own "universe," complex, seemingly out of reach for the nongovernmental world and "the man and woman in the street," often cumbersome and bureaucratic, at times ignorant about or insensitive to Indigenous Peoples' issues and their voices. It can be also seen as "too political," meaning that it is about politics among states or regions of states and about strong international economic or geopolitical interests. Looked at from the outside, the interstate system may also appear to follow the economic and political waves of our globalized world, raising the question, for individuals and communities, "What does this all have to do with me?"[1]

At the same time, it is clear to anybody who has experienced the UN human rights system that nongovernmental organizations (NGOs) have had considerable impact on the UN's human rights work – such that the way the UN human rights system developed and is still developing would be unimaginable without that input, struggle, diplomacy, and engagement. Theories of institutions and the observation of power structures of the UN can make us wonder about the power nonstate actors can have.[2] By nonstate actors we mean NGOs, academia, even individuals who care to focus and strategize for change. The possibility for human ingenuity and initiative within the bureaucracy becomes obvious. More than anything else, the contradictions in the UN also become obvious. As in any human enterprise, there are, also in the UN, various tendencies, forces, and actions that come into play, such that the result can almost never be predicted in exact terms, which means that there is always room and possibility for people to try out options.

It is only a relatively recent phenomenon, since the establishment of the United Nations Permanent Forum on Indigenous Issues (UNPFII) in 2000, that Indigenous Peoples' voices on alternative modes of development started being heard at the international level and with such a high profile. In fact, it would be no exaggeration to say that the very few alternative visions of development that reach this high level of visibility in the UN and provide a critique to the dominant model of economic globalization are expressed

---

1 Parts of this chapter are based on Elsa Stamatopoulou "Walking the Talk? Including Indigenous Peoples' Issues in Intergovernmental Organizations," in *Indigenous Peoples' Rights in International Law*, ed. Roxanne Dunbar-Ortiz et al. (Kautokeino: Gáldu and Copenhagen: IWGIA, 2015).

2 Cornelius Castoriadis pointed out that as the conscious questioning of society's instituted representations, philosophy develops hand in hand with politics, which Castoriadis described as society's lucid attempt to alter its own institutions. In his book *The Imaginary Institution of Society*, he demonstrates that the world and its institutions are not articulated once and for all but are constantly subjected to human creativity. Castoriadis, *The Imaginary Institution of Society*, trans. Kathleen Blamey (Cambridge, MA: MIT Press, 1998).

by Indigenous Peoples. As Carson Kiburo, Endorois in Kenya, Executive Director of the Jamii Asilia Centre, stated in response to a question I raised, "Indigenous Peoples are not dividing the territory of any state; we just want to participate and self-determine our future."[3]

The issue of development and Indigenous Peoples is a broad one – in fact, the issue of development is also a very broad one for states and the intergovernmental system as a whole, and it is an area where substantial resources, efforts, policies, and politics are devoted. Economic and social development is also part of the mandate of the UNPFII, which has systematically dealt with the issue at each of its sessions. Whether the Forum's topic is Indigenous children, Indigenous women, the Sustainable Development Goals (SDGs), or climate change, the Forum systematically studies and monitors the issues and makes recommendations on Indigenous Peoples and development. This is how the Permanent Forum opened the chapter of its recommendations on "development with culture and identity" in the year 2010:

> 4. Development paradigms of modernization and industrialization have often resulted in the destruction of the political, economic, social, cultural, education, health, spiritual and knowledge systems of indigenous peoples. There is a disconnect between dominant development paradigms and indigenous peoples due to the way indigenous peoples are often viewed. For example, indigenous peoples' "development" is understood to be their assimilation into the so-called "civilized world." Also, indigenous peoples' cultures and values are seen to be contradictory to the values of the market economy, such as the accumulation of profit, consumption and competition. Further, indigenous peoples and their cultures are seen as "obstacles" to progress because their lands and territories are rich in resources, and indigenous peoples are not willing to freely dispose of them.[4]

Three specific articles of the United Nations Declaration on the Rights of Indigenous Peoples (UNDRIP) are of fundamental importance for Indigenous Peoples' development with culture and identity: Articles 3, 32, and 37.[5]

---

3 Kiburo interviewed by the author, 7 March 2022. The list of persons with whom discussions were held appears in Annex 1. The questions discussed with interviewees are listed in the introduction.

4 UN Permanent Forum on Indigenous Issues, Report on the Ninth Session (19–30 April 2010), UN Doc. E/2010/43 (2010), para. 4.

5 UN General Assembly, Resolution 61/295, United Nations Declaration on the Rights of Indigenous Peoples, UN Doc. A/RES/61/295 (13 September 2007), www.un.org/development/desa/indigenouspeoples/wp-content/uploads/sites/19/2018/11/UNDRIP_E_web.pdf.

Article 3

> Indigenous peoples have the right to self-determination. By virtue of that right they freely determine their political status and freely pursue their economic, social and cultural development.

Article 32

> 1. Indigenous peoples have the right to determine and develop priorities and strategies for the development or use of their lands or territories and other resources.
> 2. States shall consult and cooperate in good faith with the indigenous peoples concerned through their own representative institutions in order to obtain their free and informed consent prior to the approval of any project affecting their lands or territories and other resources, particularly in connection with the development, utilization or exploitation of mineral, water or other resources.
> 3. States shall provide effective mechanisms for just and fair redress for any such activities, and appropriate measures shall be taken to mitigate adverse environmental, economic, social, cultural or spiritual impact.

Article 37 states, among other things:

> 1. Indigenous peoples have the right to the recognition, observance and enforcement of treaties, agreements and other constructive arrangements concluded with States or their successors and to have States honour and respect such treaties, agreements and other constructive arrangements.

1. Methodological and Conceptual Questions

Two major methodological questions have been linked to the topic of development and Indigenous Peoples: free, prior, and informed consent, and data collection and disaggregation – the first, in order to ensure that Indigenous Peoples' voices and visions find their way and are respected in actual decision-making; and the second, in order to reveal the inequalities and the real situation of Indigenous Peoples, inequalities that are often hidden under national averages. Linked to the question of data collection is the issue of indicators on Indigenous Peoples' well-being and sustainability. Extraordinary work of analysis has been done by the Permanent Forum and others on this, as well as by Indigenous Peoples themselves of course. One of the results of these efforts is the creation of the Indigenous Navigator, which is a framework and set of tools for and by Indigenous Peoples to systematically monitor the level of recognition and implementation of their rights. By using the Indigenous Navigator, Indigenous organizations and communities, duty bearers, NGOs, and journalists can access free tools and resources based on community-generated data.[6]

At the same time, a question underlying the legitimacy of the debate on development has been the very concept of development. What does development mean? How do we define it when it comes to Indigenous Peoples? Who defines it? The concept is often highly suspected by Indigenous Peoples due to devastating acts that have impacted their lives in the name of development. Thanks to Indigenous Peoples' advocacy, UN bodies often use the terms well-being, living well/*vivir bien – sumak kawsay, suma qamaña, laman laka*, or *gawis ay biag*, in various Indigenous languages – when it comes to Indigenous Peoples (instead of the term "development"). The UN also places value on subsistence economies; for example, on pastoralism or on hunting and gathering, instead of considering them ancient, inferior, forgotten, or negative socioeconomic practices. Yet when it comes to actual decisions, many questions arise: Who says that a program or project constitutes "development" for an Indigenous community? The UN and its agencies, a rich bilateral state donor, an NGO or a church working in the so-called "field," a corporation, or the government of the country? Or the Indigenous Peoples themselves?

Indigenous Peoples have advocated for self-determined sustainable development, a human rights-based approach to development and development with culture and identity. It is these three frameworks that outline their visions of well-being and development.

Two sets of rights guaranteed by the UNDRIP underpin development with culture and identity: (a) the set of rights defining Indigenous Peoples' full and effective participation and their right to self-determination, and (b) cultural rights.

In other words, the adoption of the UNDRIP now requires new approaches to development. It encourages the building of genuine partnerships with Indigenous Peoples, so that their voices will contribute to development with culture and identity and so that, according to Article 3, Indigenous Peoples will actually "freely pursue their economic, social and cultural development." States are required to respect these voices, even when they reflect different visions and cultural perspectives of human development than their own.

B. Navigating the Maze of the Interstate System

We have to visualize the map of the UN system and of the numerous UN funds, programs, and agencies in order to appreciate the system's immensity

---

6 https://indigenousnavigator.org/, accessed 6 October 2019.

and complexity.[7] Each of these UN entities is a world of its own, with its own dynamics, culture, and governing system. Each of these has its own general assembly or executive committee, composed of states' delegations. Each of these has its policies, programs, and budgets decided by its assemblies and executive committees. Each has its own history and its staff.

Moreover, the inputs of each state delegation to those entities are not necessarily part of a consistent policy of the specific state but rather are fragmented and even contradictory sometimes because states' governments are not necessarily coherent within themselves. It would not be uncommon to see the position taken by a state in one UN organization or body contradicting its position in another. For example, the World Health Organization (WHO) and the UN Population Fund (UNFPA) coincide in their concern for health, but UNFPA has been much more open and active on Indigenous issues than WHO, where Indigenous issues have been met with a certain resistance. States' delegations do not necessarily have coherent positions in the governing bodies of WHO and UNFPA. They may pursue different interests and positions in these different bodies. Policies are supported by different ministries within a government. For example, a specific state may take a supportive position and project a positive public image for Indigenous Peoples in the UNPFII but a nonsupportive one in WHO or in the United Nations Educational, Scientific and Cultural Organization (UNESCO). Lack of coherence can be due to different interests pursued by states in different platforms. For example, a state government may wish to show a positive public face at the UNPFII, which is attended by hundreds of Indigenous representatives and other advocates, while it may not wish to commit to additional resources for Indigenous health at WHO, where the discussions are among states. Lack of coherence could also be attributed to weak coordination within state governments and to under-resourced civil services that would need to navigate these complex international organizations.

When the UNPFII "appeared" on the international scene in 2002, with its first session and the mandate to mainstream, integrate, and coordinate Indigenous issues in the UN system, it was viewed by several UN organizations, funds, and programs, as "the new kid on the block." Some staff, and cadres of well-established organizations with many decades of life, first looked at the Forum as an annoyance, with little patience for its duty to tell them what they could do better. Then, in 2007, with the adoption of the UNDRIP, the UN system saw itself addressed in a new international normative instrument, an innovative norm in UNDRIP, that specifically addresses the obligations of the UN system in Articles 41 and 42:

---

7 For the UN System chart, see www.un.org/en/pdfs/un_system_chart.pdf, accessed 7 October 2023.

Article 41

The organs and specialized agencies of the United Nations system and other intergovernmental organizations shall contribute to the full realization of the provisions of this Declaration through the mobilization, inter alia, of financial cooperation and technical assistance. Ways and means of ensuring participation of indigenous peoples on issues affecting them shall be established.

Article 42

The United Nations, its bodies, including the Permanent Forum on Indigenous Issues, and specialized agencies, including at the country level, and States shall promote respect for and full application of the provisions of this Declaration and follow up the effectiveness of this Declaration.

There is a robust international normative framework that surrounds the UN and facilitates advocacy, despite the obstacles that state politics may pose. The nongovernmental world pioneered a number of human rights instruments. The adoption of the very first UN human rights treaty, the 1948 Convention on the Prevention and Punishment of the Crime of Genocide, was a powerful example of "one man's struggle," that of Raphael Lemkin.[8] Other major NGO initiatives range from the creation of the human rights complaints procedures, the preparation of treaties and declarations, such as the Convention against Torture and Other Cruel, Inhuman or Degrading Treatment or Punishment; the Convention on the Rights of the Child and its optional protocols; and the Declaration on the Right and Responsibility of Individuals, Groups and Organs of Society to Promote and Protect Universally Recognized Human Rights and Fundamental Freedoms, to the International Convention for the Protection of All Persons from Enforced Disappearance and the UNDRIP. It has been an empowering experience for many to see international institutions and international law being reshaped through the dynamic interface between the increasingly powerful Indigenous Peoples' movement and the UN system.[9]

What was previously discussed about civil society and human rights has similarities to Indigenous Peoples and human rights at the UN, given the political sensitivity of human rights for states. To include an issue that has been long neglected and rendered invisible in the aims of an international

---

8 Bartolomé Clavero, *Genocide or Ethnocide, 1933–2007: How to Make, Unmake, and Remake Law with Words* (Milan: Giuffré, 2008).

9 I told this story in the first article I published. Elsa Stamatopoulou, "Indigenous Peoples and the United Nations: Human Rights as a Developing Dynamic," *Human Rights Quarterly* 16, no. 1 (February 1994), https://doi.org/10.2307/762411.

organization is no easy task: it involves changing public policies, laws, and resource allocations. More than anything, it involves a change of registry in the minds of those pulling the strings of an organization, a change of institutional culture on a specific public interest issue in the case of Indigenous issues. Mainstreaming, as this effort to include a new topic is sometimes called, is also about public officials, international and national, gaining in-depth understanding of the issue that is to be included. The United Nations system has had these mainstreaming experiences with human rights and with gender, originally.[10] Later, the strategy of mainstreaming became popular for other topics. The word "mainstreaming" has sometimes been used to indicate the need to be multidisciplinary in public policy analysis and methodologies. Although mainstreaming processes at the international level might seem esoteric and bureaucratic – and they sometimes are – there is a lot at stake behind them for the public good. They represent a site to debate and mold ideas that will then be launched into the world. They are the tip of the iceberg, an important indicator of where major currents of public policies are headed, and those currents eventually do have an impact on human beings and communities.[11] Mainstreaming processes therefore deserve attention, input, and critique.

1. Specificity in Addition to Universality

The adoption of specific policies on Indigenous issues by UN agencies has been a standard and perennial recommendation of Indigenous Peoples and of the Permanent Forum from its early sessions. As a result, a considerable

10 Since the late 1990s the UN Secretary-General established four Executive Committees, internal bodies to coordinate specific issues: one on peace, one on humanitarian affairs, one on economic and social affairs, and one on development (the latter called UN Development Group, UNDG; it was later renamed UN Sustainable Development Group). The Secretary-General, in consultation with the High Commissioner for Human Rights, decided that, instead of establishing a separate committee on human rights, human rights would be mainstreamed in the work of all the other committees. As part of the New York Office of the High Commissioner, I was closely involved in those processes and later focused more on mainstreaming human rights in development. Eventually, in 2003, the UNDG adopted the human-rights based approach to development.

11 To show the currents of ideas, ideologies, and interests that surface in mainstreaming debates, let me mention that, while in the 1990s the concept of "decentralization" was used to measure democracy, by 2008, the Organization for Economic Cooperation and Development (OECD) had pushed "harmonization" as the ideal, which was essentially advocating, albeit indirectly, for centralization. It was not a surprise that the launch of "harmonization" coincided with most of the European Union and other Western countries, except the Nordics, implicitly abandoning their advocacy for the human rights-based approach to development (which is strong on participation and decentralization) and their political engagement with social policies.

number of agencies have adopted or revised such policies, among them the United Nations Development Program (UNDP; its policy predated the establishment of the Permanent Forum and was revised in 2013), the International Fund for Agricultural Development (IFAD), the European Bank for Reconstruction and Development (EBRD), the World Bank, Food and Agriculture Organization of the United Nations (FAO), and UNESCO. Agency reports to the Permanent Forum have been an important way for agencies to engage with Indigenous issues. Such reports are submitted annually, detailing activities on Indigenous issues and the follow-up given to the Forum's recommendations. This practice also gives the opportunity for the agencies to state how they are implementing their obligations under Articles 41 and 42 of the UNDRIP as well as the Forum's recommendations. It is also obvious that when the agencies report to the Permanent Forum, this can also enrich the policy know-how of states on integrating Indigenous issues in national policies and programs.[12]

During the period 2000–2015, the Millennium Development Goals (MDGs) were the focal development goals of the international community. Over the years, the Secretariat of the Permanent Forum analyzed MDG country reports, programming papers of select UN country teams, papers of the Common Country Assessments and UN Development Assistance Frameworks, as well as UN Resident Coordinator reports and human development reports in order to ascertain whether those had integrated Indigenous Peoples' issues or Indigenous Peoples' participation. The analysis has demonstrated that, with very few exceptions, Indigenous Peoples' issues were not part of these development processes. This has led to the realization that, at this point, training of many UN country teams (UNCTs) is urgently required – that is, intensifying the training that is offered and that has been limited to a small number of UNCTs. Such training, together with the momentum of the UNDRIP, the UN Development Group (UNDG) Guidelines on Indigenous Peoples' Issues, and the System-Wide Action Plan following the 2014 World Conference on Indigenous Peoples, should strengthen action for the integration of Indigenous issues where it matters most: at national and local levels in connection with the SDGs, which are the international development agenda until 2030.

12 In addition to the public dialogues with the Forum, monitoring of how the agencies implement the Permanent Forum's recommendations is also done through an analytical database of recommendations updated annually by the Secretariat of the UNPFII and placed on its website (see https://unpfii.desa.un.org/). Reports by the Secretariat of the Permanent Forum periodically indicate the percentage of recommendations of the Permanent Forum that have been implemented, the percentage that are in the process of implementation, or recommendations where implementation has not been reported or started.

2. *Indigenous Peoples' Indirect Participation*

At a more political level, the Permanent Forum, in its own right, has pursued formal representation at meetings of intergovernmental bodies and conferences, as for example at the World Trade Organization (WTO), the Commission on Sustainable Development, UNESCO, the Commission on the Status of Women, the Governing Council of IFAD, the World Intellectual Property Organization (WIPO), and others. The account of the Forum's efforts to participate at a WTO meeting, as elaborated earlier, is indicative of the difficulties.

Negotiating such representation has not always been easy and at times has not been achieved, either due to procedural difficulties or the political reticence of states. The representation of the Forum at other UN bodies is clearly not the same as Indigenous Peoples representing themselves and not what Indigenous Peoples have been seeking through their efforts at the UN General Assembly for "enhanced participation" after the World Conference on Indigenous Peoples. Understanding the difficulties that the Permanent Forum – itself a UN body – has faced in such representation is an indicator of the exclusivity and "silo mentality" that often prevails in these international policy bodies, despite much discussion of coordination and harmonization within the UN system. Indigenous Peoples' participation in international bodies is not a bureaucratic or technical issue but a profoundly political one involving states as well.

Several examples under Section D ("Obstacles and Opportunities for Participation") illustrate these concerns.

C. Strengthening Indigenous Peoples' Participation[13]

From the 1950s to the early 2000s, Indigenous issues were dealt with mainly by the International Labor Organization (ILO) and the Office of the High Commissioner for Human Rights (OHCHR); previously called the Center for Human Rights and, earlier, Division of Human Rights). After the establishment of the Working Group on Indigenous Populations (WGIP) of the Sub-Commission on Prevention of Discrimination and Protection of Minorities in 1982, the ILO was the only UN organization to attend the meetings at the beginning and to interact with Indigenous participants and experts of the WGIP for a number of years. This had beneficial effects on the ILO's work on Indigenous Peoples' rights. Indigenous Peoples had the opportunity to also voice their critique of ILO Convention No. 107 on Indigenous and Tribal Populations as assimilationist, in light of the higher human rights standards that were in the making through the drafting of the UNDRIP by

---

13 This section relies on the author's research for Stamatopoulou, "Walking the Talk?"

the Working Group. In the long run, the participation of ILO in this global dialogue with Indigenous Peoples at WGIP paved the way for ILO's adoption of ILO Convention No. 169 on Indigenous and Tribal Peoples in Independent Countries.[14]

Starting in the later part of the 1980s, some UN agency representatives would arrange informal meetings among themselves to discuss Indigenous Peoples' issues. In addition to the Center for Human Rights – precursor to the OHCHR – and the ILO, representatives of the UNDP, UNESCO, and the WHO would also start joining. These meetings were mostly the result of the initiative of staff with commitment and engagement on Indigenous Peoples' rights, rather than part of any formal institutional arrangements.

One of the goals of the first International Decade of the World's Indigenous People, proclaimed by the UN General Assembly in 1993, was to strengthen international cooperation to solve the problems faced by Indigenous Peoples in such areas as human rights, the environment, development, education, and health. Yet in the reports on the first Decade by the Secretary-General and the OHCHR,[15] it was found that in spite of important advances during the first Decade in the area of interagency cooperation and institutional developments, the Indigenous Peoples in many countries continued to be among the poorest and the most marginalized. States expected a mobilization of international agencies toward the goal of the first Decade. With a few exceptions, based on committed individuals' initiatives, the UN agencies were unable to engage in an adequate way, although the two International Decades managed to increase awareness of Indigenous Peoples' issues'[16] The results of the Decades in terms of inclusion of Indigenous participation in the work of international agencies were not satisfactory.

---

14 For a discussion of this "transition" in the ILO's dealing with Indigenous Peoples, see Athanasios Yupsanis, "The International Labour Organization and Its Contribution to the Protection of the Rights of Indigenous Peoples," *Canadian Yearbook of International Law* 49 (2012), https://doi.org/10.1017/S006900580001033X.

15 Report of the Secretary-General on the Preliminary Review by the Coordinator of the International Decade of the World's Indigenous People on the Activities of the United Nations System in Relation to the Decade, UN Doc. E/2004/82 (25 June 2004); Implementation of the Programme of Activities for the International Decade of the World's Indigenous People, UN Doc. A/59/277 (17 August 2004); Final Report of the United Nations High Commissioner for Human Rights Reviewing the Activities within the United Nations System under the Programme for the International Decade of the World's Indigenous People, UN Doc. E/CN.4/2005/87 (4 January 2005).

16 The First International Decade of the World's Indigenous People (1995–2004) was proclaimed by UN General Assembly resolution 48/163. The Second International Decade of the World's Indigenous People (2005–2014) was proclaimed by UN General Assembly resolution 59/174. It is known that UN Decades constitute "soft" mandates for UN agencies: they are unfunded by any regular budget allocations and rely a lot on the good will and initiatives of UN agency actors and some governmental donors as well as the social group concerned.

In 2000, the Economic and Social Council (ECOSOC) established the UNPFII,[17] with the central mandate of integrating Indigenous issues in the UN system. According to the enabling resolution, the Permanent Forum is to serve as an advisory body to the ECOSOC

> with a mandate to discuss indigenous issues within the mandate of the Council relating to economic and social development, culture, the environment, education, health and human rights; in so doing the Permanent Forum shall: (a) Provide expert advice and recommendations on indigenous issues to the Council, as well as to programmes, funds and agencies of the United Nations, through the Council; (b) Raise awareness and promote the integration and coordination of activities relating to indigenous issues within the United Nations system.[18]

Taking the mandate literally, one might think that UNPFII's main goal is to do what previous UN actions had failed to do: integrate Indigenous issues into the UN system. While this may seem like a more inward-looking process, within the UN, and the mandate of the Permanent Forum may appear narrow, the so-called mainstreaming process unleashes a dynamic and dialectic approach that can have an impact beyond the UN system, at country level, in terms of participation of Indigenous Peoples. In other words, if one sees the UN system as the entry point that needs to be influenced in order to integrate Indigenous issues in public policies, there can be a compounded, spiral effect on public policy much beyond the originally targeted UN agencies. This makes the mainstreaming effort worthwhile.

The word "mainstreaming" has sometimes been used to indicate the need to be multidisciplinary in public policy analyses and methodologies. Although mainstreaming processes at the international level might seem esoteric, there is a lot at stake behind them for the public good. They represent a site to debate complex issues and an important indicator of where major currents of public policies are headed. Those currents eventually do have an impact on human beings and communities. It is reiterated here that mainstreaming processes therefore deserve attention, input, and critique.

1. Strategies for Inclusion and Participation

Over the decades, but especially since the establishment of the UNPFII and the focused advocacy of Indigenous Peoples, a number of strategies have

---

17 UN Economic and Social Council, Resolution 2000/22, Establishment of a Permanent Forum on Indigenous Issues, UN Doc. E/2000/22 (28 July 2000), www.un.org/esa/socdev/unpfii/documents/about-us/E-RES-2000-22.pdf.
18 UN Doc. E/2000/22, para. 2.

been used to increase Indigenous participation in the work of international agencies. They are briefly described and analyzed in this section. The strategies include the following:

1. Creation and strengthening of the Interagency Support Group on Indigenous Peoples Issues (IASG): The IASG was originally created by the High Commissioner for Human Rights in 2002 to support the Permanent Forum. From eight intergovernmental agencies that were members in 2002, the IASG has grown to some forty members. Many agencies appoint focal points on Indigenous issues. The IASG holds annual meetings, with a rotating Chair, while the Secretariat of the Permanent Forum acts as Co-Chair. The mandate of the IASG is to support UNPFII and other Indigenous-related UN bodies. The IASG creates and strengthens formal and informal relations and cooperation between the UNPFII and other Indigenous-related UN bodies and agencies as well as a network of support.
2. A system of agencies reporting to the UNPFII and the Expert Mechanism on the Rights of Indigenous Peoples (EMRIP) annually. In-depth or other dialogues with the agencies are encouraged.
3. A system of UNPFII official visits to the UN agencies, engaging at high level, awareness raising within each agency and promoting implementation of the UNDRIP and the Forum's recommendations.
4. Promoting the adoption of Indigenous-specific policies within each agency, with relative success.
5. Monitoring of the programmatic instruments of the UNCTs on the ground (such as Common Country Assessments/UN Development Assistance Frameworks, CCAs/UNDAFs), to identify to what extent Indigenous Peoples' issues had been included and Indigenous Peoples had been consulted. Some good examples were found, but inadequate examples prevailed, where Indigenous Peoples were not even mentioned. Such papers of analysis were distributed to all UNCTs in order to raise awareness and promote change.
6. An interagency group on Indigenous women was created. It promoted awareness and prepared case studies of good examples of UN projects with Indigenous women as participants and beneficiaries.
7. Preparation of case studies that analyzed how programs addressing Indigenous Peoples were delivered and whether the results were successful (IFAD studies; Indigenous Women-related; UNESCO papers on education).
8. Preparation and adoption of the UNDG Guidelines on Indigenous Peoples' Issues in 2008 to promote the implementation of UNDRIP.
9. Promoting the establishment of Indigenous Peoples' consultative committees to advise UNCTs and agencies on policies and programs (Ecuador, Bolivia, and the Latin American Region as a whole).

10. Capacity-building of UNCTs: an Action Plan was created to train UNCTs on Indigenous issues and to implement training of trainers as well as preparation of a training manual and related material.

2. International Agencies' and States' Interactions

A number of questions arose very soon after the establishment of the Permanent Forum given the very complexity of IGOs. Does their mandate fit Indigenous Peoples' issues? How do IGOs interpret their mandate? What is the limit of action by the secretariats, the civil servants, of these agencies? Do states not have the ultimate power of decision-making in IGOs through the established governing bodies of each agency? What about political obstacles that could be placed by such governing bodies in the integration of Indigenous issues and Indigenous participation in specific agencies?

A colleague from a UN agency asked me, when I was heading the Secretariat of the UNPFII, with a grave sense of doubt in his tone, how one could expect the agencies to implement free, prior, and informed consent (FPIC) for Indigenous Peoples. He pointed out that it is states that have the upper hand and ultimate power, and they are generally reticent to accept the principle. His question suggested that agency bureaucracies would be overruled by their governing bodies composed of states if the bureaucracies moved outside of prescribed political boundaries and limits. I responded that, in my view, within the parameters of agency action in their practical work, agencies have a responsibility to follow UN principles and standards; in this case, that meant following the UNDRIP, which clearly recognizes free, prior, and informed consent.

Linked to this type of question, there have been other, more practical, obstacles to the inclusion of Indigenous issues in the work of interstate agencies. How should one approach agencies that had never dealt with Indigenous issues – that is, agencies that had no information, knowledge, or expertise? How could they be convinced to overcome their formal position of "our agency has no mandate on Indigenous issues," to understanding that they actually do, that it is a matter of interpretation, of nondiscrimination, of making Indigenous Peoples visible in their work, after they – the agencies themselves – see and recognize Indigenous Peoples and their issues as part of the society the agencies are supporting. In this way, the agencies can then relate to Indigenous Peoples as subjects, with their own voices and representative institutions and requiring respect as individual human beings and as collectivities.

Some theoretical reflections underline some contradictions of the UN, a phrase I use in a positive way. Any student of international relations will know that the UN as an organization is not just the sum of its constituent parts – the states that comprise it – but something beyond that sum, brought together under common goals, as stated in the UN Charter. On the one hand, the UN is an organization of states, that presumably only look after their own limited interests, as understood by the governments in power, and that want to avoid criticism of their behavior internationally. On the other hand, those very states, acting under the principles of the UN Charter, have adopted international human rights treaties by voting at the UN General Assembly. They have subsequently ratified those treaties, thus subjecting themselves to the scrutiny of the UN human rights treaty bodies. We therefore understand that the UN system is not a monolithic entity. Instead, it offers a potential for positive action through the numerous actors at play. This element is crucial for mainstreaming efforts regarding Indigenous issues.

Borrowing liberally from the concept of relative autonomy in political theory,[19] we can also see that the various institutions within the UN system have relative autonomy. For example, the Secretariat of the UN is one of the organs of the UN under the Charter, and as such, it not only carries out the orders of the political bodies of the UN, such as the Human Rights Council or the General Assembly, but has the possibility to act in ways that are relatively independent. Article 100 of the UN Charter proclaims the independence of the international civil service.[20] This means that agency officials have the capacity, within some parameters, to act with a certain autonomy.[21]

When the UNPFII was ready to hold its first session in 2002, the UN High Commissioner for Human Rights, whose Office was servicing the Forum at its first session, established the IASG. Its mandate was to support and promote the mandate of the UNPFII within the United Nations system. This mandate was later expanded to include support for Indigenous-related mandates throughout the intergovernmental system. The IASG Chairmanship rotates annually so as to strengthen the engagement of each agency on Indigenous issues. In a gesture of solidarity and advocacy, the IASG later changed its name to Inter-Agency Support Group on Indigenous *Peoples'*

19 According to the *Oxford Dictionary of Politics*, relative autonomy is "the theory that any social totality has four separate and distinct sets of practices – economic, political, ideological, and theoretical – which act in combination, but each of which has its own relative autonomy according to the limits set by its place in the totality." *A Concise Oxford Dictionary of Politics and International Relations*, 4th ed. (2018), s.v. "relative autonomy."

20 UN Charter, 26 June 1945, www.un.org/en/about-us/un-charter/.

21 There is considerable literature on international organization theory and organization theory, which both study the phenomena of organizations. Authors also explore the anthropology and psychology of organizations. An especially interesting article is Sungjoon Cho, "Toward an Identity Theory of International Organizations," *Proceeding of the International Meeting (American Society of International Law)* 101 (2007). The author points out that the paradigm shift in perceiving an international organization from a passive, inorganic tool to an autonomous, organic entity provides us with a theoretical foundation under which we can delve into a unique and case-specific institutional development of an international organization.

Issues. Originally composed of nine agencies, the IASG had become, by 2012, a group composed of some forty UN and other intergovernmental entities, including International financial institutions (IFIs).

The formalization of the IASG from 2002 onward strengthened its capacity to act alongside the focal points within each agency. The UN Permanent Forum on Indigenous Issues and the Inter-Agency Support Group on Indigenous Peoples' Issues opened the horizon to new opportunities for integrating Indigenous voices and issues, and these have become more extensive since the adoption of the UNDRIP. After the IASG was established, the UNPFII and agencies started developing synergies to strengthen each other. The IASG also became a support group of professionals who could give each other tips and strategize on how to raise awareness, overcome obstacles, and promote the mainstreaming and implementation of Indigenous rights in their organizations. IASG membership started spreading, and its annual meetings became the focus of specific Indigenous issues of interagency cooperation.

The UN agency colleague I referred to earlier who wondered about the limitations of the agencies' capacity to respond to the UNPFII's recommendations to mainstream Indigenous issues also had another concern. Why was the explicit mandate of the Forum to address agencies and not states directly? Was that not too narrow? If we were to interpret the "minds" of states, one could say that obviously many states did not necessarily want to establish a high-level body, such as the Permanent Forum, with extraordinary Indigenous participation, to make recommendations to them directly about how they should deal with Indigenous Peoples' issues across the board. Making the agencies the targeted recipients of the Forum's recommendations was a step removed from states, plus the agencies could certainly improve their performance on the topic and do some good on the ground, thus also lightening some of the burden of states. Moreover, if agencies could establish good systems for Indigenous Peoples' participation, they would set good examples that states could follow.

3. Significance of Articles 41 and 42 of UNDRIP

The adoption of the UNDRIP in 2007 signaled a new era for UN agencies' work on Indigenous Peoples' rights, by explicitly referring to UN agencies in two articles:

Article 41

The organs and specialized agencies of the United Nations system and other intergovernmental organizations shall contribute to the full realization of the provisions of this Declaration through the mobilization, inter alia, of financial cooperation and technical assistance. Ways and means of ensuring participation of indigenous peoples on issues affecting them shall be established.

Article 42

The United Nations, its bodies, including the Permanent Forum on Indigenous Issues, and specialized agencies, including at the country level, and States shall promote respect for and full application of the provisions of this Declaration and follow up the effectiveness of this Declaration.

Indigenous Peoples' participation in the work of international agencies is mandatory according to Article 41 of UNDRIP. The right to self-determination is fundamental among the rights included in the Declaration that also bind UN agencies. In fact, the representation of Indigenous Peoples, through their own governance structures, in the work of the international agencies is an expression of external self-determination of Indigenous Peoples.

The IASG held an extraordinary meeting in 2008, before the seventh session of the UNPFII, to discuss the impact of the adoption of the Declaration on the work of the agencies. The ILO and OHCHR hosted this meeting in Geneva. Each agency was invited to prepare a paper with reflections on the implications of the adoption of the Declaration on its work.

In its report to the Permanent Forum that year, the IASG included another strong statement and critique, this time on the topic of integrating the Declaration and ILO Convention No. 169 into UN system operations.[22]

A number of common operational and institutional challenges were identified in that report. These included conflicting priorities within agencies, competition over limited resources, limited low capacity of staff, absence of Indigenous staff, and lack of institutionalized mechanisms for dialogue with Indigenous Peoples. The report said that

> agencies will need to find ways and means of ensuring the participation of indigenous peoples. Some agencies have experiences with the establishment of institutionalised mechanisms for participation of indigenous peoples which can serve to inspire more comprehensive efforts in the future.

According to the report, meeting participants recommended that "IASG explore ways and means of establishing institutionalised mechanisms for indigenous peoples' participation in the planning, implementation and evaluation of UN country programmes affecting them, e.g. through national consultative bodies" and that "IASG members prioritise training and capacity-building

---

22 Report on the Inter-Agency Support Group (IASG) on Indigenous Peoples' Issues Special Meeting on United Nations Declaration on the Rights of Indigenous Peoples, 26 and 27 February 2008, UN Doc. E/C.19/2008/CRP.7 (27 March 2008). See the "Documents" section of the website for the UNPFII's seventh session, https://social.desa.un.org/issues/indigenous-peoples/unpfii/unpfii-seventh-session.

for meaningful participation of indigenous peoples in decision-making at the national level."[23]

The statement of the IASG demonstrates the boost that the adoption of UNDRIP and the synergies with the Permanent Forum gave to the inclusion of Indigenous issues. Even though not all ideas materialized in the short-term, they captured trends in actions that agencies expressed the will to follow in the mid- to long-term.

In 2009, at its discussion of Article 42 of the UNDRIP and the question of how the Forum would approach its new mandate under this article, the Forum also adopted a significant statement on the legal validity of the Declaration and its own mandate under Article 42.[24] After asserting that the purpose of the Declaration is to constitute the legal basis for *all* activities in the areas of Indigenous issues, meaning also the activities of agencies, the Forum pointed out that the task of the UNPFII in the years to come, would be "to act within its capacity to transform the Declaration in its entirety into living law."[25] Implementation of this living law would have been fulfilled when the Indigenous Peoples had achieved practical results. The Forum stated that the Declaration "forms a part of universal human rights law," that "the basic principles of the Declaration are identical to those of the main human rights covenants," and that the Declaration is a general instrument of human rights.[26] The Forum made it clear that the Declaration is the basis and measure of all action by intergovernmental organizations on Indigenous Peoples' issues.

Systematization of Practice

As mentioned earlier, the IASG was established in 2002. Its membership has continued to expand within the UN system and outside it. The Permanent Forum has repeatedly recommended that all agencies appoint focal points on Indigenous issues, with a work plan and resources, so that agency staff formalize their functions and raise the profile of Indigenous issues. Thirty-five UN entities were part of the IASG as of 2012,[27] albeit it with different levels

---

23 UN Doc. E/C.19/2008/CRP.7, p. 5.
24 UN Permanent Forum on Indigenous Issues, Report on the Eight Session (18–29 May 2009), UN Doc. E/2009/43 (2009), annex, 19–22.
25 UN Doc. E/2009/43, 19.
26 UN Doc. E/2009/43, 19.
27 Commonwealth Secretariat, Department of Economic and Social Affairs (DESA), Department of Political Affairs (DPA), Department of Public Information (DPI), Economic Commission for Latin America and the Caribbean (ECLAC), the European Commission's External Action Service, Food and Agriculture Organization (FAO), Fondo Indígena, Inter-American Development Bank (IADB), International Fund for Agricultural Development (IFAD), International Labor Organization (ILO), International Land Coalition,

of engagement, and many of them have formally appointed focal points on Indigenous issues, although not all on a full-time basis. It is interesting to note that non-UN-related agencies have gradually started joining the IASG, even as observers. Among them, the Commonwealth Secretariat and the European Commission's External Action Service. IFIs have also joined, including the World Bank, the Inter-American Development Bank, and the IFAD.

The adoption of the UNDRIP brought new dynamism in the relation between the IASG and the UNPFII and between individual agencies and the UNPFII as well.

One of the most notable actions of agencies working together was the cooperation among IASG members around the adoption of the UNDG Guidelines on Indigenous Peoples' Issues in 2008.[28] Given the complexity and high profile of the UNDG, it was a major achievement that the IASG was asked to draft these guidelines and that the UNDG subsequently adopted and formally disseminated them to all UN country teams. The Guidelines, which reflect and operationalize the UNDRIP and highlight the elements of a development with culture and identity, have since become the subject of training for UNCTs spearheaded by the Secretariat of the UNPFII, with funding from IFAD and other sources.

4. Adoption of Specific Policies on Indigenous Peoples' Issues

The adoption of specific policies on Indigenous Peoples' issues by the UN and other agencies has been a standard and perennial recommendation of the Permanent Forum since its early sessions. As a result, a considerable

---

International Organization on Migration (IOM), Office of the Coordinator for Humanitarian Affairs (OCHA), Office of the High Commissioner for Human Rights (OHCHR), Secretariat of the Convention for Biological Diversity (SCBD), UNAIDS, UN Conference on Trade and Development (UNCTAD), UN Development Program (UNDP), UN Environment Program (UNEP), UN Education, Science and Culture Organization (UNESCO), Secretariat of the UN Framework Convention on Climate Change (UNFCCC), UN Forum on Forests (UNFF), UN Population Fund (UNFPA), UN-HABITAT, UN Children's Fund (UNICEF), UN Industrial Development Organization (UNIDO), UN-Women, UN Institute for Training and Research (UNITAR), UN Staff College, UN University Institute for Advanced Studies (UNU-IAS), World Food Program (WFP), World Health Organization (WHO), and the World Bank.

28 United Nations Development Group, Guidelines on Indigenous Peoples' Issues, UN Doc. HR/P/PT/16 (2008), www.un.org/esa/socdev/unpfii/documents/UNDG_guidelines_EN.pdf. The UNDG is one of the four thematic executive committees established by the UN Secretary-General in the 1990s. The UNDG brings together all the UN agencies, funds, and programs, as well as departments of the UN Secretariat that deal with development. The UNDG, at the principals level, adopts policy directives addressed to UN country teams around the world, promotes training, and offers a global supervision of the UN's development work on the ground. UNDG processes are sometimes slow or cumbersome, with considerable push and pull from various agencies and, implicitly, states, and require a lot of time and skill investment to get results.

number of agencies have adopted or revised such policies, among them UNDP (its policy predates the establishment of the Permanent Forum and was due for revision later on), IFAD, EBRD, and the World Bank. Agency reports to the Permanent Forum have been an important way for agencies to engage with Indigenous issues. Such reports are submitted annually, detailing activities on Indigenous issues and the follow-up given to the Forum's recommendations. However, a more targeted and focused system was inaugurated in 2009 when the Forum introduced the practice of holding public dialogues with UN agencies. It was a memorable moment at the eighth session of the Forum in 2009 when six UN agencies submitted reports and sent high-level delegations for a public dialogue with the Forum in the presence of states and Indigenous Peoples. After examining agency reports, the UNPFII then adopted conclusions and recommendations regarding each agency.[29] Resembling something like the periodic dialogue between human rights treaty bodies and states, this new method of work has the potential to become a strong tool for the integration of Indigenous issues into agency work, especially if Indigenous Peoples and governments also participate more actively. This practice, although toned down in the last decade, also gives agencies the opportunity of stating how they are implementing their obligations under Articles 41 and 42 of the UNDRIP as well as the Forum's recommendations.

Over the years, the Secretariat of the Permanent Forum had also analyzed MDG country reports, programming papers of select UN country teams, papers of the Common Country Assessment and UN Development Assistance Framework, as well as UN Resident Coordinator reports and human development reports, in order to ascertain whether these were integrating Indigenous Peoples' issues or including Indigenous Peoples' participation. The analysis demonstrated that, with very few exceptions, Indigenous Peoples' issues were not part of these development processes. This has led to the realization that, at this point, training of many UNCTs is urgently required – that is, up-scaling of the training that was offered, which had been limited to a small number of UNCTs. Such training, together with the momentum of the UNDRIP and the UNDG Guidelines on Indigenous Peoples' Issues, could strengthen action for the integration of Indigenous issues where it matters most: at national and local levels.

On a more political level, the Permanent Forum has pursued formal representation at meetings of intergovernmental bodies and conferences, such as the WTO, the Commission on Sustainable Development (while it existed), UNESCO, the Commission on the Status of Women, the Governing Council of IFAD, WIPO, and others. Negotiating such representation has not always

---

29 For the recommendations on the first six agencies that held a public dialogue with the Forum, see UN Doc. E/2009/43, annex.

been easy and at times has not been achieved – for example, in the cases of the first two bodies mentioned earlier – either due to procedural difficulties or the political reticence of states.

Indigenous Peoples' participation has continued to be an advocacy focus of the IASG: the creation of a regional Indigenous Consultative Group composed of Indigenous leaders for the UN system in Latin America has been a good example. Originally launched by the United Nations Children's Fund (UNICEF), it later became a group that advised all UN agencies. From a national perspective, an interesting experience with respect to UN programs was developed in Nicaragua, where a program advisory committee was set up between the UN System and Indigenous Peoples' representatives, as a strategic space for the fulfillment of the provisions of the UNDRIP regarding self-determination, inclusion, and consultation.[30] National advisory committees were also established in Kenya and Bolivia, but these committees had difficulty functioning.[31]

5.   *Achievements within International Organizations*

A number of modest achievements have been made in including Indigenous Peoples' issues within intergovernmental agencies, and the most important ones have been previously captured. Much more remains to be done, and it is crucial to keep in mind that, as in any political process, achievements are not permanent unless supported continuously. In other words, it is possible to slip backward as well.

The most important facilitating factors in mainstreaming have been the UNPFII and the UNDRIP. As analyzed before, the Permanent Forum carries the integration of Indigenous issues in the UN system within its core mandate and has developed strategies and methods of work to engage the agencies actively, especially under Articles 41 and 42 of UNDRIP. The strength of the Forum, however, lies not just in its sixteen expert members but largely stems from the presence of numerous Indigenous Peoples' representatives and many states that annually attend its sessions and follow its work in various ways throughout the year. The strength of such participation also has an impact on agencies.

The UN system's previous experiences of mainstreaming human rights since the late 1990s have facilitated the effort to mainstream Indigenous issues. The adoption of the Common Understanding for a Human Rights-Based Approach to Development by the UNDG in 2002 created a model for the adoption of the UNDG Guidelines on Indigenous Peoples' Issues in

---

30 Program committee established jointly by OHCHR and UNDP.
31 See UN Expert Mechanism on the Rights of Indigenous Peoples, Contribution to the Study on Indigenous Peoples and the Right to Participate in Decision-Making, UN Doc. A/HRC/ EMRIP/2010/3 (7 May 2010).

2008.[32] Interagency and intra-agency processes could and can thus be targeted in a more informed way so as to pursue a faster inclusion of Indigenous issues.

The IASG has played a positive role in mainstreaming, creating a spirit of "strength in unity" and spearheading catalytic initiatives, such as the adoption of the UNDG Guidelines on Indigenous Peoples' Issues. The existence of an increasingly solid knowledge base and experience on Indigenous issues leads to good practices upon which agencies can build. The experiences of some agencies in establishing institutionalized mechanisms for the participation of Indigenous Peoples can facilitate more comprehensive efforts in the future. The expanding awareness of Indigenous issues within the agencies is yet another facilitating factor, as are the training efforts on Indigenous issues.

The interest, advocacy, pressure, and engagement of Indigenous Peoples themselves with the agencies plays an irreplaceable role and underscores the moral prerogative for the agencies to carry out their obligations under the Declaration and to be relevant to groups in society – in this case, Indigenous Peoples, who need and are entitled to their support. The continuing commitment of a number of states as policy facilitators and catalysts, and as financial donors, is a major facilitating factor for the integration of Indigenous issues. Lastly, since international organizations are "living things" in which people can make a difference, one should not underestimate the facilitation that committed individuals, including Indigenous persons who work in agencies, can offer in taking risks and "piercing" bureaucracies.

6. Avoiding "Over-Institutionalization"

Despite the benefits of institutionalizing Indigenous issues, so that they are an integral part of agencies' attention and action, it is imperative to recognize the danger of over-institutionalization and bureaucratization and to avoid being boxed into a "normality" that leads to the loss of the topic's particularities. People working on Indigenous issues in agencies should not be lulled into seeing them as routine. There is in most cases an urgency about Indigenous Peoples' issues, given the adverse situations into which they have been forced as a result of systemic discrimination, marginalization, loss of livelihood, and other effects of colonialism over centuries. It is a moral imperative for agencies to have an active and dynamic attitude to the integration of

---

32 See "The Human Rights Based Approach to Development Cooperation: Towards a Common Understanding among UN Agencies," HRBA Portal, 2003, https://hrbaportal.org/the-human-rights-based-approach-to-development-cooperation-towards-a-common-understanding-among-un-agencies.

Indigenous Peoples' issues, keeping an open avenue of communication with Indigenous Peoples themselves. Advice and programs from UN bodies and secretariats will be ineffective or unwelcome unless agencies also develop the sensibility to be relevant to the Indigenous Peoples they are meant to support. This point is far beyond the simple technical efficiency of an agency. It should be kept in mind that, beyond discussions of programmatic efficiency of an agency, Indigenous Peoples cannot be "absorbed" by an interstate organization such as the UN because their right to self-determination is primordial for their sustainability and well-being. Deep understanding among UN agency staff of this specific point is crucial for respect of the UNDRIP, including its Article 41.

At the sessions of the Permanent Forum and outside them, in their countries, Indigenous Peoples engage with the agencies. Programs and projects of agencies have sometimes had results that Indigenous Peoples have been involved in and welcomed. IFAD has undertaken considerable efforts to establish good practices with Indigenous Peoples' own participation.[33] Indigenous Peoples have also used the sessions of the Permanent Forum to develop positive relations with UN agencies and sought the intervention of the Forum to change some agency policies and practices.[34] No agency likes to be critiqued by Indigenous Peoples publicly, and this offers room for diplomacy. There is, however, untapped potential for Indigenous leaders to weigh in and present critical, albeit constructive, evaluations of agencies in the public space of the Forum and to achieve results.

The strategy of integrating Indigenous issues in intergovernmental public policies and eventually in governmental public policies that will halt the marginalization of Indigenous Peoples will need to be multipronged. The interaction between the Indigenous Peoples' movement and the UN in the past four decades and the adoption of the UNDRIP places the United Nations in a special position to help reverse historical injustice and move from guilt over the past to responsibility for the future.

---

33 Some of these good practices were documented in a study done under the aegis of the Secretariat of the UNPFII and the Tebtebba Foundation: Victoria Tauli-Corpuz, ed., *Good Practices on Indigenous Peoples' Development*, UN Doc. E/C.19/G646 (Baguio City and New York: UNPFII, 2006). See also International Fund for Agricultural Development, *Policy of Engagement with Indigenous Peoples* (Rome: Palombi & Lanci, 2009), www.ifad.org/documents/38711624/39417924/ip_policy_2009_e.pdf/.

34 One example in 2003 was the critique by Indigenous leaders from the Chittagong Hill Tracts of Bangladesh regarding a UNDP program that had not respected free, prior, and informed consent (FPIC) of the Indigenous Peoples, a principle included in UNDP's policy on Indigenous Peoples (the UNDRIP had not yet been adopted at the time). The Indigenous leadership appealed in writing for the Forum's intervention to stop the program until FPIC would be achieved. The diplomatic intervention of the Forum's Chairperson, Ole Henrik Magga, resulted in an evaluation mission and a subsequent postponement of the UNDP program for about a year. The case is analyzed later in this chapter.

D. Obstacles and Opportunities for Participation

Specific examples given in this section illustrate the difficulty of entrenched international institutional systems to comprehend the significance of Indigenous Peoples' direct participation in programs that concern them. At times, there has also been a reluctance to accept the Permanent Forum's recommendations that ask for focused attention on Indigenous issues. Some examples, however, have been positive, and opportunities have been found or created by Indigenous Peoples' representatives and agency officials to welcome Indigenous participation and work on Indigenous issues in a constructive way.

1. Challenges within the Interstate System

The effort to mainstream Indigenous issues, or any other subject, in an intergovernmental agency is complex. Those who pursue the mainstreaming – for example, the UNPFII, its Secretariat, and Indigenous Peoples themselves – must have good knowledge of the agency they are trying to mainstream the issue in, to see the potential and obstacles and develop networks and strategies. This requires time and staff resources, but also persistence, collegiality, strength, and long-term vision, so as not to lose steam from attitudes that are negative, ignorant, or dismissive or that simply come from overworked people.

Lack of awareness and knowledge of Indigenous issues among UN officials and the reluctance of agencies to accept recommendations of the Permanent Forum are challenges. Particularly challenging is the occasional reluctance of high-level agency officials, due to the politicization of Indigenous issues.[35] It is also true that agency governing bodies may be reticent on Indigenous issues and some states may try to put pressure on agency secretariats and that this may limit agency action or progress in Indigenous affairs. Although awareness and knowledge have improved, the combination of a high turnaround rate among UN agency officials and the slow pace of trainings compared to the need on the ground have resulted in inability, until now, to adequately respond to this challenge.

UN programming processes at headquarters and at the country level lack adequate inclusion of Indigenous Peoples' own voices, despite some good examples. This difficulty is coupled with the insufficient human and financial resources for Indigenous issues in the UN system. For example, as research

---

35 For example, in the process of preparing statements for a high official, I had to respond to comments in the margins of the drafts that questioned that Indigenous Peoples were facing discrimination; that it was a matter of social justice to deal with their issues; that the UN and states had to protect Indigenous Peoples' way of life; and that it was important to disaggregate data, including in the area of the MDGs, so that the adverse situation of Indigenous Peoples would not be not hidden behind national averages.

has revealed, MDG-related actions and other development instruments lacked adequate inclusion of Indigenous Peoples and their issues.[36]

The situation of Indigenous Peoples in countries in armed conflict and postconflict situations needs more attention. It is still a large gap that Indigenous issues have been inadequately integrated in the work of the UN in the peace and humanitarian areas.[37]

Engaging a number of intergovernmental agencies in the Permanent Forum's work, and thus in the mainstreaming of Indigenous issues in their work, is still a challenge. This includes the WTO, the International Tourism Organization, the African Development Bank, and the International Monetary Fund, among others.

Changing agencies' operational culture to "see" those who have been marginalized and made invisible by states remains a major challenge. Agencies must take many steps to change their ways of work and to recognize Indigenous Peoples as collectivities and subjects of human rights, both individual and collective, to respect Indigenous Peoples' self-determination and governance structures and to have them as interlocutors around the table. My involvement with some operational projects in the UN regarding Indigenous Peoples made me realize that one of the most difficult points to convince UN officials about is that the Indigenous Peoples themselves should be asked what the content of a project should be and that free, prior, and informed consent should be respected, instead of assuming somehow that UN staff would know better and should act accordingly.

2. A "Personalized" Encounter with Globalization: The WTO

At its second session in May 2003 the UNPFII decided to send a representative to a WTO meeting in the fall of the same year in Cancun, Mexico.[38] The Forum was concerned about WTO's Trade-Related Aspects of Intellectual

---

36 See reviews conducted by the Secretariat of the UNPFII, including *Integration of Indigenous Peoples' Perspective in Country Development Processes: Review of Selected CCAs and UNDAFs*, no. 3 (UNPFII, January 2008); *Human Development Reports and Indigenous Peoples: A Desk Review* (UNPFII, 2009); *MDG Reports and Indigenous People: A Desk Review* (UNPFII, January 2006); *Desk Review of Select Resident Coordinator Reports: 2001–2003* (UNPFII, February 2007); and related reviews, listed at www.un.org/development/desa/indigenouspeoples/resources/other.html.

37 Notable exceptions were the statement of the UNPFII after the tsunami in Indonesia on 31 January 2005 on the disaster, and the efforts of the Permanent Forum to engage with the UN Department of Peacekeeping Operations (DPKO) through the adoption of recommendations and various meetings, albeit with rather poor results. The Forum was asking DPKO to develop a system of screening for UN peacekeepers involved in crimes against Indigenous people in their home countries, so that they would be prevented from serving as UN troops.

38 UN Permanent Forum on Indigenous Issues, Report on the Second Session (12–23 May 2003), UN Doc. E/2003/43 (2003). There are various references to WTO in this report of the Permanent Forum.

Property Rights Agreement (TRIPS), which confirms the rights of individuals and corporations to patent life forms – something that is against Indigenous Peoples' traditional beliefs, practices, and interests. The TRIPS agreement is advocating for countries to allow corporate scientific institutions to search for and patent Indigenous plant varieties that have beneficial properties. So in 2003, the Forum expressed the wish to send one of its members, Mililani Trask, an Indigenous leader from Hawaii, to the WTO meeting in the fall of 2003.

In July 2003, I was in Geneva for another UN meeting and decided to devote one afternoon to personally make contact with officials in WTO to ensure Ms. Trask's accreditation to their meeting. I would do that in my capacity as Chief of the Secretariat of the UNPFII at the time. I had experienced the obstacles of "entering" WTO before. WTO is considered part of the UN system. This may come as a surprise to a careful observer, given how divorced WTO appears to be from many normative and policy pronouncements of the UN, especially those in the human rights area. Dominated by finance ministries of states, and with a strongman's presence of the Global North, the WTO had not allowed the UN High Commissioner for Human Rights, Mary Robinson at the time, to receive accreditation to the 1999 WTO Ministerial Conference in Seattle, Washington. The Conference was launching a new millennial round of trade negotiations, and the High Commissioner wanted to bring in the human rights angle to this topic. The UN had just marked the fiftieth anniversary of the Universal Declaration of Human Rights in 1998, breathing a moment of post-Cold War optimism. Mary Robinson, former President of Ireland, was the most charismatic High Commissioner for Human Rights, and Kofi Annan was the most pro-human rights UN Secretary-General that has held that office in recent times. It was a beneficial and inspiring coincidence that those two personalities were serving at the UN at the same time. The Secretary-General's Office was also involved in the effort to accredit the High Commissioner to the Seattle meeting. It was a deep disappointment, although not a surprise, that WTO put up a wall to stop even the highest UN human rights official from attending and bringing the human rights elements to the launch of the new global trade talks.

Back in Geneva, I used my full UN credentials as Chief of the Secretariat of the UNPFII to enter the WTO building at 154 Rue de Lausanne, the Centre William Rappard, as the building is called, in a beautiful garden by the lake of Geneva. I was directed to the first office, which passed me on to the official responsible for accreditation to the Seattle meeting. He was in charge of NGOs. I explained that the Permanent Forum is not an NGO but an official UN body, a functional commission of the ECOSOC. I explained its mandate and composition and said emphatically that this distinguished UN body had adopted a recommendation to send a representative to the WTO meeting.

I was then passed on to a policy bureau on the second floor. It was explained to me that the WTO had no category for accrediting UN bodies to participate at its meetings. This was a very different practice from that of the Permanent Forum, where a number of UN bodies and agencies participate and are actually encouraged to do so. Despite my explanations, at this point I was referred to a public relations office to seek possible solutions to my quest. More than two hours had already passed of me being sent from one office to the next. Imagine my surprise when I found myself referred, after two and a half hours, back to the first floor and to the very first office I had visited. It was a Kafkaesque experience. Needless to say, WTO did not accredit Ms. Trask as member of the Permanent Forum to its ministerial meeting. She was brought in as part of the delegation of the Department of Economic and Social Affairs (DESA), as a courtesy of DESA (the Secretariat of the UNPFII is situated within DESA). But this was very different from WTO acknowledging that a UN body carrying Indigenous Peoples' voices could participate under its rightful name and bring in Indigenous issues.

This anecdotal encounter with "the tip of the iceberg of globalization," in the form of the WTO, demonstrated not bureaucratic ineptitude but a profound political determination to control the narrative and rhetoric – and certainly, to keep out critical voices that could bring up human rights and Indigenous Peoples issues.

These small, seemingly invisible battles to accredit the UNPFII and then open the door of the interstate organizations to the direct participation of Indigenous Peoples themselves have been happening over the years with mixed results. Positive results have been achieved in some international bodies and organizations, including the Convention on Biological Diversity (CBD), the WIPO, and the IFAD, a particularly promising example.

3. *Is Being "for All Children" Enough for Indigenous Children? UN Children's Fund*

In 2003 the Permanent Forum decided to have Indigenous children and youth as a special theme of its second session. UNICEF was quite forthcoming in sending a senior official to make a presentation and respond to questions of the Forum about the organization's work on Indigenous children – education and health, including maternal health, being a core mandate of UNICEF. The Permanent Forum adopted a number of recommendations addressed to UNICEF that year and in subsequent years.[39] It was important for the Forum to engage productively with UNICEF, given its prestige and resources, as well as the fact that it was a human rights-inspired agency, having the Convention

---

39 UN Doc. E/2003/43, para. 5 (b), 8–16, and 21.

on the Rights of the Child as its guide, especially since the Convention has specific provisions on the Indigenous child.[40]

The Forum's recommendations to UNICEF included the recommendation to adopt a policy on Indigenous Peoples and to appoint a UNICEF goodwill ambassador for Indigenous children and youth.[41] UNICEF, however, did not follow these and other recommendations. At the time, UNICEF's argument was that UNICEF is for *all* children and that therefore Indigenous children do not need special attention. It was disconcerting that UNICEF took this position, especially given its human rights inclination for a long time and the fact that it based its work on a human rights instrument – the Convention on the Rights of the Child. In other words, UNICEF could not see that part of supporting human rights is to see the inequalities, their roots and specificities, including cultural ones, and to take specific measures to address those.

The need for specific measures to address inequalities is a fundamental human rights principle, one already well-established since the 1960s, in the 1965 Convention on the Elimination of all Forms of Racial Discrimination. UNICEF was resisting the Permanent Forum's push for specific measures, otherwise also known as positive action or affirmative action. Fortunately, UNICEF came around to some extent over time and understood substantively what this was about. Some of their specialists admitted to me UNICEF's realization over the years that investment in development programs in Indigenous communities did not bear fruit and in particular they were not sustainable – the desired long-term effect would just fizzle out once UNICEF's project ended. Through its own analysis, I was told, UNICEF had realized the reason: the communities did not have ownership of the projects, and there was no genuine and representative participation by the communities' own governance structures. The organization had been treating Indigenous Peoples as anonymous peasants and groups, not as organized societies and peoples.

UNICEF again held a public dialogue with the Permanent Forum in 2011.[42] The Forum continues to address recommendations to this important organization during its annual sessions. As of the time of writing of this text, UNICEF had not yet adopted a policy on Indigenous Peoples' issues or appointed a goodwill ambassador for Indigenous children and youth.

---

40 Specifically, Articles 17, 29, and 30 of the Convention. UN General Assembly, Resolution 44/25, Convention on the Rights of the Child, UN Doc. A/RES/44/25 (5 December 1989). The UN Committee on the Rights of the Child, in 2009, adopted General Comment No. 11 on "Indigenous Children and Their Rights under the Convention on the Rights of the Child," UN Doc. CRC/C/GC/11 (12 February 2009).

41 UN Doc. E/2003/43, para. 13–14.

42 Recommendations to UNICEF in 2011 appear in para. 51 and 60–77 of UN Permanent Forum on Indigenous Issues, Report on the Tenth Session (16–27 May 2011), UN Doc. E/2011/43 (2011).

A UNICEF Executive Director has yet to address the Permanent Forum as of the time of writing of this book. In international political symbolism, the level of UN officials participating in the UNPFII also matters, as it is an indicator of the importance the organization gives to Indigenous Peoples' issues.

4. UN Development Program and the Chittagong Hill Tracts of Bangladesh

UNDP was involved early on in Indigenous affairs since the time of the WGIP. It was the first UN development entity to adopt a policy on Indigenous Peoples in 2001. Since its inception, the UNPFII was supported by the IASG, where UNDP has been an active participant from the outset. UNDP has also provided crucial support in the development, adoption and dissemination of the UN Development Group Guidelines on Indigenous Peoples' Issues.[43]

From its inception, the Permanent Forum has seen UNDP as a natural and crucial partner, based on UNDP's paradigm of human development and its policies on Indigenous Peoples and human rights. In August 2001, UNDP issued a policy note entitled "UNDP and Indigenous Peoples: A Practice Note on Engagement." This practice note indicated among UNDP's priority areas "democratic governance and human rights"; and by democratic governance, UNDP meant participation of Indigenous Peoples, which was explained as follows:

> 27. By incorporating the "right to development" in its work, UNDP fosters the full participation of indigenous peoples in its development processes and the incorporation of indigenous perspectives in development planning and decision-making. This right is of particular significance to indigenous peoples because in their experience, development has tended to be imposed upon their communities from outside, often resulting in violations of their "right to development," by damaging ancestral lands, water and natural resources.
>
> 28. Consistent with United Nations conventions such as ILO Convention 169, UNDP promotes and supports the right of indigenous peoples to free, prior informed consent with regard to development planning and programming that may affect them.[44]

---

43 The UN Development Group was later renamed to UN Sustainable Development Group; the adopted Guidelines appear at https://unsdg.un.org/resources/united-nations-development-groups-guidelines-indigenous-peoples-issues. The Guidelines assist the United Nations system to mainstream and integrate Indigenous Peoples' issues in processes for operational activities and programs at the country level.

44 UN Development Program, UNDP and Indigenous Peoples: A Practice Note on Engagement (2001), para. 27–28.

UNDP has had a long engagement with Bangladesh in the area of the Chittagong Hill Tracts (CHT). The grave problems faced by the Indigenous Peoples of the CHT were part of the UN's Indigenous agenda from "day one" of its involvement with Indigenous Peoples' rights. Already in 1982, at the first session of the WGIP, a paper was presented by the Anti-Slavery Society about the situation in CHT.[45]

The heavily militarized area of CHT – with a population of a million and a half, a waning majority Indigenous population, made up of eleven Indigenous Peoples, constantly displaced, discriminated, and minoritized by the state, including by the military and settlers sponsored by the state – was and is an area characterized by conflict. In 1997, the CHT Peace Accord was signed between the government of Bangladesh and PCJSS (Parbattya Chattagram Jana Samhati Samiti) leader Shantu Larma, the main figure of a previous armed struggle of Indigenous Peoples. The Accord stipulated a series of steps where Indigenous Peoples were to gain self-government in the CHT region, including and especially the establishment of a Regional Council as the center of this autonomous authority, with three Hill District Councils. After the Accord, Shantu Larma became the Chairman of the Regional Council.

In June 2003, an urgent appeal was addressed to the UNPFII at the UN in New York from Shantu Larma. He complained against UNDP for breaking with its own policy regarding consultation with the Indigenous Peoples in CHT and, in particular, not respecting processes of free, prior, and informed consent with regard to development. Larma's letter requested that the UNDP project simply stop immediately until the proper procedures of consultation had taken place.

The then Chairperson of the Permanent Forum, Ole Henrik Magga, concerned by the issues raised in the letter, including their implication on the conflict/postconflict situation in the CHT, decided that this was a case where the good offices of the Permanent Forum vis-à-vis UNDP were warranted. By good offices the Chairman meant a mediation of the Forum at first so that the issues raised in the complaint could be solved. This was unchartered territory for the Permanent Forum in terms of *how* to exercise its authority vis-à-vis the UN system organizations, which, after all, is part of its mandate. The Forum's mandate includes addressing economic and social development, culture, the environment, education, health, and human rights in three ways: (a) by providing expert advice and recommendations on Indigenous issues to the ECOSOC, as well as to programs, funds, and agencies of the United Nations; (b) by raising awareness and promoting the integration and coordination of activities relating to Indigenous issues within the United Nations system; and (c) by preparing and disseminating information on Indigenous issues.[46]

---

45 UN Sub-Commission on Prevention of Discrimination and Protection of Minorities, Report of the Working Group on Indigenous Populations on Its First Session, UN Doc. E/CN.4/Sub.2/1982/33 (25 August 1982), annex.

46 Economic and Social Council, Resolution 2000/22.

The complaint of the Indigenous leader, Shantu Larma, was shared with UNDP headquarters in New York. A number of consultations were undertaken with UNDP to see what action could be taken that would be true to the situation – meaning, what action could be taken that would substantively address the complaint of the Indigenous leader. It was a pleasant surprise to find out that, instead of being defensive, UNDP was open and proactive to address the situation. The entourage of UNDP's progressive Administrator at the time, Mark Malloch Brown of the United Kingdom, entered into informal discussions with the Permanent Forum's Chair and its secretariat on the best way to move forward. After all, UNDP had a high profile in human rights and Indigenous affairs at the time and had recently, in 2001, adopted its Practice Note on Engagement with Indigenous Peoples. In addition to its own policy commitments, UNDP would certainly prefer not to have a negative public commentary during the session of the Permanent Forum in New York. While various considerations of this sort could have contributed to this positive stance of UNDP, the next question was *how* to move forward in a way that would be both effective and diplomatic within UNDP itself and its country office, within the interagency system cooperation, vis-à-vis the government of Bangladesh, and vis-à-vis international public opinion, that included UNDP's donors, the Permanent Forum as the major policy body of the UN on the matter, and of course, the Indigenous Peoples of CHT themselves.

The solution found was that UNDP would send a mission to review the CHT project in Bangladesh, to review the progress and take stock of the experience and lessons learned so far. The mission, funded by UNDP, was planned to take place during two weeks in January 2004. The mission was composed of a former senior UNDP official, an Indigenous expert from Asia, and the Acting Chief of the Secretariat of the Permanent Forum. The Secretariat official was to participate in the mission in her personal capacity as an independent adviser, and for this purpose, she was released from her department (the DESA) within the framework of interagency cooperation, for the duration of the mission. UNDP would cover the travel cost and daily subsistence for the mission.

The mission was deployed in January 2004 and held extensive meetings and consultations with UNDP officials in Dhaka and CHT, with government officials, with the Regional Council Chair, and the Chairs of the three Hill District Councils, Indigenous and non-Indigenous civil society organizations, and others. It was interesting to be able to cross-check how different parties viewed consultations held by UNDP with the Indigenous Peoples. UNDP viewed them as adequate, while Indigenous leaders did not. By analyzing the details of discussions, the mission found that the consultations had not been substantive and adequately respectful of the Indigenous authority but had rather been formulaic and that the consultations had not been given the appropriate time frame. This had led to a lack of confidence in the consultations on the part of the Indigenous leadership regarding UNDP, and hence the Indigenous leadership had to appeal to the Permanent Forum to intervene to stop the launch of the proposed program. The mission presented its report to UNDP, and a few months later, UNDP paused the beginning of the program so as to ensure effective consultations and participation of the Indigenous Peoples.

Subsequent developments of UNDP's CHT Development Facility demonstrated the continued dramatic situation of Indigenous Peoples in the CHT. With foreigners banned from entering CHT since 2011, UNDP was the only international entity with a presence. It was the "eyes and ears" of the international community.

International human rights organizations and bodies, including the Permanent Forum, continue to monitor the situation while conditions on the ground for Indigenous Peoples have worsened. The Bangladesh military, a major player in the CHT within Bangladesh, is also, ironically, a major troop-contributor to UN peacekeeping operations. Troop participation in such operations is a significant revenue source for the military of this country and also a source of prestige. The grave situation of the Indigenous Peoples in the CHT epitomizes, on the one hand, the continuing contemporary practices of settler colonialism with devastating effects for the well-being and sustainability of Indigenous Peoples and, on the other hand, the impact of geopolitics and economic interests that explain much of the silence on this matter from the international community toward Bangladesh.

The case of Indigenous participation in UNDP programming in Bangladesh shows that Indigenous Peoples definitely have recourse when they face issues of genuine participation in the UN's work on the ground. The Permanent Forum is certainly one possible recipient of such appeals for mediation and, as shown in the CHT case just analyzed, can have an impact.[47]

Over the years, a number of Indigenous representatives have privately complained to the Secretariat of the Permanent Forum that, while agencies make positive speeches at the Permanent Forum and speak to the Indigenous delegates in New York, this is often not possible at the country level, where Indigenous representatives cannot even access the offices of UN agencies.[48] Indigenous Peoples have found it significant in their struggles to come to the UN and pursue the respect of their rights by states. They therefore have every reason to expect UN agencies to set an example of such respect to their dignity, especially when it comes to Indigenous participation and free, prior,

---

47 See analysis by Lars-Anders Baer in UN Permanent Forum on Indigenous Issues, Study on the Status of the Chittagong Hill Tracts Accord of 1997: Submitted by the Special Rapporteur, UN Doc E/C.19/2011/6 (18 February 2011); see also Tone Bleie, "The Politics of Shaming and Sanctions: Rewriting the Anatomy of the Bangladeshi State," in *Indigenous Peoples' Rights and Unreported Struggles: Conflict and Peace*, ed. Elsa Stamatopoulou (New York: Institute for the Study of Human Rights, Columbia University, 2017), https://doi.org/10.7916/D82R5095.

48 Such complaints were repeatedly made to the author when she was Chief of the Secretariat of the UNPFII.

and informed consent. Articles 41 and 42 of the UNDRIP prescribe this as an obligation of UN agencies, especially when it comes to Indigenous Peoples' participation in issues and programs affecting them.

5. Is UN Expertise Adequate to Decide UN Projects in Indigenous Communities? UN DESA

Another example of how challenging it is to instill a culture of partnership with Indigenous Peoples in international organizations was a project assigned to the UN DESA through the UN Development Account.[49] The Secretariat of the Permanent Forum on Indigenous Issues (SPFII), later renamed as Indigenous Peoples and Development Branch/Secretariat of the Permanent Forum on Indigenous Issues, has been part of DESA since 2003.

Through the UN Development Account, in 2005, SPFII was assigned $450,000 for a project called "Engaging indigenous women: local-government capacity-building through new technologies in Latin America."[50] A draft prepared by staff outside SPFII essentially described the project as one of distribution of computers to local government bureaucracies. There was no reference to participation of Indigenous women in that draft proposal. SPFII accepted the project by saying we would only agree to the title of the project, as that could not be changed, but that we would prepare a concept note for the project ourselves. Geographically, we proposed, it would deal with the main Andean countries: Ecuador, Peru, and Bolivia. We spent a year planning this and were conscious that we needed to create a good example of Indigenous participation and free, prior, and informed consent. There was no provision in the strict framework of the Development Account for any travel to consult with communities and their organizations. We were supposed to imagine ourselves, "as experts," what the content of the project would be. We therefore had to do all necessary consultations via email and phone. We identified the most representative Indigenous Peoples' organizations that dealt with the topic of governance and new technologies in the geographical area the project would be in. Once we identified the organizations, we then asked them *what should be the content of the project.* This was the most important point – that the people themselves would exercise their self-determination and say what technologies were useful to them, in their circumstances, and how those could support Indigenous women's participation in local governance. However, this was also the point that was extremely difficult for DESA's committee responsible for approving projects to take in; they had difficulty

---

49 The Development Account is a capacity development program of the UN Secretariat aiming at enhancing capacities of developing countries in the priority areas of the United Nations Development Agenda; see www.un.org/development/desa/da/.

50 I was Chief of SPFII at the time.

understanding that the Indigenous People themselves would identify the content of the project. They thought that rather we, DESA's "expert" staff, would do so from afar. We explained the meaning and significance of free, prior, and informed consent (FPIC) and stated that, as SPFII, we could not accept to do a project that would not respect FPIC. We were able to convince our colleagues and the project evolved successfully over a three-year period.[51]

This first project set a good example for Indigenous participation in DESA projects. Other good projects form the Development Account have followed in which Indigenous Peoples' participation and partnership have been integrated.

6. Leadership in Climate Change Solutions

Indigenous Peoples have clearly placed climate change on the global agenda as a human and human rights issue as well as an environmental and development issue. Climate change is also examined internationally through the angle of development. In December 2005, a delegation of Inuit, headed by the then President of the Inuit Circumpolar Council, Sheila Watt-Cloutier, traveled to the Inter-American Commission on Human Rights in Washington, DC, to provide first-hand testimony of how global warming is destroying their way of life and to accuse the US government, the Bush administration, of undermining their human rights – "the right to be cold," as this was called – that is, their right to their culture, to their way of life.[52] In 2007, Sheila Watt-Cloutier was nominated for the Nobel Peace Prize.

It is significant and symbolic that Indigenous Peoples have been in the front leading the huge climate change demonstrations in New York in 2014 and during Climate Week in September 2023. Indigenous Peoples have been the most visible social group in international climate change negotiations.

Since early on in its work that started in 2002, the UNPFII has reflected the voices of Indigenous Peoples claiming justice and substantive participation in climate change solutions. It was impressive when, in 2005, the Intergovernmental Panel on Climate Change (IPCC) visited the UNPFII, asking to present their special reports on *Carbon Dioxide Capture and Storage* and on

---

51 An account of this project appears on the website of the Secretariat of the UNPFII, "Technical Cooperation Projects on Indigenous Peoples," www.un.org/development/desa/dspd/indigenous-peoples.html.

52 The petition was seeking relief from human rights violations resulting from the impacts of climate change caused by acts and omissions of the United States; see "Petition To the Inter-American Commission on Human Rights Seeking Relief from Violations Resulting from Global Warming Caused by Acts and Omissions of the United States," 2005, https://climatecasechart.com/non-us-case/petition-to-the-inter-american-commission-on-human-rights-seeking-relief-from-violations-resulting-from-global-warming-caused-by-acts-and-omissions-of-the-united-states/.

Safeguarding the Ozone Layer and the Global Climate System.[53] The UNPFII was then a young body, just holding its fourth session. But the experts of the IPCC knew the significance of Indigenous Peoples in this field – in identifying the first signs of climate change, in applying traditional knowledge for solutions, and in creating visions for another kind of development for the well-being of humanity and the environment.

Over the years, various studies were requested by Indigenous Peoples on climate change topics, and the UNPFII conducted a number of them. The most recent one was in 2021,[54] and it underlined that "by living in harmony with nature, indigenous peoples have developed traditional ancestral knowledge that has been a source of resilience, enabling them to devise climate change mitigation and adaptation strategies."[55]

In 2008, the session of the UNPFII was devoted to the special theme "Climate change, bio-cultural diversity and livelihoods: the stewardship role of indigenous peoples and new challenges." At that and subsequent sessions, the Forum adopted a series of rich policy recommendations regarding climate change adaptation and mitigation measures. It conducted a number of studies and inspired global and regional conferences, including the Indigenous Peoples' Global Summit on Climate Change in Alaska in 2009.

Indigenous Peoples' aspirations and advocacy have been focused on the following six main themes. These themes also resonate in the advocacy of the Global Alliance of Territorial Communities.[56] In summary, the main themes are (a) engagement with Indigenous Peoples, their substantive participation, and recognition of their stewardship role; (b) emphasis on the importance of Indigenous traditional knowledge and its contributions to climate change adaptation and mitigation measures; (c) respect of the UNDRIP by states, intergovernmental organizations, and the private sector, especially regarding Indigenous Peoples' full and effective participation and FPIC; (d) respect for land rights, protection and titling (official recognition); (e) financing directly to Indigenous Peoples regarding mitigation and adaptation measures; and (f) measures to protect the environment.

Another achievement of the Indigenous Peoples' movement to have their direct participation recognized can be seen in the Local Communities and

---

53 Intergovernmental Panel on Climate Change, *Carbon Dioxide Capture and Storage* (Cambridge: Cambridge University Press, 2005), www.ipcc.ch/report/carbon-dioxide-capture-and-storage/; IPCC and Technology and Economic Assessment Panel, *Safeguarding the Ozone Layer and the Global Climate System: Issues Related to Hydrofluorocarbons and Perfluorocarbons* (Cambridge: Cambridge University Press, 2005), www.ipcc.ch/report/safeguarding-the-ozone-layer-and-the-global-climate-system/.

54 UN Permanent Forum on Indigenous Issues, Indigenous Peoples and Climate Change: Note by the Secretariat, UN Doc. E/C.19/2021/5 (12 January 2021).

55 UN Doc. E/C.19/2021/5, para. 4.

56 The Alliance represents thirty-five million people living in forest territories from twenty-four countries in Asia, Africa, and Latin America. See https://globalalliance.me/, accessed 11 October 2023.

Indigenous Peoples Platform Facilitative Working Group, established by the Conference of the Parties to the UN Framework Convention on Climate Change (COP 24), in December 2018. Representatives of Indigenous Peoples and of states are equally represented in the Facilitative Working Group.

States' action on climate change issues has been inadequate until now. What should be the focus and actions of the broad civil society? How should people be mobilized? How can Indigenous Peoples help bring together various social movements around climate change? Indigenous participation in the climate change international debates has to be safeguarded and expanded.

7. Opportunities for the Future

How can we interpret the reluctance of some international agencies to accept the UNPFII's recommendations? We now understand that long-term processes of awareness raising are required. We also need improved and robust monitoring of the agencies' work on Indigenous issues.

UN programming processes at headquarters and at the country level lack adequate inclusion of Indigenous Peoples' own voices, despite some good examples. This difficulty is coupled with insufficient human and financial resources for Indigenous issues in the UN system. For example, MDG-related actions lacked adequate inclusion of Indigenous Peoples and their issues. On the other hand, good examples of such inclusion at headquarters level can be found in IFAD's creation of the "Indigenous Peoples' Forum at IFAD," a platform of dialogue between IFAD staff, Indigenous Peoples, and governments' representatives (discussed later in this chapter), and in the UN-REDD Program's inclusion of Indigenous leaders on its Policy Board, the highest decision-making body.[57]

Changing agencies' operational culture to "see" those who have been marginalized by the states remains a major challenge. Agencies must take many steps to change their ways of working and to recognize Indigenous Peoples as collectivities and subjects of human rights, both individual and collective, to recognize Indigenous Peoples' governance structures and to include them as interlocutors around the table. Involvement with some operational projects in the UN regarding Indigenous Peoples made me realize that one of the most difficult points to convince UN officials about is that the Indigenous Peoples themselves should be asked what should be the content of the project and that free, prior, and informed consent should be respected, instead of assuming somehow that UN staff would know better.

The adoption of the UNDRIP and the work of the UNPFII have facilitated the inclusion of Indigenous issues in the work of agencies. As mentioned earlier, the Permanent Forum carries the integration of Indigenous issues

---

57 See the United Nations Collaborative Program on Reducing Emissions from Deforestation and Forest Degradation in Developing Countries (UN-REDD) website, www.un-redd.org/.

within its core mandate and has developed strategies and methods of work to engage the agencies actively, especially under Articles 41 and 42 of UNDRIP. The force of the Forum, however, does not come only from its sixteen members but instead stems largely from the presence of numerous Indigenous Peoples' representatives who annually attend its sessions and follow its work in various ways throughout the year. The force of such participation also has an impact on agencies.

Indigenous Peoples' interest, advocacy, pressure, and engagement with the agencies play an irreplaceable role and underscore the moral prerogative for the agencies to carry out their obligations under the Declaration and to be relevant to groups in society – in this case, Indigenous Peoples and their communities – who need and are entitled to their support. The commitment of states and individuals as policy facilitators can clearly make a difference.

The human rights-based approach to development (HRBA) in the UN system has been a facilitating factor for Indigenous issues on the ground for some time. It advocates strongly for empowerment, nondiscrimination, attention to the most vulnerable, participation, and accountability. Unfortunately, the weakening of the HRBA in the UN in the last ten-plus years, due to states' interventions, including those of donors, has also weakened this facilitating factor for the inclusion of Indigenous issues. In a 2012 report evaluating the application of HRBA to UNICEF programming, it becomes clear that the HRBA is being considerably weakened in an agency that used to be at the forefront of the efforts in this area.[58]

8. The Human Rights-Based Approach

The human rights approach has participation as one of its foci and offers a number of analytical tools:[59]

1. It provides the concept that human rights (civil, cultural, economic, political, social) are *intercomplementary*, *interdependent*, and *interrelated*.
2. A human rights analysis identifies the *duties of states* in four main categories, which are human rights concepts: respect, protect, fulfill,

---

58 UN Children's Fund, *Global Evaluation of the Application of a Human Rights-Based Approach to UNICEF Programming* (New York: UNICEF, 2012), 106–111, www.unicef. org/policyanalysis/rights/files/UNICEF_HRBAP_Final_Report_Vol_I_11June_copy-edited_ translated.pdf. The evaluation was presented to UNICEF's Executive Board in January 2013.

59 This is according to international human rights theory and practice developed by human rights treaty bodies, UN human rights rapporteurs, resolutions adopted by states at the United Nations, and via policies adopted by the UN system agencies – in addition to the academic literature around the human rights approach. See also UN Sustainable Development Group, "The Human Rights Based Approach to Development Cooperation: Towards a Common Understanding among UN Agencies" (UNSDG, September 2003), https://unsdg.un.org/resources/human-rights-based-approach-development-cooperation-towards-common-understanding-among-un.

remedy. *Respect* refers to the duty of the state to not interfere with the free exercise of human rights. *Protect* refers to the duty of the state to intervene and prevent nonstate actors from interfering with the free exercise of human rights. *Fulfill* refers to the duty of the state to take specific positive measures, especially in terms of budgets, to support the implementation of rights. *Remedy* refers to the state taking measures for those affected by the denial or violation of their human rights; for example, special measures for Indigenous communities whose languages are at risk of extinction due to, in large part, earlier negative boarding school practices.

3. The human rights approach provides *specificity based on international law obligations of states* – namely, based on human rights instruments. The human rights approach is linked to *accountability*. It helps answer the question of who is responsible, who, concretely, is the duty bearer in a specific context. States must take specific measures, legislative, administrative, judicial, and other. This in turn means that the international human rights mechanisms of the UN or of regional organizations can monitor how states implement their obligations under international law and can adopt statements and recommendations for the respect of these rights. It also means that Indigenous Peoples and NGOs can cooperate with the international human rights bodies in holding states accountable in the monitoring and promotion of human rights. The human rights regime, in other words, gives a concrete legal and policy framework and surrounds, supports, and enhances Indigenous Peoples' rights. The human rights regime also provides mechanisms of monitoring and redress and of possible international cooperation and assistance.

4. A human rights approach brings in the fundamental norm of *nondiscrimination and equality*; this includes paying attention to the most vulnerable.

5. A human-rights approach places emphasis on *participation* – in this case, the participation of Indigenous Peoples in decision-making regarding laws, programs, and projects that may affect them.

The HRBA in the UN system was a facilitating factor for Indigenous issues on the ground for some time, but as mentioned earlier, the weakening of the HRBA in recent years due to states' interventions has also weakened this facilitating factor. It remains to be seen whether the presence of human rights language in the Sustainable Development Goals (the 2030 Agenda) will bear fruit on the ground for Indigenous Peoples.[60]

---

60 See analysis of the SDGs later.

E. Sustainable Development Goals and Indigenous Participation[61]

The Sustainable Development Goals (SDGs) represent the UN global development agenda until 2030. It is therefore important to ask what the involvement of Indigenous Peoples is and what the perspectives are for their well-being to be positively affected by the SDGs.

The SDGs, or Agenda 2030, are clearly a stronger framework than the Millennium Development Goals (MDGs) for the pursuance of Indigenous Peoples' human rights and well-being. Indigenous Peoples participated dynamically in the process of preparation of the document and advocated strongly for the inclusion of their issues.[62] Not only are Indigenous Peoples specifically mentioned several times in the text of the 2030 Agenda, but the overall thrust of the document around some structural impediments of development and the emphasis on human rights, nondiscrimination, and inclusion, as well as a reduction of inequalities, is a positive framework for Indigenous Peoples. One of its overarching goals is "to realize the human rights of all."[63] Many goals are framed in ways that reinforce the commitments most states have already undertaken under the ten core international human rights treaties.

In addition, most SDGs and many targets are directly relevant for Indigenous Peoples, even if there is no explicit reference to Indigenous Peoples. Last but not least, we note some of the basic philosophical approaches of Indigenous Peoples underlying the document and alluding to other possible paradigms of development than the dominant one, which has proven unsustainable for the planet as well as being unjust and feeding inequalities among states and within states. We note conceptual references to the possibility of another model including the reference to improved modes of production and consumption,[64] references to harmony with nature,[65] and references to

---

61 This section is based on Elsa Stamatopoulou, "Indigenous Peoples and Agenda 2030," working paper presented at the 2015 UN Expert Group Meetings on Indigenous Peoples and Agenda 2030 for Sustainable Development, organized by the UN DESA's Division of Social Policy and Development, New York, 22–23 and 26–27 October 2015.

62 The UN's 2030 Agenda is presented in UN General Assembly, Resolution 70/1, Transforming Our World: The 2030 Agenda for Sustainable Development, UN Doc. A/RES/70/1 (21 October 2015). An online version of the report is available at https://sdgs.un.org/2030agenda.

63 2030 Agenda, preamble.

64 2030 Agenda, Goal 8, target 8.4 is "Improve progressively, through 2030, global resource efficiency in consumption and production and endeavour to decouple economic growth from environmental degradation, in accordance with the 10-year framework of programmes on sustainable consumption and production, with developed countries taking the lead."

65 For example, in the sentence about "prosperity" in the 2030 Agenda preamble: "We are determined to ensure that all human beings can enjoy prosperous and fulfilling lives and that economic, social and technological progress occurs in harmony with nature."

Mother Earth.[66] Yet Agenda 2030 does not represent a paradigm shift in the area of development.

It is clear that for the proper monitoring of the SDGs, the participation of Indigenous Peoples at national and global levels needs to be ensured.

1. Lessons Learned from the Millennium Development Goals

The MDGs, adopted in 2000, did not include reference to Indigenous Peoples, and Indigenous Peoples did not participate in the process of their negotiation. In 2005, thanks to advocacy by the UNPFII and some States, some reference was included, in the General Assembly resolution that year, to the need to respect Indigenous Peoples' traditional knowledge and to the need for the UN to adopt the UNDRIP. The UNPFII devoted the special themes of two sessions (fourth and fifth, in 2005 and 2006) to examining the MDGs and their relevance to Indigenous Peoples and made significant recommendations on how the MDGs should be applied in order to not harm Indigenous Peoples on the way but instead improve their well-being.[67]

It has by now been documented that, aside from rare exceptions, the implementation of the MDGs hardly included Indigenous Peoples and their issues in processes or in programs at national level. SPFII reviewed the most relevant MDG country reports: forty-six desk reviews of MDG country reports, between the years 2006 and 2010. In total, only twenty-six out of the forty-six MDG country reports made some reference to Indigenous Peoples – that is, only 56.5 percent of all the reports reviewed. Those references, however, to Indigenous Peoples were hardly adequate; in fact, in most cases they were very weak. Moreover, there was hardly any evidence of any participation of Indigenous Peoples in MDG planning, implementation, and evaluation processes.

Among conclusions and recommendations of the desk reviews, it was found that in countries where Indigenous Peoples make up a small minority, it seemed tempting for states to marginalize them further when implementing development policies. The cultural and linguistic barriers that Indigenous Peoples face increase this risk, as contextualized and directed policies are often needed to surmount obstacles. Given the inherent costs

---

66 2030 Agenda, para. 59: "We recognise that there are different approaches, visions, models and tools available to each country, in accordance with its national circumstances and priorities, to achieve sustainable development; and we reaffirm that planet Earth and its ecosystems are our common home and that 'Mother Earth' is a common expression in a number of countries and regions."

67 See reports of the UNPFII, Provisional Agenda: Permanent Forum on Indigenous Issues, Fourth Session, UN Doc. E/C.19/2005/1 (18 January 2005) and Provisional Agenda: Permanent Forum on Indigenous Issues, Fifth Session, UN Doc. E/C.19/2006/1 (19 January 2006).

and difficulties of developing such programs as mother-tongue instruction for small demographics, there is risk that states will opt for programs aimed at larger groups in order to improve their national level results and averages.

In Indigenous-majority countries such as Bolivia, the need to squarely address Indigenous issues is more obvious, for it would be nearly impossible to successfully reach the MDGs without addressing the needs and rights of Indigenous Peoples in such countries. But for countries where Indigenous Peoples are numerical minorities, it is clear that further efforts were needed to include Indigenous issues and emphasize the importance of an equal share in the benefits of MDG-related development across all segments of the population, including Indigenous Peoples.

All the desk reviews prepared by the Secretariat of the UNPFII over the years have consistently highlighted several important conclusions and recommendations: (a) Free, prior, and informed consent of Indigenous Peoples should be sought in all development initiatives that affect them; and (b) states and the UN system should improve the collection and disaggregation of data regarding Indigenous Peoples because improved disaggregation of data is indispensable to properly monitor progress.[68]

The SPFII also conducted desk reviews of Common Country Assessments/UN Development Assistance Frameworks (CCAs/UNDAFs), as well as UN Resident Coordinator reports. These reviews revealed a tremendous participation gap for Indigenous Peoples and an absence of their issues in the efforts to implement the MDGs.

There are various explanations and lessons, which can be taken into account as attention now focuses on the SDGs implementation:

1. The lack of specific language on Indigenous Peoples in the MDGs contributed to the invisibility of Indigenous Peoples and their issues, as well as to their nonparticipation in MDG processes of states and of UN agencies. It would be no exaggeration to say that Indigenous Peoples' participation was not even a question on the table for policy makers, with rare exceptions (e.g., Bolivia).
2. The emphasis on national averages, and the eagerness of national and international actors to show progress on MDGs at a national level, left Indigenous Peoples' realities in the shadow. Data collection and disaggregation as per Indigenous Peoples was basically absent.
3. The absence of indicators specific to Indigenous Peoples similarly contributed to the invisibility of Indigenous Peoples and their issues.

68 The desk reviews are posted on DESA/DSPD-SPFII website, www.un.org/development/desa/indigenouspeoples/resources/other.html.

In the meantime, however, under the umbrella of the UNPFII, meticulous, specialized, and methodical work has been done over a number of years by Permanent Forum members, Indigenous Peoples, and their organizations around the world.[69] This work was carried out in cooperation with UN agencies (FAO, IFAD, ILO) and experts to prepare Indigenous-specific indicators that capture Indigenous Peoples' well-being, poverty, and sustainability.[70] The results can be used to include Indigenous Peoples and their issues in the implementation of SDGs more successfully.

2. Priorities of Indigenous Peoples in the SDGs

Indigenous participation in the MDGs and the SDGs has evolved positively. Indigenous Peoples participated very actively in the SDG processes as of 2014. Based on relatively negative experiences with MDGs, they also pushed for the formulation of indicators specific to Indigenous Peoples because they realized that unless specific references to Indigenous Peoples are made in those, Indigenous issues would again become invisible.

There are six specific references to Indigenous Peoples in Agenda 2030: three are in the political declaration, two in the targets, and one in the section on follow-up and review (see further). However, these references do not necessarily capture the priority issues for Indigenous Peoples, nor do they, by any means, represent the only relevant areas of Agenda 2030 for Indigenous Peoples. Even where Indigenous Peoples are not explicitly mentioned, other references are of direct relevance to their human rights and well-being, including references to ethnicity, culture and cultural diversity, women, vulnerable groups (although this term is critiqued), data collection, and of course, human rights. In several references, Indigenous Peoples are listed together with other "vulnerable" groups, a characterization that has been viewed with some criticism by Indigenous representatives, given their recognized status as specific collectivities, peoples, with rights of self-determination and other rights. Despite this, the existing references in the document constitute an important achievement for Indigenous Peoples and a step up from the Millennium Development Goals, which had no explicit references to Indigenous Peoples.

---

69 Meetings were held and documentation prepared in connection with Central and South America and the Caribbean, the Arctic, North America, Africa, Asia, and the Pacific.
70 Much of this material has been compiled in a publication of Tebtebba Foundation (Indigenous Peoples' International Centre for Policy Research and Education), *Indicators Relevant for Indigenous Peoples: A Resource Book* (Baguio City, 2008); see the website of Tebtebba, www.tebtebba.org. See also the UNPFII reports for recommendations on indicators over a number of years, as well as reports of members of the Permanent Forum submitted to various sessions (website of SPFII, www.un.org/indigenous).

The specific references to Indigenous Peoples' rights in the 2030 Agenda are quoted:[71]

"Declaration" section:

[Paragraph] 23. People who are vulnerable must be empowered. Those whose needs are reflected in the Agenda include all children, youth, persons with disabilities (of whom more than 80 per cent live in poverty), people living with HIV/AIDS, older persons, *indigenous peoples*, refugees and internally displaced persons and migrants.

[Paragraph] 25. We commit to providing inclusive and equitable quality education at all levels – early childhood, primary, secondary, tertiary, technical and vocational training. All people, irrespective of sex, age, race or ethnicity, and persons with disabilities, migrants, *indigenous peoples*, children and youth, especially those in vulnerable situations, should have access to life-long learning opportunities that help them to acquire the knowledge and skills needed to exploit opportunities and to participate fully in society.

[Paragraph] 52. "We the peoples" are the celebrated opening words of the Charter of the United Nations. It is "we the peoples" who are embarking today on the road to 2030. Our journey will involve Governments as well as parliaments, the United Nations system and other international institutions, local authorities, *indigenous peoples*, civil society, business and the private sector, the scientific and academic community – and all people.

SDG targets:

[Target] 2.3: By 2030, double the agricultural productivity and incomes of small-scale food producers, in particular women, *indigenous peoples*, family farmers, pastoralists and fishers, including through secure and equal access to land, other productive resources and inputs, knowledge, financial services, markets and opportunities for value addition and non-farm employment.

[Target] 4.5: By 2030, eliminate gender disparities in education and ensure equal access to all levels of education and vocational training for the vulnerable, including persons with disabilities, *indigenous peoples* and children in vulnerable situations.

Follow-up and review, national level:

[Paragraph] 79. We also encourage Member States to conduct regular and inclusive reviews of progress at the national and sub-national levels which are

---

71 See 2030 Agenda, https://sdgs.un.org/2030agenda, for all references; emphasis of "indigenous peoples" added in each quotation.

country-led and country-driven. Such reviews should draw on contributions from *indigenous peoples*, civil society, the private sector and other stakeholders, in line with national circumstances, policies and priorities. National parliaments as well as other institutions can also support these processes.

Beyond the targets that specifically mention Indigenous Peoples, other goals and targets have been highlighted by Indigenous representatives during SDGs negotiations. They relate to the major human rights and development issues faced by Indigenous Peoples around the world, as well as the rights affirmed in the UNDRIP. Proposals have been made to develop corresponding indicators to measure the implementation of these goals and targets. As described further, this could be done through disaggregation by ethnic/Indigenous status or other measurements, either as part of the global indicators or through alternate data collection efforts at the regional and national levels.

The goals Indigenous representatives identified as important for them during international negotiations toward the SDGs are as follows:

Goal 1. End poverty in all its forms everywhere

Goal 2. End hunger, achieve food security and improved nutrition and promote sustainable agriculture

Goal 3. Ensure healthy lives and promote well-being for all at all ages

Goal 4. Ensure inclusive and equitable quality education and promote lifelong learning opportunities for all

Goal 5. Achieve gender equality and empower all women and girls

Goal 8. Promote sustained, inclusive and sustainable economic growth, full and productive employment and decent work for all

Goal 10. Reduce inequality within and among countries

Goal 13. Take urgent action to combat climate change and its impacts

Goal 15. Protect, restore and promote sustainable use of terrestrial ecosystems, sustainably manage forests, combat desertification, and halt and reverse land degradation and halt biodiversity loss

Goal 16. Promote peaceful and inclusive societies for sustainable development, provide access to justice for all and build effective, accountable and inclusive institutions at all levels

Goal 17. Strengthen the means of implementation and revitalize the global partnership for sustainable development

The 2030 Agenda already includes the elements of the human rights-based approach, as developed over the years in the UN's theory and practice and mentioned earlier, even if those elements are not neatly organized in one segment. Agenda 2030 is after all a long document.[72]

---

72 See "The Human Rights Based Approach to Development Cooperation" adopted by the UN Development Group in 2003, HRBA Portal, https://hrbaportal.org/the-human-

3.   *Indicators for Measuring Progress for Indigenous Peoples*

The lessons from the MDG experience regarding Indigenous Peoples clearly show that Indigenous-specific indicators are a critical entry point for the implementation of the SDGs and the inclusion of Indigenous Peoples and their issues.

Given the rich work conducted in the past several years on Indigenous-related indicators, there are a few specific thematic areas of fundamental significance for Indigenous Peoples' well-being and sustainability. Those few themes correspond to the normative framework of the UNDRIP, the Outcome Document of the 2014 World Conference on Indigenous Peoples, and the policy framework advocated over the years by UNPFII.

Main themes identified as needing to be addressed by indicators are (a) disaggregation of data; (b) lands, territories, and resources; (c) free, prior, and informed consent; (d) special targeted measures; (e) access to justice and redress mechanisms; and (f) participation and representation in decision-making and in relevant bodies.

These key themes give rise to measurable, concrete indicators formulated to fit under the various priority goals and targets of Agenda 2030. Some are already agreed upon indicators, such as ILO's and CBD's "status and trends in traditional occupations." Some Indigenous-specific indicators could ride on some already existing ones that disaggregate data by ethnicity, by adding reference to Indigenous Peoples in those.

While Indigenous representatives at the SDG negotiations had originally proposed six indicators, the major broad indicator that constituted their final proposal was one regarding land, as follows:

> Percentage of women, men, indigenous peoples, and local communities (IPLCs) with secure rights to land, property, and natural resources, measured by (a) percentage with legally documented or recognized evidence of tenure, and (b) percentage who perceive their rights are recognized and protected.[73]

The aforementioned indicator was not included among the formal SDGs indicators adopted. However, the strategic question among Indigenous representatives was, in what contexts, other than the formal SDG context, could the SDG-related indicators be pursued?

Based on extensive experience, there is agreement on the importance of community-based monitoring and the necessity of developing monitoring mechanisms, that go from the local to the national and global levels.

---

rights-based-approach-to-development-cooperation-towards-a-common-understanding-among-un-agencies.

73   This indicator was circulated in various papers shared by Indigenous representatives during negotiations.

Indigenous Peoples have continued to develop their own capacity to monitor indicators at the local level, in order to be able to do "shadow reporting" at the national and global levels. They also build on various experiences, systems, and initiatives on monitoring indicators at the community level that were developed over the years – for example, the Indigenous Navigator, existing monitoring processes under the Convention on Biological Diversity (CBD), the Arctic Social Indicators, and REDD+ indicators.[74]

4. Data Collection with, on, and for Indigenous Peoples

Data collection and disaggregation has become central to the human rights-based approach because statistics can reveal differences based on gender, ethnic origin, religion, and other elements that have historically marginalized people.

The very first international meeting organized on data collection and disaggregation related to Indigenous Peoples was under the auspices of the UNPFII. It was historic and brought together Forum members, statisticians, and Indigenous rights and development experts from States, Indigenous Peoples, and UN agencies. At the opening of this extraordinary expert meeting in 2004,[75] the then Officer-in-Charge of the Statistics Division noted that consideration of the issue of Indigenous Peoples and data collection was groundbreaking work.[76] The collection of reliable data would allow judgments to be made about the effectiveness of development programs that had a direct impact on the quality of life of the world's Indigenous Peoples. Indigenous issues were the important emerging theme in social statistics.

Questions discussed in that historic 2004 meeting included the following: Who are we collecting data for? How do we collect the data? What should be measured? Who should control information and the data? What is the data for? Why do Indigenous Peoples in resource-rich areas experience poor social conditions and the lack of social services? To what degree is remoteness responsible? How should free, prior, and informed consent of Indigenous Peoples be implemented in data collection?

---

74 See Indigenous Navigator, a comprehensive framework for community-based monitoring of UNDRIP, www.indigenousnavigator.org; Convention on Biological Diversity, "Draft Monitoring Framework for the Post-2020 Global Biodiversity Framework for Review," www.cbd.int/sbstta/sbstta-24/post2020-monitoring-en.pdf, accessed 19 July 2022; Joan Nymand Larsen, Peter Schweitzer, and Andrey Petrov, eds., *Arctic Social Indicators – ASI II: Implementation* (Copenhagen: Nordic Council of Ministers, 2014), https://doi.org/10.6027/TN2014-568; Sheila Wertz-Kanounnikoff and Desmond McNeill, "Performance Indicators and REDD+ Implementation," in *Analysing REDD+: Challenges and Choices*, ed. Arild Angelsen et al. (Bogor: Center for International Forestry Research, 2012), www.cifor.org/knowledge/publication/3827/.

75 UN Permanent Forum on Indigenous Issues, Report of the Workshop on Data Collection and Disaggregation for Indigenous Peoples, UN Doc. E/C.19/2004/2 (10 February 2004).

76 Author's archives.

Several critical recommendations on data collection and disaggregation came out of that 2004 UNPFII expert meeting and subsequent experiences that have Indigenous Peoples' participation as a focus and that are obviously crucial for the implementation of the SDGs and any other work of actors external to Indigenous Peoples under the umbrella of development.[77] The most central recommendations are listed next:[78]

(1) States should be encouraged and supported to include questions on Indigenous identity with full respect for the principle of self-identification. It is important to develop multiple criteria with local indigenous peoples' active and meaningful participation accurately to capture identity and socio-economic conditions. It is desirable to have long-term, standardized data based on this principle.

(2) Data collection concerning indigenous peoples should follow the principle of free prior and informed consent at all levels and take into account both the Fundamental Principles of Official Statistics as established by the United Nations Statistical Commission on the basis of the Economic Commission for Europe's Decision C (47) of 1994 . . . and the collective rights of indigenous peoples. . . .

(3) Data collection should be in accordance with provisions on human rights and fundamental freedoms, and with data protection regulations and privacy guarantees including respect for confidentiality.

(4) Indigenous peoples should fully participate as equal partners, in all stages of data collection, including planning, implementation, analysis and dissemination, access and return, with appropriate resourcing and capacity-building to do so. Data collection must respond to the priorities and aims of the indigenous communities themselves. Participation of indigenous communities in the conceptualization, implementation, reporting, analysis and dissemination of data collected is crucial, at both the country and international levels. Indigenous peoples should be trained and employed by data-collection institutions at the national and international levels. The process of data collection is critical for the empowerment of the communities and for identifying their

---

77 See UN Permanent Forum on Indigenous Issues, Report on the Third Session (10–21 May 2004), UN Doc. E/2004/43-E/C.19/2004/23 (2004); the report of the expert meeting is contained in UN Doc. E/C.19/2004/2.

78 The recommendations quoted are contained in UN Doc. E/C.19/2004/2, para. 33, subparagraphs 1–5 and 9. The full list of recommendations is in para. 33, subparagraphs 1–24.

needs. Indigenous communities should have the right to have data (primary and aggregated) returned to them, for their own use, noting the importance of the confidentiality of such data, particularly as it applies to individuals who have participated. In conducting data-collection exercises, states should involve indigenous peoples from the earliest stages (planning and community education) and ensure ongoing partnerships in collecting, analyzing and disseminating data.

(5) Data collection exercises should be conducted in local indigenous languages to the extent possible and, where no written language exists, should employ local indigenous peoples (as translators/interpreters as well as advisors) to assist in the collection process. . . .

(9) For international organizations, data collection should be mainstreamed. . . . It should also be used to assess the impact of development assistance and to promote social dialogue at the national level.

The work conducted by the UN Statistics Division, of the DESA, is indeed crucial and can be useful for the challenges that data collection poses with regard to Indigenous Peoples. As indicated in DESA's report to the UNPFII at its eighth session in 2009,[79]

the Statistics Division incorporates the indigenous population dimension in all of the aspects of official statistics at the national and international levels, emphasizing the need to capture and disseminate data pertaining to these population groups. More specifically, the United Nations Principles and Recommendations for Population and Housing Censuses, Revision 2 elaborates in detail the need to disaggregate statistics on the basis of ethnocultural characteristics, especially with respect to Indigenous Peoples. . . .[80]

Despite the fact that ethnicity is not a core topic in many national population and housing censuses, the Statistics Division, as part of its series of

79 UN Permanent Forum on Indigenous Issues, Information Received from the United Nations System and Other Intergovernmental Organizations: Report of the Department of Economic and Social Affairs, UN Doc. E/C.19/2009/3/Add.4 (2 March 2009), para. 77–78. As stated in paragraph 76 of the report, "the mandate of the Statistics Division may be summarized into four main areas: developing international statistical standards and methodological guidelines; collecting and disseminating internationally comparable statistics; providing support to national statistical agencies in terms of improving statistical capacity; and servicing the United Nations Statistical Commission as the apex of the international statistical system."

80 See UN Statistics Division, Principles and Recommendations for Population and Housing Censuses, Revision 2, UN Doc. ST/ESA/STAT/SER.M/67/Rev. 2 (2008), https://unstats.un.org/unsd/demographic-social/Standards-and-Methods/files/Principles_and_Recommendations/Population-and-Housing-Censuses/Series_M67Rev2-E.pdf.

special topics, collected, processed and disseminated data on ethnocultural characteristics.[81]

If we take stock of where things are in data collection regarding Indigenous Peoples, we can see that by this point significant work has been done at the international level. Indigenous participation is a key element of data collection. International analysis and recommendations are there, available for states and others to use at the national level, if they have the political will and resources: I am uncertain that these exist. Therefore, continuing advocacy at all levels about this seems wise.

F. How to Define Good Examples of Indigenous Peoples' Participation?

1. Learning from Examples of International Agencies

Given that Indigenous Peoples' participation in programs and projects concerning them is so crucial, and also such a difficult point to drive home in practice most of the time, the Secretariat of the UNPFII collaborated with the IFAD to do a review of IFAD projects concerning Indigenous Peoples. The review was to ascertain the factors that made for a successful or less successful project. The results showed that successful examples were those that had substantively and from the beginning engaged the Indigenous Peoples' communities and sought their free, prior and informed consent.[82] A broader analysis of IFAD's good example is presented in the next segment.

In addition, in a study by the Inter-Agency Group on Gender Equality on Indigenous women and the UN system, eighteen cases were presented, through which agencies tried to identify what the elements of good examples were.[83] It is interesting that one of the conclusions was that

increasing decentralization and devolution to local governments, and its effects on local-level power and public investment, are opening up new spaces for indigenous participation in local government administration and management of territories, communities and neighborhoods, with a legitimacy that is sustainable over time.[84]

81 See https://unstats.un.org/unsd/demographic/sconcerns/popchar/.
82 Tauli-Corpuz, ed., *Good Practices on Indigenous Peoples' Development*.
83 Secretariat of the Permanent Forum on Indigenous Issues and Inter-Agency Network on Women and Gender Equality Task Force on Indigenous Women, *Indigenous Women and the United Nations System: Good Practices and Lessons Learned*, UN Doc. ST/ESA/307 (New York: UN, 2007), www.un.org/esa/socdev/publications/Indigenous/indwomen07.htm.
84 *Indigenous Women and the United Nations System*, conclusion no. 9, p. 114.

The first and last of the six recommendations of the aforementioned study focus on participation:

1. The United Nations system, Governments and all actors involved should promote the establishment of true participatory mechanisms for the involvement of indigenous peoples, especially women, in decision-making processes related to any projects or programmes impacting on their lives. . . .

6. United Nations organizations should ensure and support the full participation of indigenous peoples, and indigenous women, as equal partners in all stages of data collection, including planning, implementation, analysis and dissemination, access and return, with the appropriate resourcing and capacity-building for achieving this objective. Data collection must respond to the priorities and aims of the indigenous communities and indigenous women themselves, and be gender-focused and disaggregated.[85]

The issue of participation of Indigenous Peoples at all levels, including programs and projects of international agencies, has become a significant part of UN messaging since the 1993 International Year of the World's Indigenous People.[86] The motto of the first International Decade of the World's Indigenous People was "Partnership in Action," and that of the Second Decade was "Partnership for Action and Dignity." The first two of the five objectives of the Second Decade had to do with participation, as they proposed promoting "non-discrimination and inclusion of indigenous peoples in the design, implementation and evaluation of international, regional and national processes regarding laws, policies, resources, programmes and projects"; and promoting

full and effective participation of indigenous peoples in decisions which directly or indirectly affect their lifestyles, traditional lands and territories, their cultural integrity as indigenous peoples with collective rights or any other aspect of their lives, considering the principle of free, prior and informed consent.[87]

It is obvious that Indigenous Peoples' participation is lagging behind existing policy pronouncements. Starting in 2007, with the adoption of the Declaration, the bar was placed higher: the right of Indigenous Peoples to self-determination and the right to free, prior, and informed consent became

---

85 *Indigenous Women and the United Nations System*, 115–116.
86 The formal title of the International Year did not include the 's' in "peoples" at that time.
87 "Second International Decade of the World's Indigenous People," *UN DESA website*, www.un.org/development/desa/indigenouspeoples/second-international-decade-of-the-worlds-indigenous-people.html, accessed 20 July 2022. The Decade ran from January 2005 to December 2014 and was established by General Assembly resolution A/RES/59/174.

pronounced international legal norms. ILO Convention No. 169 also includes free, prior, and informed consent; this right is stronger and applies to more areas in the Declaration. There is clearly a participation gap for Indigenous Peoples at the country level, and the analysis of documentation regarding the MDGs showed just that.[88]

Whether things are improving during processes of the SDGs remains to be seen. A report by the Indigenous Peoples' Major Group for Sustainable Development on the 2019 session of the High-Level Political Forum (HLPF), which is the global review process of the SDGs that is held every July at the UN, stated:

> At the 2019 HLPF session on the Voluntary National Reviews (VNRs), only one Indigenous Peoples' representative was able to make a statement on behalf of all the Major Groups and Stakeholders. While many of the VNRs acknowledge "marginalized groups" as those left behind, most States do not provide mechanisms for their meaningful participation. There are also no specific plans, targets and budgets to address the specific condition of Indigenous Peoples. In fact, most countries with Indigenous Peoples neither mentioned Indigenous Peoples as distinct groups nor did they make reference to their collective rights and contributions to sustainable development. Further, there is a continuing lack of awareness on the SDGs at the grassroots level including by Indigenous communities who face serious risks to their rights and wellbeing in the implementation of economic growth targets in the implementation of the SDGs. . . .
>
> As 24 countries with Indigenous Peoples will present their reports on the implementation of the SDGs at the HLPF 2020, it is important for Indigenous Peoples in these countries to engage with their respective states and demand consultations and participation in decision-making in relation to the implementation of the SDGs. It is critical for Indigenous Peoples to be reflected in the national SDG action plans with specific measures and strategies to fully address the structural barriers and challenges they face in order to ensure the respect, protection and realization of their rights, wellbeing and aspirations for sustainable development as distinct peoples.[89]

---

88 During the author's tenure as Chief of SPFII, analyses were prepared annually of MDG country reports in order to ascertain to what extent Indigenous Peoples' issues were included and whether there were references of Indigenous Peoples' participation in MDG processes. These analyses were used to brief the UNPFII.

89 The website of the Indigenous Peoples Major Group for Sustainable Development can be found at https://indigenouspeoples-sdg.org/index.php/english/. The aforementioned commentary and quote were circulated by the Indigenous Peoples Major Group in 2019 after the holding of the HLPF of that year. Much of the text of this commentary is repeated in this article: Joan Carling, "Indigenous World 2020: The Sustainable Development Goals (SDGs) and Indigenous Peoples," *IWGIA website*, 11 May 2020, www.iwgia.org/en/the-sustainable-development-goals-sdgs-and-indigenous-peoples/3658-iw-2020-sdgs.html.

The aforementioned critique of the situation by the Indigenous Peoples Major Group is indeed eloquent. The lessons learned from the rich practice of UN bodies and agencies could be useful for states as well. While some states do not formally recognize Indigenous Peoples, or do not recognize them under this terminology, it is by now well-known that the term "Indigenous Peoples" has prevailed as a general or generic term. In some countries, there may be preference for terms other than "Indigenous Peoples." There are some local terms (such as tribes, first peoples, aboriginals, ethnic groups, *adivasi, janajati*) or occupational and geographical (hunter-gatherers, nomads, peasants, hill people, rural populations, etc.) that, for all practical purposes, can be used interchangeably with "Indigenous Peoples." In some cases, the notion of being Indigenous has pejorative connotations, and some people may choose not to reveal their origin. External actors must respect such choices, while at the same time working against the discrimination of Indigenous Peoples.

The most fruitful approach is to identify, rather than define, Indigenous Peoples in a specific context and, most importantly, based on the fundamental criterion of self-identification, as underlined in a number of human rights documents, especially the UNDRIP.

The heart of the matter in the implementation of Agenda 2030 is that "nobody should be left behind," as is declared in UN meetings, and therefore all efforts should be made on the part of states, in cooperation with agencies, to address the substance of Indigenous Peoples' challenges, with their full participation, and by showing the requisite political will. The UN agencies should be facilitating this in all ways possible.

2. The Good Example of the International Fund for Agricultural Development

IFAD has been among the first UN system organizations actively and creatively involved with the work of the UNPFII. Given that each organization has its own history, culture of work, and protocol, what stands out in connection with IFAD are two things: the visible engagement of high-level management with Indigenous Peoples' issues and a dynamic culture of exchange and learning within – a culture that creates an atmosphere of openness and allows for resilience, flexibility, and change. Evaluating IFAD's work on Indigenous Peoples' issues in the last ten-plus years, it should be said that, in terms of public policy results, it is commendable and ambitious for IFAD to be measuring results publicly and visibly, so soon after the adoption of its 2009 Policy of Engagement with Indigenous Peoples.[90] Given that all evaluated projects reviewed were designed prior to IFAD's Policy on Indigenous Peoples, this exercise was testimony to IFAD's dynamic approach to Indigenous and other issues.

---

90 www.ifad.org/en/-/document/ifad-policy-on-engagement-with-indigenous-peoples. The author had the opportunity to study the evaluation efforts of IFAD.

There have been a number of facilitating factors in IFAD's work: the size and nature of IFAD-financed projects – comparably smaller than those financed by other IFIs; concentrating on rural and agricultural development for poverty reduction; and a unique focus on targeting, participatory approaches, community development, empowerment, and inclusion. These factors have enabled IFAD to follow a proactive approach and to support Indigenous Peoples. IFAD's comparative advantage also stems from inter-linkages of its activities at different levels: experience on the ground, various instruments at the corporate level (the policy, a dedicated desk in the Policy and Technical Advisory Division), broad partnerships, and networks, as well as the roles played by IFAD at the international level.

Among major IFAD achievements, we should underline IFAD's substantial contribution to the international processes and its advocacy. The Indigenous Peoples' Assistance Facility (IPAF) has been a flagship program and a unique instrument that has helped IFAD develop partnerships and trust with Indigenous Peoples' organizations, and it has also contributed to their empowerment. The 2009 Policy of Engagement with Indigenous Peoples is highly relevant to IFAD's overall corporate strategies and to Indigenous Peoples. There are indications that the attention to Indigenous Peoples' issues is becoming more visible, even though there are still challenges in implementation, and the trends are not consistent across the board. The Indigenous Peoples' Forum (IPF) is another major institutional achievement for IFAD, as it constitutes a formal consultative process with Indigenous Peoples. IFAD is the only agency expanding the institutional dialogue with Indigenous Peoples to the African region.

In terms of the areas that need strengthening, some are especially important:

1. There is a need to strengthen consistent policy implementation at an operational level.
2. There is a limited understanding of Indigenous Peoples' issues among some of IFAD's country program managers/officers.
3. Key issues related to investment projects include the need for tailored approaches and for better monitoring with disaggregated data and specific indicators.
4. Among the principles of engagement in the policy, there has been lack of clarity about how to operationalize the requirement of free, prior, and informed consent (FPIC).

Regarding the lack of clarity on operationalizing the FPIC requirement, mentioned in item 4, it would be important to (a) clarify for which types of projects and in which cases FPIC at project design stage would be required, whether and how this should/could be practically and pragmatically done (including what would constitute a "consent"); and (b) understand and appreciate the possible implications on the budget for design work and projects, as well as the timeframe.

Given IFAD's leadership role, it would indeed be crucial for IFAD to clarify FPIC in its operations. In that sense, IFAD cannot allow itself to "become victim of its own success." Attention to the time flexibility required for meaningful participation of Indigenous Peoples is indispensable for development with culture and identity. What has significantly helped IFAD reach this commendable level of leadership on Indigenous issues is the high-level profile of these issues at the institutional/management level. This approach should obviously continue.

In the sessions of the UNPFII and in their countries, Indigenous Peoples engage with UN agencies. Agencies' operations have sometimes had results that Indigenous Peoples have been involved in and welcomed. IFAD has made considerable efforts to establish good practices with Indigenous Peoples' direct participation. Indigenous Peoples have also used the sessions of the UNPFII to develop relations with UN agencies, to promote global or national Indigenous issues, and to seek the intervention of the Forum in order to change some agency policies and practices.

3. Conclusion

Based on all the work done on development, data collection, and indicators over the years and on the experiences of Indigenous Peoples, states, and interstate agencies, the conclusion is that Indigenous Peoples' genuine participation is an indispensable element for any program or project in the area of development to be a "good example."

The concept of a "good example" is well captured in a 2015 publication, prepared by the Secretariat of the UNPFII in cooperation with IFAD, which identifies the minimum essential criteria of a good practice:[91]

> [1.] Indigenous peoples are acknowledged as rights holders and programmatic strategies prioritize the importance of free, prior and informed consent;
>
> [2.] Indigenous peoples are recognized as key decision makers and as experts in matters that affect them;
>
> [3.] Emphasis is placed on the full and effective engagement and participation of indigenous peoples at all stages of the programme;
>
> [4.] Strong partnerships are established between UN agencies (or through the UN Country Teams) with local institutions, Member States, and Indigenous peoples; and

---

91 Secretariat of the United Nations Permanent Forum on Indigenous Issues. *Partnering with Indigenous Peoples: Experiences and Practices* (2015), 1–2, www.un.org/esa/socdev/unpfii/documents/LibraryDocuments/partnering-with-ips.pdf. See also *Indigenous Women and the United Nations System*, another collection of promising practices.

[5.] A culturally sensitive approach to programming, including an understanding of norms and practices of indigenous cultures, is incorporated into policy and programme design and implementation.

The projects studied for the aforementioned publication provide compelling evidence that the success of UN operations depends on Indigenous Peoples' role and engagement in the process. This should build on the principles of the UN Development Group Guidelines on Indigenous Peoples' Issues and, especially, on the UN Declaration on the Rights of Indigenous Peoples. The goal is to ensure that Indigenous Peoples actively participate in UN programs at all levels, including as implementing partners; project or activity coordinators or facilitators; experts, advisors, and resource persons; program or project committee members; and monitors and evaluators. States and Indigenous Peoples can certainly draw some useful conclusions from such good examples and lessons.

Including Indigenous Peoples' issues within intergovernmental organizations is a complex yet worthwhile enterprise, given the role that international public institutions can play in promoting social justice globally and at the national level.

This chapter discussed how Indigenous Peoples have been questioning the dominant development paradigm – in fact, the very concept of "development" – through their participation, especially at the international level, since the beginning of the Working Group on Indigenous Populations and, later, at the UN Permanent Forum on Indigenous Issues, as well as in major international debates on the Millennium Development Goals (MDGs) and the Sustainable Development Goals (SDGs). The MDGs and SDGs have been central battlegrounds on such issues, where Indigenous Peoples have articulated what could constitute a just development for people and the planet.

Given the emphasis on development in the international system, and the involvement of Indigenous Peoples in such policy efforts, this chapter unveiled opportunities and also challenges for Indigenous participation. The issues woven together under the concept of development, including environment, climate change, and traditional knowledge, also help us understand what self-determined development would mean for Indigenous Peoples.

Bibliography

Bleie, Tone. "The Politics of Shaming and Sanctions: Rewriting the Anatomy of the Bangladeshi State." In *Indigenous Peoples' Rights and Unreported Struggles: Conflict and Peace*, edited by Elsa Stamatopoulou, 155–191. New York: Institute for the Study of Human Rights, Columbia University, 2017. https://doi.org/10.7916/D82R5095.

Carling, Joan. "Indigenous World 2020: The Sustainable Development Goals (SDGs) and Indigenous Peoples." *IWGIA*, 11 May 2020. www.iwgia.org/en/the-sustainable-development-goals-sdgs-and-indigenous-peoples/3658-iw-2020-sdgs.html.

Castoriadis, Cornelius. *The Imaginary Institution of Society*. Translated by Kathleen Blamey. Cambridge, MA: MIT Press, 1998.

Cho, Sungjoon. "Toward an Identity Theory of International Organizations." *Proceeding of the International Meeting (American Society of International Law)* 101 (2007): 157–160.

Clavero, Bartolomé. *Genocide or Ethnocide, 1933–2007: How to Make, Unmake, and Remake Law with Words*. Milan: Giuffré, 2008.

Convention on Biological Diversity. "Draft Monitoring Framework for the Post-2020 Global Biodiversity Framework for Review." Accessed 19 July 2022. www.cbd.int/sbstta/sbstta-24/post2020-monitoring-en.pdf.

Intergovernmental Panel on Climate Change. *Carbon Dioxide Capture and Storage*. Cambridge: Cambridge University Press, 2005. www.ipcc.ch/report/carbon-dioxide-capture-and-storage/.

Intergovernmental Panel on Climate Change and Technology and Economic Assessment Panel. *Safeguarding the Ozone Layer and the Global Climate System: Issues Related to Hydrofluorocarbons and Perfluorocarbons*. Cambridge: Cambridge University Press, 2005. www.ipcc.ch/report/safeguarding-the-ozone-layer-and-the-global-climate-system/.

International Fund for Agricultural Development. *Policy of Engagement with Indigenous Peoples*. Rome: Palombi & Lanci, 2009. www.ifad.org/english/indigenous/documents/ip_policy_e.pdf,www.ifad.org/documents/38711624/39417924/ip_policy_2009_e.pdf.

International Labor Organization. Convention No. 107: Indigenous and Tribal Peoples Convention. ILO, 1957.

International Labor Organization. Convention No. 169: Indigenous and Tribal Peoples Convention. ILO, 1989.

Larsen, Joan Nymand, Peter Schweitzer, and Andrey Petrov, eds. *Arctic Social Indicators – ASI II: Implementation*. Copenhagen: Nordic Council of Ministers, 2014. https://doi.org/10.6027/TN2014-568.

Report on the Inter-Agency Support Group (IASG) on Indigenous Peoples' Issues Special Meeting on United Nations Declaration on the Rights of Indigenous Peoples, 26 and 27 February 2008. UN Doc. E/C.19/2008/CRP.7, 27 March 2008.

Secretariat of the Permanent Forum on Indigenous Issues. *Desk Review of Select Resident Coordinator Reports: 2001–2003*. New York: UNPFII, February 2007.

Secretariat of the Permanent Forum on Indigenous Issues. *Human Development Reports and Indigenous Peoples: A Desk Review*. New York: UNPFII, 2009.

Secretariat of the Permanent Forum on Indigenous Issues. *Integration of Indigenous Peoples' Perspective in Country Development Processes: Review of Selected CCAs and UNDAFs*, no. 3. New York: UNPFII, January 2008.

Secretariat of the Permanent Forum on Indigenous Issues. *MDG Reports and Indigenous People: A Desk Review*. New York: UNPFII, January 2006.

Secretariat of the Permanent Forum on Indigenous Issues. *Partnering with Indigenous Peoples: Experiences and Practices*, New York, 2015. www.un.org/esa/socdev/unpfii/documents/LibraryDocuments/partnering-with-ips.pdf.

Secretariat of the Permanent Forum on Indigenous Issues and Inter-Agency Network on Women and Gender Equality Task Force on Indigenous Women. *Indigenous Women and the United Nations System: Good Practices and Lessons Learned*. UN Doc. ST/ESA/307. New York: UN, 2007. www.un.org/esa/socdev/publications/Indigenous/indwomen07.htm.

Stamatopoulou, Elsa. "Indigenous Peoples and Agenda 2030." Working paper presented at UN Expert Group Meetings on Indigenous Peoples and Agenda 2030 for Sustainable Development. New York, 22–23 and 26–27 October 2015.

Stamatopoulou, Elsa. "Indigenous Peoples and the United Nations: Human Rights as a Developing Dynamic." *Human Rights Quarterly* 16, no. 1 (February 1994): 58–81. https://doi.org/10.2307/762411.

Stamatopoulou, Elsa. "Walking the Talk? Including Indigenous Peoples' Issues in Intergovernmental Organizations." In *Indigenous Peoples' Rights in International Law: Emergence and Application*, edited by Roxanne Dunbar-Ortiz, Dalee Sambo Dorough, Gudmundur Alfredsson, Lee Swepston, and Petter Wille, 172–199. Kautokeino: Gáldu and Copenhagen: IWGIA, 2015.

Tauli-Corpuz, Victoria, ed. *Good Practices on Indigenous Peoples' Development*. UN Doc. E/C.19/G646. Baguio City: Tebtebba Foundation; New York: UN Permanent Forum on Indigenous Issues, 2006.

Tebtebba Foundation. *Indicators Relevant for Indigenous Peoples: A Resource Book*. Baguio City: Tebtebba Foundation, 2008.

UN Charter, 26 June 1945, www.un.org/en/about-us/un-charter/.

UN Children's Fund (UNICEF). *Global Evaluation of the Application of a Human Rights-Based Approach to UNICEF Programming*. New York: UNICEF, 2012. www.unicef.org/policyanalysis/rights/files/UNICEF_HRBAP_Final_Report_Vol_I_11June_copy-edited_translated.pdf.

UN Committee on the Rights of the Child. General Comment No. 11 (2009) on "Indigenous Children and Their Rights under the Convention on the Rights of the Child." UN Doc. CRC/C/GC/11, 12 February 2009.

UN Development Group. Guidelines on Indigenous Peoples' Issues. UN Doc. HR/P/PT/16, 2008. www.un.org/esa/socdev/unpfii/documents/UNDG_guidelines_EN.pdf.

UN Development Program. UNDP and Indigenous Peoples: A Practice Note on Engagement, 2001.

UN Economic and Social Council. Resolution 2000/22, Establishment of a Permanent Forum on Indigenous Issues. UN Doc. E//RES/2000/22, 28 July 2000. www.un.org/esa/socdev/unpfii/documents/about-us/E-RES-2000-22.pdf.

UN Expert Mechanism on the Rights of Indigenous Peoples. Contribution to the Study on Indigenous Peoples and the Right to Participate in Decision-Making. UN Doc. A/HRC/EMRIP/2010/3, 7 May 2010.

UN General Assembly. Resolution 44/25, Convention on the Rights of the Child. UN Doc. A/RES/44/25, 5 December 1989.

UN General Assembly. Resolution 61/295, United Nations Declaration on the Rights of Indigenous Peoples. UN Doc. A/Res/61/295, 13 September 2007. www.un.org/development/desa/indigenouspeoples/wp-content/uploads/sites/19/2018/11/UNDRIP_E_web.pdf.

UN General Assembly. Resolution 70/1, Transforming Our World: The 2030 Agenda for Sustainable Development. UN Doc. A/RES/70/1, 21 October 2015. https://sdgs.un.org/2030agenda.

UN High Commissioner for Human Rights. Final Report of the United Nations High Commissioner for Human Rights Reviewing the Activities within the United Nations System under the Programme for the International Decade of the World's Indigenous People. UN Doc. E/CN.4/2005/87, 4 January 2005.

UN Permanent Forum on Indigenous Issues. Indigenous Peoples and Climate Change: Note by the Secretariat. UN Doc. E/C.19/2021/5, 12 January 2021.

UN Permanent Forum on Indigenous Issues. Information Received from the United Nations System and Other Intergovernmental Organizations: Report of the Department of Economic and Social Affairs. UN Doc. E/C.19/2009/3/Add.4, 2 March 2009.

UN Permanent Forum on Indigenous Issues. Provisional Agenda: Permanent Forum on Indigenous Issues, Fifth Session. UN Doc. E/C.19/2006/1, 19 January 2006.

UN Permanent Forum on Indigenous Issues. Provisional Agenda: Permanent Forum on Indigenous Issues, Fourth Session. UN Doc. E/C.19/2005/1, 18 January 2005.

UN Permanent Forum on Indigenous Issues. Report of the Workshop on Data Collection and Disaggregation for Indigenous Peoples. UN Doc. E/C.19/2004/2, 10 February 2004.

UN Permanent Forum on Indigenous Issues. Report on the Eight Session (18–29 May 2009). UN Doc. E/2009/43, 2009.

UN Permanent Forum on Indigenous Issues. Report on the Ninth Session (19–30 April 2010). UN Doc. E/2010/43, 2010.

UN Permanent Forum on Indigenous Issues. Report on the Second Session (12–23 May 2003), UN Doc. E/2003/43, 2003.

UN Permanent Forum on Indigenous Issues. Report on the Tenth Session (16–27 May 2011). UN Doc. E/2011/43, 2011.

UN Permanent Forum on Indigenous Issues. Report on the Third Session (10–21 May 2004). UN Doc. E/2004/43-E/C.19/2004/23, 2004.

UN Permanent Forum on Indigenous Issues. Study on the Status of Implementation of the Chittagong Hill Tracts Accord of 1997: Submitted by the Special Rapporteur. UN Doc. E/C.19/2011/6, 18 February 2011.

UN Secretary-General. Implementation of the Programme of Activities for the International Decade of the World's Indigenous People. UN Doc. A/59/277, 17 August 2004.

UN Secretary-General. Report of the Secretary-General on the Preliminary Review by the Coordinator of the International Decade of the World's Indigenous People on the Activities of the United Nations System in Relation to the Decade. UN Doc. E/2004/82, 25 June 2004.

UN Statistics Division. Principles and Recommendations for Population and Housing Censuses, Revision 2. UN Doc. ST/ESA/STAT/SER.M/67/Rev. 2, 2008. https://unstats.un.org/unsd/demographic-social/Standards-and-Methods/files/Principles_and_Recommendations/Population-and-Housing-Censuses/Series_M67Rev2-E.pdf.

UN Sub-Commission on Prevention of Discrimination and Protection of Minorities. Report of the Working Group on Indigenous Populations on Its First Session. UN Doc. E/CN.4/Sub.2/1982/33, 25 August 1982.

UN Sustainable Development Group (UNSDG). *The Human Rights Based Approach to Development Cooperation: Towards a Common Understanding among UN Agencies.* UNSDG, September 2003. https://unsdg.un.org/resources/human-rights-based-approach-development-cooperation-towards-common-understanding-among-un.

Wertz-Kanounnikoff, Sheila, and Desmond McNeill. "Performance Indicators and REDD+ Implementation." In *Analysing REDD+: Challenges and Choices*, edited by Arild Angelsen, Maria Brockhaus, William D. Sunderlin, and Louis V. Verchot, 233–246. Bogor: Center for International Forestry Research, 2012. www.cifor.org/knowledge/publication/3827/.

Yupsanis, Athanasios. "The International Labour Organization and Its Contribution to the Protection of the Rights of Indigenous Peoples." *Canadian Yearbook of International Law* 49 (2012): 117–176. https://doi.org/10.1017/S006900580001033X.

EPILOGUE

The global Indigenous Peoples' movement arose out of numerous local and national struggles. It is one of the most robust social movements today, with major achievements already to its credit. Yet its advocates fully expect its dynamism, vision, and action to continue across generations. Correcting and reversing injustices doesn't happen all at once.

This book has tried to tell the stories and analyze the strategies that allowed this movement to attain a strong presence in the interstate system that few, if any, expected. By accompanying the Indigenous Peoples' movement over five decades, this book has been able to unveil, in the midst of tremendous diversity, a profound unifying logic that weaves distinct cultures, political situations, and philosophies into a compelling whole.

This thread, I have argued, is the commitment to self-determination – self-determination as a right, as a goal, as a process aiming at justice, and as an everyday practice that Indigenous Peoples carry out themselves, demanding that it be respected by states and others.

Active participation at the international level is a crucial part of Indigenous external self-determination, expanding over time in-depth and breadth. This self-determination has generally won acceptance by states and their organizations. It is not without its challenges, but it is accepted.

Corrective exceptionalism, the theoretical term this book has put forward to explain how Indigenous Peoples won this unprecedented status in interstate organizations, cannot correct everything. The great historical injustices with which Indigenous Peoples have had to struggle – colonialism, mass killings and individual assassinations, land grabbing, settlement, discrimination, marginalization – have visible effects today, but they are also ongoing phenomena, even if they are not given these names by states or majority societies.

Correcting these wrongs is a long and harsh struggle. It is a struggle that the privileged – whether conscious or unconscious of their privilege – often perceive as a threat to reduce their accustomed power. In fact, it is a competition for resources and their redistribution. It is also a struggle for the recognition of what is right.

Ethics has not been foreign to the analysis of the Indigenous Peoples' movement that this book has presented. But there is another point about the ethical dimension of this story that I want to underline here. Several people have been privileged to be informed about the history and situation of Indigenous Peoples by the Indigenous advocates with whom we have been lucky enough to interact. I recognize that not everyone has had the same access to this knowledge. But that knowledge is an indispensable bridge between Indigenous and non-Indigenous people. Human solidarity requires that we seek and learn more from Indigenous knowledge than we start out with.

For future generations, can we imagine an era when solidarity and justice will prevail in state, societal, and other worlds? Will our ethics allow us to see that the questions Indigenous Peoples raise are not just about "them" but concern us all? "*Seguimos*" ("we continue") is something we often say instead of "goodbye" after international Indigenous meetings – awareness, resilience, action, hope, we continue.

ANNEX 1:
LIST OF PERSONS INTERVIEWED

The author is deeply grateful for the generosity, time, and insights that these extraordinary leaders offered to the questions discussed in this book. The list of questions appears in the introduction. Over the decades of her work with Indigenous Peoples, the author has had numerous discussions with Indigenous representatives and others that informed her knowledge and views on various complex issues.

- Claire Charters, Professor at Te Wāhanga Ture, Faculty of Law, Waipapa Taumata Rau, University of Auckland, Aotearoa, New Zealand, and a well-known Indigenous rights advocate
  2 November 2018
- Antonella Cordone, senior official at the International Fund for Agricultural Development (IFAD)
  7 May 2016
- Myrna Cunningham, Miskita senior Indigenous rights advocate from Nicaragua, President of Fondo Indígena, Executive Director of CADPI (Centro para la Autonomía y Desarrollo de los Pueblos Indígenas), President of Pawanka Fund, former Chairperson of UNPFII, and a surgeon
  17 May 2016
- Kenneth Deer, of the Mohawk Nation of the Kahnawake territory, an award-winning journalist, an educator, and an internationally known Indigenous rights activist, and an active participant in the development of the UN Declaration of the Rights of Indigenous Peoples
  6 April 2016

- Binota Moy Dhamai, Indigenous leader and Indigenous rights activist from Bangladesh, Chairperson (2022) of the UN Expert Mechanism on the Rights of Indigenous Peoples
  March 2022
- Lola Garcia-Alix, an executive of IWGIA (International Work Group on Indigenous Affairs) for a long time, former Executive Director and now Senior Advisor on Global Governance, and a well-known advocate for Indigenous Peoples' rights
  29 April 2016
- Moana Jackson, New Zealand lawyer of Ngāti Kahungunu and Ngāti Porou descent, specializing in constitutional law, the Treaty of Waitangi, and international Indigenous issues; and an advocate and activist for Māori rights, leading work on constitutional reforms and the rights of Indigenous Peoples internationally
  16 May 2017
- Mikaela Jade, Indigenous rights advocate in Australia, founder and CEO of Indigital, a business that aims to help embed Indigenous stories and history into the mainstream, by using augmented reality technology
  16 May 2016
- Carson Kiburo, Endorois of Kenya, Executive Director of the Jamii Asilia Centre, and former Co-Chair of the UN Global Indigenous Youth Caucus
  7 March 2022
- Wilton Littlechild, Grand Chief for Treaty #6 in Western Canada and a senior world-renowned Cree Indigenous leader
  28 January 2017
- Oren Lyons, Onondaga Nation Faithkeeper, senior human rights advocate
  20 September 2016
- Les Malezer, Aboriginal leader, Chairperson of the Foundation for Aboriginal and Islander Research Action (FAIRA) in Australia, and a person that held various international Indigenous-related mandates
  8 April 2016
- Aehshatou Manu, Mbororo of Cameroon, National Women Coordinator of the Mbororo Social and Cultural Development Association
  29 November 2016
- Aroha Mead, Māori Elder and an active leader at international fora for decades
  5 April 2016
- Chhing Lamu Sherpa, Indigenous Sherpa leader in Nepal, Founder and member of Mountain Spirit
  21 November 2016
- Rodion Sulyandziga, Udege leader in the Russian Federation, founder and director of the Center for Support of Indigenous Peoples of the

North\Russian Indigenous Training Center (CSIPN/RITC), and member of UN EMRIP

30 January 2017

- Victoria (Vicky) Tauli-Corpuz, Igorot senior leader in the Philippines and former UN Special Rapporteur on the Rights of Indigenous Peoples as well as former Chairperson of the UNPFII

18 October 2016

- Howard Thompson, Mohawk of the Haudenosaunee, Elder and senior Indigenous rights advocate

January 2018

INDEX

Printed in the United States
by Baker & Taylor Publisher Services